KU-597-755

Profit and Crises

Profit and Crises

ARGHIRI EMMANUEL

Translated from French by N.P. Costello

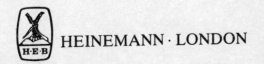

HEINEMANN · LONDON

Heinemann Educational Books Ltd
22 Bedford Square, London WC1B 3HH
LONDON EDINBURGH MELBOURNE AUCKLAND
HONG KONG SINGAPORE KUALA LUMPUR NEW DELHI
IBADAN NAIROBI JOHANNESBURG
EXETER (NH) KINGSTON PORT OF SPAIN

This book was first published under the
title *Le Profit et les Crises* by
François Maspero et Cie in 1974.

© François Maspero 1974
© in English translation: Heinemann Educational Books 1984
First published in English 1984

ISBN 0 435 84354 0

British Library Cataloguing in Publication Data

Emmanuel, Arghiri
Profit and crises.
1. Developing countries—Economic conditions
2. International economic relations
I. Title II. Le profit et les crises, *English*
382′.09172′4 HC59.7

ISBN 0-435-84354-0

QUEEN MARY
COLLEGE
LIBRARY

Phototypesetting by Castlefield Press, Northampton
Printed in Great Britain by Biddles Ltd, Guildford, Surrey

Contents

Foreword

This book constitutes a major contribution to the analysis of particular contradictions in the capitalist mode of production, especially those arising from the existence of profit and demonstrated in movement of prices and crises of overproduction. Arghiri Emmanuel supplies decisive answers to questions that have hitherto remained unilluminated, notably because they have been developed in quite different directions by authors who are otherwise close in outlook, or even sometimes by one and the same writer, a clear indication of how inadequately these problems have been resolved.

Emmanuel's abundantly detailed text opens the way not only to a proper analysis of overproduction, price movements and economic crises but also to a more precise formulation of numerous other problems such as company profits, inflation and 'stagflation'. From this base progress can now be made in areas where Marxist analysis had previously come more or less to a standstill, while official theories provided plainly illusory solutions whose only purpose was to support particular class practices.

Of course, even with its great qualities this work cannot but contain either gaps or debatable points. As far as I am concerned the latter are essentially the same as those discussed in my remarks attached to the author's previous work *Unequal Exchange*.

To round off this brief foreword I would like to say that in my view this book is an extension of Marx's analyses. Here we find a clear, systematic and explicit treatment and development of a collection of propositions that Marx set out either in brief form or in terms that are open to mistaken or contradictory interpretations. A case in point is where Marx seems to be discussing circulation of capital when in fact his remarks are devoted to a specific problem concerning product realisation. By clarifying these questions in a rigorous and outstandingly logical manner, Arghiri Emmanuel has made a contribution of the first order to our understanding of the capitalist mode of production, an understanding that is vital to all those striving to combat the exploitation and oppression that capitalism still inflicts on the vast majority of mankind.

Charles Bettelheim

Preface to the English Edition

In 1974, when I completed the first French edition, the original oil crisis had just occurred. It was to put an end to over a quarter century of crisis-free growth, a period unprecedented in the history of capitalism. The so-called 'recessions' of that period, including that of 1970–71, were no more than minor fluctuations below the prevailing rate of growth, leaving this growth rate on average two-and-a-half times as high as the average annual rate of expansion in England over the century preceding the First World War, a century which saw that country dominate the world industrially.

My lengthy ninth chapter was therefore devoted to an explanation of this 'miracle', despite the warning signals of its impending end. This was quite natural. In the framework of my arguments as a whole, unemployment is the system's normal condition. What are unusual and, consequently, stand in need of explanation, are those situations in which the system manages to reproduce itself up to the limits determined by its endowment of factors, especially if these situations outlast cyclical business recoveries, as was indeed the case with the extraordinary long stretch of full employment (or quasi-full employment) after the last war.

Nonetheless, I did not ignore these 'warning signals'. Right at the start of Chapter 9, I expressed my belief that this exceptional period was no more than a reprieve, that 'there is nothing to say that . . . an overproduction crisis . . . will not break out before this book reaches publication (p. 293)'; and further (on p. 366, note 67), I suggested that everything now depended on the size of the oil surpluses and on the behaviour of the industrial countries in response to these surpluses.

I made it clear that, in my view, the problem was not the price of oil in itself, but firstly, the extent to which the oil countries would be capable of really *receiving* this price, in the sense of absorbing its counterpart of extra imports and, secondly, the protectionist measures which the industrial countries might adopt out of panic, in order to palm off on each other their own shares of the overall trade deficit with OPEC.

A retrospective examination of events since 1974 gives me no reason to revise my ideas. In fact, in so far as the oil crisis has been the main cause of the current depression – and I believe that it has been – it is not as the payment of a bill that it has played this role. If it were really a matter of payment – between countries only the delivery of extra real values to cover the change in price can legitimately be termed 'payment' – I do not believe that this would have been a major problem. For at the time of the first price hike in 1974 – and, *a fortiori*, the second in 1979–80 – the consumer countries had more than enough excess capacity to produce these values at practically zero social cost and to deliver them to the oil producing countries without growing poorer or even reducing their growth rates.

The calculation is simple. In OECD there were already some seven million unemployed, and more than enough idle means of production to equip them. Since value-added per employee was, at that time, on average $14,000 per year, mobilisation of this potential would have allowed the production of more than $90 billion of extra value-added. But the increase in the price of oil only added up to around $60 billion. OECD countries could therefore have paid it by setting to work only part of their idle potential, human and material. Even if we were to allow that the capitalist system cannot react in this positive way to such a revaluation of imports, by increasing employment enough to make up for the loss resulting from the worsening of the terms of trade, then this loss, compared with the total annual GNP of the OECD countries, would have represented a levy of only 1.5% per year. This would easily have been outweighed by productivity growth and demographic expansion of the workforce, even allowing for the persistence of unemployment.

But not only is the system incapable of reacting positively to such 'shocks': it is, in certain circumstances, led to react negatively. In this way, instead of mobilising the unemployed to produce the counterpart of the oil, the mechanisms set in motion resulted in throwing 10 million extra workers out of a job after the 1974 rise, and a further 10 million after 1979–80.

Why is this? Because it turned out that the oil producers were not in a position to collect the whole sum due to them. In a sense, they were too poor to be able to absorb the price that their joint political action had enabled them to fix. Between 1974 and 1978, they were only able to *absorb* half of the extra income, the rest being kept in the form of financial holdings.

If the consumer countries were planned economies, this partial respite from payment would have been a godsend, because it would have allowed them to deal with the frictions and bottlenecks resulting from the mobilisation of their resources, by spreading the necessary adjustments out over time. But for market economies this is a poisoned gift. For it results in a deficit on the balance of trade, and it is this which these economies are totally incapable of dealing with. (This was seen after the First World War when the allies eventually had to renounce their claim on most of the reparations imposed on Germany in the Versailles Treaty because of the system's inability to digest them.) The OECD countries, then, acting out of panic and in disarray, each trying to escape from the danger zone at the expense of the rest, adopted a series of deflationary measures which had the effect of causing two or three times the harm which these very measures were supposed to cure.

The table shows OECD estimate, published in March 1982 and referring to the second oil crisis, which is interesting in this regard.

OECD countries' loss of real income due to the 1979–80 oil price rise and the policies adopted to deal with it (expressed as a percentage of the GNP of the OECD area)

	1980	*1981*
Losses due to worsening of the terms of trade	1¾	1¾
Loss of GNP		
caused by extra OPEC savings	3	4¼
caused by OECD countries' policies	¼	1¾
TOTAL	5	7¾

It is not clear on what basis the OECD experts distinguish between the loss caused by OPEC's 'savings' and that caused by the measures adopted by OECD countries in response to this saving. A human community can only lose from its suppliers' abstention from demanding full payment for their supplies – this is what the OECD calls 'savings' – as a result of certain contradictory 'measures' which its economic system forces it to adopt. In the last analysis, crises are nothing other than '*a failure of the system because of the operation of the system itself*', in Immanuel Wallerstein's very apt phrase. Leaving aside all other considerations on the merits and demerits of the system of planning, it is hard to see how the Soviet Union could suffer any loss or disturbance because its Western partners agreed – as they do today – to supply a proportion of the commodities it needs on credit which can be rescheduled for ever. Indeed, no country of the Eastern bloc has ever been known to avoid a deficit on its trade balance as long as the credit extended by its suppliers made it possible to finance this deficit.

This 'credit' must also include 'credit money'. Imagine a situation in which the Soviet Union's Western suppliers were to accept, in payment for their supplies, roubles which they would then sterilise in their reserves, or which they would have fun turning into petro-roubles or Euro-roubles, as the oil-producing countries do today with dollars. Not only would the Soviet Union find it acceptable for its exports to be reduced thereby, it would be delighted. As I say in my work, to export is to give and to give is to become poorer. To import is to receive and to receive is to become richer. This is the natural order of things. The market economy reverses this and stands the world on its head. Here one gains from losses and loses from gains. This 'perversity' is the main object of my work, and in everything which has taken place in the world since its first draft, I can find no better illustration of it than the effects of the oil surpluses on the economies of the centre.

However this may be, the OECD study referred to above shows clearly that it is the deflationary effect, 4¼ + 1¾ = 6% (in 1981), and not the inflationary effect, 1¾%, which constitutes by far the largest loss of substance. This is remarkable in an organisation which has for so long firmly insisted on the absolute priority of the struggle against inflation.

Imagine that oil was produced by countries with large domestic markets, such as Holland or the Scandinavian countries, and that these countries had set up an OPEC and increased their prices in the same way and by the same proportion. Or imagine that it was not through an increase in royalties and taxes but through an increase in the remuneration of factors representing consumable domestic revenues, that the actual OPEC oil was made more expensive. In both cases, the demand on the international market of either of these groups of countries would have risen by as much as their export receipts, and the oil purchasers would have been required to satisfy this demand, and so to settle in full their oil bill with real values. Thus, in the worst case, in which these countries were unable to increase employment and had to supply the extra commodities at the expense of domestic consumption, there would have been a primary transfer of wealth from these countries towards the oil countries, amounting (according to the OECD estimate) to 1¾% of GNP. No secondary effect and no crisis.

The result would be the same if the oil-producing countries, though still poor, as indeed they are, were planned countries, able to take investment decisions upstream despite the absence of 'prior outlets' downstream. The result would again be the same if it were the consuming countries which were planned, in which case, as we said earlier, the suppliers' inability to absorb commodities, far from causing problems, would on the contrary have reduced the stress on their productive apparatus.

In reality, the crisis occurred because the suppliers and the consumers were countries with market economies, but the former were forced to hoard because of the inelasticity of their national markets.

But this is not the only point which has in my view been borne out by events. The way in which the industrial countries are trying to solve the problem is another. Incapable of surmounting their rivalries and launching an internationally coordinated boost to consumption – a boost which take place without any danger of disequilibrium in the balances of trade and payments, since trade within the zone affords a sufficient degree of autonomy to the zone in relation to the rest of the world – they fall back on different variants of supply-side economics. The industrial countries would again be trying to realise the age-old dream of the capitalist system, to invest independently of and in inverse proportion to final consumption. The constant failure of these attempts seems to me fully to confirm the position I developed in Chapter 10, that the fundamental contradiction of the market economy is the fact that its decision-makers cannot but treat investment and consumption as directly proportional magnitudes, whereas they are by nature inversely proportional.

Finally, one last thing which is noteworthy in post-1974 developments is, in Gabriel Thomas's phrase, the impudent health of the balance of trade of those countries that revalue their currencies and the baneful sickness which afflicts those countries which depreciate theirs, despite the fact that these changes in exchange rates considerably exceed the respective differentials in the rates of inflations, and thus despite the fact that, corrected for monetary variations, the export prices of the former have risen considerably more than those of the latter. This is a spectacular refutation of the postulate that the elasticity of demand is greater than unity, which I challenged in my work.

All these points only strengthen my conviction that, apart from the reformulation of certain passages (few in number), which are only meant to fill some gaps in my arguments, pointed out to me by the apposite remarks of Nicholas Costello in the course of the translation, none of the essential points of my work stand in need of revision on the occasion of this English edition.

Arghiri Emmanuel
September 1982

1 Introduction

A basic postulate

I announced my intention to write this work in the introduction to my study on *Unequal Exchange*.[1] At that time I mentioned it only in passing, while on the subject of a certain kind of protectionism which traditional economic doctrine since Quesnay has generally condemned, but without bothering to explain why it crops up again and again.

I wrote then that in order to take account of this phenomenon, one must reject the basic postulate of political economy, that the sum of revenues generated in a given period is equal to the value of the new production of that same period. I added that the beginnings of a rejection of this equation are to be found in Sismondi, but that he stops short on this point, in his hotchpotch of ideas which are as rich as they are unsystematic. Finally, I put forward the opinion that an *implicit* rejection of this equation is to be found in certain of Marx's formulations, especially when he is dealing with overproduction, or over-accumulation of capital; but that, in Marx's work as a whole, this rejection could not stand up against the *explicit* schematisation of this very equation, in the chapters on simple and expanded reproduction, and in the passages where he is studying the realisation of the product.

Since no one has completed Marx's work, the challenge of this apparent 'contradiction' between the contents of different notebooks and scraps of paper does not seem to have been accepted right up to now. Lenin, in his desire to prove to the populists that capitalism is quite capable of generating growth, stressed the equilibrating factors.[2] And all those who are more concerned with the disequilibria, such as Rosa Luxemburg for example, have always attributed them, in one way or another, to disproportions between branches of production which are inevitable under capitalism, the controversy dealing exclusively with the nature and effects of these disproportions.

As a result of this, the classical postulate of the accounting – and

1. *Unequal Exchange*, London, 1972.
2. *See footnote on following page.*

therefore indestructible – equality between the aggregate value added in production and the sum of distributed revenues has not been refuted, even by the most radical and scientific critique of the market economy, Marxism. The subject of the present work is the challenging of this sacrosanct equation.[3]

It goes without saying that the full meaning of this refutation is not limited to an explanation of protectionism. The latter is only a secondary and localised manifestation of a structural and general disequilibrium of the capitalist mode of production. It is this disequilibrium itself which will be studied in this work. The aim I have set myself is to show that we are dealing with an essential contradiction of this mode of production; and that, on the level of the realisation and reproduction of the product, the original contradiction between social production and private appropriation resolves itself, or transforms itself, into this contradiction.

It may therefore seem strange that I approach this contradiction, so to speak, obliquely, from the aspect of its manifestation in international trade. This is because I think that this domain shows more clearly than any other the impasse which economic science has

2. 'The more rapid the process of accumulation, i.e. the excess of production over consumption, the better, taught the classical economists, who, though they were not clear about the process of the social production of capital, and though they were unable to free themselves from Adam Smith's mistaken view that the social product consists of two parts, nevertheless advanced the perfectly correct idea that production creates a market for itself and itself determines consumption. And we also know that Marx's theory [. . .] took over this view of accumulation from the classical economists' (Lenin, *Collected Works*, vol. 2, p. 148). And a few pages further on, 'Hence, "consumption" develops *after* "accumulation", or *after* "production"; strange though it may seem, it cannot be otherwise in capitalist society' (p. 155, emphasis original).

3. I would like at the outset to avoid a possible misunderstanding. What we are concerned with here is precisely the equality between production and revenues, and not that between production and effective demand. Marxism has formally and explicitly challenged this latter equality,

However, the two equations have often been clumsily conflated in the 'Theory of Markets', and have not always been properly separated in economic thought. Keynes distinguishes between them from the outset and rejects the latter, calling it a Euclidean postulate, but unreservedly accepts the former. 'The conclusion that the *costs* of output are always covered in the aggregate by the sales-proceeds resulting from demand, has great plausibility, because it is difficult to distinguish it from another, similar looking proposition which is indubitable, namely that the income derived in the aggregate by all the elements in the community concerned in a productive activity necessarily has a value exactly equal to the *value* of the output' (*General Theory*, p. 20).

Lenin went so far in the defence of this *indubitable* equation, and distinguished it so little from the other, that Plekhanov was able at one time to see in him a second Russian partisan of Say, the first being Tugan Baranovski (note to 1905 edition of *Our Controversies*).

been led into by the postulate of the material impossibility of general overproduction. Here we have a rare case of a permanent and absolute divorce between science and business, between theory and praxis. It will not – I believe – be useless to ponder this for a short while before getting down to the root of the problem. A certain concreteness of view and, so to speak, demystification in advance, may be gained from this topsy-turvy world, the contradictions of which we shall then have to reproduce through reflection on it.

The 'mirage' of a surplus balance of payments

The protectionism which I mentioned in the part of my last work referred to above was not List's protectionism, in which the custom's tariff plays the role of a *handicap* designed to equalise the chances of a nascent national industry with those of its fully grown foreign competitors; i.e., the kind that helps a *specific* branch of production that is worthwhile in itself on the basis of comparative costs to get through its infancy.[4]

Nor was it that of Manuilesco or certain modern theories of growth which see industrialisation as an end in itself, an autonomous factor of development, independently of all considerations of geo-economic viability or comparative costs, which Graham calls the protection of 'infant capitalism' instead of 'infant industry'.[5] Nor was it the specific protectionism of reprisals against a particular foreign country which is striking at one's own products with aggressive customs duties; nor the kind aimed at curing a chronic deficit in the balance of trade which is exhausting one's reserves. The kind of protectionism I was referring to was all round and unconditional protectionism, including, apart from custom's tariffs, the whole range of possible measures to promote exports and restrict imports. The aim of these measures is quite simply to *sell*, to sell anything,

4. In reality List only systematised the 'infant industry' argument. The argument itself is to be found in many different parts of economic literature. Not only in Alexander Hamilton and John Stuart Mill, as is generally recognised, but also, long before List, in various eighteenth and nineteenth century authors such as Andrew Jarranton and William Wood. Sismondi (*Nouveaux Principes*, book I, chapter XI) and Fr. Ferrier both speak of it. Finally, it is to be found in the most eminent mercantilists. Thus Forbonnais estimates the maximum protective tariffs for a new industry to be 15%, so that the inclusion of transport charges, commissions, etc. gives a margin of from 18 to 20%, which should be enough *if the industry is viable in itself* (*Eléments du commerce*, I, p. 251). Compared with the tariffs of today, these percentages, though recommended by an eminent mercantilist, seem remarkably moderate.

5. See Frank D. Graham, 'Some aspects of protection further considered', *Quarterly Journal of Economics*, February 1923.

anywhere, anyhow, to sell more to the rest of the world than one buys from it, and thus to ensure a balance of trade *not in balance, but in surplus*.

This last kind of protectionism was not exclusively the result of an ephemeral aberration of mercantilist policies. It is the constant element of foreign economic policy at all times, in all countries with market economies. If there has been any fluctuation, this has only been on the level of economic thought. We should further stress that it is only called an aberration from a certain level of economic abstraction upwards. Below this level, even in the technical language of economists, a favourable balance and a surplus balance are synonyms.

It is not enough to state that this policy is absurd and pointless at the international level, since, whatever one does, the world balance of exports and imports cannot be in surplus or deficit, and that the only effect of blanket customs duties in all countries is to lower the level at which this equilibrium is attained, to the detriment of all concerned. What is known as the system of nationalism was not concerned with the world equilibrium or optimum. The politicians and economists of the time declared unambiguously and without any hypocrisy that their aim was to get rich on the backs of others. They were even convinced, and they said as much, that there was no other way of getting rich.[6] Though less frank nowadays, those in charge of foreign trade in all the different countries still pursue essentially the same ends.

It was irrelevant that the adoption of this behaviour could lead to a general fall in world trade, which would harm one's own interests. The point was, how could a *specific* country hope to enrich itself by means of a permanent surplus balance, always assuming that it could attain the situation, at the expense of the rest of the world. For we are no longer talking about a current surplus aimed at building up reserves as a form of insurance against eventual future deficits. We are dealing fairly and squarely with surplus as an end in itself. If a surplus balance is held to be favourable, there is no reason to wish that it be temporary.

Now, whereas economists have disagreed about the theorem that commodities are paid for with commodities and that supply equals

6. 'But the city in its commerce should only think of itself and never of other peoples', said Aristotle (*Politics*, book IV, chapter V, para 5).

Colbert thought that the sum total of world trade, the number of boats and output of manufactured articles, were relatively fixed; and therefore that any expansion by one country in this domain could only be accomplished at the expense of some other country. Thus, he concluded, trade is like a war.

effective demand within each national economy, once we come to foreign trade there is no room for disagreement, whether for economists or for simple common sense. Between countries, no payment is materially possible, except either in the form of goods and services (including monetised metals), or in the form of securities. But since securities can only be used for the eventual importation of goods or services through the use of the revenue from these securities or the principal itself, there is in the long term only one means of international payment: goods and services. If this is the case, a permanent balance of payments surplus, through the very fact that it makes these goods and services undesirable, amounts to giving the surplus away to the rest of the world as a present.

To put it another way, the country that attains a permanent surplus balance can only accumulate gold and silver ingots, or foreign assets. The question arises: in the former case how can one believe that this or that kind of money is wealth, since, by rejecting the idea of a deficit balance in the present or future, one has precluded oneself from ever using this hoard?; in the latter case what is the use of these stocks and shares destined to be accumulated for ever, if, the surplus being permanent, they can never be converted into any kind of use-values?

The countries with surplus balances send abroad real values, which have cost national labour and resources. In the former case they receive others – gold and silver – which are just as real, and which have cost the rest of the world just as much, but which, once obtained, are worth scarcely more than the cellars in which they are buried, as in La Fontaine's well known verse. In the latter case, they receive stocks and shares which have only cost the rest of the world ink and paper, and which, in Leon Say's expression, are worth less than blank paper, since they have been dirtied with writing.[7]

Yet this frantic search for a surplus for surplus's sake has been an unshakable feature of the economic policies of all states, ever since commodity relations, capitalist or pre-capitalist, have developed within and between nations. This takes us back a long way – certainly to the High Middle Ages, perhaps to the Graeco-Roman world and, according to some, back to the Phoenicians.[8] Selling without buying has always been considered a victory, buying without selling, a

7. If we export commodities payable only in gold, 'we should be acquiring an asset of complete worthlessness to ourselves, so that we might as well have made a gift; while the outside world as a whole is "worse off", relatively to the gift situation, by the amount of real resources devoted to gold production' (Howard S. Ellis, 'Bilateralism and the future of international trade', p. 430, *Essays in International Finance*, n°. 5, Summer 1945, reprinted in *Readings in the Theory of International Trade*, pp. 408–36.

8. See A. H. L. Heeren, *Historical Researches*, vol. I, p. 328.

defeat, while the most elementary logic shows that, at least at the international level, the former amounts to giving without receiving, and the latter to receiving without giving.[9]

If, from time to time, this trade war between nations has been suspended or attenuated by bilateral or multilateral agreements, as in the short interval of free trade in the middle of the nineteenth century, this was simply a matter, through the play of reciprocal concessions, of guarding against a general contraction of world trade while the balance of forces at the time had reached a certain equilibrium and did not allow any of the parties involved any reasonable hope of beating the others by means of a permanent surplus. The actual principle of the advantageousness of a surplus was never challenged anywhere outside textbooks of political economy. As soon as the uneven rate of development changed this balance of forces, the agreements were smashed to pieces, and trade wars restarted more ferociously than ever. This was well and truly the case at the end of the free-trade truce in the 1880s, which respectable economists expressed their horror about by calling it neo-mercantilism. This does not explain it at all – it merely names it – and the phenomenon we are talking about was in sore need of an explanation.

Simplistic anti-mercantilism: naivety or blindness?

Since the time of Quesnay and Adam Smith, political economy has adopted the position of considering this trade policy of the capitalist states as a technical error, engendered by the 'chrysohedonic illusion'. It has got round the problem superbly. Leaving aside the naivety of this position, the explanation itself is totally gratuitous. Not only did the mercantilists never express the slightest chrysohedonism, but the most representative of them took pains explicitly to dissipate this illusion in the minds of their readers.

Thus Davenant, after having declared that 'Whatever Goods we make up of Foreign Materials, and sell in the Markets abroad all above the Cost of the Materials is a clear Gain to England',[10] affirms no less strongly that 'the real and effective Riches of a Country, is its native Product', and that 'Gold and Silver are indeed the Measure of Trade, but the Spring and Original of it, in all Nations, is the Natural, or Artificial Product of the Country, that is to say, what their Land, or

9. As Furniss points out, over the seventeenth and eighteenth centuries any country that sold Britain more than it bought from her was considered virtually as an enemy, while any country with which Britain had a surplus balance could obtain all the favours of H.M. Government and the help of her diplomatic representatives.

10. C. Davenant, *An Essay upon the Probable Methods*, pp. 96–7.

what their Labour and Industry produces.[11] And to illustrate his point of view, he points out that 'in Persia and some of the Eastern-Nations (where 'tis believ'd there is more Gold and Silver than in any other Part of the World) the Common People are under the last Degree of Poverty. . . .'[12] He also thought that through universal agreement anything, and especially credit, could perfectly well replace gold, and in his *New Dialogues* he went into ecstasies over the Bank of Amsterdam's system, where no gold or silver were to be seen passing through the cash-desks: all operations were carried out by transfers from one account to another.

Montchretien pleaded ardently for colonial expansion in order to secure markets for French products, but was careful to stress at the same time that it is not gold and silver or pearls and diamonds which make a state wealthy, but the goods necessary for the life of its citizens.[13]

This supposed fetishism of money would anyway have been completely incompatible with the quantitative theory of money, accepted more or less explicitly by the great majority of these writers, and the first known traces of which are to be found in the works of Jean Bodin, one of the earliest mercantilists:

> I find that the dearness that we see comes approximately because of four or five reasons. The principal and almost only reason (though no one up to the present has touched upon it) is the abundance of gold and silver, which today in this realm is greater than it has been for four hundred years . . .', and also '. . . The principal factor that raises the price of all these things everywhere is the abundance of that which gives value and price to things.[14]

Forbonnais' quantitative formulation is much more precise: 'Imagine two self-sufficient countries, with equal populations, no external relations, possessing an equal number of the same foodstuffs; that in one of them the mass of foodstuff is represented by 100 pounds of some metal, and in the other by 200 pounds of the same metal. What is worth one ounce in one will cost two ounces in the other.'[15]

Can one really believe that money is a form of wealth in itself when one is a partisan of the quantitative theory and convinced that the value of money is inversely proportional to its quantity? Having such

11. C. Davenant, *Discourse on the Public Revenues*, p. 15. This leads Marx to say that 'it must not be thought that these mercantilists were as stupid as they were made out to be by the later Vulgar–Freetraders' (*Theories of Surplus Value*, I, p. 174).

12. *Discourse on the Public Revenues*, p. 64.

13. A. de Montchretien, *Traicté de l'oeconomie politique*, p. 241.

14. J. Bodin, *Response of Jean Bodin*, p. 23.

15. V. de Forbonnais, *Eléments du commerce*, vol. II, p. 90.

a nominalist and relativist conception of money as the quantitative theory while at the same time holding money to be true and absolute wealth would have been such a gross contradiction that it could only be explained by mental deficiency. Thinking that such writers as Forbonnais, Davenant, Mun, etc. were mentally deficient is, to say the least, hardly tenable. Yet this is the position that orthodox political economy has adopted.

In their desire to demystify money, the classics were knocking down open doors. Long before them, and long before Quesnay, such authors as William Petty, Boisguillebert and Vauban had done the job of dispelling any illusions that might have survived. Quesnay's definition of money as an intermediary pledge between sales and purchases, however appealing it may be, does not differ greatly from that of Boisguillebert: a pledge for the handing over of real things. (Anyway, neither of them added much to Aristotle: an intermediate commodity whose purpose is to facilitate exchange between two other commodities.)

The Common Report of the Three Estates to the Estates General declared in 1484: 'Money is to the body politick what blood is to the human body.' This is a good summary of the mercantilist epoch's conception of money: money, the bearer of nutritive substances, rather than a nutritive substance itself. 'Money is but the Fat of the Body politick', William Petty was later to declare, 'whereof too much doth as often hinder Agility, as too little makes it sick.'[16] Money is only the oil that facilitates the movement of the wheels of commerce, said Hume, one of the last Mercantilists. Forbonnais illustrated the futility of accumulating gold and silver, by citing the examples of Spain and Portugal, which impoverished themselves by 'neglecting the arts and culture of Europe, in order to gather silver and gold in these new provinces'.[17] To the examples of Spain and Portugal, Vauban added those of Peru and India, 'which abound in Gold and precious Stones, and yet want Bread'.[18]

However much you search in mercantilist writings, you will find no suggestion of this 'chrysohedonic illusion' which their critics accuse them of so often. Josiah Child, a convinced mercantilist and ardent partisan of all kinds of state intervention up to the most aggressive, such as the Navigation Act, was nonetheless in favour of the free exit of gold and silver from the country, whether monetised or not. '[Coin and Bullion] seems [. . .] most plentiful when there is least occasion for it, and on the contrary, most scarce, as the occasions for the

16. *Verbum Sapienti* in *The Economic Writings of Sir William Petty*, vol. I, p. 113.
17. *Eléments du commerce*, vol. I, p. 29.
18. S. Vauban, *A Project for a Royal Tythe*, p. 2.

employment thereof are more numerous and advantagious. . . .'[19]

Giovanni Botero adopted the same position: 'But of what use is all the wealth of Croesus and Midas to a ruler who, when he is attacked by sea, has no timber to make ships and galleys, no artificers, sailors, navigators, no tackle nor any other essentials? . . . He who has nothing to buy is as poor as he who has nothing to spend.'[20] He goes on to explain that, in all cases, one should only accumulate as much money as corresponds to the surplus of the balance of trade, a conception not very different from that of Thomas Mun, who declared that only the money coming from the surplus of the balance of trade is profitable, explaining that, 'if we melt down our plate into Coyn [. . .] it would cause Plenty of mony for a time, yet should we be none the richer'.[21]

These two last positions, those of Botero and Mun, show clearly that, in the eyes of the mercantilists, the utility of a surplus balance of trade does not in the least consist in the building up of a hoard, although an influx of precious metals is welcome as the sign and consequence of a surplus balance. *In what, then, does it consist?* This is the question which political economy has neglected to pose, convinced as it has been that it is pointless to look for reasons for such a paranoiac kind of behaviour.

19. Josiah Child, *A new Discourse of Trade*, p. 145ff.

20. *The Reason of State*, book VII, p. 141.

21. *England's Treasure by Forraign Trade*, p. 52ff. An analogy can be drawn between this conception and the current reaction of various countries, on the occasion of the first international monetary crisis. The 'commercial' dollar is welcomed; the 'financial' dollar is rebuffed. Germany and Japan are inundated by a flood of dollars. They get worried, react, take measures to stem the flood. But at the same time, these same countries protest vigorously against Nixon's protectionist measures aimed at improving the US balance of trade, thereby recovering a portion of these dollars which are encumbering them so much. Now in theory the most profitable way to get rid of these dollars would be, precisely, to realise them, i.e. to allow them to be converted into US or other commodities.

The formal distinction which France has just established between the financial and the commercial dollar is an even better illustration of this parallelism with mercantilist doctrine, which distinguished, as we noted above, between money coming from the trade surplus and all other money. The financial dollar is allowed to float and depreciate; one wants to get rid of it. But everything is done to maintain and even increase one's surplus on sales abroad; and thus to obtain as many commercial dollars as possible.

Now, once in the possession of a foreign country, a commercial dollar does not differ in the slightest from a financial dollar. It is still the same dollar: a claim on the US. Whether it comes from commercial or financial dealings, this dollar is just as inconvertible, and the claim deriving from it is just as irrecoverable in either case. Therefore these countries do not want to sell in order to obtain dollars: they want to sell in order to sell.

The survival of the mercantilist 'illusion'

It is interesting to note that, in the contemporary era, states have not abandoned the search for a surplus, although events have done the job of dispelling the chrysohedonic illusion by the elimination of its very object. States no longer have the excuse that the free-traders gave for the mercantilists, since they no longer receive gold as the counterpart of their surplus on sales. They receive inconvertible dollars which they hasten to declare undesirable, while being careful not to refuse them.*

Taking political realities into account, let us imagine that political pressure from the US compels the central banks of certain countries, which are more or less US vassals, to create more of their own currency, buy these excess dollars with it, and put the dollars in their treasuries with no hope of using them in the future, while not only is this against their own interests, but also the traditional statutes of the central banks of emission previously expressly forbade it. However, this pressure is not the only reason why the surplus countries hesitate to leave the dollar to its fate. The fear of losing the American market is another, just as compelling if not more so. Anyway, politics is not the only argument of the Americans themselves. They use another: if you don't want our dollars, then stop selling your junk to us. And everything goes to show that this argument is every bit as compelling as political pressure.[22]

The same language was used before the last war by the German Minister of Economics, Dr Schacht, to the Balkan countries, who were complaining about the permanent surplus in their clearings with Hitler's Germany. And in this particular case, in order to buttress the monetary 'illusion', the Balkan states had neither its material basis – gold or silver – nor even its universality, its *socialisation* on a world scale, as in the present case of the dollar. Yet, in general, and with

*Translator's note: This was written in the early 1970s.

22. Here it must be said that, for each country taken separately, what is in question is not its exports to the US alone, but its exports towards the whole of the rest of the world. For, ever since the dollar standard was set up, no country could cease buying all the dollars offered to it without effectively revaluing its currency, and it cannot revalue it in relation to the dollar without automatically revaluing it in relation to all the other currencies that have retained their old fixed parity in relation to the dollar. (The only parry – and it is only slightly effective – is the dissociation of the financial dollar from the commercial dollar and the adoption of a dual exchange rate.)

Therefore, in effect, the dilemma that the US places all other countries in, taking advantage of their disunity, is not 'accept dollars or cut back your sales on the American market', but 'support the dollar or revalue, and thereby reduce your sales throughout the world'.

This, obviously, does not yet explain why countries still prefer to sell for useless pieces of paper rather than cut back their sales.

more or less objections, they played the game, and the clearings lasted up till the war in 1940, which several of these states were the victims of, after having contributed to its preparation with their supplies without any counterpart.

Can one really reproach the mercantilists of the sixteenth and seventeenth centuries for selling useful commodities for sterile gold? Rather than restrain their sales, today's states prefer to sell for less than that: for credit balances in a clearing account which they know will never be re-absorbed, for dollar balances which will never be used. How did matters reach such a point? What is this system which so debases the product of human labour as to make it less desirable than doubtful or even clearly fictive claims?

To think that such an aim, as to continuously sell more to the rest of the world than one buys from it, could have been pursued so systematically over so many centuries by all countries and all governments without exception as the result of an error in formal logic is a fantastic supposition. It is scarcely credible that so many economists have been satisfied with it. This phenomenon deserved a deeper examination.

The Marxist view on protectionism

Marxism has not made a systematic study of this question because the quarrel between free-trade and protection has been considered, in Lenin's phrase, 'a question of bourgeois policy'. Nonetheless it offers a more plausible explanation. The phenomenon of protectionism results from the dominant position of the interest groups and capitalist strata who stand to gain by it.[23]

This is Lenin's position: 'Protection . . . serves the interests not of the entire bourgeois class, but merely of a handful of all-powerful magnates. . . .'[24] This is also Rosa Luxemburg's view when she describes the frenetic rise of protective tariffs at the time of the US civil war:

> Messrs Morrill, Stevens and the other gentlemen who advanced the war as a lever for enforcing their proctectionist programme initiated the practice of weilding the implement of a customs policy quite openly and cynically to further private profiteering interests of all descriptions. Any home producer who appeared before the legislative assembly with a request for any kind of special tariff to fill his own pocket saw his demands readily

23. It is because free trade, by developing the extreme antagonism between the bourgeoisie and the proletariat, accelerates the process which carries within itself the means to get free of capitalism and 'hastens the Social Revolution', that Marxists have on various occasions come out in favour of free trade, without any deeper commitment (see K. Marx, *Speech on the Question of Free Trade*, delivered in Brussels in 1848, *Collected Works*, vol. 6, p. 465).

24. Lenin, *The Economic Content of Narodnism* in *Collected Works*, vol. 1, p. 436.

granted, and the tariff rates were made as high as any interested party might wish.[25]

Also, according to J. Duret, protectionism became necessary under monopoly regimes in order to 'protect' the domestic monopoly super-profits.[26]

This explanation, though coherent, falls short, which is not surprising given that the Marxist writers we are concerned with deal with protectionism as a marginal problem.[27] It falls short, because the protectionism we are talking about, that which tries to ensure a permanent surplus of exports over imports, has such a perennial and continuous character as to extend far beyond any conjunctural situation of the predominance of one capitalist group over another. It all suggests that we are dealing, not with the circumstantial interests of this or that group of capitalists, but with the vital and permanent interests of the entire capitalist class, of the very survival of its economic system.

Anyway, the Marxist authors we have quoted, and above all Lenin, were not dealing with this kind of protectionism, but only with the protection of certain *disproportionately developed* branches, which are therefore incapable of realising the exchange of their products on the domestic market (we will return to this point when we examine theories of disproportion). But when capitalism can be driven, as we said above, to accept even non-payment in order to be able to drain off its surplus, we are dealing with a phenomenon which Lenin, for example, refused to countenance:

> Do we deny that capitalism needs a foreign market? Of course not. But the question of a foreign market has *absolutely nothing to do with the question of realisation* [. . .] The romanticist says the capitalists cannot consume surplus-value and therefore must dispose of it abroad. The question is: do the capitalists supply foreigners with products gratis, or do they throw them into the sea? They sell them – hence, they receive an equivalent; they export certain kinds of products – hence, they import other kinds.[28]

Lenin's classical side is to the fore in this passage. Do the capitalists supply foreigners with products gratis? The individual capitalist, no. Of course not. Although 'clearing' marks or inconvertible dollars

25. *The Accumulation of Capital*, p. 399.
26. See J. Duret, *Le Marxisme et les Crises*, p. 26.
27. The Marxists were not the first to attribute protectionism to the action of a social class or stratum. Bastiat had already pontificated: 'In England, the protectionist system had two supports: the economic error and Feudal power' (*Le Libre Echange*, in *Oeuvres completes*, vol. II, p. 232).
28. V.I. Lenin, *Economic Romanticism* in *Collected Works*, vol. 2, p. 162. Emphasis original.

may be the reflux of his exports, he himself is paid in his national currency. But for the capitalist state as a whole, matters are somewhat different. We must agree on the meaning of the word 'gratis'. Formally, no, the surplus commodities are not supplied gratis. They are covered by claims, by debts. But, even without using the extreme examples of clearing marks or reserve dollars, where the realisation of the claims is materially impossible even if the creditor states demand it – which they are careful not to do in order not to compromise their sales abroad – it is clear that these claims can only be recovered if a country's trade balance goes into deficit. As such an eventuality is rigidly excluded from the economic policy perspective of capitalist states, it can be said that these claims are just as unrecoverable as pre-war marks, or today's dollars.

These commodities, Lenin says, 'they sell them – hence, they receive an equivalent'. Yes, but we must see what kind of equivalent. 'They export certain kinds of products – hence, they import other kinds.' Not necessarily, no. The equivalent is not necessarily other goods or services. It may be claims representing an export of capital. These claims may even be entirely fictive. The need to sell in order to disburden the domestic market is so great that states nonetheless continue to accept them. Though unthinkable for Lenin, this is however what the Balkan states did before the last war, and what Germany and Japan are doing now. The question of the foreign market is not unconnected with that of realisation, as Lenin thought it to be.[29]

External protectionism: the by-product of a fundamental internal disequilibrium

Anticipating the central theme of this study, we may say that everything suggests that the search for a surplus on foreign trade is conditioned by some fundamental constraint proceeding from the interior of the market economy system, that the functions of realisation and reproduction of the product within the country are in constant danger of deadlock by a permanent overflow which can only be reabsorbed by an external outlet, that this bloodletting abroad

29. One should however add that this 'classicism' of Lenin's was, to a certain extent, an echo of that of Marx. Thus in *Theories of Surplus Value* Marx approvingly quotes this passage from an anonymous Ricardian work directed against Malthus: 'The object of selling your goods is to make a certain amount of money; it never can answer to part with that sum of money for nothing, to another person, that he may bring it back to you, and buy your goods with it: you might as well have just burnt your goods at once, and you would have been in the same situation' (*Theories of Surplus Value,* vol. III, p. 60).

makes it possible to decongest the domestic market and release forces that increase its activity.

The apparent aberrance of the trade policy of each national capitalist formation would then only be a symptom of a profound structural contradiction in its internal functioning, the external disequilibrium between sales and purchases being intended to compensate for an inverse internal disequilibrium. A struggle to give without receiving, this *is* something completely topsy-turvy, but what is topsy-turvy is not mercantilist thought, but the real world which it reflects. This real world turned common sense upside down as the result of a radical change in the social relations of production on the day when, in Blanqui's expression, a 'strange contradiction' arose in human society, in which 'artificial and frantic production has taken the place of the regular and peaceful labour of earlier times, and the ability to sell has been restricted by a limitation of the ability to buy'.

The underlying cause of this phenomenon is no technical error, nor any internal rivalry between the capitalists, though this last factor may in some circumstances aggravate the contradiction. A permanent surplus in the balance of trade, supposing that it can be achieved, certainly constitutes a loss of substance for the national economy. But if it is possible, by this method, to unlock the internal mechanism of reproduction, and thereby to increase the level of activity and employ factors that would otherwise have remained unutilised, to 'wake up the dormant and idle productive forces of a country', in List's expression, then this loss may very well be outweighed by a larger gain in terms of the total volume of the domestic product.

From the moment when commodity relations became predominant, and the power of economic decision-making passed from the community to the individual, a complete reversal of the function of social production took place. Instead of consuming as much as we are materially capable of producing, we can only produce according to the rate and fluctuation of sales. Now the sale is no longer simply one phase of the distribution of the product; it is presupposed in its very existence since it is the condition for its creation. At this point, the marginal social cost of a commodity which is the object of an additional sale may be not only nil, but, so to speak, negative. This is the case if, not only does the production of this actual commodity depend upon its being sold, but its sale is also likely to stimulate the sales, and therefore the production, of other commodities which will be produced with overabundant and idle factors.[30]

Under the hypothesis of full employment, and above all on the basis of the axiom of the equality of total production and total purchasing power, the two premises of the classical economists, this whole structure collapses. All that then remains of the mercantilist approach is a commonplace piece of nonsense: the preference for the symbol which represents commodities over the commodities themselves. This is all that economists since Quesnay and Adam Smith have been able to find in the theories of their predecessors on the one hand, and in the protectionist practice which survived them on the other. But the coherence of their doctrine was certainly not the only factor determining the attitude of the economists. A certain consciously or unconsciously apologetic attitude, from the time when the system itself began to be challenged, could not but condition their thought to a certain extent. The admission that it is necessary to throw a portion of the product of human labour overboard in order to make the economic machine work, would have meant recognising that the established order is the ultimate absurdity. It was more convenient to believe that it was simply a matter of the blindness of the princes who govern it and the experts who advise them.

Under-employment: a corollary of the market economy

The mercantilists were in a different position. Because of the lack of detractors of the existing system, they were, firstly, free from apologetic inhibitions; and secondly, they lived in a world which had never approached what may be described by the term 'full employment'. Such a hypothesis would have seemed a complete fantasy to them. Since political economy was not yet a science, they spoke on the basis of their intuition and the experiences they had lived through. The main phenomenon which conditioned their reflections and their research was the huge, silent and amorphous under-employment of the pre-industrial trading society, the memory of which has subsequently been blurred by the registered, officialised and demanding, although incomparably smaller, unemployment of developed capitalism.[31]

Forbonnais, who was perhaps, with Davenant, the most systematic – one is tempted to say scientific – mercantilist author, tells us that the gold and silver sent us from abroad are only 'conventional wealth'. But, however conventional it may be, 'this wealth, by circulating

30. 'A Hundred Bales of Cloth that are burnt or sunk in the Mediterranean are as Beneficial to the Poor in England, as if they had safely arriv'd at Smyrna or Aleppo, and every Yard of them had been Retail'd in the Grand Signior's Dominions' (Mandeville, *The Fable of the Bees*, vol. I, p. 465).

31. According to Jacques Marchand, under-employment was the historical fact which, at least in part, led to the emergence of the mercantilist doctrine (see *La Renaissance du mercantilisme à l'époque contemporaine*).

domestically, will procure a comfortable existence for a greater number of citizens'.[32]

How can the additional money coming from an export surplus act as a stimulus to economic activity if, according to the quantitative theory generally accepted by the mercantilists, any increase in the quantity of money, whatever its source, only results in diminishing its value to a strictly proportional extent? And however this may be, what sense is there in seeking this surplus, since the price increase resulting from the inflow of money will, according to the same law, lead to an increase in imports and decrease of exports, which will re-establish equilibrium and therefore even involve the return abroad of the surplus previously gained?

Thomas Mun had already said that 'plenty or scarcity of mony makes all things dear or good or cheap; and this mony is either gotton or lost in forraign trade by the over or under-ballancing of the same'.[33] A superficial criticism has seen, in the search for a surplus, the image of a dog chasing its tail. And this is correct, if one abstracts from the time factor. The classics' analysis – all classicism is to a certain extent static – did make this abstraction. The dynamics of the mercantilist reasoning, admittedly expressed in unscientific terms, escaped them.

Once it had become a science, political economy took about a century to rediscover dynamic formulations in the true sense of the word, that is, formulations in which one studies the variations of the dependent variables of a system, not only as a function of the successive data, but also as a function of the evolution of these same variables over time.[34]

It makes no difference whether the quantity of money in circulation is 100 or 1000. As quantitativists, the mercantilists were perfectly aware of this. But it does make a difference whether the quantity of money is increasing from 50 to 100, or decreasing from 1500 to 1000. In the first case there is *inflation*, in the second *deflation*, with all the attendant phenomena on the level of employment, although in the first case there is less money in absolute terms than in

32. *Eléments du commerce*, vol. I, p. 78. See also vol. II, p. 68, where Forbonnais draws a distinction between natural wealth (agriculture), artificial wealth (industry), and conventional wealth (precious metals), established to represent real wealth.

33. *England's Treasure by Forraign Trade*, p. 51.

34. The highest speed at which we can negotiate a given corner without skidding depends not only on the condition of the vehicle and the shape of the road, but also on the speed at which we were driving *before* we reached this bend. We may be safer at 40 m.p.h. than at 30, if, in the first case, we are accelerating, i.e. if we have just reached 40 m.p.h. from 30 m.p.h., and if, in the second case, we are decelerating, i.e. if we have just reached 30 m.p.h. from 40 m.p.h.

the second.[35] In the first case economic activity is stimulated; in the second it is depressed.

There are numerous mercantilist writings which explain clearly that what counts in their eyes is not the quantity of money at any given point in time, but its changes over time. Forbonnais extensively analyses the relativity of the notion of the surplus balance. And Hume left us the most coherent formulation:

> It is of no manner of consequence . . . whether money be in a greater or less quantity. The good policy of the magistrate consists only in keeping it, if possible, still increasing, because by that means he keeps alive a spirit of industry in the nation, and increases the stock of labour in which consists all real power and riches. A nation, whose money decreases, is actually at that time weaker and more miserable than another nation which possesses no more money, but is on the increasing hand.[36]

There is an interval between the entry of money into circulation and the price increases and another interval between the increase in the price of goods and the increase in the price of labour-power. Finally, money may very well be nominal, but at least one price does not change – that of previously incurred debts – and another only changes indirectly – that of taxes. So the influx of money arouses activity *before* the opposing forces which it engenders affect the re-equilibrating movement of foreign accounts. And by the time this moment arrives, the conditions are already propitious for a renewed export drive on the basis of the increased domestic activity, and a renewed surplus on the balance of trade.[37]

Under-employment in undeveloped capitalism

All this, of course, only proves one thing: that one can at the same time, and without contradiction, believe that money is active and still accept the quantitative theory; but it does not show how the influx of money from a surplus balance can stimulate the economy, nor does it prejudice the well-foundedness of this thesis. It will anyway be

35. This is something which Suzanne de Brunhoff, for example, fails to take into account in her recent work, *L'Offre de monnaie*, and it is this which makes it impossible for her to understand how an entirely nominal currency can have any effect on the economy.

36. *Writings on Economics*, p. 209.

37. Suzanne de Brunhoff (L'Offre de monnaie) wonders how money can be 'socialised' without being tied to any real value. She forgets that money, even when entirely inconvertible and nominal, is invested by law with the power to pay off, at a fixed parity, already constituted debts and taxes. This is a fixed reference point which means that money's quantitative variations would not lack significance and real effects, even if all prices and all current remunerations were adjusted *instantly* to these variations.

impossible to grasp completely the basis of this process without a proof of the *necessity* of under-employment in a market economy. All we know so far is that it is an observed fact, and therefore a *possibility*. But our main concern here is to show that mercantilist thought was conditioned by a constant preoccupation with maximising employment.[38]

There are scarcely any important writings of this epoch which do not bear the marks of this preoccupation. It seems to have been greater than any other. B. Mandeville saw it as the most important of all. Vanderlint recommended the development of consumption as the only means of promoting employment. Laffemas, Sully, Montchrétien and Colbert got down to detailed evaluations of the loss of production which society suffers as a result of unemployment and suggested many measures to reabsorb it. They even came out against a certain kind of disguised unemployment which they found in the overgrowth of the tertiary sector, in which they higgledy-piggledy included beggars, vagabonds, lawyers, financiers, monks and curates. To these Forbonnais added haberdashers, second-hand clothes dealers and lottery ticket sellers.

William Petty was equally obsessed by the unemployment of his time: 'If we cannot dispose of our cloth to others, 'twere better to give it for Wine or worse, than to cease making it; nay, better to burn a thousand mans' labour for a time, than to let those thousand men by non-employment lose their faculty of labouring'.[39]

The estimates of the unemployment of their time bequeathed to us by these authors are terrifying. Davenant, quoting King's figures, estimates the paupers at about one million out of a total population of 5½ million, or around 20%, which would correspond to around 40% of the active population. This is proportionately more than has ever existed under developed capitalism, the crisis of the 1930s included. Let us add that, since the last war, the number of unemployed in

38. The physiocrats were to be completely uninterested in employment. James Stewart, who followed them very closely, revived this question. A few other heterodox economists (before Marx) continued to be concerned about it. Thus, replying to Adam Smith (the tailor does not try to make his own shoes), Ferrier said: 'Certainly, the head of a family, all the children of which are gainfully employed, would be very wrong to turn them from gainful work in order to employ them at making their own clothes . . . but as long as some of the children are out of work, it is a very great economy for the home if he takes advantage of their time' (*Du gouvernement considéré dans ses rapports avec le commerce*, p. 271). And further on, 'there is no family, nor nation, whose workers may not grow in number, in talent and in industry' (*ibid.*, p. 287).

39. *Treatise of Taxes* (1662) in *The Economic Writings of Sir William Petty*, vol. I, p. 41.

England has never exceeded the million, out of a population of 55 million.

The form under which unemployment appeared was that of vagabondage, with its accompaniment of crimes and riots of despair, an unprecedented wave of which descended on continental Europe and England from the sixteenth century. Begging, according to Ravenstone, became a universal phenomenon. Waves of repression of unheard-of ferocity followed. Criminality seemed to grow as fast as the attempts to suppress it. 'The zeal of Henry VIII is supposed to have hanged one-fiftieth part of the people of England, without producing any improvement in the morals of the nation.' He concludes that this almost led to the dissolution of society.[40]

The fluctuations in the English poor-rates give an indication of the level of underemployment. According to B. Franklin, these rose in the eighteenth century, in certain parts of the country, to 25% or 30% of annual revenues. Arthur Young estimates the poor-rates and the voluntary charities at £5 million, to which, he says, must be added the establishments founded for the poor and the property assigned to them at parish level, which raise the total to more than double this sum. (According to P.–E. Lemontey, this corresponds to 300 million French francs.[41] If we relate this sum to the annual wages of a worker in this period, which varied between £15 and £20, and if we assume that each pauper received half the wages of a man at work, we obtain about 1½ million unemployed out of a total population, in 1770–80, of about 7½ million, or 20% of the total population, 45% of the active population, which corresponds, one century later, to the figures of Davenant quoted above.[42] It was in these conditions, and around the same time, that a science of political economy, based essentially on the assumption of full employment, came into being; this would be an inexplicable oddity in the development of human

40. P. Ravenstone, *A Few Doubts*, p. 464.

41. P.–E. Lemontey, *Oeuvres complètes*, vol. I, p. 208.

42. W. Petty estimates the average per capita consumption in England in the seventeenth century at £6 13*s* 4*d* per year. But this was only an average. At a time when the spread of citizens' consumption was very wide, the per capita consumption of the working class must have been well below this figure, without even mentioning the unemployed worker, and his even lower consumption. The same W. Petty estimates the average consumption of a whole family of six people in Ireland at £2 12*s* 0*d* per year (*The Political Anatomy of Ireland*, in *The Economic Writings of Sir William Petty*, vol. I, p. 188). Even if we allow that parish relief alone would ensure the unemployed English worker a much higher standard of living than the Irishman in work, we must conclude that £10 million had to cover more than 1½ million unemployed.

ideas, unless we regard this assumption as apologetic in nature, though probably unconsciously so.[43]

It was only from the middle of the nineteenth century onwards that unemployment was brought down to the orders of magnitude to which we are accustomed, and which correspond to the nature of developed capitalism. The numbers are noticeably lower than in the preceding period, despite a very widespread belief that the opposite is the case. Thus, from 1860 to 1920, unemployment in Great Britain never exceeded 10% of the number of workers. It fluctuated between 10 and 20% from 1920 to 1930, reaching a maximum of 22% during the great crisis. However, this figure only represents slightly over half what emerges from the figures for the chronic unemployment of the seventeenth and eighteenth centuries as quoted above.[44]

Production and purchasing power

Whether reduced or not, unemployment is still the age-old experience of man. A set of phenomena constantly reappears in the market economy, which can only be understood as a permanent overabundance of factors and products in relation to the market's capacity for their absorption.

These phenomena are well summed up in Tugan Baranowski's simplified formula: 'In the capitalist economy, it is more difficult to sell than to buy'.[45] In modern terms, we may say that the capitalist economy is a buyer's market ('The customer is always right!'). The sale is not automatic: it is a feat (in Marx's expression, a transsubstantiation as difficult and as painful as the passage of the Hegelian 'Idea' from Necessity to Freedom).

43. But well after the emergence of classical political economy, at the start of the nineteenth century, authors such as Colquhoun considered that 'the great object will be, to find productive employment for the people . . .' (*A Treatise on the Wealth* [. . .] *of the British Empire*, p. ix).

Perhaps rather less severely than in England, and with the difference in date due to the later adoption of the new mode of production, the problem of unemployment was nonetheless apparent in France. Buret calculates the official number of paupers (those who had obtained relief in hospices) in France in 1833, at 1,120,961, representing, in his opinion, three times as many actual paupers, out of a population of around 32 million (*De la misère*, vol. II, p. 60).

44. But as late as 1842, as R. C. O. Matthews notes, the English unemployment figures are more like those of the 1930's than any intervening period (see *A Study in Trade Cycle History*).

45. '. . . the superiority of supply over demand is not only no accident under the present economic system – it is the general rule' (*Les Crises industrielles en Angleterre*, p. 189).

'Finally, I believe', writes Domar, 'that a capitalist society (without sufficient government participation has an inherent deflationary tendency . . . and I doubt whether the problem of unemployment has been solved for good' (*Essays in the Theory of Economic Growth*, p. 5).

Since it turns out that these phenomena are cyclical in nature, and thus result in sometimes very serious crises, economists have not been able to ignore them entirely, despite their unshakeable attachment to the equality of production and revenues: $P = R$. So they have constructed an incalculable number of explanatory theories, each more complicated than the last, without ever challenging this fundamental equation. The very number of these theories, and the subtlety of their nuances and their differences, in relation to each other, shows them to be unsatisfactory. The correct solutions to great problems are generally more simple.

Once again anticipating the rest of this work, I would like to say straight away that I believe that no solution can be found within the framework of this equality. The rush to sell, this 'general anxiety to sell' and 'general disinclination to buy', which were noted by John Stuart Mill despite his classicism, remain mysterious and inexplicable phenomena. If production were equal to revenues within the nation, then equilibrium would be structurally assured, at least as a tendency, and any positive or negative margin in the foreign balance could only destroy this equilibrium since, in this case, we would have:

$$\text{Production} - \text{Export Surplus} < \text{Revenues},$$

or

$$\text{Production} + \text{Import Surplus} > \text{Revenues}.$$

Then the only rational policy would be the search for a neutral, and therefore strictly equilibrated, foreign balance. The desire for a foreign surplus would not be explained.

Let us allow with Keynes that $P = R$ at various levels of employment: this can explain the protection of certain sectors and branches, even if they are not viable in terms of comparative costs; but it cannot explain the search for a surplus balance, and a lasting one at that.

I have already pointed out the distinction that should be made between these two aims. Since under-employment has, since Keynes, become a respectable hypothesis in political economy, distortions of comparative costs have become generally acceptable in certain circumstances, except for a few liberal fanatics.

We should add that this idea is not entirely new. Long before Keynes, several economists had pointed out that, given under-employment, the cost of factors to the entrepreneur is not the same as their social cost; and that, therefore, an international division of labour according to costs does not have much meaning.

Let us recall John Law's declaration, as appealing as it is surprising for his period: 'If 50 Men are set to Work, to whom 25 Shillings is payed per day, and the Improvement made by their Labour be only equal to, or worth 15 Shillings, yet by so much the Value of the Country is increased'.[46] (One might add: although the entrepreneurs who hired them would have lost 10 shillings.)

Let us also recall the discussion between J.–B. Say and Cournot:

> The transportation of hemp from Riga to Havre', says J.–B. Say, 'costs a Dutch shipowner 35 francs a ton [. . . This shipowner] proposes to the French government, which is a consumer of Russian hemp, to take charge of this transportation for 40 francs a ton. ... The French government, from a desire to favour French ship-brokers, prefers to employ French vessels, in which the same transportation will cost 50 francs, and which would have to charge 55 francs to provide the same profit. What will happen? The government will have spent 15 francs a ton to provide 5 francs for its citizens; and as it is the citizens who also pay the taxes, from which public expenditure are met, this operation will have cost Frenchmen 15 francs, to provide a profit of 5 francs for other Frenchmen.

Cournot replies:

> This reasoning would be unanswerable if the French ship-broker should charter a foreign vessel, for instance an American ship, manned by American seamen, and victualled with American supplies, to go to Riga for Russian hemp to carry to Havre [. . .] he (J.–B. Say) reasons as if the national income had only been increased to the extent of the broker's profits by the operation under consideration. But of the 55 francs per ton which are to be divided [. . .] why should the part of the broker be picked out rather than those of the captain, of the mate, of the steersman, or of the sailors [. . .] the carpenter or the ropemaker who worked on the building of the vessel [. . .] This difference can only be explained by tacitly supposing that the French ship-broker would be unable to find employment either for his skill or his capital [. . .] and [. . .] that the crew would find employment on other vessels, or that other trades would offer them equivalent wages [. . .] But the supposition made concerning the ship-broker is quite as gratuitous as the opposite supposition . . . .[47]

(The 'opposite supposition' which Cournot describes as gratuitous is that of full employment.)

But neither John Law nor Cournot, any more than Keynes and the modern economists, would have accepted that the product of the 50 men 'set to Work' in the first example, or the transporting of hemp in the second, should be 'given away' in the form of a foreign surplus, on the pretext that, having been produced with idle factors, they cost nothing to the nation. For such an outflow without any counterpart to

46. *Money and Trade Considered*, pp. 13–14.
47. A. Cournot, *Researches into the Mathematical Principles of the Theory of Wealth*, pp. 167–9.

be advantageous to the nation, the social cost of the goods or services under consideration must be, not nil, but 'negative', i.e. their non-production, or their being overstocked, must be prejudicial and dangerous for the subsequent workings of the national economy.

In other words, a state of under-employment cannot by itself explain the search for a surplus balance. As long as one is in equilibrium at $P = R$, one has no interest in setting to work the idle factors whose product, having flowed off abroad without any counterpart, adds nothing to P or to R. To explain the search for a surplus balance, the under-employment must be in *cumulative* disequilibrium, such that the non-use of these idle factors threatens to throw an additional quantity of factors out of use.[48]

If $P > R$, if there is *general* overproduction, compared to purchasing power, and if this situation, by exerting a downward pressure on prices, is such as to aggravate *both* this inequality *and* the under-employment which underlies it, then all becomes clear. For then the act of dumping the surplus of P over R abroad without any counterpart, although it does not directly allow us to valorise this surplus, which is lost in one way or another, may however make it possible to restore equilibrium between supply and demand, and thus indirectly prevent more serious losses.

If $P > R$, and if this inequality is intolerable because of the tensions which it generates, then any export surplus, which reduces P without affecting R, will have the effect of reabsorbing some of the disequilibrium between the domestic supply of commodities and purchasing power. In this case there would be nothing aberrant in a policy aimed at achieving the equation $P - E = R$.[49] This policy might even be taken one step further and aim at a surplus in the foreign balance greater than the difference between P and R, i.e. a situation where $P - E < R$. This substitution of an inflationary disequilibrium for a deflationary one is desirable to the extent that, through the cumulative tensions and effects which it engenders, it is liable to lead to a rise in the level of employment.

48. 'The aim of increasing employment *per se* is hardly an economic aim. . . . The aim of economic as well as technical thinking is to find ways to increase the yield of a given effort or to decrease the effort needed for getting a certain yield. To produce more and to work less is the essence of technical and economic progress. From the economic point of view, more employment makes sense only if it means more output and higher standard of living.' (Charles Bettelheim, *Studies in the Theory of Planning*, pp. 294–5.)

Employment can obviously not be an aim in itself. The increased activity must increase the national revenue indirectly, if not directly. Without this, employment *per se* becomes a joke, a bit like the gesture of Diogenes, who, during the siege of Corinth, set about rolling his barrel, so that he should not be idle while every one else was busy.

49. Here E stands for the surplus on the trade balance.

We must therefore prove that, if the system is left to itself, P will necessarily be greater than R, i.e. that at any given point in time, the sum of the prices of commodities of all kinds – articles of consumption and means of production – which have already been produced and are on the market is greater than the sum of distributed revenues of all kinds – profits, wages, rents, etc. – and therefore than the aggregate purchasing-power of that point in time. If this can be shown, not only will we have explained the protectionism we have spoken about, which is only a by-product of this disequilibrium, but we will have found the basis of a coherent set of causes and determining conditions for the under-employment which is endemic in the commodity mode of production, for depressions, for the system's inherent tendency to deadlock and for the crises that overcome this tendency by provisionally re-establishing the equilibrium.

Then a new light will have been shed on this curious fetishism of the *sale* which dominates the behaviour of economic agents in the capitalist mode of production and which makes the sale, defined as one stage of exchange, dissociate itself from this stage, become autonomous, and finally contradict and block exchange.

The commercialisation of human relations

Whether on the international level, or even on the domestic level of the nation, this mania for selling which we have been discussing does not figure in the traditional scientific schemas. According to these schemas, the sale is only a moment of exchange, which is itself an indispensable corollary of the division of labour. Therefore it does not constitute a specific macroeconomic problem.

Selling without the intention of buying is equivalent to giving up one's share in the social product. It is an irrational attitude and as such, while it may interest other disciplines, it is no part of the subject-matter of political economy, all of the laws of which are grounded in the hypothesis that each individual pursues his own material interests in good earnest.

Hoarding may break the chain of exchanges, whether domestically or in foreign trade. But this can only be an accident. The dishoarding of some should normally compensate for the hoarding of others, according to the law of averages. As Marx says, there are capitalists who sell without buying, but there are others who buy without selling. Non-Marxists have gone further: while there may be disequilibrating residues in one direction or the other, their effects are neutralised by the forces which they themselves engender, and which are opposed to them. It is enough to let economic laws do their work. These disequilibria only exist in the short term. In the long term, the system is in stable equilibrium.

In the domestic framework of perfect competition, savings are equal to investment, and hoarding is impossible at the level of society as a whole; in the international framework of free trade and good convertibility, the monetary metals will of their own accord share themselves out from country to country throughout the world economy in such a way as to give rise to prices that equilibrate the balances of all countries. If, domestically, competition is imperfect, and above all if, internationally, the aberration of protectionism develops, political economy can only throw up its hands in despair.

However, an aberration which has lasted for centuries, or even for millenia, deserves a deeper examination. For the passion for selling and the 'allergy' against buying are not innate characteristics of the human race. They are a product of commodity relations. And commodity relations are only one phase in the history of humanity. Put an African tribesman at the top of Oxford Street and give him a wad of bank-notes. By the time he reaches the bottom of the street, he will not have a penny left. Goods are offered to him all along the way, and it seems that these sheets of paper he has been given entitle him to take them. So can I have this jacket? Fine. What? You want one of these sheets of paper? Which one? Here you are. And this tie? Another piece of paper I suppose? Here, take this one. And so on, until he has no more pieces of paper left to exchange for the beautiful objects displayed before his eyes. Money has fulfilled its fundamental role, that of a voucher giving one the right to a part of the social product. The bearer hurried to use this right. This is the natural order of things.

Of course, things did not happen exactly like this for our tribesman when he lived in his tribe. There, he participated in the common labour in his capacity of a member of the community, without any particular rights accruing to him from this; in the same way, he participated in social consumption without any reference to the quantity or quality of the labour he had supplied. There was no conceivable link between his obligation to work and his right to consume, and no measure could intervene between the two. Labour and other resources being limited, and man's needs unlimited, the only problem was that of scarcity. That a good could fail to find a taker, or that the community should refuse the labour of one of its members, were things that defied the imagination.

There certainly was a social division of labour and a social division of the product. But there was neither private exchange nor trade. The various labours were just as concrete and irreducible to each other as the different goods that composed the social product. No common measure could exist, whether between the different applications of labour, between the different goods consumed, or between the first on the one hand and the second on the other.[50]

Then strange conquerors arrived in the land and imposed their laws. They themselves organised the labour and subsequently distributed the product. But this was done in a strange way. Instead of directly giving people the goods they needed, they gave them pictures painted on paper, or engraved on metal, which were then exchanged for the goods in specific places.

While rather complicated, the new system nevertheless came to the same thing as the old, at first glance and on the whole. One worked and one consumed. The African got rid of all the pieces of paper and all the coins as quickly as possible, and consumed roughly as before, and perhaps even better than before. But suddenly at the end of one week, there were less notes and coins than usual, and so he could not obtain enough food in exchange. Yes, of course, he had missed two days of work that week. But what had that got to do with it? Through what aberration could his labour become the measure of his consumption? Certainly, he could well understand that his laziness might be penalised in one way or another. But that someone could coldly sit down and calculate the quantity and value of his work, like that of a horse or a machine, that passed all understanding.

50. Here Adam Smith makes a fundamental mistake. Since he is incapable of imagining a division of labour without the private exchange of a commodity economy, but he notes that there is no human society without a division of labour, he concludes that man has, by nature, a propensity to exchange. Now, the division of labour and some way of distributing the product are in fact attributes of man's nature, but what does not go without saying, and what Adam Smith asserts gratuitously, is that the only possible mode of distribution is the exchange of commodities.

The division of labour – national or international – does not of itself imply trade – domestic or foreign. In the primitive community, there was certainly a division of labour, but there was no trade. In present 'socialist' societies, we are in the presence of exchange of a special kind, where, apart from a few special areas – kolkhoz markets, artisans, etc. – one of the parties to the exchange is the community itself. This is therefore a mixed system of distribution and transactional exchanges. Finally, in the higher phase of socialism, such as it is conceived in theory, the division of labour will give rise to no private exchange at all.

As for the international division of labour, while it has so far always functioned on the basis of transactional exchanges – which has made it possible to say that foreign trade precedes domestic trade since primitive communities already exchanged their products amongst each other – there is no theoretical necessity that it should always be so. One can very well conceive of a world socialist system in which the world division of labour and division of production are consciously and centrally organised.

But the point when things were really mucked up, the point when the new system definitively failed in his eyes, was the day when he turned up for work normally at the stated hour, only to be told that there was no work. This time he had no pieces of paper at the end of the week and he could buy nothing. At all times in his village, there were never enough hands, and that was why not everything people wanted could be produced. Now he was told that there were too many hands, because too many goods had been produced. Too many, compared to what? The man only had two hands and a whole host of unsatisfied needs. How could it be that there were too many hands and too many goods at the very point when the goods which had already been produced were being refused to those who had the most need of them?

The above is not a Robinson Crusoe story or a witticism. In the case of black Africa, this process occurred fairly recently. Its last phase took place, depending on the country, between the 1930s and the immediate post-war period. This was a passage without transition from a shortage of workers to unemployment. The Africans who had scarcely left the primitive community, or what was left of it, which was very much alive on the level of personalised relations, underwent this mutation without ever completely internalising it. The fully developed commodity relations artificially implanted by the European coloniser dislocated the material foundations of tribal society, but did not have time to impregnate the Africans with the ideological superstructure in advance. Man is then split in two. He is worn down and mutilated in his material life; he becomes unravelled. So he constantly seeks refuge in his 'backward' ancestral values, and there he reconstitutes his humanity and repairs the ravages of reality as best he can.[51] It is by refusing to integrate himself in commodity relations that this man, through his very irrationality, manages to a certain extent to escape alienation. By undergoing these relations as an *external* constraint, he is sorely oppressed, but in this oppression he remains a subject.

He refuses to accept the transformation of products into commodities and, even more obstinately, that of concrete labour into abstract labour. The separation of wealth from its material basis and

51. This time-lag in the superstructure makes the mercantilisation of the foundations themselves very precarious and fragile. The vestiges of communal relations seem particularly tenacious, and are one of the factors giving rise to the 'dualism' which brakes development along the capitalist road – but this is a different subject.

its incarnation in money are things which have not yet been sufficiently internalised by him. Money, when he has it, lasts basically as long as it takes to walk through a market.[52]

The sale as an end in itself

If man behaves in a commodity society in a way completely opposite to what we have sketched above, this is because he is conditioned by a specific characteristic of commodity societies. Over the centuries and millenia of commodity relations, while the products of labour have become profane through the very fact of their transformation into commodities, and the general equivalent has become sacred, the sale has been elevated to the central position in man's economic activity. One of the repercussions of this, to the extent to which the sale has become a feat in itself, has been the development of an aversion to purchasing, which has become to a certain extent atavistic.[53] But however atavistic it may be, this aversion is in no sense a fact of nature; it has no existence prior to the disequilibria of commodity society and can, therefore, not explain them.

The precondition of this *aversion to purchasing* is obviously the replacement of barter by two autonomous acts: purchase and sale. But this is only a precondition, and in no way a cause.

Anyway, purchase and sale are not the two abstract halves of a barter, as the dominant tendency of political economy would have it. They are two concrete, independent and complete acts.

Monetary exchange is not a technically perfected form of barter. Between the more or less occasional barter of primitive society and the monetary exchange of a commodity society, there is a discontinuity and a qualitative leap.

To decompose barter into sale and purchase is artificially to superimpose on barter categories which are not only alien to it, but its very

52. Which greatly scandalises the whites, who see in this a lack of maturity and an irresponsibility which justify colonial tutelage. Sometimes, however, the black does hoard for a certain while. This generally concerns a specific sum, destined for a specific object, whose value is greater than his current receipts and expenditure. This is not a *general* abstention from buying in order to amass *general* wealth. Money, for him, has not completely lost its original character of a simple certificate giving one access to concrete products. It is not yet, for him, as abstract as the verbiage printed on it; it is not yet a value as abstract as it is for Westerners. This all is despite the fact that the most 'developed' or the most mercantilised of them already have Swiss bank accounts . . . .

53. Cato the elder said: 'Patrem familiae vendacem, non curarem esse oportet' (It is fitting that the head of a family should be a seller and not a buyer).

opposite. Barter is an indivisible and irreducible objective entity. The 'exchange of commodities', contrariwise, is, considered as an entity, nothing more than a mental construct. It is also a simple accounting notion which may be useful for economic calculation, but which does not correspond to any real phenomenon. As long as there is real *exchange,* there are no *commodities,* but only products, and from the moment when products are transformed into commodities, exchange disappears. It is replaced by two autonomous acts which are only linked by the intervention of the monetary equivalent. But they are linked not in the illusory process of an exchange, but in that of the circulation of capital. It is only on the precondition of this complete autonomisation of the two acts that the sale was able to become an aim in itself.

This seems to us to be Marx's position. It is not the simple fact of inserting into the process of exchange – product against product – an intermediate element – *product against money against product* – nor simply the interval in time and in space between the two operations which the intervention of this element makes possible which is the real break and qualitative leap. What does constitute this break and this leap is the reversal of the sequence and its transformation into *money against product against money*. This is the opposite of the preceding form, and its negation.

Money becomes the beginning and the end of the cycle. By so doing, money negates exchange. But by negating exchange, it also negates the product and transforms it into a commodity. And it is only then that the product becomes a commodity in the full meaning of the term. However, this transformation takes place *immediately,* i.e. through the same qualitative leap, in such a way that the sequence: *money against product against money*, which we wrote above, does not exist in reality – and we pass without any transition from *product against money against product* to *money against commodity against money*.[54]

In fact, it is just as impossible to have a product as an intermediate term, as it is to have a commodity as a pole of the cycle. The very

54. 'Money is no longer an intermediary in exchanges; it penetrates to the deepest level and interposes itself between the production of goods and their appropriation.' (B. Schmitt, *La formation du pouvoir d'achat*, p. 147).

Nogaro's formulation is weaker: 'Money shatters barter; it resolves it into two independent operations which are mutually ignorant of each other.' (*Le rôle de la monnaie dans le commerce international*, p. 55). In reality, money does not merely shatter barter; it transforms it into its opposite.

concept of a commodity implies that its sale is the aim, and posits the commodity as the transitional form of capital.[55]

It is true that, before passing to the form M–C–M (money–commodity–money), Marx first of all studies the form C–M–C (commodity–money–commodity), but he studies it as a transitional form, belonging to a hypothetical mode of production, in which society is composed exclusively of independent worker-producers, and where men exist in 'only one economic capacity, that of owners of commodities, a capacity in which they appropriate the produce of the labour of others, by alienating that of their own labour'.[56] This is therefore a logical construct, in which Marx abstracts from wage-labour and capital. Now while simple commodity relations do exist, *both* in feudal society *and* in capitalist society (*and* even in Graeco-Roman slave society), historically there does not exist any mode of production based exclusively on these relations and characterised by them.[57]

It may be said that, in the form C–M–C, the metamorphosis of the product into a commodity is not yet complete. 'The independent form, i.e. the money-form, which the value of commodities assumes in the case of simple circulation, serves only one purpose, namely the exchange of *products*, and vanishes in the final result of the movement. On the other hand, in the circulation M–C–M, both the money and the commodity represent only different modes of existence of value itself . . . .'[58]

For the metamorphosis from product to commodity to be complete, money must leave the intermediate position and come to

55. An anecdote which went the rounds during the last war is, it seems to me, a very good illustration of this 'trans-substantiation' of the product into a commodity. The scene is London, 1943. The black market is at its peak. Commodities pass through several hands before reaching their final consumer. A batch of 100 crates of sardines passes in this way through the hands of several middlemen. The first buys it for £10 a crate and sells it for £12. The second resells it for £14, and so on. Months pass. The batch is now in the hands of a dealer who got it for £25. In response to an invitation for tenders, this last dealer sells it to the Ministry of Supply for £30 a crate. Civil servants arrive to take delivery, and inspect the merchandise. First crate opened: damaged. Second: likewise. A third, taken from a different lot: the same.

The dealer watches them, but cannot see what they are leading up to. 'You're trying to make a fool of us all', say the inspectors, 'How dare you offer us these sardines?' 'And why not?' asks the dealer. 'They're inedible! Are you blind or something?' 'But . . .', he replies, bewildered, 'but . . . they're not for eating.' 'Oh, and what are they for then?' 'No, don't you see, you buy them, you sell them, you buy them, you sell them, you buy them, you sell them . . . .'

56. *Capital*, vol. I, p. 110.

57. Nonetheless, New England in the eighteenth century seems to be a case in which simple commodity relations were, if not the only kind, then at least dominant.

58. K. Marx, *Capital*, vol. I, pp. 151–2, corrected from the 1875 French translation supervised by Marx (emphasis added).

occupy the poles, as the beginning and end of everything.[59] For the commodity to be completely a commodity, it is not enough for it to be produced for others – in primitive barter certain goods were already, in part, produced for others; it must become pure value, in the form of capital.

Barter is always present and implicit in the form C–M–C, except that the latter permits a rupture in time and space.[60] What negates and annihilates barter is the passage from this formula to the formula M–C–M.

> The form which circulation takes when money becomes capital, is opposed to all the laws we have hitherto investigated bearing on the nature of commodities, value and money, and even that of circulation itself. What distinguishes this form from that of the simple circulation of commodities, is the inverted order of succession of the two antithetical processes, sale and purchase. How can this purely formal distinction between these processes change their character as it were by magic?[61]

It is true that in the reproduction schemas of Volume II Marx returns to the formula C–M–C and even congratulates Quesnay for having adopted it in his 'Tableau economique', as opposed to the mercantilists, who for their part stuck to the formula M–C–M. But it is also true that the reproduction schemas belong to the most classical side of Marxist doctrine. Being static, these schemas express the system's *possibility* of equilibrium and constitute a rigorous proof of the equality between the value created during a production period

59. Here we must dispel a possible misunderstanding. There is no need whatsoever for the money to be materially substituted for the commodity. It is enough for the commodity, having been sold, to be replaced by a credit drawn up in money, whether this credit is a claim on the central bank (fiduciary money), a claim on a private bank (bank money), or even a simple private debt. The quality of the claim itself has no importance here. What counts is the acceptance of the commodity by the purchaser and his agreement on the price.

60. It was by sticking exclusively to this rupture that Dieterlen was able to think that the essential characteristic of monetary exchange is that it is a non-simultaneous barter (see *Au-delà du capitalisme*, p. 103).

There is a very dangerous temptation for the social sciences to see present phenomena simply as new variants of past phenomena. Purchase and sale follow on historically from barter; therefore they can only be a decomposed form of barter. The economists went on to reconstitute barter on the basis of purchase and sale. Since purchase and sale are a non-simultaneous form of barter, then barter can only be a simultaneous form of purchase and sale. Thus John Stuart Mill: 'In the case of barter, the selling and the buying are simultaneously confounded in one operation.' (*Some Unsettled Questions*, vol. II, p. 70).

All this is very rash. One has no right to define purchase and sale by what differentiates them *in appearance* from barter, nor barter by what differentiates it from purchase and sale.

61. K. Marx, *Capital*, vol. I, p. 154.

and the revenues distributed on the basis of this same production. The 'Tableau economique' on the one hand, and modern national accounting models on the other, are in essence built on the same principle.[62] In both of these realisation is no problem – it is presupposed.

However, even the simple dissociation in time of barter into purchase and sale, expressed in the formula C–M–C – and the conception of money as the agent of this disjunction – are a great step forward compared with the classical Ricardian and physiocrat doctrine of money as completely passive, a simple technical accessory and 'tool of commerce', rather like the publican's wine glasses, in Quesnay's expression.[63]

E. Daire's reply to this conception of money is perhaps the best, because the most concise. Money, he says, is not a measure like a yard, a mile, etc., but it is used as a measure. The yard which facilitates exchange is not, like the money, one of the terms of the exchange.[64]

In passing to the formula M–C–M and placing money at the poles, another great step is taken. Barter is now not merely disjointed, broken in two, but negated. The sale appears clearly, not only as an independent act, but as an aim in itself, the crown and *raison d'être* of all economic activity.

But these steps can only establish the preconditions for disequilibrium. They do not show us its cause. They reveal to us a necessary condition, but not the sufficient condition. It is obvious that the phenomenon which we are trying to understand, and which is a perennial experience of humanity, i.e. the permanent difficulties met with in trying to ensure the sale of the social product despite the number of human needs which remain unsatisfied, is materially impossible in conditions of barter. We would not have insisted so much on this metamorphosis of barter if there was not such confusion on this point.[65]

But it is just as clear that the simple existence of the sale as an autonomous act is no foundation or explanation for the difficulty of selling, and the disequilibria. Nor is it enough to note the regular and

62. 'All accounting is made in double entries . . . and this may be taken for another statement of Say's Law, as Jean Coutrot once said. This principle lies at the basis of national economic accounting, and to this extent it has all the appearances of a justification of Say's Law.' (J. Denizet, *Monnaie et Financement,* pp. 29–30).

63. 'Productions are always bought by productions, or by services; money is only the medium by which exchange is effected . . .' (Ricardo, *Principles*, chapter XXI, p. 275).

64. E. Daire, *Economistes financiers du XVIIIe siècle*, p. 507.

durable existence of these disequilibria in the real world. Their theoretical *necessity* must be proved.

All the same, before harnessing ourselves to this task, we believe it necessary to examine, on the one hand how a theory, the 'Law of Markets', which on the contrary teaches the necessity and the indestructibility of equilibrium, was able to triumph and dominate the science right up to the present day; and on the other hand how its opponents, and above all those like the Marxist critics, who have attacked the conclusions of this theory the most violently, have at the same time been able to accommodate themselves, at least tacitly, with its basic postulate: production equals purchasing power.

This is what we shall try to do in the three chapters which form the first part of this work.

It is only in the second part that we shall attempt the theoretical refutation of this postulate and that, on the basis of this refutation, we shall try to explain the disequilibria and overproduction crises of the capitalist mode of production, not *despite the basic equality* of production and revenues, as has been attempted up to now, but *on the basis of their inequality*, i.e. on the basis of the excess of production at any one point in time over the revenues of that same point in time.

65. Marx put these questions in focus with perfect clarity: 'If the commodity could not be withdrawn from circulation in the form of money or its retransformation into money could not be postponed, as with direct barter – if purchase and sale coincided, then the possibility of crisis would . . . disappear . . . and if we say that the simple form of metamorphosis comprises the possibility of crisis, we only say that in this form itself lies the possibility of the rupture and separation of essentially complementary phases.' (*Theories of Surplus Value*, vol. II, p. 508).

However, there has been one economist – only one to our knowledge – who maintains that there can be a crisis of overproduction even in conditions of barter. This is P. Lambert, who, in a text entitled 'La Loi des débouchés', published in the *Revue d'économie politique* in 1952, has quite a few original things to teach us: 'Even if we allow', he writes, 'that money is only a pure intermediary . . ., it does not follow that production . . . creates for itself a sufficient market. . . . The baker has made more bread than the cobbler wants; the cobbler has made more pairs of shoes than the baker wants, and so on: there is . . . logically [sic] a crisis of overproduction; the same phenomenon may arise without money, at the current rates of exchange. The baker now offers three loaves instead of two, for one pair of shoes, while the cobbler offers one pair of shoes for one loaf. The previous rate of exchange re-establishes itself, and each retains his surplus.' You cannot help wondering whether this is meant to be a joke: the cobbler is quite happy to give one pair of shoes for a single loaf, but, 'logically', he refuses the deal as soon as he is offered three loaves in exchange!

PART I The Law of Markets and the Phenomenon of General Overproduction

2 The Conditions for Equilibrium

The equality of production and purchasing-power

Before political economy became a science, economists contented themselves with descriptions of their own experiences and did not inquire any deeper. General overproduction was an obvious and permanent fact of life. Business booms could only mitigate it. But whatever the state of business, it was, as we said in the Introduction, much more difficult to sell than to buy. Barring exceptional circumstances – blockades, sieges, natural calamities – shop-windows and warehouses were chock-a-block with goods, and there was clearly insufficient purchasing power. One hundred francs in cash was automatically convertible into any commodities of equal value. One only had to ask. But commodities to the value of one hundred francs were not automatically convertible into one hundred francs proper. A buyer would have to be found first. This asymmetry found expression in everyday language: one *orders* a commodity when one has money; one does not order money when one has a commodity.

In a market economy, money is an *immediately* social value; a commodity only becomes so through the mediation of the sale. Xenophon saw this basic difference clearly, when he proposed that the State of Athens hire slaves to work the silver mines of Laurion. (At that time silver was the only monetary standard; gold was still only a simple commodity.) Silver-mining, he wrote,

> is quite different from other industries. An increase in the number of coppersmiths, for example, produces a fall in the price of copper work, and the coppersmiths retire from business. The same thing happens in the iron trade . . . . But an increase in the amount of the silver ore discovered and of the metal won is accompanied by an increase in the number of persons who take up this industry. Neither is silver like furniture, of which a man never buys more when once he has got enough for his house. No one ever yet possessed so much silver as to want no more; if a man finds himself with

a huge amount of it, he takes as much pleasure in burying the surplus as in using it.[1]

The mercantilists took note of this age-old state of affairs, but they never bothered to establish the theoretical possibility, still less the theoretical *necessity* thereof. After them, by breaking through, as is right and proper, in modern terminology, from phenomenon to 'essence', from 'ideology' to 'science', from the visible to the invisible, Quesnay, Adam Smith and Ricardo banished the idea of structural general over-production from political economy. Their 'invisible' was in diametrical contradiction with the 'visible' reality. There could be no over-production, neither compared with needs, which are unlimited, nor compared with revenues, which are only the bookkeeping counterpart, the other side, of the value created in production.

Each constituent element of the value of a product corresponds to a revenue. Since the sum of the parts is equal to the whole, the sum of revenues, and therefore of purchasing power, must be equal to the value produced.

Like all tautologies, this proof was incontrovertible. Essentially the same thing is being repeated on both sides of the equation under a different name. On one side there are the goods already produced or in existence, on the other side the property rights attached to them. Since there is neither product nor value without an owner, the two must be equal.

This is exactly the same approach as that of commercial double-entry bookkeeping. It is based on the equation: assets = liabilities + equity. Any *valuable* good – i.e. a good whose acquisition costs money – gives rise to an equivalent claim (property right): this claim is what constitutes and measures its character of being valuable. Those goods that constitute assets are put at the disposal of the enterprise subject to payment. Their sum total is therefore no different from the sum of the amounts falling to the rightful claimants – creditors and shareholders. This is a definitional equation, which is

1. *Scripta Minora*, p. 207. 'Price, like relative value in general', writes Marx, 'expresses the value of a commodity (e.g., a ton of iron), by stating that a given quantity of the equivalent (e.g., an ounce of gold), is directly exchangeable for iron. But it by no means states the converse, that iron is directly exchangeable for gold. In order, therefore, that a commodity may in practice act effectively as exchange-value, it must quit its bodily shape, must transform itself from mere imaginary into real gold. . . .' (*Capital*, vol. I, chapter III, p. 105.)

'Because money is the metamorphosed shape of all other commodities, the result of their general alienation, for this reason it is alienable itself without restriction or condition.' (*Ibid.*, p. 112).

therefore indestructible, however its terms may vary in the course of transactions.

In the same way, by definition, the social product is nothing but the sum of the goods whose production costs money, to the exclusion of all others. This implies that all the goods that constitute social output are matched from birth with corresponding claims belonging to various categories of citizen.

The price of a good put on sale is composed of three portions: the commodities consumed during and in consequence of its production, the remuneration of the workers employed in its production, and the remuneration of the non-working claimants – capitalists, landowners, the state (indirect taxes), etc. The first portion only adds on one side what it withdraws from the other. An existing commodity is destroyed, and its value is incorporated in the price of a new commodity. What has really been *created* in production is therefore the two other portions of the price, i.e. the remunerations of the workers and the non-workers. In their hands, these remunerations constitute purchasing power. Therefore, what has really been created in production is equal to the purchasing power distributed as a result of this same production.

Changes in the price of the commodity under consideration do not alter this equation at all. Such changes can only result from or result in corresponding changes in one or several of the three components of price. Therefore, whatever the price of a commodity may be, the portion of this price *created* by a given stage of production, what is known as *value added*, is strictly equal to the new purchasing power created by this same stage of production.

If this holds for each individual commodity, it must also hold for commodities as a whole. Therefore, absolutely nothing can lead to any inequality between the production of a given period and the revenues (or purchasing power) created during this same period. The only way things can go wrong is if there is a qualitative non-correspondence between the two, a disproportion in the use-values which the social product is composed of. Too many socks and not enough shoes have been produced. 'Too many' and 'not enough' are each defined in relation to the other. For to each general level of production there corresponds a different proportion of needs. It follows that thc only possible kind of overproduction is partial over production, arising in one or several specific industries. It can only exist in relation to and at the same time as an equivalent under-production in other specific industries. The only possible disequilibrium is that of disproportion.

Marxist terminology even supplies us with an adequate model to clarify the above. The value of a commodity, V_i, is equal to the sum of the constant capital consumed, c_i, the variable capital, v_i, and the surplus value, s_i. The sum of the values produced is equal to the sum of these three parts:

$$\begin{array}{l}
c_1 + v_1 + s_1 = V_1 \\
c_2 + v_2 + s_2 = V_2 \\
\quad\vdots \\
c_n + v_n + s_n = V_n \\
\hline
\Sigma c + \Sigma v + \Sigma s = \Sigma V
\end{array}$$

The transformation of values into prices of production does not affect the equality of these sums at all.

A commodity's price of production, P_i, is equal to the sum of the constant capital consumed, c_i, variable capital, v_i, and profit, pr_i. The sum of the prices is equal to the sum total of the three parts:

$$\begin{array}{l}
c_1 + v_1 + pr_1 = P_1 \\
c_2 + v_2 + pr_2 = P_2 \\
\quad\vdots \\
c_n + v_n + pr_n = P_n \\
\hline
\Sigma c + \Sigma v + \Sigma pr = \Sigma P
\end{array}$$

If we leave aside the constant capital consumed, which compensates for itself as we said above, it is clear that the two other components of price, v and pr, are at the same time revenues, those of the workers and the capitalists respectively. Consequently, there can be no difference between the total price of the goods produced and aggregate purchasing power.

Any further redistribution of this purchasing power, from the bearers of v and pr towards other beneficiaries – land-owners, traders, the state, etc. – will only transfer existing purchasing power from one economic subject to another. The sum totals will not be affected by this. It is therefore enough to refer back to an earlier situation of equilibrium, which can be the dawn of time if necessary, to show that any production since then can only have added equal sums to equal sums, in such a way that nothing can ever have given rise to an excess of commodities offered for sale at a given point in time over the purchasing power facing them at the same point in time.

So general overproduction appears to be a mathematical impossibility.

The 'over-production' controversy

This is the most captivating theorem that political economy has ever developed.[2] Its triumph was total. All objections were swept aside with disconcerting ease. First of all, of course, those which I shall call the naive conception of overproduction, which is a part, at least, of Malthus's and Sismondi's arguments, and which can be broken down into two points: (a) a supposed excess over human needs; (b) the comparison of the whole of social output with effective demand for consumption goods alone, as if production consisted of the latter alone, i.e. a failure to take productive consumption into account.

The cards were stacked in Ricardo's favour. When Malthus reproached him for neglecting the question of 'the wants and tastes of mankind' and pointed out to him that it is not only the proportions between commodities, but also their relation to these 'wants and tastes', which determine prices, Ricardo replied that he took the wants and tastes of mankind to be unlimited. And that put an end to the discussion.[3] And when it was put to Ricardo that the capitalist does not *consume* all his profit, since he accumulates part of it, Ricardo replied that one can only accumulate by buying labour or instruments of production and that, consequently, accumulation increases demand just as much as consumption does.[4] As Marshall was to put it later, one buys commodities and labour as much with the portion of revenue which one saves as with that which one spends.

And that was that. Accumulation is not a problem in itself. Marx's

2. As captivating for the mind as were the physicians' ether or phlogiston. It possessed all the characteristics of that notorious 'epistemological break' which the partisans of Althusser talk about so much nowadays, that passage from the visible to the invisible which is presented to us as the necessary and *sufficient* condition for passing from ideology to science. But, just like ether and phlogiston, and however *invisible* it might be, this equation between production and purchasing-power is, as we shall try to show in this study, no more *true* than ether or phlogiston. In fact, it is not enough to contradict the world of phenomena for one to automatically attain to the truth, as a doctrine recently very fashionable in France seems to imagine.

3. However, this reference to 'wants', which is the most primitive version of the overproduction argument, was taken up again by such an eminent Marxist as Kautsky in some astonishingly weak passages of his *Marxism and the critic Bernstein*: 'If more is produced than is needed at the moment, prices fall. If less is produced, they rise above their average level. The impossibility of selling commodities at their cost-price is therefore an inevitable periodical phenomenon of market production and this impossibility . . . is the very basis of crises.' And later: 'We are not dealing here with the retroactive force of local or partial disturbances, but with general overproduction.'

4. Letters exchanged on 11 and 16 September 1814. *The Works and Correspondence of David Ricardo*, vol. VI, pp. 131–4.

reproduction schemes were later to provide Ricardo's argument with a rigorous theoretical formulation.

Simple reproduction

If there is no accumulation – the case which Marx calls simple reproduction – equilibrium can be expressed by dividing social production into three Departments: means of production, articles of workers' consumption and articles of capitalists' consumption; in the three following equations:

$$\begin{array}{l} c_1 + v_1 + pr_1 = P_1 \\ c_2 + v_2 + pr_2 = P_2 \\ c_3 + v_3 + pr_3 = P_3 \\ \hline \Sigma c + \Sigma v + \Sigma pr = \Sigma P \end{array}$$

It is then enough to define the conditions:

$$\begin{array}{l} \Sigma c = P_1 \\ \Sigma v = P_2 \\ \Sigma pr = P_3 \end{array}$$

for the realisation of the product to be possible and for over-production, even *partial*, to be ruled out.

Since Σc is directly (productive) consumption and P_1 is a part of the social product, they cancel each other out if they are equal. Σv and Σpr represent respectively the revenues of the workers and the non-workers, while P_2 and P_3 represent the consumption goods that have reached the market; their respective equalities, which have been laid down above as conditions, mean that purchasing power equals production, as much for the economy as a whole as for each Department taken separately.

If these conditions are not satisfied, there will be sectoral over-production and underproduction, but still no difference between the totals, and therefore no general overproduction. For it is quite clear that any divergence between one or several *P*s and the sums facing them must necessarily correspond to a strictly equal and opposite divergence of one or several other *P*s, since the sum of the *P*s is, whatever happens, equal to the overall sum of *c*, *v* and *pr*. Since the sum total remains unchanged, the sum of the positive and negative divergences of its component parts will be equal to zero. The possible over-production of one or several sectors therefore compensates for an equivalent under-production in one or several other sectors. General over-production is impossible.

Let us take a numerical example:

c		v		pr (20%)		Output	
1000	+	500	+	300	=	1800	means of production
500	+	250	+	150	=	900	articles of workers' consumption
300	+	150	+	90	=	540	luxury goods
1800	+	900	+	540	=	3240	

All the equilibrium conditions are satisfied and there is neither general nor partial overproduction.

This is of course an ideal situation, in which all the equilibrium conditions are met. Since these equilibrium conditions express the division of social resources between capital and labour (1800 and 900) in the three departments and since, in the capitalist system, this division is not planned, but is the result of a great number of individual decisions, without any coordination, it may happen that this precise combination does not emerge. This means, quite simply, that a certain quantity of capital and labour will be displaced, compared to the scheme above, from one department to another. Any such displacement unbalances the system. Suppose that 100 capital and 50 labour are displaced from department I to department II. We will have:

c		v		pr (20%)		Output
900	+	450	+	270	=	1620
600	+	300	+	180	=	1080
300	+	150	+	90	=	540
1800	+	900	+	540	=	3240

The result is overproduction by 180 in department II (1080 articles of workers' consumption produced, as against a total of workers' revenues of 900). But there is strictly equivalent under-production in department I (1620 capital goods, equipment, raw materials, etc., produced, whereas we need 1800 to replace those which have been consumed in the course of the same cycle of production).

Reproduction on an extended scale

Nothing is changed if we take account of accumulation, i.e. in Marxist terminology if we pass from simple reproduction to reproduction on an extended scale. In this case, the unconsumed portion of profits must quite simply be added to constant capital consumed. If we call the consumed part of profits pr_c and the capitalised part pr_k, the equations become:

$$
\begin{array}{l}
c_1 + v_1 + (pr_{c1} + pr_{k1}) = P_1 \\
c_2 + v_2 + (pr_{c2} + pr_{k2}) = P_2 \\
c_3 + v_3 + (pr_{c3} + pr_{k3}) = P_3 \\
\hline
\Sigma c + \Sigma v + \Sigma pr = \Sigma P
\end{array}
$$

The equilibrium conditions are:

$$
\begin{aligned}
\Sigma c + \Sigma pr_k &= P_1 \\
\Sigma v &= P_2 \\
\Sigma pr_c &= P_3
\end{aligned}
$$

Just as in the case of simple reproduction, if this ideal situation is not attained, the partial overproduction which will result in one or several sectors will *necessarily* be compensated for by a strictly equivalent under-production in one or several other sectors.

Let us look at a numerical example here too:

						Profit				
c		*v*		**Consumed**		**Capitalised**			**Output**
1150	+	575	+	172.5	+	172.5	=	2070
500	+	250	+	75	+	75	=	900
150	+	75	+	22.5	+	22.5	=	270
1800	+	900	+	270	+	270	=	3240

The gross product is 3240. Having subtracted the 1800 of material inputs (constant capital consumed, in Marxist terminology; intermediate consumption plus depreciation, in non-Marxist terminology) we are left with a net product of 1440, composed of 270 of capital goods (equipment, raw materials, etc.), 900 of workers' consumption goods and 270 of luxury products, facing which there is an aggregate purchasing power, likewise of 1440, composed of 270 of accumulated (saved) profits, 900 of wages and 270 of profits destined for the capitalists' personal consumption. Just as in the preceding example, there is neither general nor partial over-production.

If, in the anarchic conditions of capitalism, this ideal division is not attained, and if we suppose, as we did earlier, that the resulting sub-optimal situation corresponds to a displacement of 100 capital and 50 labour from Department I to Department II, we will have:

				Profit					
c		*v*		**Consumed**		**Capitalised**		**Output**
1050	+	525	+	157.5	+	157.5	=	1890
600	+	300	+	90	+	90	=	1080
150	+	75	+	22.5	+	22.5	=	270
1800	+	900	+	270	+	270	=	3240

The result is partial overproduction by 180 in Department II, since 1080 of workers consumption goods have been produced there, in contrast to distributed wages of 900; and partial underproduction in Department I, where only 1890 of capital goods have been produced, whereas, on the one hand, we have to replace 1800 of these goods used up in the course of production, and on the other, we have to satisfy a specific purchasing power for this kind of goods deriving from the sum of capitalised profits. This underproduction is also 180.

But here also the net product, 3240 − 1800 = 1440, is equal to the sum of purchasing power: 900 + 270 + 270 = 1440. There is not and there cannot be general overproduction.

The saving/consumption trade-off

It follows not only that accumulation is no evil, but that it is the condition *sine qua non* for the growth of production and for progress.

The mercantilists and Malthus after them, trusting in appearances, had said that it is spending, and even prodigality, which encourages production and gives men work. Adam Smith, J.–B. Say and Ricardo battled energetically against this 'paradox'. It is frugality which enriches a nation.[5] Sismondi himself, despite his belief in the possibility of overproduction, could only approve of this condemnation: 'Encouraging consumption is a poor way to set about developing trade'.[6] 'Royalty dispenses charity by its profuse expenditure', Louis XIV had said. 'A truly alarming dogma, and one that shews the ruin of France to have been reduced to principle', was J.–B. Say's reply.[7]

'What, I would ask', exclaimed Malthus, to illustrate the need for luxury consumption, 'would become of the demand for commodities,

5. 'Every prodigal appears to be a publick enemy, and every frugal man a publick benefactor.' Adam Smith, *The Wealth of Nations*, vol. I, p. 340.
6. *De la richesse commerciale*, p. 115.
7. *Treatise on Political Economy*, vol. II, p. 281.

if all consumption except bread and water were suspended for the next half-year? What an accumulation of commodities! *Quels débouchés*! What a prodigious market would this event occasion!'[8] (Ricardo could have told him the answer: for these six months the profits would be used to build modern bakeries and water-towers in order to have more bread and better quality water later on.)

'If every person were satisfied with the simplest food, the poorest clothing, and the meanest houses, it is certain that no other sort of food, clothing and lodging would be in existence,'[9] Malthus continues. (No! Factories could perfectly well be turning out machines designed to produce fine food, sumptuous clothes and luxurious houses later on.[10])

Sismondi, who was not averse to contradicting himself, followed Malthus and Chalmers, despite his contrary affirmation quoted above, and in several other parts of his work came out against the idea that saving is of benefit to society.[11] Adam Smith, on the other

8. *Principles of Political Economy*, p. 363, footnote.

9. Preface to *Principles of Political Economy*, p. 8.

10. This exploit has already been managed by some underdeveloped socialist countries. It may well be unlikely, or even impossible, when the power of decision-making is in the hands of independent producers in competition with each other, but this difficulty or impossibility derives, not from any objective mathematical necessity, as Malthus imagined, but from the motivations of these independent producers, which should, in this case, be explained. This is what is attempted by Keynes, who quotes Malthus's first passage above (*General Theory*, p. 364).

11. Or perhaps it is not a real contradiction. For Sismondi, equilibrium between production and consumption can only be established if the rich consume their revenues, neither more nor less. Like Malthus and other contemporaries, he only saw in capital the part destined for wages and he ignored the material means of production. So he thought that, if the rich consumed more than their revenues, they would eat into their capital, and the workers would die of hunger for want of the funds to set them to work; if they accumulated their revenue – accumulation is here identical to hoarding – the workers would still die of hunger because they counted on this revenue to exchange against their labour. And if the capitalist neither eats into his capital nor hoards? If he capitalises a part of his revenue? Then, says Sismondi, he increases the claim that he gives to labour this year, but the poor will make a loss the next year, when the product of this additional labour will find no purchaser willing to replace this capital. (*Nouveaux principes*, vol. I, book III, ch. IV, pp. 89–108.)

When, in some passages, he does take material inputs into account, he constructs models based on the peculiar conditions of agriculture in which the only consumption product, wheat, is at the same time the only means of production (seed), such that there is a natural proportionality between its two uses. So the physiological limit of consumption is very quickly reached. If, every year, the farmer turns his surplus into additional seed, who will eat all this wheat? But here his example plays a nasty trick on him. For, if there are neither machines nor technical progress, and if the farmer sows the surplus every year, he must engage new workers in exactly the same proportion, and there will be no lack of mouths to feed. To get out of this, no argument is too far-fetched for Sismondi. For example, 'Human generations do not grow as fast as subsistence' (*Ibid.*, p. 97), which Malthus would not have liked at all.

hand, followed Quesnay and Turgot. J.–B. Say, James Mill, Ricardo, MacCulloch and Senior sided with Smith. John Stuart Mill adopted an intermediate, if not agnostic, position. Lauderdale, for his part, pointed out the danger of excessive saving, but did not go any further. Cairnes, more faithful to classicism, came out in favour of savings.

Productive consumption

We have just described in its most elementary form what has been accepted as a basic truth of political economy from its origins as a science right up to the present day. In this form, it has been adopted by all schools, including Marxism, Marginalism, neoClassicism and the Keynesian revolution. The 'famous' discussion between Ricardo–Say and Malthus–Sismondi reached a definitive conclusion. The main cause for the relatively easy defeat of the supporters of general overproduction was their glaring error concerning the nature and function of accumulation.[12]

Rereading the arguments formulated by Malthus and Sismondi on the one hand, by Ricardo and Say on the other, it is incomprehensible how the latter were able to defeat the former so decisively with so little intellectual effort. Without even mentioning Say, who was of far lesser stature than the other three, and who most often contented himself with using flowery language and side-stepping the issue, Ricardo himself is far from having refuted the arguments of his adversaries point for point.

But alongside their valid arguments which deserved more attention, the opponents of the equality between production and purchasing power insisted, on the one hand, on confusing accumulation with simple hoarding; and on the other hand, on ignoring the consumption of means of production. When they drew up the balance-sheet of the national accounts, they distinguished perfectly well between profits and wages on the revenue side. On the output side they saw only consumption goods. From there onwards, everything became confused and jumbled up, and their good ideas were lost in the resulting morass. The capitalists only had one stomach, like everyone else. How could they consume a quantity of wheat equivalent to their profits? Of course there were luxury

12. However, this mistake of Malthus's and Sismondi's, which, by ignoring the material inputs to production, leads to the conclusion that the realisation of surplus-value is impossible, was still repeated by Proudhon several decades later. He in fact continued to maintain that the levy deducted by the owners from the value of the product deprives the workers of part of their purchasing power and thus prevents the smooth sale of output.

products. But, on the one hand, luxury too had its limits; and on the other, luxury was excluded on principle from the way of life of the classic capitalist. It was the characteristic of a different class, the land-owners. And in this way, at last, the sumptuous expenditure of these idlers became healthy for economic equilibrium. Since those who produced did not consume sufficiently, capitalism had need of a class which would consume without producing. Without this, the system was deadlocked.

The Ricardians had no trouble in explaining that the social product is not composed solely of final consumption goods, whether ordinary or luxury, but also comprises means of production. From the point of view of realisation, these means of production are commodities like any others and form part of aggregate supply. Accumulating means buying these specific commodities in order to make one's capital give fruit. While productive by destination, these purchases are just as much a consumption as any others. There is certainly an excess of production over *personal* consumption, but this excess is made up for by *productive* consumption. There is no overall excess.

This was so dazzling that the other points of the discussion were obscured. Once their gross error on this point was recognized, the detractors were definitively beaten, and no one listened to them any more. Their other arguments seemed all the more suspect, as they had only been put forward as secondary supports. When Lenin, for example, later criticised Sismondi because 'the failure to understand that production creates a market for itself leads to the doctrine that surplus value cannot be realized',[13] he only addressed this particular point, which he dealt with in the following terms:

'What seemed to Sismondi to be simply an error, a contradiction in Ricardo's doctrine – that accumulation is excess of production over revenue – actually corresponds in full to reality and expresses the contradiction inherent in capitalism.'

(By 'revenue', Lenin here means: revenue destined for unproductive consumption. This is clear from the rest of his argument.)

'This excess is *necessary* for all accumulation, which opens a new market *for means of production without correspondingly expanding the market for articles of consumption, and even contracting this market.*'[14]

Yet Sismondi, besides making this mistake, made some particularly remarkable points, which were all the more interesting as they were said for the first time. But these points were vitiated by his

13. *Collected Works*, vol. II, p. 148.
14. *Ibid.*, p. 159, emphasis original.

original error, and Sismondi himself never managed to extricate himself and distinguish clearly between the differing arguments, neither in his formulations, nor, it appears, in his own thoughts. Curiously enough, Lenin himself quotes one of these arguments of Sismondi's in his critique: 'From reproduction comes revenue, but *production in itself is not yet revenue*: it acquires this name and functions as such only after it is realised, after each article produced finds a consumer who has the need or the desire for it'.[15]

This is a crucial thesis, which, for the first time to our knowledge, introduces the time factor into the process of realization.[16] But Sismondi was wrong to use the word 'consumer', which shows that he was still only thinking of personal expenditure and final consumption goods, and Lenin directs his fire at this error, without realising that there was something more in the guilty sentence: 'Thus, the identification of revenue with "production" (i.e. with all that is produced) leads to the identification of realization with *personal* consumption.'[17]

Now Sismondi's error in question, even if it is present in the last sentence of the passage, has nothing to do with the thesis that he is proposing here. His essential argument is independent of the error and is to be found in what precedes the word 'consumer'. Replace this word with 'purchaser', and one would naturally and correctly understand it to refer to the totality of social output, hence including means of production: but the argument would still stand. It concerns the fact that purchasing power, though it derives from production, does not exist as such *before* realization, and consequently that the realization of current production cannot be based on the purchasing power deriving from this same production. Its ultimate implication is the structural *inequality* of production and purchasing power and thus leads to the necessity or the possibility of general overproduction. Whether correct or not, it was sufficiently important and unprecedented to deserve to be examined on its own merits, abstracting from the incidental mistake which Sismondi made in the same passage by identifying 'realization with *personal* consumption'.

The 'Law of Markets' and sectoral disequilibria

In this way, the doctrine of the strict equality between production and purchasing power triumphed. It took on the name of 'Say's Law of Markets', which seems rather inaccurate. For either this includes all the conclusions which J.–B. Say drew from it, in which case the

15. *Ibid.*, p. 148.
16. It contains the germ of our own argument, as presented later on in this study.
17. *Collected Works*, vol. II, p. 148, emphasis original.

doctrine is far from unanimously accepted, or it refers to the basic principle – 'production equals revenues' – in which case Say's paternity is rather overdone. In this reduced form, the principle has been put forward, in one way or another, in Say's own time and sometimes well before him, by several other economists, such as James Mill (in his controversy with Spence[18]), Adam Smith, Le Trosne, etc.[19] It was already present and active in Quesnay's *Tableau économique*, all the functions and relations of which were conditioned by it.

Of course, this overall equality does not exclude, as we have seen, sectoral inequalities deriving from what is known as the anarchy of the market, i.e. the fact that the power of decision-making, as concerns the division of social resources between the different branches of production, is vested in a whole host of independent producers and the fact that, apart from the market's *ex post* corrections and sanctions, there is no mechanism for the *ex ante* harmonisation of production.

However, on the one hand, these disequilibria, however possible and even probable they may be and whatever the consequences may be, remain, logically speaking and *at this point in the discussion*, accidents – technical errors on the part of investors – and therefore cannot constitute the basis for any real *law* of crises. On the other hand, even if we allow that certain further theses on under-employment and crises, notably Marxist and Keynesian, which we shall examine later on, prove the structural necessity of these phenomena, these theses in no way contradict the *essence* of the Law of Markets, which is, we repeat, the overall equality between the value added in one cycle of production and the revenues (purchasing power) distributed during or as a result of the same cycle of production.[20] J.–B. Say not only accepted the existence of these

18. cf. also his *Elements of Political Economy*, pp. 232–3: 'But if the demand and supply of every individual are always equal to one another, the demand and supply of all the individuals in the nation, taken aggregately, must be equal. Whatever, therefore, be the amount of the annual produce, it never can exceed the amount of the annual demand. . . . A nation . . . never can be without a market.'

19. Josiah Tucker had declared formally in 1752 that it is impossible for 'all the trades and all the crafts to be simultaneously overburdened with men'.

20. One single thesis of Marx's attempts, as we shall see later, to refute this equation; it is that of the time lag between depreciation and the replacement of fixed capital. We are speaking of course of a real thesis, which has reached us completely and systematically worked out; we are not talking about simple allusions and incomplete ideas, such as that of the over-accumulation of capital, to which we have already referred.

Continued on page 48

partial disequilibria, he even used them to explain the contradictions between theory and the phenomena of the real world. If there is overproduction in one place, there must be equivalent under-production somewhere else.

Nor did James Mill miss stating: 'If there is in the market a foodstuff or a commodity whose quantity is greater than the demand for it, there must be another whose quantity is less than demand'.[21]

Ricardo did not deny the possibility of a crisis resulting from a simple disproportion in the distribution of social labour. This was even the sole explanation which the classical economists provided for crises, as an experienced fact of life. 'If there be more sellers than buyers of one thing, there must be more buyers than sellers for another', John Stuart Mill would say.[22] And Jevons agreed later: 'Overproduction is not possible in all branches of industry at once, but it is possible in some as compared with others'.[23] In saying this, Jevons certainly did not feel that he was refuting the 'Law of Markets'.

20. *Continued from page 47*

Thus Bourguin was able to write: 'Marx points out the many occasions on which crises may occur. But these contingent crises are still only partial breaks in equilibrium, accidental discordances. Marx shows convincingly that these breaks are likely to occur, but it is in no way clear from his presentation that they are inevitable, that they are part of the essence of capitalist organisation.' (*Les systèmes socialistes*, pp. 321–2.) Bourguin might be right were it not for the theorem on the disparity between the two periodicities, that of depreciation and that of the replacement of equipment. Without prejudging the well-foundedness of this theory, we can say that within it, general over-production and crisis are fairly and squarely theoretically implied by the structure of the capitalist system.

21. *Elements of Political Economy*, chapter IV, sec. III.
22. *Essays on some Unsettled Questions*, p. 69.
23. *Theory of Political Economy*, p. 220.

3 Purchasing Power and the Will to Purchase

We have seen how the postulate that value produced equals purchasing power developed into an unchallengeable dogma. General overproduction came to be regarded as a theoretical impossibility, 'an unintelligible proposition' in Scrope's phrase.[1] We have also seen how an attempt was made, in what we have characterised as the 'naive view of overproduction', to refute this postulate by invoking a shortfall of *personal* consumption on the part of the capitalists and a consequent shortfall of overall demand for consumption goods in relation to total production – thus failing to take into account the *productive* consumption of producer goods in the context of reproduction on an extended scale; how this attempt was brushed aside, and how Sismondi's more pertinent but clumsily expressed remarks concerning the time lag between production and realization were ignored. It therefore remains to be seen how, once this postulate had been accepted, political economy was able to reconcile the mathematical equality between production and revenues with the 'phenomena' of over-production which accompany the depressions and periodic crises of the capitalist system.

To formulate the problem in these terms is obviously to resolve it, since there is only one possible reply to the question posed: if purchasing power, in its totality and independently of its specificity, is at all times equal to the total value of the commodities on sale, only one factor can – at least in the first instance – explain the difficulties actually encountered in realising the product; this is a lack of the *will* to purchase.

This is indeed what appears as the immediate cause in every single theory of the business cycle. Behind the very varied definitions and formulations, from simple conjunctural disproportion between industries resulting from anarchy of production, through to Keynes's liquidity preference, by way of Marx's hoarding, or the slowdown in investment caused by a fall in prices, therefore to a fall in the rate of profit, and structural disproportionality between the Departments – what Lenin calls a disproportion between productive consumption and individual consumption – there must always be some economic

1. G. Poulett Scrope, *Political Economy for Plain People*, p. 175.

agent who interrupts the chain of exchanges by failing to purchase after having sold.

In this regard, it is immaterial whether the initial cause is a fall in the propensity to consume which in turn discourages investment, or a reduction in incentives to invest, caused by other factors, which results in unemployment and underconsumption. It is equally immaterial whether the failure to purchase is initially motivated by the desire to build up a 'hoard'; or whether, with some industries overproducing and others underproducing, this failure is simply a result of the fact that the bearer of purchasing power cannot find the commodities he wants on the market, and does not want to buy those he can find. If revenues are equal to the total value of output, any failure to realise the latter is only *possible* because of a refusal by someone, somewhere, to make use of this revenue.

This would be a mere truism, and Domar would be exaggerating when he said that hoarding refutes Say's Law, were it not for the fact that, in the confusion which has characterised this controversy, the Ricardians went so far that they seem to deny the very possibility of a failure to purchase after having sold.

'Effectual demand', objected Malthus to Ricardo, 'consists of two elements, the *power* and the *will* to purchase . . . I by no means think that the power to purchase necessarily involves a proportionate will to purchase; and I cannot agree . . . that in reference to a nation, supply can never exceed demand. A nation must certainly have the power of purchasing all that it produces, but I can easily conceive it not to have the will.'[2]

Ricardo rejected this objection. Why should the owner of purchasing power fail to make use of it? One only produces in order to consume or to sell, and one only sells one commodity in order to obtain another, more useful commodity, whether this usefulness is in terms of current consumption or of its contribution to future production.

Indeed, it is not enough merely to posit the theoretical possibility of a lack of will to purchase. Overproduction would then be an accident, beyond the purview of science. It was necessary to show concretely that this lack is, if not necessary, then at least probable, i.e. that it can be explained in terms of individuals' rational economic behaviour.

To this question, Malthus had no answer beyond his 'naive' reference to the 'wants and tastes' of mankind. Ricardo eventually

2. Malthus to Ricardo, 11 September 1814, *The Works and Correspondence of David Ricardo*, vol. VI, pp. 131–2.

lost patience with this. 'I consider the wants and tastes of mankind as unlimited'[3], he replied, putting an end to the discussion.

Malthus is not alone in referring to the desire to purchase, in reference to disequilibria between supply and demand. Thomas Tooke wrote, in open challenge to the 'Law': 'The error is in supposing the *disposition* or *will* to be co-extensive with the power.'[4] Likewise, in line with the Saint-Simonians, Proudhon spoke of the sterilisation of disposable purchasing power. He saw the main advantage of his system – the replacement of money by exchange vouchers – to lie in ridding society once and for all of this 'scourge of trade', hoarding.[5] Alfred Marshall adopted the same argument as Malthus and Tooke against the Ricardian thesis of the theoretical impossibility of overproduction: 'But though men have the power to purchase they may not choose to use it.'[6] Hobson and Mummery took the same view.[7] Knut Wicksell, noting the general fall in prices between 1875 and 1900, despite the low rate of interest, concluded that J.–B. Say's Law of Markets was false, since demand could exceed purchasing power through credit, or fall short of purchasing power through hoarding.

In the same line as Proudhon and Saint-Simonians, Silvio Gesell also found the root of all evil in the very qualities of traditional money – qualities which enable it to be stored, and thus withdrawn from circulation. This money, he said, makes it possible to defer demand. In his opinion, money has too many qualities to be used for the circulation of commodities. The 'Free Money' which he proposed had this in common with the Saint-Simonian 'exchange vouchers': both lacked all the qualities of real money, making them ephemeral, transitory, thus not liable to hoarding.[8]

'It is conceivable that sellers might by *choice*, for a certain period, buy less than they sell, less than they could buy. But it is inconceivable for people to be *unable* to buy as much as they sell', wrote Aftalion. 'I am willing to accept that the seller may temporarily

3. Ricardo to Malthus, 16 September 1814, *ibid.*, p. 134.
4. T. Tooke, *An Inquiry into the Currency Principle*, p. 79.
5. P.–J. Proudhon, *Organisation du crèdit et de la circulation* (1848), *Oeuvres complètes*, vol. VI, p. 124.
6. *The Economics of Industry*, p. 154.
7. *Physiology of Industry*, pp. 100ff.
8. 'Money which goes out of date like a newspaper, rots like potatoes, rusts like iron, evaporates like ether, is alone capable of standing the test as an instrument for the exchange of potatoes, newspapers, iron and ether.' (*The Natural Economic Order*, p. 213.) 'Free-Money' is endorsed once a month and replaced once a year. John Law expressed roughly the same view when he stated that the precious metals are not an appropriate medium of circulation, and that the best currency is paper, precisely because it has no intrinsic value.

refuse to turn purchaser and may instead hoard. But it is inconceivable for society to be materially incapable of buying back what it has produced. There may be *deferred capitalist consumption*. There cannot be *capitalist under-consumption* due to a lack of purchasing power relative to output.'[9]

What is really remarkable is that this recognition by economists that the desire to purchase may not accompany purchasing power – a recognition which is really quite platitudinous – is used as often against the Law of Markets as in its defence. Some, like Aftalion, tell us that a failure to sell does not necessarily prove that purchasing power is less than production. There may be a lack of the will to purchase. This does not conflict with the 'Law'. The rest, such as Thomas Tooke and Wicksell, state that, since a lack of the will to purchase has the same effect as a lack of purchasing power, the assertion that aggregate supply cannot exceed aggregate demand is false. This reflects a lasting confusion in political economy between the possibility and the necessity of overproduction, a confusion which carries over to the distinction between the capitalist economy's general tendency to depression and the cyclical form in which problems of realization of output appear over time.

To say that purchasing power must be accompanied by the will to purchase is to say nothing at all, in the sense that this banality, as we have seen, unites the strongest enemies and the most zealous supporters of the 'Law'. The real question is whether or not, under capitalist relations, this will to purchase is *actually* co-extensive with purchasing power; and if there is a disjunction, what laws and concrete mechanisms determine it. A positive reply to the first question does not prejudice the position one adopts on the second. Between the two, there is all the difference between conjunctural accidents, which may be ignored, and structural disequilibrium, which must be explained.

There has been so much confusion about this that when Marshall distinguishes correctly between the two questions, and replies positively to the former in *Economics of Industry* and negatively to the latter in *Pure Theory of Domestic Value*, J. A. Hobson and, later, Keynes, found this inconsistent. However, Marshall was quite clear. He started by pointing out that it is incorrect to *rule out* any excess of supply over demand a priori, on the basis of thc mathematical equality of production and purchasing power, since demand requires not only purchasing power, but also the will to purchase. He went on to study the self-same 'will to purchase', and concluded that there is

9. *Les crises périodiques de surproduction*, p. 311, emphasis original.

no structural deficiency which might prevent the whole of revenue from being spent.

Whether or not Marshall was in fact correct, there is no internal contradiction in his analysis. We of course think that Marshall's basic position was wrong, in so far as he was not willing to challenge the real kernel of the Law of Markets, which is the equality between production and revenue. But his rigorous and scientific approach on the one hand, and his negative results on the other, show that it is pointless to try to explain the disequilibria of the capitalist system as occurring *despite* this equality. A lack of the 'will to purchase' is no explanation. For one of the following must apply: either it is a mere accident, and can then not explain anything, since the phenomena of overproduction and crisis are so perennial and regular in the capitalist system that they cannot possibly be matters of chance; or else it is constantly present in the system, in which case it itself needs to be explained. The search for this explanation is indeed what has occupied those economists who in one way or another accept the existence of a structural tendency in market economies towards underemployment of the factors of production.

Marx's view of hoarding and overproduction crises

Marx never produced a systematic analysis in the form of a self-contained work on economic crises, any more than on overproduction in general. On the specific problem of realisation of the product under the capitalist mode of production, there is one in chapters XX and XXI of volume II of *Capital*, with the schemes of simple and extended reproduction, but this, on the contrary, shows the theoretical *possibility* of this realization and defines the conditions for it to occur.[10] By referring to the two six-part plans for his *Economics* which Marx put in his Preface to the 1859 *Critique of Political Economy* and the 1857–59 Introduction to *Grundrisse*,[11] as well as the five-part plan in notebook M of 1857,[12] one can conclude that Marx postponed the study of crises to the last section of his work, which was of course never written. This section was meant in a sense to crown his work, with the study of the world market 'in which

10. Although Marx warns us that these conditions 'change into so many conditions of abnormal movement, into so many possibilities of crises, since a balance is itself an accident owing to the spontaneous nature of this production'. *Capital*, vol. II, p. 499.

11. *A Contribution to the Critique of Political Economy*, p. 19; *Grundrisse*, p. 264. These manuscripts were published in full under the title *Grundrisse des Kritik der politischen Oekonomie*, and in English as *Grundrisse: Foundations of the Critique of Political Economy*, London, 1973.

12. *Grundrisse*, p. 108.

production is posited as a totality . . . but within which . . . all contradictions come into play'.[13]

Matters could not be otherwise for an author who constantly stressed the international vocation of the capitalist system and the constant dialectical movement between the resolution of partial or local contradictions and their enlarged reproduction on a higher level and on a more vast scale. According to the vicissitudes of economics and politics, the system's contradiction might be resolved provisionally in this or that country by a local revolution. This was one possibility. But the objective material limits of the capitalist mode of production and, thus, the ultimate necessity of its destruction, still only emerged on a world scale. 'Crises are then the general intimation which points beyond the presupposition, and the urge which drives towards the adoption of a new historical form.'[14]

On both these counts, crises could only adequately be studied and theorised in the very last chapter of a work based equally on the two principles of the universality and the outdatedness of the present system. Marx did not have time to complete his plan – his theory of crises was never worked out. But there are many long deliberations both on the structural disequilibria of the capitalist system which lie at the root of crises, and on crises themselves, scattered throughout his writings, in the most varied contexts.[15] These writings can in general be divided into two kinds: some concern the abstract preconditions for crises of over-production, while others deal with the concrete mechanisms of the process.

The first arise out of the general theme of hoarding. They appear in different forms, with an extraordinary wealth of analyses and ideas, in all of Marx's posthumously published manuscripts and rough notes – here they are intertwined with the second. But, setting aside a few historical and descriptive passages, they are also the only kind to appear in the works published during Marx's lifetime, and here they are concentrated in the first volume of *Capital* and in the 1859 *Critique of Political Economy*.[16] These are consequently the only

13. *Ibid.*, p. 227.
14. *Ibid.*, p. 228.
15. Apart from some remarks in passing in *The Communist Manifesto, Wage-labour and Capital, Speech on Free Trade* and *The Poverty of Philosophy*, the most noteworthy passages are the following:
1. *Capital*, vol. 1, pp. 197–209, 229; vol. II, pp. 77–86, 188–9, 262–3, 288–9, 318–22, 404–24, 459, 471–5, 494–507, 521–5; vol. III, pp. 118–19, 249–57, 266, 304–5, 360–1, 416–29, 447–9, 460, 482–93, 530, 565–74.
2. *Theories of Surplus Value*, vol. II, pp. 492–546; vol. III, pp. 21–2, 57–63.
3. *Contribution to the Critique of Political Economy*, pp. 85–146.
4. *Grundrisse*, pp. 125–30, 147–8, 200, 236, 410–16, 419–20.

16. Besides, they are found in corresponding chapters of the two works: in chapter III of *Capital*, entitled 'Money, or the Circulation of Commodities', and chapter II of the *Critique*, 'Money or Simple Circulation'.

ones to have been thoroughly worked out and completed. But, as we have already had occasion to say and as Marx himself repeated countless times, they only establish the possibility of crises, and never their cause.

The second, those that in our opinion are the materials for the unwritten chapter, deal with the structural (material) causes and conditions of the hoarding of capital, as well as their cumulative effects due to the opposition between productive capital and loan capital. They are directed towards the discovery of an ultimate cause which would make overproduction crises not merely possible and probable, but necessary, and even, if this can be said, not only historically but also theoretically necessary.

It has to be recognized that this ultimate cause, this *primum movens*, is never clearly defined anywhere in these texts in varying states of completion, as published posthumously on the basis of Marx's rough notes. A thousand times the reader thinks he grasps this cause; a thousand times it slips through his fingers. Each time, we are of course referred back to the primary contradiction between social production and private appropriation of the product. But that is not enough. All secondary contradictions and all disequilibria derive from this contradiction in one way or another. What we need is the concrete process through which this fundamental contradiction comes to be reflected in a crisis of over-production. Marx knows this and says as much, as we shall see, on several occasions. He also tells us in which areas he is looking for this cause, and supplies us with a mass of circumstantial evidence and confirmatory signs. But as late as Chapter XXII of volume III of *Capital*, written in 1865, he declares that 'the analysis of this cycle itself [the industrial cycle] . . . cannot be given here',[17] and even in 1873, well after all these texts on economics had been written, one of his letters to Engels shows that he was not at all satisfied with what he had discovered and that he was still looking for information to use as a basis finally to construct his theory of crises.[18]

There is another important question which was completely ignored by Marx: whether over and above the periodicity and the fluctuations of the cycle, the capitalist system, and even commodity production in general, have, in their structure and laws of motion, an inherent tendency towards a permanent excess of supply over demand which would transcend cycles and crises. Despite a few rare approaches in this direction, which we shall examine in the course of this account, Marx appears to reject this hypothesis:

17. *Capital*, vol. III, p. 358.
18. Letter of 31 May 1873; see *below*, p. 57, note 22.

> Let us suppose that the whole of society is composed only of industrial capitalists and wage-workers. Let us furthermore disregard price fluctuations, which prevent large portions of the total capital from replacing themselves in their average proportions and which, owing to the general interrelations of the entire reproduction process as developed in particular by credit, must always call forth general stoppages of a transient nature. Let us also disregard the sham transactions and speculations, which the credit system favours. Then, a crisis could only be explained as the result of a disproportion of production in the various branches of the economy, and as a result of a disproportion between the consumption of the capitalists and their accumulation.[19]

This argument leads, *a contrario*, to the conclusion that in ideal conditions for the functioning of capitalism, when the equilibrium proportions are met between Departments on the one hand, and between saving and the capitalists' personal consumption on the other, crises would disappear entirely. But such a position – deeply classical – is a serious handicap in the attempt to discover a basis for the theoretical necessity of overproduction crises, and this perhaps explains why Marx did not find it. For once this thesis is accepted, there is only one place left to look for the causes of disequilibrium: in the excessive complexity of the equilibrium conditions: and this is what Marx does in volume II of *Capital*. This position is also shared by a great number of Marxists. The system is so complex that equilibrium can only occur by accident. Engels, Lenin and several others adopted this from Marx. But this is not a scientific law of general overproduction. Either the basic causes of this general overproduction are already *present* in the system's own conditions of functioning, i.e. the best conditions theoretically possible, and crises are only their extension, as violent as they are ephemeral, while still remaining entirely the product of the functioning of these laws of motion in their purest form, or crises are merely an *effect* of the system's working badly, however probable and recurrent, or even inevitable, they may be in practice. For practical inevitability concerns only the past, and nothing which has been inevitable in the past can, by virtue of this alone, be considered as *ineluctable* in the future. Now, the only use of theory is to predict and transform reality, that is to predict and transform the future.

As opposed to those who embraced this approach, Marx was never fooled by it. The complexity of the equilibrium conditions for the processes of simple reproduction and reproduction on an extended scale, he admits, only creates the *possibility* of crises, 'occasions for running abnormally'.[20] The law of crises must still be found.

19. *Capital*, vol. III, pp. 483–4.
20. *Ibid*., vol. II, p. 500.

Marx seemed to be searching for this law when he wrote in March 1858: 'For me, the main task is to discover an element determining these cycles in the immediate material conditions of large-scale industry.'[21] And he was speaking of this same law when, fifteen years later in May 1873, he said that his search had been fruitless.[22] Nonetheless, no one up to now has dealt as thoroughly as Marx with the two points which we distinguished above and which we shall deal with separately below. The first, studied in the works published during his lifetime, and therefore to be found in its complete and definitive form, concerns the possibility of crisis that exists in the act of hoarding. The second, incomplete, which is so to speak the object of exploration in all directions, and so both uncertain and extremely rich and fertile, only featuring in the posthumous publications, concerns the structural causes of crises.

Hoarding as a possible breach of equilibrium

As we have just said, no one to our knowledge has developed or refined the theme of hoarding as much as Marx, and his position on this question was expressed with perfect clarity. Since purchasing power is equal to the value of production put on sale – this kernel of the 'Law' was never in question – the *necessary* condition of any crisis of overproduction, or even of any disturbance in the process of the realisation of the product, is a temporary abstention from making use of this purchasing power by a certain number or a certain category of its bearers. But this abstention, this disjunction between purchase and sale, is in no way a *sufficient* condition. One must distinguish between the possibility (*Möglichkeit*) and the reality (*Wirklichkeit*) of overproduction and crisis.

21. Letter from Marx to Engels, 5 March 1858.

22. Letter from Marx to Engels, 3 May 1873: 'I have imparted to Moore here, a problem with which I have long been grappling in my inner furnace. But he believes that the matter is insoluble, at least for the meanwhile, because of the numerous factors which must first be discovered, and which compose the elements of the problem. This is what it is about: you know those tables which show prices, discount rates, etc., along with their fluctuations in the course of the year, represented by zigzagging curves which go up and down. I have tried on several occasions to calculate – in order to analyse crises – these peaks and troughs in the way one analyses irregular curves, and I believed it possible (and I still believe it possible, with the help of carefully enough chosen documentation) to determine mathematically, on this basis, the essential laws of crises. Moore, as I have said, does not believe that the thing is feasible at the moment, and I have decided to give it up for now.' (The 'problem' which Marx is talking about here, the same one he discussed in his letter of 5 March 1858, is the disjunction between the rate of depreciation and the rate of replacement of equipment, which we shall discuss later on.

> No one can sell unless someone else purchases. But no one is *forthwith* bound to purchase, because he has just sold. . . . To say that these two independent and antithetical acts have an intrinsic unity – are essentially one – is the same thing as to say that this intrinsic oneness expresses itself in an external antithesis. If the interval in time between the two complementary phases . . . *become too great*, if the split between the sale and the purchase become too pronounced, the intimate connection, their oneness, asserts itself by producing – a crisis.[23]

The mistake that Marx attacks in the classics is of having considered money as a mere technical accessory of circulation, as a passive element. This conception ruled out the possibility of a specific demand for money. If money is not demanded for its own sake, but only as a means of purchase, it is quite clear that one can only sell one commodity in order to buy another, and all problems of realization disappear, since the more commodities one has on sale, the more one wishes to buy. Commodities are purchased with commodities. The only thing that can go wrong is for the quantities of different kinds of commodities produced not to correspond with the preferences of purchasers, given the level of aggregate revenues at that point in time. Then there will be overproduction in certain industries, which must be the counterpart of strictly equal under-production in certain other industries: gluts on one side, and shortages on the other. These distortions will themselves give rise to the re-equilibrating forces. First of all price movements in opposite directions, which change the actual scales of preferences of the purchasers, since these scales are functions of revenues and prices; and later a transfer of factors from the overstocked industries to the understocked ones, the temporal margins needed for the readjustment being ensured by the elasticity of these stocks.

Marx attacked the inaccuracy of this notion. Money is no mere technical means of circulation. It is itself a commodity, and one with a very specific nature in the sense that its use-value consists in crystallising, in storing value in its already realized, socialised, i.e. socially recognized form. One can therefore try to acquire it in its own right and for its own qualities, in order to hold on to it, at least for a certain length of time. What is more, this commodity has the following peculiarity: it is opposed to all other commodities and expresses their values, so that its demand is the supply of all other commodities and its supply is the demand for all other commodities. Consequently, any excess of the demand for money over its supply really reflects an excess of the aggregate supply of commodities over their aggregate demand.

23. *Capital*, vol. I, p. 115, emphasis added.

At this point one can say, if one likes, that there is no general overproduction, since there is at least one commodity, money, whose demand exceeds its supply; and in this way the Law of Markets can be saved. But this would only be to deprive it of all substance, since our problem is not that of the metaphysical realisation of all commodities, including the money-commodity, but that of the concrete realisation of all commodities *except money*, which, for its part, is a 'realised' commodity from its very birth and however much of it there may be.

'The supply of all commodities', Marx replies to Ricardo and John Stuart Mill, 'may, at a given moment, be greater than the demand for all commodities, because the demand for the universal commodity, money . . . is greater than that for all particular commodities or because the incentive to convert commodities into money, i.e. to realize their exchange-value, defeats the incentive to reconvert them into use-values.'[24]

After having been relegated to the ranks of technical accessories of economic activity, 'money then suddenly appears not as the medium of circulation, but once more as the only adequate form of exchange-value, as a unique form of wealth, just as it is regarded by the hoarder . . . the sole form of wealth for which people clamour at such times . . . and compared with it all other commodities – just because they are use-values – appear to be useless, mere baubles and toys'.[25] The money becomes petrified to a hoard, and the seller becomes a hoarder of money. . . . Along with the extension of circulation, increases the power of money, that absolutely social form of wealth ever ready for use.'[26]

However, while this dissociation in time between purchase and sale does mean that there is no necessity for supply of commodities always to equal demand for them, it in no way refutes the other part, the kernel of the Law of Markets, i.e. the equality between the value of production and revenues. Even after this point has been made, the kernel in question is still so unchallengeable that a Marxist economist such as Ronald Meek could call it a mere truism. In fact, this dissociation can only diminish the *will to purchase; purchasing power*, for its part, is in no way affected, and is still strictly equal to the overall value of the commodities produced and put on sale. Likewise, this temporary abstention from using existing purchasing power only gives rise to the mere *possibility* of disequilibrium, an adventitious disturbance. Marx is conscious of this:

24. *Theories of Surplus Value*, vol. II, p. 505.
25. *Critique of Political Economy*, p. 146.
26. *Capital*, vol. I, pp. 131–2.

> All these antitheses and contradictions, which are immanent in commodities, . . . develop their modes of motion, in the antithetical phases of the metamorphosis of a commodity. These modes therefore imply the possibility, and *no more than* the possibility, of crises. The conversion of this mere possibility is the result of a long series of relations, that, from our present standpoint of simple circulation, have as yet no existence.[27]
>
> The difficulty in selling . . . arises simply from the purchaser's ability to defer the reconversion of his money into a commodity.

Kautsky's edition adds here:

> The commodity must be converted into money, money has no need to be immediately converted into a commodity.
>
> We have said that this relation implies the possibility of a crisis . . . Since purchase and sale can be separated, they contain the potential for crises. Their coincidence is always a critical moment for the commodity. *But they can also follow on after each other smoothly.*[28]

And further:

> The general possibility of crises subsists . . . in the temporal and spatial non-coincidence of purchase and sale. But this is in no way the cause of a crisis.[29]

The classics were wrong to claim that there is no possibility of crisis. This possibility exists and it lies *solely* in the separation of sale from purchase.[30]

Once this precondition has been stated, development of a theory of crises required proof of two points: that there exist, in capitalist relations of production, permanent or recurrent factors leading to hoarding on the macroeconomic level; and that their effects are cumulative, that is to say that they themselves give rise to new impulses towards an even greater contraction of demand. Here we take up the second point of Marx's search, which is, as we have said, far from being as clear as the first.

The causes of hoarding and the inevitability of overproduction

Since hoarding destroys the equality between the aggregate value of the supply of commodities and actual purchases, any cause of hoarding also indirectly, but necessarily, results in a failure to sell, and to search for these causes is to search for the causes of over-

27. *Ibid.*, p. 115, emphasis added.
28. *Theories of Surplus Value*, vol. II, p. 509, emphasis added.
29. *Ibid.*, p. 515, emphasis added.
30. *Ibid.*, p. 508, emphasis added.

production crises. However, these causes must be rooted in the actual nature of the capitalist mode of production, and must not be the result of impurities and contingent features; and the hoarding which they engender must be *net* hoarding at the level of society as a whole.

Temporary abstentions from purchasing after having sold, if they are fortuitous, or if they result from a general *unvarying* propensity to defer the use of purchasing power, cannot be the basis of any necessary disequilibrium, whether structural or even conjunctural, since, according to the law of probability, in both these cases purchases reaching maturity at any point in time should compensate for purchases deferred at that same point in time.

Without even mentioning the perennial character of the phenomenon of overproduction in market economies, which transcends the business cycle – even for regularly recurrent conjunctural disequilibria to be possible, there must be periodic *structural variations* in the propensity to hoard itself, i.e. in the rate of hoarding itself, or else dishoarding by some would compensate for hoarding by others. These variations themselves would then stand in need of explanation.

If one rejects the hypothesis that man has an innate desire to avoid purchasing, this propensity to build up hoards cannot be a datum exogenous to the economic system; still less can its abrupt periodic increases be so. They can only result from one of two sources: from uncertainty about the future felt by the bearers of hoarded purchasing power, i.e. from uncertainty as to the future trend of their revenues, or from material constraints of reproduction. If for the moment we only consider the first half of the alternative, a difficulty arises immediately. Under capitalist relations of production, all revenues derive from a sale, the sale of labour-power or the sale of a product. So before any uncertainty over future revenues could arise, and before people could begin to avoid purchasing, sales, as such, must already have become unreliable, as a fact of human experience. This leads us straight into a vicious circle. The difficulty of selling cannot be explained by hoarding, if hoarding is itself only explained by obstacles to selling.

It may be objected that, while it is not part of human nature to avoid purchasing, man may nonetheless have acquired the propensity, if not natural, then at least historical, to obtain access to universal wealth from the moment when money became its incarnation. This objection would be valid if the hoarding we are dealing with were that of wage-earners. But neither today, nor, all the more, in Marx's time, i.e. on the basis of roughly subsistence wages, does it seem possible to argue seriously that an excess of wage-earners' current hoarding over their current dishoarding could set off a crisis. Not only was this never claimed by Marx, but he even argued that those theories that attribute over-production crises to workers' underconsumption are false, since on the eve of crises, the volume of employment, wage-rates and the level of working-class consumption are always at their maximum.[31] While he does refer here and there to saving on the part of certain categories of wage-earners, he makes it quite clear that in his opinion these sums make an almost negligible contribution.

It is therefore only the capitalist, not the wage-earner, who may break the chain of purchases and sales and provoke a disequilibrium between supply and demand. From now on, the search for causes of hoarding must be confined to a search for factors that either lead capitalists to *decide* to abstain, or *compel* them to abstain, from productive or unproductive consumption of a part of their revenues. The factors that induce this decision to abstain operate on the level of motivations and are in a way psychological. Those that 'compel' capital to withdraw temporarily from circulation are moments of the objective process itself. In order to clarify analysis, these two categories of factors must be treated separately.

Subjective causes of hoarding

It is appropriate to recall that what we are discussing here is true hoarding, which corresponds to a revenue that is neither consumed nor invested. As an explanation of the incentives for a capitalist to engage in such hoarding, the intrinsic qualities of money are insufficient. For however perfect money's incarnation of universal wealth may be, a capitalist, for his part, is in no way enriched by abstaining from the purchase of new labour-power and new raw materials after realizing his product, when he interrupts or slows down reproduction in this way in order to build up a sterile hoard. He is impoverished by behaving in this way. (Or he misses a chance of gain, which comes to the same thing.) For him to behave in this way, his confidence in the possibility of future sales must have been seriously shaken, to the point where he foresees a greater loss through continuation of reproduction than through its interruption.

It is quite clear how the withdrawal of one capitalist from the market reduces the sales of other capitalists, and therefore their purchases, but unless crises are to be explained as the result of a mere technical error, it is once again circular reasoning to attribute the obvious overproduction and failure to sell to hoarding and to a lack of

31. *Capital*, vol. II, p. 415.

the will to purchase on the part of the capitalists, if we also accept that there would be no hoarding or lack of the will to purchase were it not for a previous or expected failure to sell.

To argue that the capitalist, in hoarding, may simply reduce his personal consumption without suspending or diminishing his (productive) purchases of labour-power and means of production would only shift the terms of the calculation in a purely formal way. Funds are not specially earmarked in advance for personal expenses or for investment; these two quantities have the same quality. If the capitalist reduces his luxury consumption, he has the choice of two destinations for the funds thus freed: to increase his investments or to amass a hoard. Logically, he will only choose the hoard if investment does not offer him a reasonable chance of gain, however small.

Although never formulated, this reasoning seems to us to underlie Marx's argument. It is implicit in the constant repetition of innumerable variations on the theme *possibility/reality, condition/cause*, of overproduction crises, of which we have already given some examples. It is undeniably compatible with the assertion that 'the general possibility of crisis is nothing other than its most abstract form; without the content and without the concrete *prime mover* which give rise to it'.[32]

The 'prime mover' of capital, and therefore of the whole process of reproduction, is the search for profit. Should we conclude from this that incentives to invest are conditioned by fluctuations of the rate of profit?

An objection arises immediately. If physical costs are given, the rate of profit can only vary as a function of price variations. If prices of outputs vary in the same proportions as prices of inputs, the rate of profit remains unchanged. If the two variations are not proportional, the rate of profit changes, and, as the case may be, it may fall.[33] But then these variations and, even more, this asymmetry between the variations, must themselves be explained in turn.

Here, however, we are not necessarily dealing with the vicious circle which we were caught in earlier, when lack of markets led to hoarding, while hoarding, in its turn, was what made the markets contract. For inputs include labour-power, and the rate of profit can begin to fall when the sale of commodities is going most smoothly, if this situation leads to a rise in wage-rates. It can therefore be assumed provisionally, without being proved, that in a situation of full

32. *Theories of Surplus Value*, vol. II, p. 509, emphasis added.

33. Here we are abstracting from Marx's law of the tendency of the rate of profit to fall which, being a long-term unidirectional variation, cannot explain the cyclical variations of overproduction.

employment – this situation is the proper starting-point for any explanation of a slowdown in reproduction and resulting unemployment – the price of labour-power increases faster than that of other commodities and that the rate of profit falls as a result.

But if the rate of profit remains positive – no one has ever claimed that during a period of prosperity a general increase in wages can absorb all the surplus-value – it remains to be shown why investment should fall as a result of a fall in this rate. The greatest confusion reigns on this question. Many Marxists usually argue as if, for a given level of savings, the level of investment was an increasing function of the rate of profit, or as if there existed, in static and absolute terms, thresholds in the rate of profit below which capital would prefer to lie idle. By putting this interpretation on Marx – one of those indisputable views which no one dreams of questioning – Marxists have laid themselves wide open to the anti-Marxist critics.

In fact this is a gratuitous assertion which no one to the best of my knowledge has ever attempted to justify. Often the increasing function which, for a given level of revenue, relates savings to variations in the rate of profit or interest within a model based on the equality of savings and investment, i.e. a model which denies the possibility of hoarding, is transferred wholesale into a model which denies this equality and which accepts the possibility of hoarding; and this function is transformed into a function which is supposed to establish a direct relation between the level of investment and these same variations. While it is quite easy to understand why, below a certain rate of interest, this or that individual should choose to spend his revenues rather than save them, it is rather more difficult to see why this or that capital, once it has been formed out of savings, should voluntarily turn itself into a totally sterile hoard rather than invest itself at a reduced rate of profit.[34] Arbitrage between personal consumption and saving/investment as a function of the rate of remuneration of this investment is one thing; but it has nothing to do with our problem, since it in no way reduces the overall value of demand, only modifying the proportions of the use-values between which this arbitrage occurs. Hoarding pure and simple, as an excess precisely of savings over investment, is a completely different matter; it diminishes the value of aggregate demand, and this is what we are looking for here.[35]

34. A reduction in profits, Sismondi said in essence, will not stop capitalists from accumulating, unless the rate falls to zero. (Cf *De la richesse commerciale*, vol. I, ch. III.) '. . . Interest has usually been regarded as the reward of not-spending, whereas in fact it is the reward of not-hoarding.' (Keynes, *General Theory*, p. 174).

The law of the tendency of the rate of profit to fall

It is true that this interpretation of Marx as accepting a *direct* functional link between the rate of investment and the rate of profit does rest on certain texts. These are the passages in the famous part III of volume III of *Capital*, in which Marx presents the 'law of the tendency of the rate of profit to fall'. They naturally stress variations in the rate of profit and make them appear as an autonomous cause of variations in the level of investment. Thus, for example, at the start of chapter XV, Marx writes that, 'the rate of self-expansion of the total capital, or the rate of profit, being the goal of capitalist production (just as the self-expansion of capital is its only purpose), its fall checks the formation of new independent capitals and thus appears as a threat to the development of the capitalist production process. It breeds overproduction, speculation, crises, and surplus-capital alongside surplus-population.'[36]

Since the tendency for the rate of profit to fall has not, for a certain number of years, been borne out by the facts, the actual theoretical

35. The choice between saving and consumption has long been confused with the choice between investment and hoarding, Ricardo also talks of a minimum rate of profit below which investment will cease. But Ricardo rules out hoarding, and his argument is consistent. Accumulation is synonymous with investment, and investment is a decreasing function of personal consumption. Variations in the volume of investment have no effect on the volume of employment.

Political economy has since discovered that investment may vary within certain limits, without any inverse variation of unproductive consumption. From this angle investment does of course provide employment. But from this same angle, the function relating it to the rate of profit disappears, since the source of these variations in investment is either the mobilisation of a hoard which, as such, earns nothing, or the creation of money *ex nihilo*, which, as such, costs nothing.

Once this is accepted, the functional relation which was appropriate in Ricardo's system becomes inconsistent, for example, when Charles Bettelheim writes that a fall in surplus-value reduces 'the incentive to invest' and 'tends to a different division of the capitalists' revenues between consumption and accumulation at the expense of the latter'. That, consequently, 'full employment can only be the exception under capitalism, since such a situation leads to a rise in wages, a fall in surplus-value and therefore a fall in accumulation, while this fall in accumulation results in a reduction of employment and the emergence of unemployment' (*Le Problème de l'Emploi*, pp. 91–2.)

The weak point of this argument is immediately apparent. A reduction of accumulation with a corresponding rise in the unproductive consumption of capitalists and/or wage-earners will not only have no deflationary effect, but will have the opposite effect, tending rather towards equilibrium and a rise in the level of employment, since it means restricting the rise of the organic composition of capital. It is on the contrary the disproportionate growth of accumulation compared to final consumption which creates problems, as we shall see later on.

36. *Capital*, vol. III, pp. 241–2.

part of the Marxist law is very much up for debate. Refutations or corrections have been suggested.[37] We refer those interested in this question to appendix I at the end of this chapter. But leaving aside this debate on the actual basis of the 'law', it is not at all clear:

(1) how the long-term and one-way movement implied by the 'law' turns into the booms and slumps of the cycle (Marx does tell us that this movement, though uni-directional, is nonetheless disturbed by the discontinuous effects of technical progress, but it is still difficult to see how this exogenous discontinuity is converted into the determinate periodicity of economic crises);
(2) how, and through what functional relation, a fall in the rate of profit can lead to a reduction in investment (not through an increase in unproductive consumption, which would be plausible, but) through a build-up of hoards.

The opposition between money-capital and commodity-capital

But there are other passages by Marx on overproduction crises. And in these passages, hoarding, for Marx, is no longer dependent on the magnitude of the rate of profit, but on its variations over time, which is a much more complex argument than appears at first glance, and also on the relation between these variations and variations of the rate of interest over time. Although incomplete, this analysis is much more subtle than has generally been acknowledged, and astonishingly dynamic and modern for its time. It rests essentially on the distinction and hence opposition between productive and loan capital.[38] The first is remunerated according to the rate of pure profit (what Marx called profit of enterprise, i.e. the average rate of profit minus the rate of interest); the second, according to the rate of

37. We refer among others to the important article written by Charles Bettelheim himself, as early as 1959, under the title 'Variations of the Rate of Profit and the Growth of Labour Productivity'; Serge Latouche's study in *IREP Documents*, no. 2, and his article, 'Concerning the tendency of the rate of profit to fall'; Y. Barel's article, 'Some contradictions of contemporary capitalism'; F. Danjou's study, 'On the tendency of the rate of profit to fall'; and finally, a commentary by Henri Denis on the study by F. Danjou already referred to, in issue 5 of the same periodical.

38. cf. Marx, *Grundrisse*, p. 413: '[The classics – Ricardo for example – say:] Since production is itself regulated by the costs of production, it allegedly regulates itself, and if onc branch of production docs not rcalisc itself then capital withdraws from it to a certain degree and throws itself on another point where it is needed. But apart from the fact that this necessity of evening-up already *presupposes* the unevenness, the disharmony and hence the contradiction – in a general crisis of over-production the contradiction is not between the different kinds of productive capital, but between industrial and loanable capital – between capital as directly involved in the production process and capital as money existing (relatively) outside of it.'

interest. Although the rate of interest depends ultimately on the average rate of profit, it varies in the short-term inversely with the rate of profit of enterprise and, within certain limits, independently of variations in the total rate of profit itself. 'If we observe the cycles in which modern industry moves . . . we shall find that a low rate of interest generally corresponds to periods of prosperity or extra profit, a rise in interest separates prosperity and its reverse, and a maximum of interest up to a point of extreme usury corresponds to the period of crisis.'[39]

It is therefore possible that at a certain point in the cycle the rate of interest should absorb such a high proportion of the total rate of profit that the rate of profit of enterprise should fall, even if the total rate of profit remains the same or even increases. However, the rate of profit of enterprise is itself only an average, covering a whole spread of individual rates of profit which always vary from industry to industry, and even from firm to firm. If this average moves too close to zero, some of its components may become negative although the average itself remains positive. In these units, all new investment would stop, or at least that part that requires external financing. Marx does not explicitly envisage this case, but it is implied by many of his discussions of the question. However this may be, these discussions deal with quite a different set of considerations from those of the long-term fall of the rate of profit.

But can it be said that in this case there is, at the level of society as a whole, a non-utilisation of purchasing-power through a fall in the volume of investment below the sum of disposable savings, what Marx calls 'the universal simultaneous formation of a hoard.'[40]? It seems not. The refusal to borrow in order to invest does not represent hoarding on the part of the enterprises under consideration (those in the lower part of the spread of rates of profit). Nor does it necessarily represent hoarding on the part of lenders either, since they can find a placing for their funds with enterprises on the other side of the average. Unless the rate of interest rises above the general rate of profit itself, all available funds will be absorbed.

But all this is, so to speak, a merely static view of things. Marx develops his analysis much further. What conditions the investment

39. *Capital*, vol. III, p. 360. The value of money-capital (the rate of interest) rises at the very moment when, and because, the value of real capital (the rate of profit) falls, despite the fact that the latter determines the former. In chapter XXXI (pp. 421ff) Marx even notes the existence of a sort of inverse function relating the quantitative variations of loan capital to those of real capital. But this second function appears to be an effect of the first.

40. *Capital*, vol. II, p. 495.

decision is not the rate of profit or interest *at that point in time*, but expectations of those involved as to future variations of these rates.

First of all, results of an investment are not measured solely by its yields in profit or interest, but also by changes in the prices of the capital-goods in which it is embodied. The same factors that cause the rate of profit to fall, i.e. in the last analysis development of the productive forces, also cause an increase in productivity of labour, a consequent reduction in the cost of material reproduction of capital and therefore in its devaluation (and this reduction also counteracts the fall in the rate of profit). But fluctuations in the rate of profit affect all capitals, whether they have already taken on the form of productive capital, or whether they are still in the form of money-capital, while the fall in the value of capital itself only affects existing productive capitals. The 'development of the productive forces of labour [occurs] at the expense of already created productive forces'[41]. As this devaluation combines with the discontinuity of technical progress itself, of which it is the result, or with the periodicity of fluctuations of the general price level within the business cycle, there are times when the capitalist can fear losing more on his principal than he stands to gain from his profits.[42]

Investment is not only a change in the form of capital. It is at the same time a purchase of commodities. While it is not in the nature of the capitalist to amass lasting hoards, he may nonetheless defer his purchases for a certain length of time, if he expects prices to drop. This is enough to cause the 'universal simultaneous formation of a hoard'. It is clear that, over such short periods of time as are affected by this kind of decision, a very small change in the value of capital itself is more than enough to compensate for the profits forgone. While it is absurd to say that a particular rate of profit may in itself be insufficient as the incentive for an already constituted money-capital to be invested, it is on the other hand quite understandable that it may be insufficient to induce acceptance of the risk of a devaluation of the principal. And it is here that the opposition between active capital and money-capital is relevant. Since a universal simultaneous depreciation of commodities is the same thing as an appreciation of

41. *Ibid.*, p. 249.

42. 'Prices do not even have to fall for the process of hoarding to get under way. If businessmen believe merely that prices are going to fall (whatever the reasons for this belief), demand will slacken, the supply of the means of exchange will lessen, and the forecasts and fears will be confirmed.' (Schumpeter, *Capitalism, Socialism and Democracy*, French edition, p. 175.)

And further on: 'Goods are unsaleable because they are too cheap and threaten to be even cheaper tomorrow. The crisis breaks out.' (*Ibid.*, p. 177.)

the specific commodity which embodies social value, any devaluation of productive capital is tantamount to a revaluation of money-capital. The only ones to profit from this revaluation will be those who have provisionally refused to invest and who have kept their capital in the form of money-capital. Under these conditions, the 'hoard' ceases to be sterile.[43]

This universal devaluation may at first seem to be immaterial from a classical point of view, i.e. in the sense that what each loses in selling he regains in buying, and in the sense that the reduction in the sum of money represented by fixed capital is exactly compensated for by the increase in the value of money itself. But Marx rejects this classical idea of passive money. Money, he points out, is not only a medium of circulation; it is also a means of payment and the measure of value including primarily contracts for loans. One does not borrow machines or buildings, even when one buys them on credit. One borrows their equivalent in money, and what one has to repay is a particular sum of money, whatever may be the new value of the machines and buildings on the day when the debt comes to maturity. In fact one always borrows money-capital. Contracts of payment are, so to speak, always to be executed on the basis of the old prices, given that 'definite, presupposed, price relations govern the process of reproduction, so that the latter is halted and thrown into confusion by a general drop in prices. This confusion and stagnation paralyses the function of money as a medium of payment, whose development is geared to the development of capital and is based on those presupposed price relations. The chain of payment obligations due at specific dates is broken in a hundred places.'[44]

On the level of society as a whole, there is of course neither gain nor loss. (Here we abstract from the loss which will occur as a secondary effect, as a result of the stoppage or slow-down in reproduction.) In the first place, what one loses is another's gain. But

43. Sweezy also proposes a functional relation between the volume of investment and variations in the rate of profit. According to his analysis, when the rate of profit falls below its usual range as the result of a rise in wages as full employment is approached, capitalists 'postpone reinvesting until conditions are once again favorable, that is to say, until either the rate of profit is back in the usual range or they have reconciled themselves to a new and lower norm for the rate of profit. In the meantime the postponement of reinvestment will have interrupted the circulation process and brought on a crisis and overproduction.' (*The Theory of Capitalist Development*, p. 142.)
This explanation appears to centre on the time it takes for entrepreneurs to be reconciled to the new rate, rather than a readjustment of the other variables of the production function to the new rate of profit.

44. *Capital*, vol. III, p. 254.

it is precisely an 'other'; this process of compensation does not operate within each capital through its alternation between the positions of seller and purchaser as the classics imagined. This 'other' is money-capital, banking capital, which is permanently in opposition to productive capital. What is more, what this 'other' gains, it gains precisely through overproduction and crisis.[45]

It is therefore not the fall in the rate of profit as such which discourages investors, but the fall in prices which generally accompanies it. Also, it is not a matter of abstention from investing; it is a matter of *speculation* concerning the *timing* of purchases.

Variations in the rate of interest and incentives to invest

At the end of this first analysis, we are still short of an explanation. The fall in prices or the expectation of a fall in prices are taken as given. We do not know what causes them. But there is a second analysis, and it is here that Marx really makes his argument dynamic, at the same time showing a keen grasp of financial affairs and their most complex and developed mechanisms. These pages bear ill their date of the mid-nineteenth century.

In developed capitalism, Marx notes, internal financing of investments and even their financing through credit and direct loans lose much of their importance. With the development of limited companies, most investments are made through subscription and the purchase of securities on the stock exchange, and pass through the banking network. These securities can either be bonds or shares. Judicially speaking, the revenue from the former is interest; that from the latter, profit. In reality, the revenue from the latter, despite its variability, is also interest.

Since the capital tied up in shares is just as divisible, just as negotiable on the stock exchange, and therefore just as liquid, as that tied up in bonds, the only qualitative difference between the two that might justify a quantitative difference between their respective yields is the variability of the dividends from shares compared to the invariability of the bond's coupon. Unless the company concerned goes bankrupt, bond-holders must be remunerated whatever the company's results; shareholders, for their part, are only provided for after, and as a function of, these results. This is what is known as the risk of profit compared with the certainty of interest which, for some Marxist economists, is the basis of the difference between their

45. Marx devotes the whole of part V of volume III to this opposition, and assembles countless statistical sources, reports of inquiries, etc., which all suggest that big bankers prosper during crises, while at the same time active capitalists face bankruptcy.

respective rates.[46] Those who argue this way forget that the risk of below average profits is compensated for by the chance of above average profits. The stock exchange, through the divisibility and mobility which it ensures, allows even the smallest capitalists to avoid this risk by spreading their investment among several companies. Finally, a sufficiently diversified portfolio of shares will, after a few years, give the same average yield as a portfolio of bonds. Investors' arbitrage between these shares and bonds constantly eradicates any gap between them and ensures this equality through resulting price fluctuations of bonds and shares.[47]

This, at any rate, is Marx's explicit position, even if he does not support it with exactly the same analysis as we have presented above. He begins by establishing a so-to-speak qualitative identity between the two revenues. 'Even if the dividends which they receive include the interest and profit of enterprise, i.e. the total profit, . . . this total profit is henceforth received only in the form of interest, i.e. as compensation for owning capital that now is entirely divorced from the function in the actual process of reproduction.'[48]

On the following page, the proviso introduced by 'even if . . .' has disappeared:

> Before we go any further, there is still the following economically important fact to be noted: Since profit here assumes the pure form of interest, undertakings of this sort [he is referring to joint-stock companies] are still possible if they yield bare interest, and this is one of the causes, stemming the fall of the general rate of profit, since such undertakings, in which the ratio of constant capital to the variable is so enormous, do not necessarily enter into the equalisation of the general rate of profit.[49]

This passage seems to express Marx's final position: the remuneration of share-capital is identified with interest not only in

46. cf, for example, H. Denis: 'To explain the rate of interest, one need only refer to the classical analysis. If the average rate of profit is known, the rate of interest can be worked out, since the spread between the two is explained as a risk premium paid by the lender.' (*Histoire de la pensée économique*, p. 538). This idea first appeared in Adam Smith.

47. This equation should not be taken too literally, since dividends proper, paid in cash, only represent distributed profits. The true yield on shares also includes undistributed profits, which are incorporated into reserves and thus reinvested in the firm. Shareholders are often compensated for this second part by the free distribution of shares as a stock dividend, and a corresponding increase in capital. If this is not done, the internal accumulation of capital will generally result in a rise in the share's quoted price and benefit the shareholders in this way. The sum of these three elements – cash dividends, stock dividends and capital gains – is the appropriate yield on a portfolio of shares to compare with the yield on a portfolio of bonds.

48. *Capital*, vol. III, pp. 436–7.

49. *Ibid.*, p. 437.

form, but also in quantity, since Marx treats it as a factor counteracting the tendency for the average rate of profit to fall.

But if the overall yield of all securities, whether of fixed or variable revenues, is subject to equalisation on the basis of the market rate of interest, and if this equalisation can only occur through the fluctuation of quotations on the stock exchange as a result of competition, it follows that an increase in the rate of interest will not only lower the quotations of bonds, but also those of all other securities quoted on the stock exchange. A fall in the rate of interest will have the opposite effect.[50]

For example, take a bond with a face value of £1000 issued when the rate of interest was 4% and therefore yielding an annual interest payment of £40. If the rate of interest should subsequently rise to 5%, the bond's market price will fall to £800, since this is the only price which will afford its purchaser the general interest rate of 5%.[51]

But, all other things being equal, i.e. if this rise in the rate of interest is autonomous and is not itself the result of a rise in the rate of profit, as has been explained above (Marx shows that it is exactly when the rate of profit levels out and stagnates that the rate of interest begins to rise and that it is during the slump that it reaches its peak), then securities with variable revenues, shares, will suffer the same fate as a result of arbitrage between the two kinds of securities.

Now we can appreciate the importance of this phenomenon and the speculation which it can give rise to. Under the assumption that a considerable part of investment is effected through the purchase of securities, the price fluctuations of these securities are immeasurably more important than their current yield. In the example above, an increase of the rate of interest from 4 to 5% represents a difference of £10 per year, and the total interest of 4% only represents £40 per year. But the resulting fall in price of the security can mean a loss of £200 in a few days. It is therefore obvious that the slightest suspicion that a rise in the rate of interest is on the cards will induce any investor to defer his purchases of securities, since the loss of interest which he will suffer by leaving his capital idle for a certain length of time is negligible when compared to that which would result from a depreciation of his capital itself.

It might be objected that purchase on the stock exchange of an already existing security is not an investment at the social level, since these securities only pass from hand to hand, and one person's

50. *Ibid.*, p. 502.

51. In fact the equilibrium rate will be slightly above 800 francs, taking account of the future repayment of its nominal value and the date of this repayment, unless it is a perpetuity.

investment must correspond to strictly equal disinvestment on the part of another. Our money-capital becomes financial capital and another strictly equal financial capital becomes money-capital. Productive capital is not affected by this. For there to be a transformation of money-capital into productive capital, there must be a new issue.

However, the rate of new issues is itself determined by variations of quotations on the stock exchange. If purchasers, foreseeing a rise in the rate of interest, create a bear market on the stock exchange and offers to sell multiply as a result of the same prediction, quotations will begin to sag even before the banks' rate of interest is raised, and even if the forecasts that it would rise were groundless. (Lastly, the forecasts, whatever their original basis, will be self-fulfilling if they are shared by a sufficient number of operators, since a fall in the quotations of securities is equivalent to a rise in the real rate of interest paid to their holders, while the banks' interest rate cannot stay below this real rate for long.)

It is apparent that in such a situation there will be less new issues, since any new issues will have to take expectations into account by offering subscribers terms as advantageous as those which they demand or expect.

Thus, as a result of speculation on a rise in the rate of interest or – which comes to the same thing – on a fall in the quotations of securities, many temporary mini-hoards are created in the hands of individuals and banks, which, taken together, constitute hoarding on the level of society as a whole.

Variations in the business climate have opposite effects on industrial capital and money-capital. During booms, prices rise, which ensure high profits for the former, but depreciates non-invested money-capital and still only affords a moderate rate of interest to loan-capital which has already found a placing. Industrial capital dominates the situation and dictates terms to money-capital During slumps, the situation is reversed. The fall in prices squeezes industrial capital's profits, but revalues money-capital. The rate of interest increases and becomes a heavy burden for the former, while it promises high remuneration for the latter. It is the latter which now dominates the former and dictates terms to it.

If active capital can only gain by reproduction, money-capital, for its part, stands to gain through inaction, through abstention from being invested. It is this temporary abstention which breaks equilibrium between supply and demand of goods, beginning with producer goods, and giving rise to cumulative effects of overproduction.

Variations in the rate of interest and cyclical movements of credit
The preceding analysis leaves the reader unsatisfied. It shows us which motivations can, in certain circumstances, induce money-capital to withdraw provisionally from production. These motivations can roughly be summed up as expectation of a rise in the rate of interest. Besides, in Marx's view, variations in the rate of interest are related to the business cycle, so that this rate, after rising slightly as business starts to recover from the slump, increases slowly but within very acceptable limits during the boom, rises faster at the height of the boom on the eve of the crisis, and reaches its peak during the crisis, falling back down to its lowest point during the slump.[52] It follows that expectation of a considerable rise in the interest rate is equivalent to expectation of a crisis. But in so far as the crisis itself is attributed to this abstention from investment, motivated by these expectations, the above analysis comes down in the end to saying that the cause of crisis is the expectation of a crisis.

This would, after all, not be the greatest of paradoxes in such a contradictory economic system as the capitalist mode of production, in which reproduction can only take place through the decisions of private appropriators whose independence denies the social character of the process. When the crazed spectators of a burning cinema block the exits, fear of fire often claims more victims than the fire itself. In the same way, when each capitalist tries to secure his own position before the rest, the crisis is aggravated to the detriment of all, or almost all. But fire must exist before man can learn to fear it, and the existence of crises must have preceded that of expectations concerning them. Specifically, what need explaining are these ups and downs of the interest rate, and the search for this explanation leads us on to the movements of contraction and expansion of credit in general, no longer just the purchase of securities which we have discussed above.

During the boom, Marx says, credit is easy. Manufacturers and traders agree mutually to postpone repayments, and everyone can buy immediately after having sold, long before the commodity sold is converted into money. 'The reflux passes off smoothly and easily. The retailer securely pays the wholesaler, the wholesaler pays the manufacturer, the manufacturer pays the importer of raw materials etc.'[53] Bills of exchange are regularly honoured when they fall due, banks and bill-brokers are quite happy to buy them.

But, since the velocity of circulation increases and supplements the

52. cf. *ibid.*, pp. 360, 488–9.
53. *Ibid.*, p. 447.

quantity of money, recourse to banks is moderate. Also, since there is a climate of confidence, bills of exchange are directly endorsed by traders, and thus circulate as additional money, joining the quantity of money already in accelerated circulation. Certain banks add their endorsements to these and thereby receive interest without advancing any money. All this makes demand for banking credit diminish. It becomes a borrower's market. The interest rate is relatively low. 'The total result is that the mass of circulating media serving the expenditure of revenue grows decidedly in periods of prosperity.'[54] We are therefore at the optimum point of the curve. The realization of the product takes place without any impediment, the workers obtain wage increases and consumption increases in the wake of the growth of production. The rise in prices on the one hand, and the maintenance of the interest rate at a favorable level on the other, lead to a bull market on the stock exchange and draw all liquid assets into production.

Entry into the 'infernal cycle'

It is at this point that overtrading comes into play. All the conditions for it have arisen together. The temptation to operate beyond one's means by taking advantage of cheap credit is too great. A sort of unproductive investment follows, in the sense that it deals in stocks of goods instead of means of production and that it relates to price differences instead of the surplus-value created in production. The 'sharpers' come onto the scene. Commodities start to circulate between speculator-middlemen and this circulation thus becomes, in a way, independent of the level of final consumption. The continued acceptability of bills of exchange serves to mask the fact that consumption is now growing slower than production.

Credit is now increasingly used, not as medium of circulation, but as means of payment. New credit operations are used to disentangle the previous operations. 'The appearance of rapid and reliable refluxes always keeps up for a longer period after they are over in reality by virtue of the credit that is under way, since credit refluxes take the place of the real ones.'[55]

Nonetheless, 'real refluxes' still increase, although insufficiently, for a certain while, and this in the last analysis is what supports the whole inverted pyramid of overtrading. In fact, as long as the

54. *Ibid.*

55. *Ibid.* But in vol. II, chapter 2, Marx had already drawn attention to the role of dealers, who make it possible for the manufacturer to restart the cycle of production as if the product had actually been realised. 'This point', he wrote, 'is important in a discussion of crises.' (*Capital*, vol. II, p. 77).

industrialist, basing himself upon the figures of his sales to middlemen, is able to renew and even extend his production, he will distribute new revenues which increase final consumption, both productive and individual, and it is this increase which, though less than the increase in production, feeds speculation and supports the process of voluntary accumulation of stocks of goods. In this way the increase in production prevents prices from collapsing and enables credit operations to reach completion without any problems.

In this way 'the entire process of reproduction may be in a flourishing condition, and yet a large part of the commodities may have entered into consumption only apparently, while in reality they may still remain unsold in the hands of dealers, may in fact still be lying in the market'.[56]

But the closer full employment approaches, the more the rate of creation of new revenues slows down, and therefore the less actual consumption grows. The gap between this rate and the rate of growth of speculative stocks of goods becomes too great and brings on the collapse of the whole edifice. 'Now one stream of commodities follows another, and finally it is discovered that the previous streams had been absorbed only apparently by consumption. The commodity-capitals compete with one another for a place in the market. Late-comers, to sell at all, sell at lower prices. The former streams have not yet been disposed of when payment for them falls due.'[57]

'The banks', Marx also writes, 'scent danger as soon as their clients deposit more bills of exchange than money'.[58] At this point they realise that their advances are being used to finance stocks instead of sales. So they begin to refuse to discount bills, to tighten credit and distrain defaulters – and the crisis breaks out. It breaks out a bit before the economy has reached the barrier of full employment. For credit to be stopped and expansion to be blocked, it is by no means necessary for expansion to be interrupted. It only requires the slowdown in the rate of expansion which occurs on the verge of full employment, 'a disturbance in this expansion or even in the normal flow of the reproduction process. . . .'[59]

During the crisis, credit practically ceases completely. The rate of interest is so high that it only attracts bad debtors, those who dig one hole to fill in another. These are refused credit by the banks. The others, the serious clients, who the banks would gladly lend to even in time of crisis, find loan-capital too expensive and do not want any.

56. *Ibid.*, p. 78.
57. *Ibid.*
58 *Ibid.*, vol. III, p. 447.
59. *Ibid.*, p. 483.

The level of bank lending falls to its lowest point, and the velocity of circulation falls faster than the prices of commodities.

The moment of hoarding. Real money

Does this imply that, during the crisis, there is hoarding at the level of the banking network, in the sense that the deposits of those with liquid assets are not fully mobilised by the banks, through granting credit to those who need it? Marx seems to think so.[60] However, on this point, he vacillates between two conflicting positions. In the first he abstracts from bank money, and even from fiduciary money. Here, the role of private banks is confined to the transfer of real purchasing power from one economic subject to another. Since their function is not simply to put the lender and borrower in contact with each other – the banks themselves assume responsibility for the transfer by taking the place of the lender – they must decide upon loans not only according to the extent of their deposits, but also according to the degree of certainty of the successful conclusion of operations. It follows that, for a given sum of deposits, the sum of their loans may vary considerably according to the business climate. When businesses are prospering, loans may reach the extreme limit of the banks' loanable funds; when business prospects are uncertain, the banks cut back on credit and allow their reserves to swell up. It is this increase in reserves which constitutes hoarding at the level of society as a whole.

This position, which is usually implicit, sometimes becomes explicit: 'The quantity of money existing in society is always greater than the part of it in actual circulation, although this swells or subsides according to circumstances.'[61] The remarks a few lines earlier in the same text leave no doubt that Marx is here thinking in terms of real money or, more precisely, gold. The term 'argent', which Marx uses for money in his French edition here, cannot refer to credit money and was never used by Marx in this sense. But however this may be, by taking the total quantity of money as given and

60. cf., for example, *Capital*, vol. III, p. 565.

Tugan Baranovski also believes that unplaced loan capital builds up during crises. Several other theorists, among them Juglar, Pareto, Spiethoff, Weber and Schmoller, explain crises by fluctuations in hoarding in general, without actually specifying where these hoards build up, or in what form. Aftalion calls this the theory of deferred capitalist consumption, and wonders in what form these uninvested savings can be held. He remarks that it is difficult to conceive of any such form. To those who invoke the growth of major national banks' cash-in-hand during the depression, Aftalion replies that these sums are negligible in comparison to the general level of economic activity. (*Les Crises périodiques de surproduction*, p. 308.)

61. *Capital*, vol. II, p. 497.

distinguishing between an active and an inactive (hoarded) part, Marx rules out any idea of credit money, since credit can in no way create inactive money; on the contrary, what credit does is either to activate existing inactive money, or to create active money *ex nihilo*.

A bit further on, Marx writes even more explicitly: 'The only assumption made in this case is that the amount of money in the country in question (the velocity of circulation, etc., being constant) should suffice for both the active circulation and the reserve hoard.'[62]

Credit money

If this were all he had said, the basic assumptions of Marx's analysis would immediately be vulnerable. Not only is the mass of (real) money present in a given country insufficient for both active circulation and the reserve hoard, as Marx asserts, but a part of active circulation, already quite considerable in Marx's day, and enormously greater today, is transacted in fiduciary and bank money. But Marx went further. In the next part of the same passage, Marx seems to introduce the idea of credit money:

> This is generally true of the first phase of capitalist production, in which even the credit system is mostly accompanied by metallic circulation, and it applies to the most developed phase of the credit system as well, to the extent that metallic circulation remains its basis. On the one hand an additional production of precious metals. . . . On the other hand the entire credit mechanism is continually occupied in reducing the actual metallic circulation to a relatively more and more decreasing minimum by means of sundry operations, methods, and technical devices. The artificiality of the entire machinery and the possibility of disturbing its normal course increase to the same extent.[63]

This passage is still vitiated by several equivocations such as 'to the extent that metallic circulation remains its basis . . .', and in chapter XXX of vol. III ('Money-Capital and Real Capital'), Marx again argues as if credit only mobilises an existing money-capital without creating any additional purchasing power:

> A manufacturer sells his product for a bill of exchange and gets this bill discounted by some bill-broker. In reality, the latter advances only the credit of his banker, who in turn advances to the broker the money-capital of his depositors. The depositors consist of the industrial capitalists and merchants themselves and also of workers (through saving-banks) – as well as ground-rent recipients and other unproductive classes.[64]

But in many other places, notably in vol. III, chapter XXXIII ('The Medium of Circulation in the Credit System'), Marx not only

62. *Ibid.*, p. 504.
63. *Ibid.*
64. *Ibid.*, vol. III, p. 484.

talks extensively about the pyramid of artificial means of circulation created by the banking network in a series of analyses which show an astonishing familiarity with the most sophisticated concrete mechanisms of banking finance, but he also enumerates them precisely in his summary.[65] Here an objection arises: as soon as credit goes beyond its original role of transferring liquid assets from one economic subject to another, and starts to create fictive liquid assets, a tightening of credit can in no way be seen as hoarding in the sense of sterilization of a revenue, which could destroy the fundamental equation, revenues = production, and thus lead to an overproduction crisis. So it seems that Marx's analysis must be rejected on logical grounds alone. This follows from either position: either credit only compensates, wholly or partly, for existing hoarding, in which case its expansion cannot lead to any net overtrading at the level of society as a whole or any inflation during booms, since the rashness of speculators without capital only counter-balances the timidity of hoarding capitalists; or credit really does create fictive capital and purchasing power, which disturb the economy through an excess of demand over supply, in which case the only effect of a contraction of credit should be a beneficial re-establishment of equilibrium, and not a crisis of overproduction.

The reasons for disequilibrium in Marx's analysis

Since these texts are insufficiently worked-out and dispersed among the most varied chapters, it is extremely difficult to arrange and synthesise them into a clear and coherent whole. Formulations which are sometimes divergent, or even contradictory, force us to adopt conjectural interpretations.

'At first glance, therefore', Marx says, 'the whole crisis seems to be merely a credit and money crisis. And in fact it is only a question of the convertibility of bills of exchange into money. But the majority of these bills represent actual sales and purchases, whose extension far

65. *Ibid.*, p. 542: 'Thus we see here how banks create credit and capital by (1) issuing their own notes; (2) writing out drafts on London running up to 21 days, but paid in cash to them immediately on issue; and (3) paying out discounted bills of exchange, which are endowed with credit primarily and essentially by endorsement through the bank – at least as far as concerns the local district.' The only item missing from this list is the extension of credit to clients in the form of current accounts, which can be mobilised by cheque or banker's draft, both of which are transfers from one account to another without any recourse to currency with an intrinsic value, and thus without recourse to any pre-existing purchasing power corresponding to a particular cost of production. But in many other passages, Marx shows indirectly that he knew of this procedure and was well aware of the mass of fictive currency which could be created in this way.

beyond the needs of society is, after all, the basis of the whole crisis.'[66]

How can *real* purchases and sales, which must represent a mass of commodities produced, exceed needs, or even – let us assume that this is what Marx means to say – existing purchasing power, since any production creates an equivalent purchasing power, according to the basic equation, revenue = production, which Marx has never rejected? Are we dealing with a non-correspondence of use-values? With a disproportion? But these are not dealt with in the chapter under consideration.

Marx argues as if equilibrium were attained in the middle of the boom, 'exactly midway between its minimum and maximum'. Once this point has been passed, 'those cavaliers who work without any reserve capital or without any capital at all and who thus operate completely on a money credit basis begin to appear . . . .'[67] It is clearly *materially* impossible for this point to be that of full employment of the factors, since production continues to grow beyond this point, even at an increasing rate, which is reflected in an accumulation of unsold stocks, financed through credit and over-speculation. But if this point corresponds to a certain degree of unemployment, it is difficult to see how it can at the same time be an equilibrium position (at least in Marx's system, which is not that of Keynes).

It is even more difficult to see how the expansion of activity beyond this point can *per se* lead to disequilibrium and price-increases – this contradicts not only Marx's system, but also that of Keynes – or how an increase of production which tends to reabsorb this unemployment can, whatever may be the motives and financial situation of entrepreneurs, be objectively described as overtrading.

'The credit system', Marx writes, 'appears as the main lever of over-production and over-speculation in commerce solely because the reproduction process, which is elastic by nature, is here forced to its extreme limits, and is so forced because a large part of the social capital is employed by people who do not own it and who consequently tackle things quite differently than the owner, who anxiously weighs the limitations of his private capital in so far as he handles it himself.'[68]

This passage is obscure. Without credit, production could not attain the limit of material possibilities, i.e. absolute full employment of available equipment and manpower, because actual owners of

66. *Capital*, vol. III, p. 490.
67. *Ibid.*, pp. 488–9.
68. *Ibid.*, p. 441.

capital are too cautious. With credit, entrepreneurs without capital get involved, and in this way production is pushed up to its extreme limit. But what harm is there in that? Why should credit operate as a 'lever of overproduction'? Overproduction in comparison to what? A lever of over-speculation, perhaps. But if this over-speculation helps to overcome the 'barrier' of the capitalists' caution and thus allows the full utilisation, or a greater utilisation, of productive potential, in what way is it pernicious? It should actually be healthy, since any additional production, whether financed with the producer's own capital or with that of another, whether resolved upon by a prudent paterfamilias, or launched by an adventurer, creates strictly equal additional purchasing power.

Does the second type of investment at the same time give rise to a specific disproportion because, for example, of the inexperience or lack of concern of these occasional entrepreneurs, leading to a bad choice of branches to invest in? If so, then, on the one hand, it should be stated which disproportion it gives rise to; and on the other, it should be admitted that at the time of the crisis, there is no truly general overproduction. But in the whole of this section, no mention is made of disproportionality. Marx is reasoning in terms of overall aggregates. Credit, and the over-speculation which it engenders, make it possible to burst through the 'immanent barrier' to production. As soon as credit wears out, over-speculation stops, and the crisis breaks out.

First of all, what is questionable is the nature of this barrier and at what level (of unemployment) it is situated. The reply that Marx gives is particularly weak: 'The maximum of credit is here identical with the fullest employment of industrial capital, that is, the utmost exertion of its reproductive power without regard to the *limits of consumption*.'[69]

Is this then the barrier of over-production? We seem to be going back in time to certain theses of Malthus and Sismondi which Marx contested bitterly. What *limits* are we talking about? Are we dealing with personal (unproductive) consumption alone? Then what do we do with productive consumption, which is precisely pushed to its maximum during this period, as a result of the dealings of these very 'cavaliers'? Marx himself admits that unproductive consumption itself grows during this period of expansion: 'These limits of consumption are extended by the exertions of the reproduction process itself. On the one hand, this increases the consumption of revenue on the part of labourers and capitalists. . . .'[70] But, quite

69. *Ibid.*, p. 482, emphasis added.
70. *Ibid.*

apart from the growth of unproductive consumption, even if we allow that this increase is less than the overall increase in production, we still have to take account of productive consumption which, for its part, is pushed to its maximum during this period by the very operations of over-speculation. This is explicitly recognised by Marx in the second half of the above sentence: '. . . on the other hand, it [the exertions of the reproduction process] is *identical* with an exertion of productive consumption'.[71]

So, if the two forms of consumption, productive and unproductive, expand in tandem with the 'exertion' of reproduction, it is impossible to see what could be the source of disequilibrium.

It is certainly quite conceivable that, if this intense circulation rests on credit and the banks one day decide to turn off the tap suddenly, then there may be blockage and collapse. It is true that, even if money's purchasing power is not created in the gold mines, but is artificially added on by banking credit, the economic system may have been able to adapt its rotations to a certain quantity of this purchasing power functioning as a medium of circulation, and that if this quantity were suddenly to be lacking, the effects would be the same as if an equivalent quantity of real purchasing power had been withdrawn through hoarding.

Since credit, as a creator of extra money, is the opposite of hoarding, its diminution could have the same effects as an increase in hoarding, and it might just be admitted that, even if productive capital should remain, on average and through the deepest point of the crisis, in debt to the banking system, a fall in the level of bank lending could be equivalent to a rise in reserves.[72]

But banks do not decide to withhold credit without a reason. And the reason is, according to Marx himself, that they realise at some point that the reflux of bills of exchange is greater than the reflux of money, i.e. the commodities whose sale has been anticipated have not really been sold and credit is being asked for in order to settle earlier credit.[73]

Therefore, before there can be any stoppage of credit, there must be a build-up of unsold stocks, and this build-up becomes inexplicable if we admit, with Marx, that there can be no general excess of the supply of commodities over purchasing power and *a fortiori*, if we are in a period of over-speculation in which the will to purchase is

71. *Ibid*, emphasis added.
72. This is one way to circumvent Aftalion's objection; he noted that during crises, there is only a fall in the level of overdrafts, a fall in the use of credit, rather than any build-up of idle savings. (cf. *Les Crises périodiques de surproduction*, p. 308.)

not merely keeping pace with purchasing power, but actually exceeds it, through the creation of fictive purchasing power through credit. Credit automatically gives rise to a strictly equivalent will to purchase. For while one may hoard the money one has earned, one obviously does not borrow in order to hoard.

It is perfectly conceivable that since the circulation time of a commodity is elastic and its protraction can be secured through credit the producer may, as long as this lasts, be prevented from seeing that demand is falling behind supply, may believe that his commodity has been consumed when it is in fact wandering from dealer to dealer, and may continue his reproduction on the same scale or on an expanded scale until the moment of collapse. But it is still necessary that final demand should actually have fallen behind supply, or else the very thing that must be proved has been taken for granted.

For unless we are dealing with a disproportion affecting one or several particular industries, it is not clear how stocks can accumulate in the hands of dealers. If, as Marx assumes, everyone purchases – we have seen that to produce is to purchase – as if his own commodities had been consumed, the commodities will in fact be consumed and, through the very fact that everyone behaves as if they had been consumed, there will be no excess stocks anywhere, and therefore no reason for a change in policy on the part of the banks.[74]

73. In actual fact, even at this point the banks do not come to an agreement to cut off credit. On the contrary, if they could agree, it is quite probable that they would decide to continue to support their debtors in order to prevent a general collapse. It is because they are in competition, and each tries to secure its own position before the rest, that credit is cut off and the crash comes. 'Although it is in [the bankers'] common interest to lend liberally, their individual interests lead them to demand the repayment of their loans instead. . . . Although it would be advantageous for all the banks to lend liberally.' A.-C. Pigou, *Keynes' General Theory – a Retrospect*, chapter VIII, para. 5.

But whether the banks act in concert or not, their behaviour is in any case predicated upon the economic situation, and cannot therefore be the ultimate cause of this situation.

74. Engels is even more ambiguous than Marx on the subject of over-trading. In 1857, in the course of an exchange of ideas with Marx on the raging crisis, which both believed capable of leading to collapse and revolution, he grapples with the question of notes of hand (accommodation bills), and, remarking that over-trading eventually becomes the general state of affairs, he writes:

'Although over-trading is not synonymous with overproduction, it is basically identical. A trading community which possesses £20,000,000 of capital has a corresponding capacity of production, transport and consumption. If, by dealings with notes of hand, this community maintains a level of business activity which would presuppose £30,000,000 of capital, production will rise by 50% while consumption will certainly also grow along with the boom, but by a considerably smaller percentage, say by 25%. After a certain while there will necessarily emerge an accumulation of

Continued on page 84

Another of Marx's arguments, which is presented as a supporting argument, is just as unacceptable. The price increases during the boom, he says, imply a contraction in real terms of the demand of wage-earners and other bearers of fixed revenues. This aggravates the disequilibrium expressed by the swelling of stocks and leading to the crisis.[75] This is of course false. For, the price increases are the result either of the injection by credit of fictive purchasing power which makes demand exceed supply, or of wage increases. If the former holds, then on the one hand this over-stocking is contradictory; on the other hand, price increases of this kind automatically lead to a strictly equal rise in profits. While they reduce the purchasing power of bearers of fixed revenues, they increase that of bearers of variable revenues by the same amount. So, if we continue to abstract from any inadequacy in use-values (disproportion), there is no aggravation of disequilibrium. In the second case (where the price increases are attributable *solely* to an increase in nominal wages), workers' real wages may at most stagnate – but in no way can they diminish.

The original equation between revenues and production – a blind alley

The preceding Marxist analysis would become perfectly coherent and would acquire irresistible explanatory power if it were accepted that there is a basic immanent (and permanent) excess of value produced over purchasing power created by the same production, i.e. that revenue is not equal to production, $R = P$, but lower than

74. *Continued from page 83*
commodities 25% greater than *bona fide* needs, that is, average needs, even during a boom. This alone would make the crisis break out, even if the money market, the barometer of trade, did not announce it in advance. Once the crash comes, not only this 25%, but also at least another 25% of stocks of goods of all kinds will be unsaleable.' (From the German. *Werke*, vol. 29, pp. 226–7.)

Engels explains nothing. Either his community really does manage to produce 50% extra, or it is merely trafficking. In the former case, there is no over-trading; in the latter, there is no overproduction. How can over-trading lead to an excess of production over consumption? Of which production? Over which consumption? Why should consumption rise by less than production since, with or without over-trading, the growth of the latter gives rise to strictly equal growth of purchasing power according to the fundamental postulate which Engels does not challenge? This being the case, since notes of hand only create extra fictive purchasing power, the only possible effect of this over-trading is disequilibrium in the opposite direction, that is to say, not enough real output facing the two kinds of purchasing power, the real and the fictive. If the play of notes of hand is interrupted, and the ficive purchasing power created by them is popped and disappears like a soap bubble, we are still left with real purchasing power, equal to real production, and everything returns to normal. There is no sign of crisis or overproduction.

75. *Capital*, vol. III, p. 491.

production, $R < P$. In this case, any additional production, by adding proportionally unequal sums to unequal sums, would, for its part and before any circulation, only increase this excess in absolute terms, while leaving it unchanged in relative terms.

If the particular kind of credit analysed by Marx (the kind which creates purchasing power *ex nihilo*, as opposed to the kind which merely transfers pre-existing purchasing power from one economic subject to another) did not exist, the excess of P over R would block the system; unsold goods would collect at all levels, and all incentives to produce would disappear. But the elasticity of inventories and speculative credit during the periods of euphoria appear to soak up this excess by sterilising the overstocks. So R + *credit* becomes equal to P, or, which comes to the same thing, P minus the overstock (sterilised and withdrawn from circulation in this way) becomes equal to R. Each capitalist launches out into production as if everything were really being sold, because everything is passing from hand to hand and because everything is settled properly financially. But this situation can only last a certain while. If P increases and, consequently, R also, their difference, $P - R$, i.e. the overstock, must increase proportionally, since any additional production is, according to the hypothesis, greater by this same proportion than the revenue which it itself engenders, and this should carry on with no limit other than absolute full employment of the factors. But both credit and the overstock financed by it have their own limits. While it can be extended far beyond the quantity of real money, credit money is nonetheless constrained by certain safety ratios. Fiduciary money can be a certain multiple of the metallic reserve; it cannot completely detach itself from this reserve. The private banks' bank money can in turn considerably exceed these banks' holdings with the central bank; but it cannot be multiplied *ad infinitum*.[76]

The overstock also has its limits. The distributive networks's absorptive capacity, while elastic, is still not infinite. It does not only depend on financing, but also to a certain extent on fluctuations of actual sales. This works in the following way: growth of stocks may well, at a given point in time, be greater than growth of sales, but only on condition that the *rate* of growth of the latter should itself be increasing. In the last analysis, over-trading is nothing but an

76. Here we are only paraphrasing some of Marx's arguments, which were of course worked out on the assumption that $R = P$, and which, therefore, did not provide the desired explanation of crises. We intend to show that once these same arguments are transposed into the framework of the assumption that $R < P$, they become extremely fertile and crucial. Eventually, we will of course have to show that this assumption is realistic; this is what we shall attempt in part II of this work.

extrapolation. One may perfectly well increase one's stocks by 10% while sales have only increased by 5%, if the day before they had only increased by 4%. But if they had increased by 6% the day before and 7% the day before that, the pressure of the overstock will begin to make itself felt. Now, as full employment is approached, the rate of growth of economic activity will inevitably drop off, even if it remains positive. When one or other of these conditions, credit on the one hand and the acceptance of an overstock on the other, runs out, the crisis will burst out.

At this point, not only will the overstock, artificially supported by credit up to this point, be thrown in one go onto the market in order to be realized, but a propensity will be created to get rid of a part of even one's normal (self-financed) stock as quickly as possible, for fear of a fall in prices. This very fear of a fall will not fail to precipitate the fall.[77] 'as soon as credit is shaken . . . all the real wealth is to be actually and suddenly transformed into money, into gold and silver – a mad demand, which, however, grows necessarily out of the system itself. And all the gold and silver which is supposed to satisfy these enormous demands amounts to but a few millions in the vaults of the Bank'.[78]

This is the most subtle point of Marx's analysis, where the contradiction between hoarding and credit money is resolved. For the crisis of overproduction to appear, there is no need for actual hoarding; it is enough for everyone to try to hoard, even if no one attains one's aim and no hoard piles up.[79] The flight from particular

77. Even the determination of what constitutes a 'normal stock' is a function not only of the level of sales, but also of its changes over time. In a graph of the level of sales over one complete cycle, each figure is met twice, once on the way up and again on the way down. Now, the volume of sales being given, the same inventory, which was viewed as normal or even insufficient on the way up, may be considered too high on the way down. What matters is not whether sales are running at 500 or 1000 per month or per week, but whether they have risen from 400 to 500 or fallen from 1200 to 1000. Once a crisis has well and truly arrived, all the phenomena of an excess of supply are found simultaneously with a lower absolute level of stocks than that prevailing during the boom, when shortages are conspicuous.

Taking account of this functional relation is the real way to make a system dynamic. In A. Paquet's very appropriate definition, 'a dynamic system is . . . a system in which the value of one or several variables depends at least in part on its own value (or on that of other variables in the system) at some earlier point in the development of the system. . . .' (*La Loi des débouchés* . . ., p. 131.)

In this respect the system used by Marx to analyse the business cycle strikes us as astonishingly dynamic in the true sense of the term, and not merely in the inaccurate sense which calls a system dynamic as long as it dates variables to trace their development over time.

78. *Capital*, vol. III, p. 574.

79. The term 'hoarding' is an incomplete concept in Keynes's view, if one is referring to an actual rise in liquid assets. The term 'hoarding', he says, should be replaced by 'propensity to hoard' (*General Theory*, p. 174).

commodities and search for the general commodity have the same effect as an actual over-abundance of the former and shortage of the latter: collapse of prices, loss of capital and stoppage of reproduction. There is no need to refute Say's Law: it becomes irrelevant. For there is no market 'glut' to be explained. Stocks are, during crises, just as small or even smaller than during booms. What have to be explained are the fall in production and the unemployment, i.e. things that are not in themselves incompatible with the fundamental equation $R = P$ since they imply equal and simultaneous diminution of the two members of the equation. This is also the only point at which Marx's analysis foreshadows that of Keynes, according to which equilibrium ($R = P$) is possible at all levels of employment.

Mutatis mutandis, a flight from money and a search for particular commodities would have the opposite effect, even if the relation between the magnitudes is the same in both cases. It is the relation between their changes which is not the same, and this latter relation is the determinant.[80]

However, this analysis could only constitute a complete theory of overproduction crises if it were possible to extract it from the 'cycle' and hook it onto some disequilibrium exogenous to the cycle, i.e. to something which, not itself being engendered by the ups and downs of the cycle, could explain the existence of the cycle itself. But in this analysis, we find nothing outside the storms of the cycle, except the Olympian calm of the postulate $R = P$, the fundamental equation between production and purchasing power, and this is why this postulate should be abandoned.

Marx never took this step, at least explicitly. As a result, his whole analysis remained essentially *within* the 'cycle'. All phenomena are regulated by a sort of balancing movement. If a slump goes very low, this is because the previous boom went too high. If credit is cut off, this is because too much was granted earlier, and this situation lasts because there are too many dubious debts to be liquidated. Symmetrically, if the subsequent recovery is vigorous and the economy overheats, this is because belts were tightened too much during the crisis. Then warehouses fill up faster than is reasonable, because forced sales emptied them more than was prudent; the production of commodities once more becomes an attractive business. And so on and so forth.

80. Only with the post-Keynesians, some three-quarters of a century later, does one find as dynamic a view of hoarding as that of Marx. For example, in Myra Curtis:

'Hoarding . . . cannot be measured simply as an amount. It consists not merely in *holding* money, since all the money in existence at any time must be held by some one, whether there is hoarding or not. It consists in *holding money immobile*.' (Myra Curtis, 'Is money saving equal to investment?', p. 613).

This movement, which is so well balanced, lacks but one thing: a first impulse. Marx is conscious of this and says so explicitly: 'The industrial cycle is of such a nature that the same circuit must periodically reproduce itself, *once the first impulse has been given*.[81]

What is this impulse? Two things are clear:

(1) It cannot be a purely accidental divergence between revenue and production. Even if, in the beginning, for some reason, there was a lack of purchasing power compared with value produced, $R < P$, the fact that all further production creates an equivalent revenue ($R' = P'$) forces us to admit that the original disequilibrium would constantly diminish, since equal sums are constantly being added to both sides of the inequality.

(2) If it is really to be a 'first' impulse, this impulse must be objective and material. It must therefore be located outside all the determinants which we have encountered so far, which eventually turned out to be no more than the economic subjects' psychological motivations and reactions. It is this first impulse, this objective and material basis, which Marx seems to have been looking for all his life, and which some of his letters to Engels quoted above seem to be referring to.

Objective causes of hoarding

We have already seen that, in a model in which revenue is equal to production, no overall disequilibrium is possible unless some part of the revenue remains unused, for whatever subjective or objective reason. If we define this failure to make use of a revenue as 'hoarding', quite apart, as we have seen above, from the question of whether this revenue actually corresponds to a sum of money in the hands of some individual, then the whole Marxist analysis which we have discussed is based on hoarding by the capitalists, and this hoarding is in a sense voluntary.

Through this approach, we have not broken out from the limits of the industrial cycle, since the 'will' of the capitalists is itself determined by the cycle. Therefore, to go further and discover the 'first impulse', it remained for Marx to examine the possibility of so-to-speak involuntary hoarding. He then noted that there are three structural (material) sources for such hoarding, sources which are therefore independent of the will of individuals: (i) the lack of synchronisation between turnover periods and working periods of capital; (ii) the contradiction between continuity of saving and discontinuity of investment; and (iii) the contradiction between

81. *Capital*, vol. III, p. 489.

continuity of depreciation and discontinuity of replacement of equipment.[82]

I. The lack of synchronisation between turnover periods and working periods of capital

This first source of involuntary hoarding is studied in chapters XV and XVI of volume II of *Capital*.[83]

In the first of these chapters, entitled 'Effects of the Time of Turnover on the Magnitude of Advanced Capital', Marx's attention is caught by the non-coincidence of the product's production periods and circulation periods. For simple material reasons, independent of the business cycle, it takes a certain length of time for a product, having left the factory, to reach its consumer. During this period, the factory cannot lie idle; it starts off a new cycle of production, for which a new capital is necessary. After long calculations and many laborious tables, Marx proves and concludes that:

> A. The different portions into which capital must be divided in order that one part of it may be continually in the working period while others are in the period of circulation, relieve one another, like different independent individual capitals, in two cases: (i) when the working period is equal to the period of circulation, . . .; (ii) when the period of circulation is longer than the working period, but at the same time is a simple multiple of the working period . . . In these cases, no portion of the successively advanced capital is set free.
> B. On the other hand in all cases in which (i) the period of circulation is longer than the working period without being a simple multiple of it, and (ii) in which the working period is longer than the circulation period, a portion of the total circulating capital is set free continually and periodically at the close of each working period, beginning with the second turnover . . . .
> C. It follows that for the aggregate social capital, so far as its circulating part is concerned, the release of capital must be the rule, while the mere alternation of portions . . . must be the exception. For the equality of the

82. The order in which we present Marx's different arguments on the subject of overproduction crises is not the same order as in the posthumous editions of these texts, and perhaps does not correspond to the chronological order of the corresponding manuscripts. We have adopted this order because it seemed the most suitable way to bring together the main ideas, which are usually incomplete, often repeated on several occasions, and always found in the middle of the most varied contexts; and in order to shorten the hundreds and hundreds of pages which go to make up this material. It does not seem to us to make much sense to enquire whether Marx 'thought' the theory of crises in this order, since Marx had postponed writing, and therefore thinking in any definitive way, the theory of crises till the end of his work, in a separate book which he did not have time to write; and since the materials whose order is in question are only first-draft notes.

83. *Capital*, vol. II, pp. 252–323.

working and circulation periods, or the equality of the period of circulation and a simple multiple of the working period, this regular proportionality of the two components of the period of turnover has absolutely nothing to do with the nature of the case and for this reason it can occur on the whole only as a matter of exception.

A very considerable portion of the social circulating capital, which is turned over several times a year, will therefore periodically exist in the form of released capital during the annual turnover cycle.[84]

The sum of these capitals which are necessarily 'released', in waiting so to speak, while circulation periods and working periods criss-cross each other, constitutes a kind of involuntary hoarding, which breaks equilibrium between production and actual purchases, if not that between production and purchasing power.

In a note published in the text, Engels suggests that these conclusions are the result of an error in calculation on Marx's part, and asserts that, whatever may be the relation between the period of circulation and the working period, there is always a release of latent, potential capital in the form of money. For those interested, we show in an appendix to this chapter that under his own assumptions, Marx made no error of calculation, and that it was Engels who misunderstood one of these assumptions. But this is a matter of detail. Whether this latent capital is formed in all circumstances, as Engels would have it, or only produced given certain conditions, as Marx demonstrates – this does not matter, since, in practice, Marx's two exceptions – (i) equal working period and circulation period; (ii) circulation period an *integer* multiple of working period – are so unlikely that, according to the law of probability, their repetition becomes impossible across more than a certain number of firms.

It is therefore undeniable that the varied criss-crossing of the product's periods of circulation outside the factory and periods of its processing within the factory compel businessmen to immobilise liquid reserves in order to be able to start a new production cycle while awaiting the payments due from the realization of the products of the preceding cycles.

Does it follow from this that the latent capitals constituted in this way are, as a sum of frozen purchasing power, a cause of disequilibrium between supply of and demand for commodities? We do not think so. In the confrontation between supply and demand, if, on the side of demand, we are short of the money corresponding to these latent capitals, we are, on the side of supply, no less short of an equivalent quantity of products, those that are circulating between the factory gates and the retail shop-window. It is *because* the

84. *Ibid.*, pp. 283–4.

commodity takes a certain length of time to get through the commercial network that the phenomenon pointed out by Marx takes place. But during this period, while the money lies dormant on one side, the commodity is unavailable on the other; it is as if it had not yet been produced. During this period, it exerts no pressure on prices, and that is all that counts. The money is subtracted from effective demand, but the commodity is likewise subtracted from 'effective supply'.

This is not the only money which lies idle periodically. The same thing happens with any money. A worker does not spend his wages the very second he receives them. If there is any need for a certain quantity of money, this is because the velocity of circulation, however great it may be, can never be infinite. But nor is the velocity of circulation of the product infinite either. No one hurries instantly to convert his money into a commodity, but nor does anyone panic and sell a commodity off cheap because it is still on his shelves ten minutes after delivery. Just as some cash-in-hand is necessary, so a certain level of stocks is acceptable, or even indispensable. The economy eventually adapts itself to the relation between these two magnitudes.

However this may be, in developed capitalism, in which the quantity of fiduciary and bank money is incomparably greater than that of the real money which serves as their basis, the relationship between these two magnitudes is in no way unfavorable to supply, since what lies idle on one side is, for the most part, extra purchasing power, while what lies idle on the other side (in the form of necessary stocks) is real 'selling-power'.

So crises cannot be explained by the relation of these two magnitudes. What might perhaps explain them is the relation between their variations. Marx is aware of this, and as soon as he broaches the subject of the disturbances which this provisionally frozen money-capital may lead to, he immediately refers to its fluctuations.

This money-capital is not necessarily kept in the company's coffers; it is deposited with banks and possibly mobilised by credit, while it must 'at the same time form one of the latter's [the credit system's] foundations'.[85] To the extent to which it is mobilised in this way, it again becomes active purchasing power in the hands of the borrower. However, the degree of this mobilisation may vary between 0 and 100%. It follows that the purchasing power which is withdrawn from the market on this account may at any given moment vary between 100 and 0%.

This is as far as we can push the meaning of Marx's argument by

85. *Ibid.* p. 286.

paraphrasing its formulation, which is allusive and not at all explicit. Can it be said on this basis that these variations are a disequilibrating factor? An aggravating factor, perhaps, at a pinch; an originating factor, certainly not. For these variations are not exogenous, they are an inseparable part of variations of the general level of bank lending, which we studied at some length above; and they are themselves determined by the ups and downs of the cycle. We are still far from the 'first impulse' we are looking for.

In the second of the two chapters in question (vol. II, chapter XVI), Marx adds to the above the case of the turnover of variable capital as the source of a specific disequilibrium, especially when the working period is very long (e.g., in railway construction). He notes the existence of an inflationary effect, since workers withdraw from the market products equivalent to their wages, while the product of their labour is not yet complete and ready to serve as the counterpart of this purchasing power.

This is another of Marx's observations which seems to us to be more advanced than the state of economic science of his time. But it should be pointed out that:

(1) Workers' consumption (variable capital) in this respect differs in no way from the consumption of constant circulating capital (intermediate consumption). Throughout the construction of a railway, not only wage-goods, but also steel, wood, cement, etc. are withdrawn from the market.

(2) If we abstract from fiduciary circulation, this is simply a matter of dishoarding compensating for previous hoarding. The sums of (real) money-capital invested during the period under consideration must in this case correspond in value to previously unsold output, which is now realised, and so everything falls into place. It is possible that they do not correspond as use-values, but that would be a matter of disproportionality, which is, on the one hand, not an effect of the investment in question and which, on the other, constitutes an autonomous disequilibrating factor.

(3) If, on the contrary, we are dealing with a money-capital created *ex nihilo* by the fiduciary or banking mechanism, then it is clear that such an injection of fictive purchasing power is certainly a disequilibrating factor. But it is disequilibrating because it is fictive, and it does not matter whether this fictive money is spent on building railways or municipal parks, or is even distributed directly as unemployment benefit. Anyway, this is a disequilibrium which generates inflation, and not the deflation of available demand which

we are looking for; it is also linked in a simple way to the whole set of incentives to invest, which are, yet again, located within the fluctuations of the business climate, and it is not a variable which is independent of these fluctuations.

II. The contradiction between continuity of savings and discontinuity of investments

Another source of temporary involuntary hoarding pointed out by Marx is the process of formation of new capitals from saved profits. In developed capitalism, the dimensions of the minimum additional unit of equipment are so great that several successive accumulations of profits are necessary before the new capital attains the requisite size. Throughout this period, the accumulated surplus-value necessarily remains in the form of potential money-capital, and represents a quantity of purchasing power withdrawn from circulation, a hoard.[86]

This is basically the same kind of hoarding as that which we studied above, differing only in that this kind appears in expanded reproduction, whilst the first kind already appeared in simple reproduction. Both have exactly the same effects from the point of view of disequilibrium, of the realization of frozen funds through credit etc., and there is no need to dwell on these points. Marx himself does not dwell on them. He only points out this form of hoarding in the margin of his chapter on expanded reproduction, simply as a possibility. 'Absurd as these assumptions would be', he writes, 'they would do nothing more than explain the possibility of a universal simultaneous formation of a hoard. . . .'[87]

III. The contradiction between continuity of depreciation and discontinuity of replacement of equipment

There is a third and last form of involuntary hoarding which, for its part, obviously captured Marx's attention, and which was the only one which he openly called 'a material basis for the periodic crises'. This is non-coincidence between the value of fixed capital, which wears out physically after a certain length of time and must be replaced, and the sum of depreciation accounted over the same period.[88]

86. cf. *ibid.*, vol. II, chapter XXI, pp. 493–7 and chapter II, pp. 84–8.
87. *Ibid.*, vol. II, p. 495.
88. *Ibid.*, p. 189. cf. also letters to Engels on 2 and 5 March 1858, in which Marx speaks of a 'determining element of the cycles'. cf. likewise *Grundrisse*, p. 720: 'We shall find other determinant causes as well. But this is one of them . . .', or *ibid.*, 'the measure of time for the motion of capital . . . is now determined, rather, by the *reproduction time* required for fixed capital'. cf. also *Capital*, vol. II, pp. 457–73.

Machines and equipment of all kinds have a physical life of several years or several cycles of production. After each working period, the instrument under consideration loses a fraction of its value, which is transferred to the product, the value and price of which are increased by an equal sum. But this fragmentation of value is not reflected in any corresponding fragmentation of use-value. The instrument remains physically complete and, despite its increasing decrepitude, continues to function as such until its death, after which it is replaced once and for all.

Here, for the first time in the whole of Marx's analysis, we have a factor which may destroy, no longer merely equilibrium between actual purchases and the supply of commodities, but the very equality between purchasing power and value produced, between *R* and *P*. Production would exceed revenues even if these revenues were spent smoothly and without delay, since this depreciation is added to the supply-value of production, while on the other side, there is neither any corresponding destruction of values, as in the case of intermediate consumption, nor the creation of any revenue, as in the case of the other elements of cost.

On the other hand, the day when the part of fixed capital in question must be replaced, the accumulated sum of the depreciation is mobilised and added to aggregate demand all in one go, while aggregate supply is only increased by the depreciation of the last year.

Suppose that the lifetime of a machine is ten years. For nine years, one-tenth of its value swells the value of the social product each year, without any counterpart on the demand side. In the tenth year, an effective demand equivalent to its entire value is created, while only one-tenth is added to the value of the social product.

At first glance, this discontinuity gives rise to no problem. If bank credit can transfer liquidity from one firm to another, and if replacements of worn-out equipment are staggered in time according to the varying lifespans and introduction dates of different kinds of equipment, then there will be, on the level of society as a whole at any one point in time, just as many complete replacements of worn-out equipment as there are depreciated used-up fractions of those which are still in service, and the former will be financed by the latter unless, once again, one considers conjunctural credit fluctuations which we have treated exhaustively above and which we could not accept as the basic cause of overproduction crises.

But Marx tries to exploit this discovery to the full. He wrote to people all over the place to find out the average lifespan of fixed capital. One of his correspondents (Babbage) told him it was five years.[89] This was clearly too short. Engels claimed that it was about thirteen and a third years.[90] Was not Engels' figure in turn a bit too high? If this were the case, then the period of industrial reproduction would coincide 'more or less with the period of repetition of the large crises', which at that time was about ten years, and this could well be the sign of a functional link between the two.[91]

At this point one cannot avoid the impression that Marx was relying in his speculations on an excessively slender empirical basis. Engels had given him a figure: 7.5%. According to him, this was the figure which industrialists generally deducted each year to cover wear-and-tear *and repairs* of machinery. This would correspond to a life of 13⅓ years (100÷7.5 = 13⅓). Without even mentioning the fact that, since this percentage also covers repairs, the actual lifespan must have been higher than 100÷7.5, and also abstracting from the industrialist's natural tendency, for a variety of reasons, to accelerate the rate of depreciation beyond what is necessary, it is still the case that these figures are only averages, which conceal an infinite variety of kinds of equipment and lifespans of these. Now, this is the very kind of calculation in which averages have absolutely no meaning. What Marx is trying to show is that there is a discontinuity in the replacement of fixed equipment. This discontinuity presupposes among other things a certain uniformity in the lifespans of these kinds of equipment. The use of an average begs the question, and is thus an error in logic, since it presupposes the very uniformity which has to be proved. Any divergences above and below this average, although they cancel out on average, spread the replacements out in time, and, by re-establishing the continuity of the process, lead to a greater convergence between the mass of replacements and the mass of depreciation over any given period of time. It goes without saying that with the development of capitalism, the diversity of the kinds of fixed equipment, and therefore the diversity of their durability, increases, so that the flow of their replacement tends to become as continuous as that of their depreciation.

But the spreading out of replacements is conditioned not only by inequality in the differing rates of wear-and-tear, but also by the staggering of introduction dates of new equipment. The spread of these dates fans out even more in reproduction on an extended scale, when installation of new equipment is not only a function of the scrapping of the old, but also of capitalised and reinvested profits.

89. Letter to Engels, 2 March 1858.
90. Letter from Engels to Marx, 4 March 1858.
91. Letter to Engels, 5 March 1858.

Marx dismisses this last objection: 'True, periods in which capital is invested differ greatly and far from coincide in time. But a crisis always forms the starting-point of large new investments. Therefore, from the point of view of society as a whole, more or less, *a new material basis for the next turnover cycle*.'[92] Just before this sentence, Marx had written: 'One may assume that in the essential branches of modern industry this life-cycle now averages ten years. However we are not concerned here with the exact figure. This much is evident: the cycle of interconnected turnovers embracing a number of years, in which capital is held fast by its fixed constituent part, furnishes *a material basis* for the periodic crises. . . .'[93]

Marx's argument, at least as formulated in this rough draft, thus ends up caught in the same circle we have already come up against several times in the course of this analysis: the circle constituted by juxtaposition of the two phrases we underlined in the last paragraph. The discontinuity of investment forms 'a material basis' for the crisis (second passage), which in turn supplies 'a new material basis' for the discontinuity of investments (first passage).[94]

92. *Capital*, vol. II, p. 189, emphasis added.

93. *Ibid.*, emphasis added.

94. An unexpected reformulation of this argument from Marx is to be found in Keynes, who adopts it without any acknowledgement of its source:

'Take a house which continues to be habitable until it is demolished or abandoned. If a certain sum is written off its value out of the annual rent paid by the tenants, which the landlord neither spends on upkeep nor regards as net income available for consumption, this provision . . . constitutes a drag on employment all through the life of the house, suddenly made good in a lump when the house has to be rebuilt. . . . Such factors may be serious in a non-static economy, especially during a period which immediately succeeds a lively burst of investment in long-lived capital.' *General Theory*, pp. 99–100.

Marx's argument is repeated so faithfully and completely as to verge on plagiarism.

J.R. Hicks also examines the periodicity of the renewal of fixed capital as a cause of the cyclical fluctuations of capitalist economies. He does not refer to Marx any more than Keynes does. Still, he approaches the question from a different angle, and his formulation is not such an exact reflection of Marx as is that of Keynes. (cf. Hicks, *A Contribution to the Theory of the Trade Cycle.*)

Finally, C.H. Douglas in *Social Credit Theory* and R.G. Hawtrey in *Capital and Employment*, also repeat this argument, the latter in the following terms: 'There is one category of costs by which incomes are not generated; that is depreciation. . . . In a community in which capital is growing the aggregate depreciation allowances will regularly exceed replacements, so that there is an unspent balance accruing to the trader's free capital.' (*Capital and Employment*, p. 99.)

While Keynes would appear to have secretly borrowed this idea, everything suggests that in the cases of Hicks, Major Douglas and Hawtrey, it is more a matter of the convergence of independent thoughts. Clearly, these writers can only be exonerated of plagiarism in so far as they had not read Marx. But this is not considered a failing in the circles of bourgeois economists.

To the best of our knowledge, Marxists have not laid great stress on this point, which Marx considered as essential, the only one in his eyes which relates to a so-to-speak physical constraint, independent of men's behaviour.[95] Engels seems unimpressed by this. In a note to the third volume, he even challenged the periodicity of crises on which Marx based his argument. He remarked that the ten-year cycle was only a very ephemeral historical occurrence. It only appeared between 1847 and 1867. In the preceding period, 'the early years of world commerce, 1815–47, it can be shown that these cycles lasted about five years'. After 1867, 'a change has taken place. . . . The acute form of the periodic process with its ten-year cycle, appears to have given way to a more chronic, long drawn out, alternation. . . .'[96]

Let us add that after Engels the ten-year cycle seemed to re-emerge, but only for one last time, with a slump from 1891 to 1895 and a boom from 1895 to 1900. After this, a five-year cycle re-appeared instead, since in the first ten years of the twentieth century, there were two slumps: 1901–04 and 1908–09. Then, with the two world wars and the very long stagnation crisis of 1929–39, any sign of ten-year periodicity or even of periodicity of any kind disappeared, since depressions from 1946 up till now have been not only more frequent and irregular, but also insignificant compared with the former crises and slumps.

The disproportions of capitalist production

Along with the other causes of disequilibrium and overproduction, Marx also dealt with lack of correspondence between the physical composition of output (i.e. the relative quantities of the commodities produced) and the structure of social demand, in terms of use-values instead of values. He dealt with this both as it arose in the course of his analyses on other subjects and, especially, in those writings which were only published after his death. These texts have therefore reached us in the same unfinished state as the others that were brought together in these posthumous publications. Although less numerous than those which we examined in the preceding section,

95. However, Jean Duret argues that 'The renewal of fixed capital . . . is the chief reason for the periodic recurrence of crises and the cyclical movements of the economy.' (*Le Marxisme et les crises,* p. 127.)

Also, Joan Robinson still presents this staggering of depreciation and replacements as Marx's main explanation of crises. cf. her introduction to Rosa Luxemburg's *The Accumulation of Capital,* pp. 19–20.

96. *Capital,* vol. III, p. 489. In this context we should point out that Domar, for example, estimates the average lifespan of fixed capital in the United States at thirty years (*Essay in the Theory of Economic Growth,* p. 158).

they are varied and multiple, varying from quite long discussions to circumstantial remarks, and even to casual or elliptical allusions.[97]

By collecting, arranging and synthesising all this disparate material, we believe it possible to distinguish two kinds of disproportions in Marx: disproportions brought about merely by the anarchy of capitalist production, and disproportions rooted in the contradictions which condition, firstly, accumulation of capital and, secondly, division of the social product between the classes. The first kind of disproportion is between industries, of whatever kind and whichever department they may belong to. It only concerns departments in so far as it concerns the industries which they are composed of. The second kind of disproportion relates directly to the different departments.[98]

1. The general anarchy of production

In a world in which the allocation of the factors of production amongst the various branches of economic activity is determined by mutually independent micro decisions of a host of competing entrepreneurs, it is inevitable that considerable divergences should constantly arise in all directions between the composition of the assortment of goods which constitutes the social product, and the qualitative structure of demand, even if the two aggregates correspond quantitatively. As capitalist production develops, the independent producer loses the personal contact which he had previously with a restricted and stable clientèle, whose tastes and needs he knew precisely, and for whom he was in a sense working on order; and he comes more and more to work for a vast, anonymous and fluctuating market, the propensities of which he does not know, and in which he is in competition with just as fluid a mass of other independent producers, whose decisions he does not know either.[99]

97. The main relevant passages can be found in: *Grundrisse,* pp. 414–16, 419–21, 443–4, 520; *Capital,* vol. II, pp. 473, 499–500.

98. Here we are referring to the three major departments into which Marx divides the social product: I: means of production; II: articles of workers' consumption; III: luxury goods for capitalists' consumption.

99. Typical in this respect is the evidence given to the banking committee of 1857 by a builder, E. Capps, which Marx quotes: 'When he was young, he said, houses were generally built to order and the payments made in instalments to the contractor as certain stages of the building were being completed. Very little was built on speculation. Contractors used to assent to such operations mainly to keep their men in constant employment and thus hold them together. In the last forty years all that has changed. Very little is now built to order. Anyone wanting a new house picks one from among those built on speculation. . . . The builder no longer works for his customers but for the market. Like every other industrial capitalist he is compelled to have finished articles in the market.' *Capital,* vol. II, pp. 237–8.

Divergences between schedules of needs (though not their overall extent, which for its part is unlimited) and the relative quantities of commodities produced must then be the rule rather than the exception. The 'invisible hand' which, according to the classics, resolves all contradictions and ensures the successful 'distribution of things necessary to life',[100] can only intervene and establish harmony between production and consumption *a posteriori*, by correcting these divergences through the sanction of the market, i.e. by penalising and eliminating through prices those producers who are on the wrong side of these divergences, with all the difficulties involved in this perpetual process of readjustment.

It could also be pointed out that such so-to-speak technical divergences between use-values produced and the structure of needs are not, as many Marxists tend to believe, the exclusive property of the free enterprise system. Planned economies are not totally exempt from them. The plan cannot calculate everything *ex ante* and, as far as consumer goods are concerned, it has to proceed through successive approximations, by trial and error. It is therefore perfectly possible that too many hats and not enough shoes should be produced, even under a socialist system. But this situation, though undesirable, does not, under socialism, have any cumulative effect or give rise to any major disturbance. Since prices are fixed, the disequilibrium will be manifested solely in variations in the level of inventories, and will be confined to this. After a certain while, an abnormal growth of the stocks of hats and an equally abnormal fall in the stocks of shoes will appear, and will indicate to the planner not only the direction of his error, but also *its precise extent*. The planner is then free to choose between two means of re-equilibration: either to transfer factors from one branch to the other, leaving prices unchanged, or to couple this transfer with a temporary modification of prices. In the first case, the transfer would be calculated in such a way as to readjust the proportions in the future, while at the same time reabsorbing the present divergence of stocks quite rapidly. In the second case, stocks would be re-equilibrated without delay by a modification of prices, and once this result had been obtained, the old prices would be restored; the transfer would be calculated exactly so as to prevent further recurrence of the disproportion in future cycles of production. The planner will choose between these alternative solutions according to certain variables: degree of perishability of the over-stocked commodity, extent of the divergence and length of time

100. Adam Smith was the first to use the expression 'the invisible hand', which has found favour with all apologists of free enterprise (*The Theory of Moral Sentiments*, pp. 184–5).

needed for the increase of production to counterbalance it, etc. Since prices are not active in the allocation of resources, there is no danger of any secondary effect. The harm done will be that inherent in the error, neither more nor less.

Matters are quite different under the capitalist system. Here, the transfer of factors from one industry to another is the business of private investors whose criterion is the rate of profit obtained or obtainable in each industry. Since the rate of profit is the difference between prices of inputs and those of outputs, the individual investor is in the last analysis guided by variations of prices. First problem: as opposed to the trend of the level of stocks, which tells us *both* the direction *and* the extent of the disequilibrium, the trend of the level of prices certainly tells us the direction, but not its quantitative extent; whence the possibility of having the disequilibrium zigzag endlessly. (If the price of furniture rises, this may mean that there is a certain shortage, but this alone does not tell us by how much. The flow of factors into cabinet-making is therefore in danger of exceeding the divergence and leading to overproduction which will in turn lead to an outflow of factors, etc.) Second problem, which is even more serious: the fall in prices does not simply discourage new investors, but may also lead to the untimely liquidation of stocks, to the closure of existing factories, to bankruptcies among the weakest or most indebted firms of the industry, the sacking of workers and therefore a fall in the general level of consumption causing over-production in other industries, in a chain reaction which may culminate in a general crisis.[101]

101. 'A crisis centring in the cotton industry may in the capitalist order put a stop to residential construction; in the socialist order it may of course happen that the production of cotton goods has to be drastically curtailed . . . but this would be a reason to speed up residential construction instead of stopping it.' (Joseph Schumpeter, *Capitalism, Socialism and Democracy,* p. 195).

Here Schumpeter is confusing two issues: disproportions between industries, which are the subject of this paragraph, and disproportions between departments, especially between consumption goods and capital goods, the latter including residential construction. This second kind of disproportion will be examined in the following two paragraphs.

Once this has been said, his observation is correct in both respects. Under socialism, there is no reason why unexpected over-production of textiles should affect the activity of any other industry such as construction; on the other hand, a *planned* contraction of the consumption and production of perishable consumer goods will release for the planner the material means simultaneously to step up the production of capital goods and consumer durables.

In his *Lombard Street,* Bagehot presents a detailed explanation of the interdependence of industries, and of how, since they are all clients of each other, any disproportion or partial overproduction tends to spread into depression and general overproduction (*Lombard Street,* pp. 125ff).

Nevertheless, lack of proportionality in production at the level of the industry is only the less significant side of our problem. Marx, as opposed to a certain number of Marxists who have considered this as the essential cause of overproduction crises, seems not to have been too preoccupied by it except in order to oppose the Ricardian conception that disproportions between industries constitute the only possibility of disequilibrium (since overproduction within one industry or country is automatically counterbalanced in another industry or country, and universal overproduction being materially impossible).[102]

In his earliest economic writings, *The Poverty of Philosophy* and *Wage-Labour and Capital*, Marx speaks of the anarchy of production and the disproportions which it gives rise to in a very general way. He refers to it as a factor which leads at the same time to perpetual divergences between supply of and demand for each commodity, consequently between prices and costs, and to a perpetual realignment of supply according to demand and of prices according to costs, through transfer of factors from one industry to another. Most of the time, Marx is concerned to show that costs do in fact determine prices in the long term, despite anarchy and disproportions.

Here and there, both in these writings and in vol. I of *Capital*, Marx links the anarchy of production with crises, referring to the fundamental contradiction between social production and private appropriation. But it is difficult to see how we can get from disproportions in both directions to general over-production, which is a disproportion in only one direction. Then, in chapters XX and XXI of *Capital*, vol. II, dealing respectively with simple reproduction and reproduction on an extended scale[103], as well as in various passages of the *Grundrisse*, Marx indicates in a general way the disturbances that can follow from a lack of proportionality, but here he is dealing with departments as opposed to industries, a subject we shall come on to later.

One sentence from the *Grundrisse* seems to us to sum up Marx's position well: 'So far in the realization process, we have only the indifference of the individual moments towards one another; that they determine each other internally and search for each other externally; but that they may or may not find each other, balance each other, correspond to each other. The inner necessity of moments which belong together, and their indifferent, independent

102. cf., for example, *Theories of Surplus Value,* vol. II, pp. 513–24.
103. cf. especially vol. II, pp. 473, 499.

existence with respect towards one another are *already* a foundation of contradictions.'[104]

As can be seen from this quotation, Marx approaches the problem of proportionality in very general terms, while he considers it as secondary. This is implied by the use of the word 'already'.

In fact, such an explanation of crises scarcely advances us beyond the Say–Ricardo Law of Markets, even if we are careful to make clear that one industry's overproduction may, in some cases, lead to such price movements, and consequently such ravages in the firms under consideration, that other industries, which either sell producer goods to these firms, or sell consumption goods to their workers, may be affected by this and find themselves in turn in a state of relative overproduction, in such a way that the crisis may spread through the whole economy stage by stage.

This explanation is still, so to speak, negative. Crises are supposed to be due to the *an*-archy of capitalist production, to the *in*-capacity of isolated independent producers to work out the exact proportion of needs. As with all negative explanations, the event is not explained in terms of any law. It becomes accidental and unpredictable. The chain reaction may or may not develop. Prices are its vehicle. Everything then comes to depend on the extent of the primary divergences, on the responsiveness of prices to these divergences and on the effects of price fluctuations on the fate of certain firms.

While we have allowed that prices are both flexible and active, this does not mean that there is a mathematical functional relation, such that the slightest overstock will make prices fall and that the smallest fall in prices will lead to the instantaneous bankruptcy of a certain number of firms. Like any living organism, the capitalist system is endowed with certain margins of manoeuvre, which enable it to absorb and break the force of shocks, at least up to a certain critical threshold. In the first place, the elasticity of inventories. Commodities which leave a factory in the morning are not auctioned off at noon and sold off towards the evening. The 'normal level of inventories' is only defined approximately, and price movements are not linked mechanically and in a so-to-speak micrometrical way to variations in the level of inventories. Prices can only change through voluntary acts on the part of the sellers, and these acts only take place at certain thresholds. No one spends his time changing all the price-tags once an hour. As long as fluctuations of inventories do not attain these thresholds, prices will not change. At the other end of the chain of causality, not every fall in prices automatically endangers the firms

104. *Grundrisse*, p. 417.

concerned. Reserves of liquid assets provide a degree of elasticity and lines of credit offer a further margin. Finally, foreign trade supplies the system with an extra margin of manoeuvre. On the one hand it makes it possible to sell off the over-producing industries' surplus, wholly or partly, and on the other, it prevents the complete emptying of the stocks of underproducing industries. Thus, while awaiting the results of internal reallocation of factors, it counterbalances part of the distortions and makes it possible, to a certain extent, to bridge the gap between the two equilibrium situations.

Consequently, if these various critical thresholds are not crossed and if, as is usually the case, there is reproduction on an extended scale, the initial disproportion will be reabsorbed, not through the liquidation of stocks, but through a greater or lesser stagnation of the existing firms, i.e. through transfers towards other industries; transfers not of factors already engaged in production, but of part of the new capitals formed by the accumulation of profits in the industries under consideration. In this case, there is no danger of any cumulative effect or generalisation of overproduction through the whole economy.[105]

It follows that, if these disproportions were the basic cause of overproduction crises, then the danger of such a crisis would diminish as capitalist economies develop, as data-processing progresses and, above all, as the volume and diversity of production increase, i.e. as the law of probability dilutes accidental deviations in an ever-growing mass of transactions and stock-in-hand.[106] Overproduction crises would then be less serious and less common in large countries than in small countries, and in developed countries than in underdeveloped countries; but this is contradicted by historical experience.[107]

This thesis is also incompatible with another fact of experience, which is that overproduction is universal from the moment it appears,

105. Taking account of the complexity of the conditions implied by Marx's mathematical schemes of volume II of *Capital,* Marxists have often argued as if the slightest disproportion between their components must block the reproduction process; rather as if we were dealing with an alchemical potion, which would explode if there were a microscopic error in the proportions of the ingredients. Clearly, if the capitalist system were at the mercy of such mini-disproportions, it would have long since collapsed. There is in fact an 'invisible hand' which saves it from such catastrophes. If it is not the hand of Adam Smith, it is that of the flexibility of inventory levels on the one hand, and a degree of price-rigidity on the other.

106. 'The larger is the number of independent entrepreneurs who meet in the market, the more will errors in their economic judgement be mutually compensating. . . .' (V.K. Dmitriev, *Economic Essays,* p. 177).

107. G. de Molinari, who also ascribed crises of over-production to ignorance of the needs of consumers, because of the size of the world market, concluded that the telegraph would solve the problem. (cf. *Etudes économiques,* pp. 38–9.)

i.e. not only after the supposed chain reaction has worked its way through the economy, but as soon as the business climate begins to deteriorate.

It is not any one commodity or group of commodities which is overabundant and cannot find a buyer, but commodities in general, just as it is commodities in general which are sold and realized without any problems during the boom just before the crisis. It may of course happen that this or that particular commodity is still selling at the height of the crisis, despite the general glut, just as this or that particular commodity may be left on the shelf when the market is at its most buoyant. But the order of magnitude of these phenomena is so low that their exceptional character is obvious to all. As such, they cannot be offered as proof that overproduction and underproduction are mutually compensating on the basis of the overall equality of supply and demand.

II. Disproportions between Departments. The rate of accumulation and the physical composition of output

A quite different kind of disproportionality concerns the quantitative relations between the three Departments into which Marx divides capitalist production:

I. Producer goods.
II. Workers' consumption goods.
III. Capitalists' consumption goods (luxuries).

For the process of accumulation to develop smoothly, various conditions concerning relations between technical conditions of reproduction and the distribution of the product between classes must be satisfied: the output of Department III must equal the sum of surplus value minus the savings of its beneficiaries; these savings must for a given period be equal to the increase in the output of Department I (assuming that the sum of wages stays constant): thirdly, assuming for the sake of simplification that wage-earners' savings are zero, the output of Department II must equal the sum of wages.

If we accept that savings are an increasing function of the sum of surplus value and that, for a given level of output, this sum is a decreasing function of wages, then it follows that to each change in the distribution of social revenue between the classes, there must correspond a change in the allocation of factors of production between Departments I, II and III, or else a disequilibrium will arise between the three categories of commodities produced and the three specific categories of demand facing them. Since distribution of the factors among the various departments depends on investment micro decisions by isolated individual entrepreneurs, while distribution of revenues depends for its part on the balance of forces between classes and the exercise of bargaining-power in general, and since these two facts are autonomous and independent of each other, there is no reason to assume that their effects should automatically be compatible.

Disequilibrium is therefore possible at any time. But it is perhaps the very permanence of this possibility which disqualifies it from serving as the basis of a law. Just as with the other disproportions discussed above, disequilibria remain possible in general, but the theoretical necessity of their appearance remains to be shown.

In some of Marx's propositions a so-to-speak parallel source of disequilibrium seems to arise. The distribution of the factors among the departments is not simply the result of decisions by capitalists and of their available capital funds; it also depends upon the degree of development of productive forces. Technological development determines a definite relation between equipment and living labour, hence a definite relation between constant and variable capital, a definite organic composition of capital. But there is a necessary correspondence between the organic composition of capital and the relation between necessary labour and surplus labour, in the sense that it is surplus labour which makes it possible to increase the organic composition through capitalisation of profits. This correspondence cannot be maintained by capitalism, since the organic composition varies according to technical factors, whereas the relation between labour and surplus labour obeys different laws and tends to be constant.

In other words, the distribution of revenue is independent of technical conditions of production, whereas these two must correspond exactly for the realization of the product to occur smoothly.

> A revolution in the forces of production further alters these relations, *changes* these relations themselves, whose foundations – from the standpoint of capital, and hence also of that of realisation through exchange – always remains *the relation of necessary to surplus labour*, or, if you like, of the different moments of objectified to living labour. It is possible, as we have already indicated earlier, that the capital as well as the living labour capacity set free owing to the increase in the productive forces must both lie dormant, because they are not present in the proportions in which production must take place on the basis of the newly developed productive forces.[108]

108. *Grundrisse,* p. 444, emphasis original.

However, this new disproportion, in so far as it differs from the last one, rests on the particularly dubious assumption that the organic composition varies as a function of technical factors. Marx clearly believes that, to make a new, more capital-intensive investment, it is not enough to dispose of enough surplus value in the form of savings; it is also necessary for the corresponding more capital-intensive technique already to exist, already to have been invented. This is true in the abstract, but could only have any practical bearing if accumulation was always sufficient in value for the universal application of the most advanced technology possible; in other words, if the accumulation fund was relatively unlimited, and the only limited (scarce) factor was technological progress.

A quick glance at the real world is enough to convince us that reality is quite otherwise. Technological progress far outstrips the economic conditions under which it is applied. Even in the country where capital is the most abundant, the US, not all building workers are equipped with bulldozers, any more than all factories are equipped with conveyor belts and computers. But bulldozers, conveyor belts and computers have all been with us for quite a while. The stock of technological inventions is many times greater than the quantity whose introduction is financially possible. To supply every worker on this planet with the heaviest and most efficient tool of those already invented or even already tried out, would require an incomparably greater quantity of capital than that already accumulated. On the contrary, the only 'scarce' factor, hence the only factor responsible for rises in the organic composition, is the sum of new capitals formed in the course of each cycle of production. There is therefore no danger of any disequilibrium between growth of the organic composition and the relation between necessary labour and surplus labour, since it is this surplus labour which makes growth of the organic composition possible and which supplies the material for it.

Charles Bettelheim's interesting study dating from 1949, which we have referred to above, contradicts this argument.[109] The accumulation of capital is not sufficient to generalise the application of technological progress, but disequilibrium is due precisely to this insufficiency. While the sum of available capital is insufficient to install a computer in all the firms of a given industry, some individual capitals are, for their part, quite sufficient to install one in some of the firms. In a centralised socialist system, these under-equipped firms would coexist with the rest in order to complete the quantity of

109. *Le problème de l'emploi.*

products which society needs, until such time as the social accumulation fund can supply them with the means to renovate themselves in turn. There would be no danger of any tension. But in the uncentralised capitalist system, these firms cannot compete, close their gates and sack their workforce.

> In this sense, it can be said that workers are not sacked because there are too many machines, as Sismondi put it, but on the contrary, because there are not enough machines to employ them, of course for a given level of technology and a given level of accumulation. . . . The sacked workers could in general be employed in less favorable technical conditions, i.e. needing less equipment, . . . but . . . in each industry, for a given firm, an organic composition lower than the dominant organic composition would mean, for this firm, worse conditions of production than for the others and, consequently, higher cost-prices . . . .[110]

This argument does not seem to us to be very convincing. Either the output of the firms that have adopted the new technique is enough to satisfy market demand, or it is not. In the first case, it cannot be said that there is not enough capital to generalise technical progress in the industry under consideration. The marginal firms are, in this case, useless, and would have to disappear under any economic system. If, at this point, the factors previously employed in these firms cannot be transferred elsewhere and become unemployed, this would be due to some other reason, not to any lack of machines. In the second case, which seems to be that envisaged by Bettelheim, i.e. the case in which the output of advanced firms is insufficient, there is no reason for backward firms to be eliminated by competition, since in this case, the market price will be determined by the costs of the least productive firm, and more productive firms will obtain a superprofit while awaiting generalisation of the technical innovation. There is, again, no danger of any disturbance because of some lack of 'machines'. Not only in the socialist system, but also in the uncentralised system, coexistence within one industry of firms with differing organic compositions is perfectly normal, and Marx did not omit to take account of this fact and speak about it.[111]

This said, neither Marx nor the Marxists have dwelt overmuch on

110. *Ibid.*, p. 106. cf. also Paul Baran, *The Political Economy of Growth*, pp. 191–5, for a restatement of Bettelheim's argument, transposed into the context of a critique of monopolistic behaviour.

111. There is however one passage in Marx which may justify Bettelheim's interpretation: 'There are not too many means of production produced to employ the able-bodied portion of the population. Quite the reverse, . . . not enough means of production are produced to permit the employment of the entire able-bodied population under the most productive conditions . . .' (*Capital*, vol. III, pp. 257–8).

these specific constraints of reproduction and accumulation. But there is another far more important constraint. This stems from a relation, held by Marxists to be intrinsic, linking the quantitative growth of Department I on the one hand, and that of Departments II and III put together on the other.

III. The contradiction between growth of the organic composition of capital and stagnation of final consumption

If the rate of accumulation of capital, and therefore the rate of growth of Department I, is greater than the rate of growth of the active population, accumulation will produce a continual increase of the organic composition, understood as the relation between the value of fixed constant capital (equipment of all kinds) and the number of workers needed to set fixed capital to work, or between the value of past labour embodied in the means of production and that of living labour engaged in production.

Now, a rise in the organic composition is not only a function of accumulation in value terms, but also expresses the application of technical progress to production. On the other hand, there is no reason why this progress should affect one Department any more than another. It follows that, in the long term, this progress will be spread out more or less evenly over the whole of production. This means that the organic composition of those Departments producing articles of consumption (II and III) will more or less follow that of the Department producing means of production (I).

But any increase in the organic composition involves an increase, whether proportional or not, in the productivity of labour. This is a necessary result because it is not in the interests of any entrepreneur to change his technology and employ more capital per worker, unless this new technology provides him with a greater quantity of produce per unit of labour.

It follows that, as a result of the accumulation of capital, the mass of articles of consumption produced per unit of labour, and therefore per wage-earner, increases as continuously and by roughly as much as the mass of means of production.

It is here that the contradiction bursts out. For while it can be allowed that capitalists' personal consumption increases by the same proportion, and that realization of the output of Department III gives rise to no problem, things are quite different in the case of Department II, since the same ultimate cause, which is the motive power of the whole process – the accumulation of capital – implies relative stagnation of wages and, consequently, of working-class consumption.

Disequilibrium is therefore a permanent and necessary effect of the accumulation of capital. Its direction is completely determined. It is a tendency towards an excess of articles of consumption in relation to consumable revenues and a shortage of means of production in relation to saved revenues. This is certainly a disproportion, but it is a specific disproportion between the aggregate values of Departments I and II. This is the expression, in the last analysis, of the fundamental contradiction between social production and private appropriation of the product. In a sense, it is a matter of the same disproportion – faster accumulation of capital than growth of population – which is, as we have seen, the basis of the law of the tendency of the rate of profit to fall, and it is no coincidence that Marx gives us the fullest summary of this explanation of crises at the end of his presentation of this law:

> The stupendous productivity developing under the capitalist mode of production relative to population, and the increase, if not in the same proportion, of capital-values (not just of their material substance), which grow much more rapidly than the population, contradict the basis, which constantly narrows in relation to the expanding wealth, and for which all this immense productiveness works. They also contradict the conditions under which this swelling capital augments its value. Hence the crises.[112]

In other words, productive consumption (which Sismondi and Malthus failed to take into account) can perfectly well compensate, in a static view of reality, for the lack of personal (unproductive) consumption and thus allow the immediate realization of surplus value. But this realization will only aggravate disequilibrium since, by definition, the aim of *productive* consumption is to increase production of all kinds even more. If textiles consumption is too low because of low wages, one can reduce the effects of the disequilibrium for a while by using a portion of the available factors to produce more steel, in order to produce better machine-tools, with which to make more efficient looms; but once this point is reached, one will have to confront the original reason why all these operations were carried out. For once part of the surplus value has finally been consumed by obtaining more efficient looms, then more textiles will have to be produced, i.e. something which cannot be consumed *productively* and, if wages are such that the population's personal consumption cannot absorb them, the contradiction will erupt.

> The capitalists' expenditures increase together with their growing income. Besides . . . continuous circulation takes place between constant capital and constant capital (even regardless of accelerated accumulation). It is at

112. *Ibid.*, p. 266.

first independent of individual consumption because it never enters the latter. But this consumption definitely limits it nevertheless, since constant capital is never produced for its own sake but solely because more of it is needed in spheres of production whose products go into individual consumption.[113]

Marx had already written in the *Grundrisse*:

It is quite the same with the demand created by production itself for raw material, semi-finished goods, machinery, means of communication, and for the auxiliary materials consumed in production, such as dyes, coal, grease, soap, etc. This effective, exchange-value-positing demand is adequate and sufficient as long as the producers exchange among themselves. Its inadequacy shows itself as soon as the final product encounters its limit in direct and final consumption.[114]

Marx hardly wrote any other significant passages on the thesis that there is a tendency towards disproportion between Departments I and II. It seems to us that Marx did not consider this disproportion as any more important than the host of other *possibilities* of disequilibrium and crisis which he discussed, as we have seen, in his writings and rough notes. It is characteristic that, on the page before the last passage we quoted, Marx declared as a preliminary that 'The point here, of course, is not yet to develop overproduction specifically, but only the *predisposition* to it, such as it is posited in primitive form in the capital relation itself.'[115]

But it remains true that, among the host of *possibilities* which Marx presents us with in turn, there are only two cases in which the roots of disequilibrium seem to extend right down to the heart of objective conditions of reproduction: the differential 'mortality' of fixed capital which we discussed earlier; and the incompatibility between comparative rates of growth of Departments I and II, as against the division of social revenue between surplus value and wages, which is the subject of this section. Did Marx rate the importance of these two sources of disequilibrium very highly, and did he intend to combine them to produce this theory of crises of overproduction and their periodicity which is missing in his works and which he intended to present in a final chapter which he never wrote? We do not know. What we do know is that Lenin placed great emphasis on the second of these sources (while completely ignoring the first) and, going as far as is possible along this track, constructed his own theory of crises on this basis, which has influenced the great majority of Marxists ever

113. *Ibid.*, p. 305.
114. *Grundrisse,* p. 421.
115. *Ibid.*, p. 419.

since. We therefore think it essential, before discussing weaknesses of this theory, to present the essence of Lenin's attempts to strengthen it. This is what we shall attempt in chapter 4.

Appendix I
Tendencies of the Rate of Profit to Vary

The rate of profit, p, is equal in Marx's formula to $s/(c + v)$, s being the sum of surplus value, c constant capital (fixed equipment and circulating capital other than wages), and v variable capital (the sum of wages), while $c + v$ is, consequently, total capital employed.

In discussions on the validity of the Marxist law of the tendency of the rate of profit to fall, participants generally start, whatever their position on the central issue, by dividing the numerator and denominator of this expression by v and thus obtaining the identity:

$$\frac{s}{c+v} = \frac{s/v}{1+c/v}$$

On this basis, the following refutation is proposed: the rate of profit varies directly with s/v and inversely with c/v. Since these two ratios vary simultaneously in the same (increasing) direction because of the same factor – the accumulation of capital and subsequent development of the productive forces – one cannot consider one of the variations in isolation, relegating the other to *ceteris paribus*, nor is it possible to determine in advance the net effect of the joint increases in the two ratios on the value of the above expression, and thus on the rate of profit. Marx says that s/v increases more slowly than c/v, and that the overall value of the expression consequently tends to fall. He justifies this by asserting that there is an upper limit to the numerator's variations, while there is no such limit on those of the denominator. But the formula above does not imply any limit of this kind; s/v can vary without limit, as much as c/v can.[1]

This kind of refutation is not at all decisive. It is true that the limit in question is not immediately apparent in the formula above. This is because the formula is inadequate. It suffices to divide the numerator and denominator by $v + s$ instead of v for this limit to emerge:

$$\frac{s}{c + v} = \frac{s/(v + s)}{c/(v + s) + v/(v + s)}$$

1. cf. François Danjou, 'Sur la baisse tendancielle du taux de profit'.

As can be seen, however much the rate of surplus-value, s/v, may increase because of the development of the productive forces, the numerator, $s/(v + s)$, can never exceed unity, while the denominator can increase without limit.

But since the second term in the denominator, $v/(v + s)$, falls as a result of this development, and tends to zero in the limit, the expression for the rate of profit tends to:

$$\frac{1}{c/(v + s)} = \frac{v + s}{c}$$

This last formula describes a situation in which, through an enormous rise in the productivity of labour, the cost of workers' subsistence goods has become a vanishing magnitude and, consequently, a value equal to the total number of hours of labour used in production, which is the same as the sum total of value added, flows to the capitalists as profit. Since variable capital has become a negligible quantity, the rate of profit will be equal to the reciprocal of the organic composition of capital, which is expressed not as c/v but as $c/(v + s)$, i.e. by the ratio of two homogeneous quantities of labour, that of the past labour incorporated in constant capital and that of the living labour which valorises the former.

At this point the substitution of $c/(v + s)$ for Marx's customary expression, c/v, merits attention.

It must first be said that the reason why the numerator and denominator of the expression $s/(c + v)$ (the definition of the rate of profit) are normally divided by v rather than $v + s$ (as *we* have done above), is precisely to reproduce, in the quotients, Marx's customary expressions: s/v and c/v, the rate of surplus value and the organic composition of capital respectively, and to study the supposed parallel rise in both of them. We have adopted different expressions. Why? Because, in the particular case of the Marxist 'law' of the tendency of the rate of profit to fall, these two expressions must be repudiated, the first as irrelevant and the second as fallacious.

As far as the first is concerned, it is enough to point out that each time, in these three chapters (XIII, XIV, XV) of volume III, that Marx says there is a limit to the growth of surplus value, he is referring implicitly, and sometimes explicitly, to one of the following: either the ratio of unpaid time to total time ($s/[v + s]$) – when total time is not given – or, more simply, to the mass of surplus value, if the total time ($v + s$) is given. In a quantitative problem like our own, the two expressions s/v and $s/(v + s)$ are completely interchangeable. They are different ratios between two magnitudes, s and v, and these ratios can of course be inferred from each other. This is really a matter of definitions and, especially with Marx, of political implications.

This is not the case for the organic composition of capital: c/v and $c/(v + s)$ are entirely different things. Marx explains that c/v is an 'index' of what he calls the 'technical' composition, which is in turn the ratio of the mass of means of production to the quantity of living labour which sets it in motion, and that this index is *only valid on the assumption of a given rate of surplus value*. If this is so, it is difficult to see the reason for using this index rather than, more simply and directly, what is indicated (which is $c/[v + s]$), especially in the particular case of a falling rate of profit, where the rate of surplus value is not taken to be a constant.

Does this mean that $c/(v + s)$ represents a 'technical' ratio? There is a troublesome equivocation in the concept of the organic composition of capital. Marx distinguishes between a technical (material) composition and an organic (value) composition. He presents the former as the proportion between 'a definite quantity of means of production, machinery, raw materials, etc.' and 'a definite quantity of labour power'.[2] In volume I of *Capital,* Marx had defined the technical composition as 'the mass of means of production, as compared with the mass of the labour-power that vivifies them'.[3] Later on in the same chapter, he speaks of the 'mass of labour in proportion to the mass of means of production moved by it'.[4]

As presented in these differing definitions, the 'technical composition of capital' is doubly unacceptable:

(1) It establishes a quantitative relation between two aggregates: a *mass* of labour-power and a *mass* of material objects. By abstracting somewhat, the first can be regarded as homogeneous. The second is not only heterogeneous by nature, but, since it features in this ratio exclusively in its materiality (in contrast to the organic composition in value terms), it is denied the only possible homogenisation, that achieved through values or prices. The technical composition of capital turns out to be a relation between one thing which is quantifiable and another which is not, and has no possible meaning as a variable.

(2) It is a contradiction in terms, since according to Marx himself, capital only exists over and above its *material* forms.

2. p. 145.
3. *Ibid.*, vol. I, p. 583.
4. *Ibid.*, vol. I, p. 773 (Pelican edition, 1976).

So the reply to our question is negative: there is nothing technical or *material* about $c/(v + s)$. c is not a *mass* but a value and, since the argument is in terms of labour-value – it is in these terms that the theory of the tendency of the rate of profit to fall is constructed – $c/(v + s)$ expresses the relation between two quantities (measured in hours) of a homogeneous and physically given substance, labour. It follows not only that the variations of this ratio are perfectly commensurable, but also that the ratio is perfectly meaningful in a static sense, in itself.[5]

As for the so-called organic composition in value terms, c/v, the ratio of constant capital to the sum of wages, it too is certainly a commensurable relation, but it can only be used for studying changes in the rate of profit if it is coupled with the assumption of a constant rate of surplus value and working-day, hence of constant hourly wages, as Marx himself admits in chapter VIII of volume III.[6] Put another way, c/v only has any meaning to the extent that one can, by means of certain assumptions, deduce $c/(v + s)$ from it. It is thus simpler to use the latter expression in the first place.

But the expression c/v is not only inadequate; it is, as we said earlier, fallacious. c/v can vary through a mere change in wage-levels, without any change in objective production conditions.[7] In this case its variations will have an effect on the rate of profit exactly opposite to what would be expected, if one were using a correct expression for the organic composition of capital. More precisely, its rises will increase the rate of profit instead of decreasing it, while its falls will have a decreasing effect instead of an increasing one.

From the above limit of the rate of profit

$$p \rightarrow \frac{v + s}{c},$$

it clearly emerges that, if c grows faster than $v + s$, i.e. if the rate of

5. In price terms the numerator, c, would express the monetary value of capital, while the denominator, $v + s$, would still express the physical quantity of (living) labour. Their ratio at any one point in time would not have much meaning, but if prices represented physical quantities of the money-commodity (convertible currency system), or if c were computed in *constant prices*, the variations of this ratio, $c/(v + s)$, would be useful in economic analysis, in the same way as those of the capital-labour ratio.

6. *Capital*, vol. III, p. 144.

7. Or, as F. Danjou points out, through mere changes in financial practices, such as the comparative periods of rotation of the wage-fund and the material elements of capital.

accumulation of capital is greater than the rate of increase of the quantity of labour expended (which tends to become equal to the rate of growth of employment), the rate of profit will eventually fall.

This is Marx's fundamental hypothesis. Doubtless considering that fluctuations in the industrial reserve army cancel each other out in the long run, he supposes that growth in the volume of employment is ultimately determined by population increases, and he considers it plausible to suppose that these increases are lower than the rate of accumulation of capital.

This hypothesis is implicit in most of Marx's arguments in this section, but it appears *explicitly* in the calculations on pages 221–2 of volume III and is stated quite clearly at the end of chapter XV. However, the way it is put contains an ambiguity which lies at the very heart of the calculation. The 'rate of accumulation' of capital is the ratio of the value of the new capital formed by reinvesting part of the profits on current production, to the value of the old capital used for this production. But this old capital has two values: that of its production and that of its *re*-production, the labour-time which was actually used in the past to produce it, and the labour-time which would be *necessary* today if it *had* to be replaced in present technical conditions, i.e. after the introduction of the new tools represented by the new capital. Profit on concluded operations will be compared to the first value, but the profit on succeeding operations will be compared to the second. The difference between the two is the depreciation of the material constituents of capital due to the rise in labour productivity, because of this very accumulation of capital.

Marx is clearly conscious of this consideration. But he confines it to 'influences counteracting the Law' as if it were an autonomous factor, whereas it is a second effect of the same cause which lies at the basis of the 'Law': the accumulation of capital. Thus, when he compares the rate of growth of employment with the rate of accumulation of capital, i.e. when we are no longer dealing with the *conditions* under which the rate of profit *may* fall, but asserting that reality is such that the rate of profit *will tend* to fall in the future, in other words, when he moves from a theorem to a law, he passes over the factor of the depreciation of capital in silence. We must therefore attempt to include it in the calculation.

If one assumes with Marx that the rate of growth of $v + s$ is lower than that of $c + v$ (accumulation of capital faster than growth of the wage-earning population), one can, without loss of generality, treat $v + s$ as a constant and $c + v$ as increasing in proportion to the difference between the two rates of growth. In other words, we can start by studying the effects on the rate of profit of the growth of capital for a given volume of employment.

There is henceforth no need to divide the two terms of the fraction, $s/(c + v)$, by anything, whether v or $v + s$. The original form of the definitional equation of the rate of profit,

$$p = \frac{s}{c + v},$$

is adequate to study its variations.

To start with, we can adopt Marx's symbol: $c + v = C$. There is in fact no longer any reason to split total capital employed into equipment and materials on the one hand, and workers' subsistence on the other. Both elements represent past labour. Thus:

$$p = \frac{s}{C}.$$

Besides, this is the only formula used by Marx in his chapter on the tendency of the rate of profit to fall.

If s falls, p certainly falls, and there is nothing more to say. The problem here is the possible rise of s.

If s rises, its rise must be decreasing, since it is limited by a constant $s + v$. As v tends to zero, the rate of growth of s will also tend to zero, and after a certain point it will be negligible. One can therefore treat s as a constant.

If s is a constant and the whole of surplus value is capitalised, then

$$C_2 = C_1 + s - C_1\delta, \tag{1}$$

where δ represents the rate of depreciation of total capital due to the increase in labour productivity, and C_1 and C_2 stand for the capitals employed in periods 1 and 2.

If the value of a given quantity of goods diminishes in proportion to rises in labour productivity, and if the value of any good is the quantity of labour necessary for its *re*-production (replacement value), then the total existing capital must depreciate in proportion to the rise in labour productivity, and the rate of depreciation is equal to the rate of growth of labour productivity.

But the rise in productivity is, according to Marx, a definite function of the rise in the organic composition:

$$\delta = f\,[C/(v + s)] = g\,(C/s),$$

where g is a simple multiple of f, determined by $\dfrac{C/s}{C/(v + s)}$, and thus by $(v + s)/s$.

If we assume that the function g is linear, with a constant coefficient a, it follows that:

$$\delta = \frac{aC}{s} \tag{2}$$

Taking (1) and (2) together, we obtain:

$$C_2 = C_1 + s - \frac{C_1^2 a}{s} \tag{3}$$

It is clear from this that the direction of change of C depends on the difference – positive, negative, or zero – between the value of the extra capital, s, and that of the depreciation of existing capital, C_1^2a/s, caused by the introduction of this newly formed capital, or, which comes to the same thing, between δ and s/C.

Three cases are possible at the start of a process of accumulation: δ may be equal to, greater than, or less than s/C, which, taken together with (2), corresponds to a being equal to, greater than, or less than s^2/C^2.

Case I

$\delta = s/C$ and $a = s^2/C^2$.

Hence, $\dfrac{C_1^2 a}{s} = s$

and, substituting from (3), we obtain: $C_2 = C_1$,

whence $\dfrac{s}{C_2} = \dfrac{s}{C_1}$

The rate of profit stays constant.

Case II

$\delta > s/C$ and $a > s^2/C^2$.

Hence, $\dfrac{C_1^2 a}{s} > s$

and, substituting from (3), we obtain: $C_2 < C_1$,

whence $s/C_2 > s/C_1$.

The rate of profit rises.

But if the rate of profit, s/C, rises through a fall in C (s being constant), s^2/C^2 also rises. Then, since δ and a are both constants, a point will be reached when $\delta = s/C$ and $a = s^2/C^2$, which brings us back to the first case, when *the rate of profit becomes a constant.*

Case III

$$\delta < s/C \text{ and } a < s^2/C^2.$$

$$\text{Hence, } \frac{C_1^2\, a}{s} < s$$

and, substituting from (3), we obtain: $C_2 > C_1$,

whence $s/C_2 < s/C_1$.

The rate of profit falls.

But if the rate of profit, s/C, falls through a rise in C (s being constant), s^2/C^2 also falls. Then, since δ and a are both constants, a point will be reached when $\delta = s/C$ and $a = s^2/C^2$, which brings us back to the first case, when *the rate of profit becomes a constant.*

Conclusion. Under these assumptions, there is in all three cases a tendency, through a kind of entropy, whatever may be the effect of the rising organic composition on labour productivity, to a state in which $s/C = \delta$, i.e. in which the rate of profit becomes equal to the rate of depreciation (fall in the value of constant capital), which is in turn equal to the rate of growth of labour productivity.

This result squares perfectly with the most important conclusion reached by Charles Bettelheim in another context and through different calculations: 'In the long run, assuming a constant rate of growth of productivity, the rate of profit tends to approach this rate of growth.'[8]

It is clear that we can now easily drop the simplifying assumptions made at the start of this analysis: (i) a constant level of employment; (ii) 100% capitalisation of surplus value.

Any variations in the volume of employment can quite simply be included under the rate of growth of productivity. As for the possibility of partial capitalisation of surplus value, one should quite simply divide the sum obtained in this way (through this introduction of the volume of employment) by the rate of capitalisation. As Bettelheim says, once more quite correctly, in the article referred to, 'the dominant spontaneous tendency appears to be a tendency to equalisation between the current rate of profit and the combined rate

8. 'Variations du taux de profit . . .', p. 86.

of growth of employment and labour productivity divided by a coefficient representing the rate of accumulation of surplus value.'[9]

Example
Rate of growth of labour productivity = 0.04 per year
Rate of growth of employment = 0.02 per year
Capitalists invest 75% of surplus value and consume the remaining 25%.
The rate of profit will tend to:

$$\frac{0.02 + [(1 + 0.02) \times 0.04]}{0.75} = 0.08106667.$$

Referring to Bettelheim once more, it can be said that once this equality is reached, 'there is static equilibrium in value terms, simple reproduction in value terms, but extended reproduction in terms of use-values'.[10]

We have assumed that a is a constant, hence an unchanging rate of growth of labour productivity. But it is apparent from the above analysis that even if this rate is not constant, the long-term result will be the same. In fact, any change upwards or downwards in this rate will only change the gap between this rate and the *current* rate of profit. But we have shown that, whatever the initial gap, positive, negative, or zero, and whatever the initial coefficient a, the rate of profit tends to approach the rate of growth of productivity. We can therefore consider each change in the value of a as the start of a new period, in the course of which the same phenomenon of convergence will appear. Of course, if the second rate runs away from the first for ever, equalisation will never occur, but the tendency towards equalisation will still be confirmed. This tendency will then express itself as a simple but very important functional relation, in terms of which the rate of profit always varies in the same direction as the product of the two rates of growth, that of labour productivity and that of employment. How do these two rates behave in reality? This is the real question.

If the fact that fluctuations in the size of the reserve army of workers cancel out over time allows one to assume that the second rate depends in the long run on the rate of demographic growth, one thereby connects this rate (that of the growth of employment) with an independent and exogenous variable which, as such, can be relegated to the *ceteris paribus*. This rate can henceforth legitimately be

9. *Ibid.*, p. 105.
10. *Ibid.*

assumed to be a constant. If, besides, the first rate, the rate of growth of labour productivity through continuous additions of capital, is decreasing, as has generally been assumed in the past, the product of the two rates will be decreasing, and one must conclude in favour of a falling rate of profit.[11]

But does this second rate, the growth of the quantity of labour employed, really derive from demographic growth, even abstracting from the reserve army? This in our opinion lies at the root of Marx's error, which neither Bettelheim nor any one else have to our knowledge pointed out in the past. It is a conceptual error which can be found in the original statement of his theory. It consists of confusing the quantity of labour employed with the size of the wage-earning population, or more precisely of confusing variations of $v + s$ with those of the physical volume of employment. In this section Marx quite simply ignores the distinction he himself worked out between abstract and concrete labour. According to his own definition, the organic composition of capital is not the relation of capital to concrete, physical living labour, but to abstract living labour. Now, though the working population, and hence the mass of physical labour, does not grow, or does not grow as fast as capital accumulates, the quantity of abstract labour that this population is capable of supplying *may*, for its part, grow independently of and well beyond any variations in the number of workers and physical number of hours which this population places at the disposal of capital. For this to happen it is sufficient for the skill structure within this working population to have changed.

Arguing in terms of the number of workers employed 'by a given capital', Marx tells us that the development of the productive forces reduces:

> the number by which the rate of surplus value is multiplied to obtain its mass. Two labourers, each working 12 hours daily, cannot produce the same mass of surplus-value as 24 who work only 2 hours, even if they could live on air and hence did not have to work for themselves at all. In this respect, then, the compensation of the reduced number of labourers by intensifying the degree of exploitation has certain insurmountable limits. It may, for this reason, well check the fall in the rate of profit, but cannot prevent it altogether.[12]

11. This contains no theoretical error, nor any hypothesis which is *obviously contrary* to reality, and Danjou (see above) is wrong to reproach Bettelheim on this point.
12. *Capital*, vol. III, p. 247.

Marx clearly assumes that the labour of these two workers is still (after the development of the productive forces which results in 'intensifying the degree of exploitation') of the same complexity as that of the previous 24. If their standard of training has changed, it may well happen that 2 workers working 12 hours supply a mass of surplus value not smaller, but considerably greater, than that extracted from 24 workers each working 2 hours, although the mass of physical (concrete) labour has fallen by half, and even if the rate of surplus value has not changed.

Marx's argument postulates a material limit to the growth of relative and absolute surplus value. A labourer working 12 hours cannot produce more than 12 hours of surplus value, even if his wages are zero. But this is not true – according to Marx's own teachings, a worker working for 12 hours by the clock may give 20, 30 or 40 hours of surplus value, even if his wages are not zero. Training decides everything. Surplus value, like value, is not measured in hours by the clock, but in hours of abstract labour.

Even if, as we suggest, the accompanying growth of the proportion of skilled labour is taken into account, it is likely, or even certain, that the organic composition has actually grown since the nineteenth century for one or several particular capitals, or even for particular entire industries. But if the growth of the proportion of skilled labour in some industries, such as services for example, has outweighed the growth of the organic composition in others, and if we also take into account the overall growth of population, calculation in Marxist terms may very well end up showing a fall in the average organic composition of social capital, and therefore a rise in the general rate of profit.

Without knowing the transformation coefficient of complex to simple labour, it is impossible to say anything about variations in the mass of surplus value nor, consequently, about variations of the rate of profit, in the framework of the Marxist system, in which the general rate of profit is the ratio of the mass of surplus value to total capital employed.

Marx reviews all the factors that counteract the 'Law' except for one: the growth of complex labour as a proportion of the total mass of labour. (I have called this proportion the 'organic composition of labour'. It can be seen here that this concept is needed to manipulate the idea of the organic composition of capital. For c/v has no meaning, not only unless a definite wage-level is given, as Marx himself points out, but also unless a definite organic composition of labour is given.) It must be said that this is not really a factor counteracting the law, but a condition which alters the construction of the theory itself.

It is possible that in Marx's time, it was plausible to maintain the hypothesis of a constant or even falling organic composition of labour as a result of technical progress. In other contexts, Marx often expressed the conviction that technological progress and the accumulation of capital tend to simplify labour and even out its qualities downwards. This is one prediction which has been refuted by the facts, if not in relation to the direct operator of machines, then at least in relation to wage-earners as a whole. For just as the labour of the former has been simplified and deskilled, their number has fallen compared with technicians and engineers on the one hand, and administrative, commercial and accounting staff on the other. Thus Colin Clark, with Professor Melman as his authority, points out that the number of administrative staff per 100 workers employed in production, which in 1900 was 10 in the US and about 8 in England, had risen to 22 and 20 respectively by the 1950s.[13] Everything suggests that for a considerable period, in developed countries, the mass of abstract labour has been growing faster than the active population, and it is by no means clear that the product of both ratios is still below the rate of capital accumulation. If it is not, the premises of the law of the tendency of the rate of profit to fall disappear.

We cannot of course blame Marx for failing to foresee this situation. What he can be blamed for is completely neglecting this variable in his presentation, whilst his whole argument relies on the comparative rates of growth of living and dead labour. The complete absence of any explicit or implicit hypothesis, one way or the other, about the variations of this variable, has resulted in Marxists being unable to take it into account when the real situation changed, and thus explain the apparent lapse of the law.

Henri Denis believes that I am wrong to blame Marx for not taking account of growth in complex labour as a proportion of the overall mass of labour. If complex labour, he points out to me, produces more value in a given period, this is because its training costs are greater. But the training costs of a skilled worker ultimately only represent the part of his active life spent learning his trade, plus the part spent transmitting his knowledge to others. Assume, he says, that a skilled worker has lost one year learning his trade and that he will lose one more teaching it to his successor. Out of an active life of, say, 20 years, there will be 2 'unproductive' years. Marx thinks, Henri Denis continues, that the value created by this worker in each productive year should be increased by 2/18. Consequently, he concludes, 'if one considers the time-unit of a worker's twenty-year

13. *The Conditions of Economic Progress*, p. 372.

active life, a skilled worker creates exactly as much value as an unskilled worker'.

This is a substantial objection. In so far as the reduction coefficient is derived from the cost of training a worker, and it is difficult to see what else it can be derived from if it is to be given *ex ante*, growth in the proportion of complex labour is cancelled out by shortening of the population's *average* active life.

But while this argument is internally consistent, i.e. in the abstract and independently of Marx's statements, I do not think that these statements allow us to attribute it to Marx. To my knowledge, there is only one passage in *Capital* from which this thesis could – very indirectly – be deduced. It is to be found in chapter VII of volume I of the French edition supervised by Marx, and it goes as follows:

> Let us accept that the labour of a jeweller is more effective than that of a spinner, that the latter is simple labour and the former is complex labour, the manifestation of a power which is *more difficult to train* and produces more value in the same period of time.

With the best will in the world, and on the basis of this passage alone, it does not really seem possible to me to base this attribution on the four words that I have italicised, found in the middle of a thousand-page work.

In his *Critique of Political Economy*, Marx postponed till later the study of 'the laws governing this reduction'.[14] The proper place for this study was precisely volume I of *Capital*. It also happens that this volume is the only one which exists in its completed form and was published in Marx's lifetime. Any supposition that it was simply omitted can therefore be ruled out, especially since this is a fundamental point in the labour theory of value, indeed a point which is considered as the Achilles heel of this theory; and since a controversy had started around it, which preoccupied Marx, as can be seen from various passages in his works. It is, in these circumstances, rather excessive to think that this 'more-difficult-to-train', put in here as an attribute of a 'power', in a quite allusive way, is the fulfilment of Marx's promise in the *Critique* to present the laws that regulate this 'reduction'.

But there is another even more important consideration. The German text corresponding to the above passage is quite different.

> All labour of a higher or more complicated character than average labour is expenditure of labour-power of a more costly kind, labour-power whose production has cost more time and labour, and which therefore has a higher value, than unskilled or simple labour-power. This power being of a

14. *Critique of Political Economy*, p. 31.

higher value, its consumption is labour of a higher class, labour that creates in equal times proportionally higher values than unskilled labour does.[15]

Such a substantial difference between the German and French texts cannot be due to the translator. It is clearly Marx himself who replaced a longer analysis in more precise and quantitative terms, such as 'of a more costly kind', 'production (which) has cost more time and labour', 'proportionally higher values', with a much shorter sentence, containing a much more imprecise and qualitative expression. Now, if Marx wanted to say that the extra value of complex labour is equal to its specific production costs, the original German text would be much more satisfactory than the short French phrase, 'more difficult to train', which has no meaning.

We are therefore obliged to conclude that when Marx revised the French translation, he consciously preferred leaving the problem unsolved to maintaining his original idea, which seemed to indicate that the value of complex labour-power is simply the sum of two homogeneous quantities of simple labour: that necessary for its own reproduction and that necessary for its training. And with good reason. For it is clear that any such idea is contradicted by capitalist reality. If this sum were the regulating magnitude of the reduction scale, one hour of the labour of the most specialised engineer who requires the longest studies, would certainly be worth not more than, say, one-and-a-half hours of the labour of the least skilled labourer, roughly taking into account the time subtracted from his active life for his own training as well as the time spent on him by his masters. Our calculations are way out. Not only do statistics show the remuneration of this kind of engineer to be many more times that of a labourer than this calculation would suggest, but theory also tells us that this must be the case. In the logic of the capitalist system, it is clear that some one who devotes 10 years of his active life to studies aimed at raising him from the status of a labourer to that of a top-class engineer, will not be satisfied with receiving in the 30 remaining years of active life what a labourer receives in 40. He will at least demand a supplement to cover interest on the capital he had to spend on supporting himself for 10 years of studies. And since, in the capitalist system, any capital, small or large, has the right to proportional remuneration, he will get it.

This is where the problems really set in. Henri Denis notes that if we add such a supplement to the actual value of skilled labour-power, the essence of the labour theory of value will be changed. This is of course true. In fact, labour-power would in this case no longer be

15. *Capital,* vol. I, pp. 191–2. cf. *Le Capital,* vol. I, p. 749.

physically given since, to make it homogeneous, we are compelled to introduce the rate of profit, or rate of interest, a variable which depends in turn on distribution and prices. Given on the other hand that the rate of surplus value must be the same however skilled or unskilled the worker employed, this factor would have an effect on the mass of surplus value itself, so that the rate of profit, far from being determined by the rate of surplus value, would instead become one of its determinants.

The logical impasse is complete. But what is to be done? If we try to escape by following Henri Denis' suggestion that the value of labour-power, however skilled, is no greater than the labour needed for its training and reproduction, we will be obliged to consider everything earned by skilled workers above this sum as a gap between the price of labour-power and its value, a sort of conjunctural super-wage, which would make the surplus value extracted from these workers fall by an equal sum.

Apart from the fact that, on the basis of existing wage-scales, this calculation would soon lead to the emergence of negative surplus value, which must be at least mildly embarrassing, I wonder whether this solution does not lead us to slip into a normative perspective, whereas the task, in Marx's own term, is to study the 'laws of reduction', i.e. the laws of fuctioning of the capitalist system *as it actually exists*. Marx is referring to this real functioning of the system when he talks of a fact of 'experience', of a reduction 'which occurs every day', which is no 'analytical artifice' but a 'procedure practised every day in all corners of the globe'.

But in the capitalist system as it exists, the excess of an engineer's wage over that of a labourer, over and above the differences in their training costs, is no accidental super-wage which can be abstracted from, but something necessary for the system's proper functioning and equilibrium, which in its own right is therefore an integral part of the 'laws of reduction' which we are examining.

We cannot go any further into this problem here. The logical impasse which we have just noted considerably compromises the very status of labour-value under developed capitalist relations, and we have examined this question in other writings. (It is in order to rescue this status that Henri Denis has recourse to the strict application of 'training costs', and he is right, in the sense that this application does in fact seem necessary to this rescue attempt.)

How is it possible, quite apart from the question of growth of the working population, to measure or even concretise the rate of growth of the mass of abstract labour, without being blocked by the difficulties of this 'reduction' which Marx himself does not seem to have been able to surmount and, we should add, without becoming the prisoner of a certain apriorism of Marxist conceptualisation? It can be done by means of the *extra* growth of labour productivity attributable to this factor. For just as no one substitutes machines for hands just to produce the same output per worker as before, in the same way no-one substitutes brains for hands unless this will produce more output per worker than before, and even sufficiently more to compensate, not for the difference in 'training costs' borne by society, but for the difference in wages borne by the entrepreneur himself. Concrete-labour productivity is a function not only of the organic composition of capital, but also of the 'organic composition of labour'. It follows that the two rates, the growth of productivity per unit of labour and that of the quantity and quality of labour, combine into one single rate: the rate of growth of output.

From then on, Henri Denis's objection becomes a question of accounting units and does not affect the concrete final result. For, once output per unit of complex labour is given, if we reduce complex labour to simple labour in proportion to training time, as Henri Denis proposes, i.e. in such a way that the sum total of abstract labour grows no faster than the population, then we are ourselves reducing the quantity of labour expended for a given social product and, therefore, we are using a heavier and more productive unit of 'abstract' labour than if we effect the reduction on the basis of wage scales.

But then the increasing effect which we lose by the fact that the numerator, s, does not increase, since it too is calculated in 'heavy' units, is reintroduced elsewhere by the fact that the denominator, C, falls relatively through its conversion into these same units, or, in other words, by the fact that the greater present productivity of our unit of labour depreciates existing capital to a greater extent.

Let us assume that an engineer's training takes up half of his 40-year-long active life, while his wages are four times those of a labourer. Let us also suppose that the product of one year's labour by an engineer is also four times that of a labourer. Finally, let us assume that the rate of surplus value is 100%.

For a capital with a value of 200 units of past labour, we replace 40 years of labourer's living labour by 20 years of engineer's labour. Then, all other things being equal, reduction by wages gives us surplus value of 40 which, compared with the capital of 200, gives a rate of profit of 20%, whereas before the replacement this was 10%.

Reduction by training costs, as proposed by Henri Denis, would give us, after the replacement of labourers with engineers, surplus value of only 20, but the value of the *reproduction* of our capital by our present society of engineers is no longer 200, but only 100. The rate of profit is therefore again 20%, as in the first calculation[16] (see the table).

It is clear that the productivity of complex labour will not necessarily rise at a rate strictly proportional to the difference in wage-rates. In our example there is nothing to stop output per engineer-hour from being three times that of a labourer instead of four. But in this case the rate of surplus value itself will change. Instead of being 100%, it will be 50% in both calculations. In this case, productivity per 'heavy' unit of labour (H. Denis' method) will not increase by 100%, but by 50%, and the corresponding depreciation of capital will not be 50%, but 33⅓%. The value of capital will fall from 200 to 133⅓, and surplus value from 20 to 13⅓. The rate of profit will be 10%, the same as before the replacement of labourers with engineers.

On the other hand, productivity in 'light' labour units (A. Emmanuel's method), instead of staying the same, will fall by 25%. (The engineer's 20 years will produce 60 units of output instead of 80.) Then capital will appreciate from 200 to 266⅔. Since the 80 'light' units of living labour will be divided between 53⅓ for wages and 26⅔ for surplus value, the latter, compared to the new value of capital, will also give us 10%, exactly the same as with the earlier calculations based on training costs. (See the table).

So the 'quantity of labour' and 'labour productivity', whose definitions are more or less opaque and controversial, turn out to be useless detours which can be circumvented. What remains to be done is to compare the rate of growth of output with the rate of growth of capital; the ratio of these two rates will represent variations in the capital-output ratio, the only relevant magnitude for studying variations in the rate of profit, as the labour-output ratio turns out to be irrelevant.

It is now legitimate to consider that the two great aggregates, current output on the one hand and existing means of production (including stocks of workers' subsistence goods) on the other, have the same structure and, consequently, their value-ratio is the same whatever standard is used (labour-values or prices of production). So these two aggregates become commensurable, which is not the case when a given quantity of products is compared with a given quantity

16. Of course the depreciation of capital due to its reduction to 'heavy' labour units has nothing to do with its depreciation due to its own accumulation. This latter depreciation is the same in both methods of calculation, and is accordingly abstracted from here.

	Constant Capital		Labour-Power	Variable Capital		Surplus Value		Net Product		Rate of Surplus Value	Rate of Profit
	Vol *A*	*Val* *B*		*Vol* *C*	*Val* *D*	*Vol* *E*	*Val* *F*	*Vol* *C + E* *G*	*Vol* *D + F* *H*	*F/D*	*F/B*
Initial situation	200	200	40 labourer-years	20	20	20	20	40	40	100%	10%
I. Replacement of 40 labourer-years by 20 engineer-years receiving wages 4 times higher but producing 80 units of output instead of 40											
1. Reduction of complex labour to simple labour by training costs: 1 engineer = 2 labourers	200	100	20 engineer-years	40	20	40	20	80	40	100%	20%
2. *Idem*, by wage-ratios: 1 engineer = 4 labourers	200	200	20 engineer-years	40	40	40	40	80	80	100%	20%
II. *Idem*, producing 60 units											
1. Reduction by training costs: 1 engineer = 2 labourers	200	133⅓	20 engineer-years	40	26⅔	20	13⅓	60	40	50%	10%
2. Reduction by wage-ratios: 1 engineer = 4 labourers	200	266⅔	20 engineer-years	40	53⅓	20	26⅔	60	80	50%	10%

Note: Vol = volume; Val = Value

of labour of given quality. By means of the comparison of two bundles of goods with the same composition – and there is no particular reason why they should not have the same composition – the 'productivity' of capital, or output per unit of capital, becomes well-defined and measurable. The productivity of labour is neither well-defined nor measurable.[17]

If this is the case, then the problem of variations in the rate of profit has been made unnecessarily complex. If s, the mass of surplus value, is a given fraction of the value of current output, then variations of s/C are inversely proportional to the capital-output ratio. Any growth of output, whatever its source, whether simply through growth in the volume of employment or through improvement in its quality, i.e. whether through a rise in the quantity of concrete labour or a rise in the quantity of abstract labour, whatever the status of these concepts, or finally through growth of labour productivity, in either of its aspects, will have the effect of lowering the capital-output ratio and, consequently, raising the rate of profit. This effect may, depending on the case, reduce, cancel out, or reverse the opposite effect of the accumulation of capital. The problem of depreciation no longer arises, since it has the same effect on both the bundles of goods whose ratios we are interested in. If the two sub-bundles, c and v, depreciate at different rates, as Danjou assumes, the only *possible* result will be to affect, not the capital-output ratio, but the ratio of output to surplus value by means of a change in the real wage. If, as we assumed above, the ratio of output to surplus value is given, then this specific depreciation has already been taken into account.

We can now argue in terms of homogeneous quantities of one single commodity. Suppose that wheat is this universal commodity, representing all the system's inputs and outputs. If 1000 tons of wheat are enough to produce 200 more (after replacing the 1000 used up), for a given quantity and quality of labour, the capital-output ratio will be 5. If the rate of surplus value is 100%, the ratio of output to surplus value will be 2. The rate of profit will then be $1/5 \times 1/2 = 0.1 = 10\%$. If the capital-output ratio rises to 6, if, for example, 2000 tons of wheat do not produce 400 tons but $333\frac{1}{3}$ tons, then the rate of profit will fall to $1/6 \times 1/2 = 0.08333 = 8\frac{1}{3}\%$. On the other hand if the capital-output

17. In fact, to eliminate all measurement problems we have to assume that the *average* organic compositions of both capital and labour in the industries producing capital goods are equal to the corresponding social *averages*. Given the greatness of the number of commodities contained in either bundle and the erratic character of both compositions in the individual industries throughout and independently of the department to which each one of them belongs, this assumption is not illegitimate.

ratio falls, the rate of profit will rise. If Y represents output, K capital and p the rate of profit, we obtain:

$$p = \frac{Y}{K} \times \frac{s}{s+v}$$

Any growth in labour input, whether extensive or intensive – i.e. whether reflecting growth of the working population or growth of its average level of skill (organic composition of labour) – will produce a rise in Y, consequently a rise in the rate of profit. Because this growth affects Y, it can be calculated directly.

In this way all the concepts that cannot be measured or rigorously defined, such as the quantity of abstract labour (L), labour productivity (Y/L), and the organic composition of capital (K/L) are in a sense short-circuited, since

$$\frac{Y/L}{K/L} = \frac{Y}{K},$$

which does not prevent us from reintroducing them if we wish to establish the functional relations between them. For, as can be seen from the above identity, Y/K varies directly with labour productivity (Y/L) and inversely with the organic composition of capital (K/L), whatever the value of L. To sum up, L alone becomes immaterial since it is the common denominator of Y and K. In addition, if wages are given as an aliquot part of Y, then variations in Y/K become the same as variations in the rate of profit.

It is now not surprising that all the critiques of the law of the tendency of the rate of profit to fall inevitably end up by focusing on the output-capital ratio or its reciprocal, the capital-output ratio. Thus Serge Latouche, using Sraffa's model, reaches the same conclusion, although he commits the same error as Danjou, that of failing to take into account the growth of capital from one period to the next, through the incorporation of part of output.[18] Similarly, to refute Latouche's conclusions, Danjou is obliged to assume 'that 10% growth of inputs corresponds to 15% growth of output. . . .'[19] Since in Sraffa's model, to which the writer is referring, 'inputs' are the whole of capital, Danjou's hypothesis corresponds to a fall in the capital-output ratio. Besides, Bettelheim (as Danjou also notes)

18. cf. S. Latouche, À propos de la baisse tendancielle du taux de profit'.

19. Danjou, p. 62. See also this writer's remarks on pp. 62–3, especially that 'if one assumes a constant wage-rate, variations in the rate of profit depend solely on the physical yield of the production process'.

concludes that what can counteract the law and even lead to a rise in the rate of profit, is a fall in the volume and value 'of the means of production needed by a worker to produce a given physical output', which is nothing but a fall in the capital-output ratio.[20] The same conclusion also emerges from Y. Barel's analysis, since his 'capital coefficient', C/np, is again nothing but the capital-output ratio, as C is identical to K, and np identical to Y.[21]

How does this ratio vary in reality? It has always been accepted as obvious that the capital-output ratio grows without limit, and this does seem to have been true during the early stages of industrialisation, if only because (fixed) capital was starting its accumulation from a very low level, close to zero. Correspondingly, the evidence suggests that there was also a long period during which the rate of profit fell.

Incidentally, the hypothesis of a decreasing rate of growth of labour, productivity, which as we said earlier (p. 121) is generally accepted, is *identical* to the hypothesis of an increasing capital-output ratio which we are discussing here. What, after all, is the meaning of a decreasing rate of growth of labour productivity? It means that output per unit of labour is rising less than proportionally to capital per unit of labour. There is therefore a fall in output per unit of capital.

At the same time that signs began to emerge that the law was weakening, economists here and there began to discover cases with a falling capital-output ratio. Such a case finally emerges from Henri Denis' model based on 'new technology'.[22] As a by-product, such a situation also makes the factor-substitution problem disappear, since the new technique is, in this case, preferable to the old one at any level of wages, and Henri Denis' diagram, it seems to us, shows just such a 'perverse' case. This assertion must of course be toned down, since the cost of the new technique must also include the non-amortized part of the value of the scrapped old equipment. But it is true that in terms of the social capital-output ratio, the result is the same. For if the introduction of this new kind of technique became widespread, firms' calculations of moral depreciation (obsolescence) would adapt to the expected rate of innovation, and this extra depreciation, by increasing the value of output, would tend to lower the capital-output ratio.

I do not for my part believe that we have yet fully entered this

20. Bettelheim, 'Variations du taux de profit'.
21. 'Des Contradictions du capitalisme contemporain'.
22. H. Denis, 'Remarques sur l'étude de F. Danjou'.

stage. A whole host of labour-saving processes, already at the blueprint stage, or even in use in some industries or regions, are still unusable today in other industries or regions, for want of sufficiently high wages to make them profitable.[23] But do not these supposedly capital-saving new techniques involve employing, not more concrete workers, but more abstract workers, for a given capital? In other words, do they not precisely imply a rise in the organic composition of labour, so that the fall in the organic composition of capital resulting from these techniques is only the result of this rise of the denominator?

If this were so, then Marx's expression c/v would once again be meaningful, once it is recognised that wage-scales are the scale of reduction of concrete (complex) to simple (abstract) labour – and, of course, that the rate of surplus value does not vary. Is this recognition not implicit anyway in Marx's repeated declarations about this reduction: 'This reduction appears to be an abstraction, but it is an abstraction which is practised every day . . .', 'experience shows that this reduction is constantly being made', 'what they ('orthodox economists') deride as an analytical artifice is quite plainly a procedure practised every day in all corners of the globe', etc.? It is tempting to reply in the affirmative, since what is actually practised every day is nothing but an equilibrium wage scale for labour-power of varying levels of skill. In this case c/v really would become a composite index of the quantity of living labour and its quality (still on the assumption of a given rate of surplus value). This would be a very useful index, since it would replace abstract ideas with something concrete and measurable. With this approach it would be easy to sidestep Danjou's objection concerning the financial turnover of variable capital, by accepting that v represents the sum of workers' annual pay, whatever the size of the funds immobilised for the sake of this pay.

In this case, however, these 'new techniques' would not strictly speaking be labour-intensive, but wages-intensive, in the sense that they really make the capital coefficient fall, not per worker but per unit of wages. This suggests that Leontief's observation might no longer appear as a paradox, since not only US exports, but the whole US domestic product, would tend to become wages-intensive.

23. Even in the most advanced countries, where wages have long been high, every day sees the invention and application of technology which, while 'new', is nonetheless capital-using and not in the least capital-saving. For example, automatic ticket machines on buses and the underground are certainly 'new technology'. Despite this, they raise the capital-output ratio, since they increase fixed capital without any rise in output (the number of bus or underground passengers).

In this light, Marx's formula would once more be correct. The reason why, by all the evidence, the rate of profit is no longer falling, say, since the last war, or that it is even rising, is that even for a constant rate of surplus value, the growth of the denominator v is faster than that of the numerator c, not only through growth in the number of workers, but even more through a rise in their level of skills, and thus a rise in average wages per worker.

This still leaves no law of a falling or rising rate of profit. There is a theorem of *variations* in the rate of profit, which identifies what factors make it fall and what factors make it rise. Depending on which factors turn out to be preponderant, there will be a fall or a rise. Marx's error lies in asserting that the former *necessarily* outweigh the latter, i.e. in turning the theorem into a 'law'.[24]

24. Here is a typical passage: 'Considered abstractly the rate of profit may remain the same, even though the price of the individual commodity may fall as a result of greater productiveness of labour and a simultaneous increase in the number of this cheaper commodity if, for instance, the increase in productiveness of labour acts uniformly and simultaneously on all the elements of the commodity, so that its total price falls in the same proportion in which the productivity of labour increases, while, on the other hand, the mutual relation of the different elements of the price of the commodity remains the same. The rate of profit could even rise if a rise in the rate of surplus value were accompanied by a substantial reduction in the value of the elements of constant, and particularly of fixed, capital. But *in reality*, as we have seen, the rate of profit *will fall* in the long run.' (*Capital*, vol. III, chapter XIII, p. 230, emphasis added).

Finally we should point out that the most accurate and notable passages of Danjou's article already referred to, are when he criticises this approach of Marx's. It is unfortunate that he goes on to verge on the same mistake by talking of a *tendency* to *rise*, which is just another word for a 'law', though in the opposite direction.

Appendix II
Working Periods and Periods of Circulation

After presenting Marx's various tables of the rotation of capital, Engels writes:

> The presentation of this chapter for publication presented no small number of difficulties. Firmly grounded as Marx was in algebra, he did not get the knack of handling figures, particularly commercial arithmetic, although there exists a thick batch of copybooks containing numerous examples of all kinds of commercial computations which he had solved himself. But knowledge of the various methods of calculation and exercise in daily practical commercial artithmetic are by no means the same, and consequently Marx got so tangled up in his computations that besides places left uncompleted a number of things were incorrect and contradictory. In the tables reproduced above I have preserved only the simplest and arithmetically most correct data. My reason for doing so was mainly the following:
>
> No matter what may be the ratio between the working period and circulation time, hence between capital I and capital II, there is returned to the capitalist, in the form of money, after the end of the first turnover and thereafter at regular intervals equal to the duration of one working period, the capital required for one working period, i.e., a sum equal to capital I.
>
> If the working period is 5 weeks, the circulation time 4 weeks, and capital I £500, then a sum of money equal to £500 returns each time at the end of the 9th, 14th, 19th, 24th, 29th week, etc.
>
> If the working period is 6 weeks, the circulation time 3 weeks, and capital I £600, then £600 are returned at the end of the 9th, 15th, 21st, 27th, 33rd week, etc.
>
> Lastly, if the working period is 4 weeks, the circulation time 5 weeks, and capital I £400, then £400 are returned at the end of the 9th, 13th, 17th, 21st, 25th week, etc.
>
> Whether any, and *if* so how much, of this returned money is superfluous and thus released for the current working period is immaterial. It is assumed that production continues uninterruptedly on the current scale, and in order that this may come about money must be available and must therefore return, whether 'released' or not. If production is interrupted, release stops likewise.
>
> In other words: There is indeed a release of money, a formation therefore of latent, merely potential, capital in the form of money. But it takes place under all circumstances and not only under the special conditions set forth in the text. So far as circulating capital I is concerned, the industrial capitalist is in the same situation at the end of each turnover as when he established his business: he has all of it in his hands in one bulk, while he can convert it back into productive capital only gradually.[1]

1. *Capital*, vol. II, pp. 287–8.

Engels is right to be irritated with Marx's confused and overelaborate style of presenting his numerical examples, but he is wrong to believe that Marx made a mistake in his calculations. Engels simply did not notice an essential, but tacit, assumption in Marx's calculations and tables: Marx divides the two periods, working and circulation, into weeks, but despite this division he assumes that the whole circulating capital needed for one cycle of production must be disposable and enter production *in one single payment* from the first day of the cycle, whatever the number of weeks of the working period. Engels, on the contrary, assumes that this same capital is used in equal fractions, with as many payments as there are weeks. Here is a clearer presentation of the four cases put forward by Marx:

Case I
The circulation period equal to the working period
Duration of one period: 3 weeks
Circulating capital needed for each cycle of production: 30

Total capital employed: 60

Date	*Operation*	*Disposable money (released)*	*Capital employed in production*	*Capital employed in circulation* I	II	III	IV	*Totals*
1 Jan	Initial capital	+60						60
1 Jan	Advance of 30	−30	30					
1 Jan	Balance	30	30					60
22 Jan	Completion and start of circulation of 1st product		−30	+30				
22 Jan	Advance of 30	−30	+30					
22 Jan	Balance	0	+30	+30				60
12 Feb	Completion and start of circulation of 2nd product		−30		+30			
12 Feb	Collection of price of 1st product and advance of corresponding money-capital		+30	−30				
12 Feb	Balance	0	+30	0	+30			60

12 Feb	Balance	0	+30	0	+30			60
5 Mar	Completion and start of circulation of 3rd product		−30			+30		
5 Mar	Collection of price of 2nd product and advance of corresponding money-capital		+30		−30			
5 Mar	Balance	0	+30	0	0	+30		60
26 Mar	Completion and start of circulation of 4th product		−30				+30	
26 Mar	Collection of price of 2nd product and advance of corresponding money-capital		+30			−30		
26 Mar	Balance	0	+30	0	0	0	+30	60

Result in conformity with Marx's conclusions: in this case I, there is no disposable ('released') money-capital after the end of the second cycle.

Case II

Circulation period longer than, but an integer multiple of, working period
Working period: 3 weeks
Circulation period: 6 weeks
Circulating capital needed for each cycle of production: 30

Total capital employed: 90

Date	*Operation*	*Disposable money (released)*	*Capital employed in production*	*Capital employed in circulation* *I*	*II*	*III*	*IV*	*Totals*
1 Jan	Initial capital	+90						90
1 Jan	Advance of 30	−30	30					
1 Jan	Balance	+60	+30					90

Continued on following page

1 Jan	Balance	+60	+30					90
22 Jan	Completion and start of circulation of 1st product		−30	+30				
22 Jan	Advance of 30	−30	+30					
22 Jan	Balance	+30	+30	+30				90
12 Feb	Completion and start of circulation of 2nd product		−30		+30			
12 Feb	Advance of 30	−30	+30					
12 Feb	Balance	0	+30	+30	+30			90
5 Mar	Completion and start of circulation of 3rd product		−30			+30		
5 Mar	Collection of price of 1st product and advance of corresponding money-capital		+30	−30				
5 Mar	Balance	0	+30	0	+30	+30		90
26 Mar	Completion and start of circulation of 4th product		−30				+30	
26 Mar	Collection of price of 2nd product and advance of corresponding money-capital		+30		−30			
26 Mar	Balance	0	30	0	0	30	30	90

Result again in conformity with Marx's conclusions: in this case II, there is no disposable ('released') money-capital after the end of the third cycle.

Case III

Circulation period longer than, but not an integer multiple, of working period
Working period: 3 weeks
Circulation period: 5 weeks
Circulating capital needed for each cycle of production: 30

Total capital employed: 90

Date	*Operation*	*Disposable money (released)*	*Capital employed in production*	*Capital employed in circulation* I	II	III	IV	*Totals*
1 Jan	Initial capital	+90						90
1 Jan	Advance of 30	−30	+30					
1 Jan	Balance	+60	+30					90
22 Jan	Completion and start of circulation of 1st product		−30	+30				
22 Jan	Advance of 30	−30	+30					
22 Jan	Balance	+30	+30	+30				90
12 Feb	Completion and start of circulation of 2nd product		−30		+30			
12 Feb	Advance of 30	−30	+30					
12 Feb	Balance	0	+30	+30	+30			90
26 Feb	Collection of price of 1st product	+30		−30				
26 Feb	Balance	+30	+30	0	+30			90
5 Mar	Completion and start of circulation of 3rd product		−30			+30		
5 Mar	Advance of 30	−30	+30					
5 Mar	Balance	0	+30	0	+30	+30		90
19 Mar	Collection of price of 2nd product	+30			−30			
19 Mar	Balance	+30	+30	0	0	+30		90
26 Mar	Completion and start of circulation of 4th product		−30				+30	
26 Mar	Advance of 30	−30	+30					
26 Mar	Balance	0	+30	0	0	+30	+30	90

In conformity with Marx's conclusions, money-capital of 30 is released intermittently in this case and is disposable between the eighth and ninth weeks, then between the eleventh and the twelfth, and so on.

Case IV
Circulation period shorter than the working period
Working period: 6 weeks
Circulation period: 3 weeks
Circulating capital needed for each cycle of production: 30

Total capital employed: 60

Date	*Operation*	*Disposable money (released)*	*Capital employed in production*	*Capital employed in circulation* I	II	III	IV	*Totals*
1 Jan	Initial capital	+60						60
1 Jan	Advance of 30	−30	+30					
1 Jan	Balance	+30	+30					60
12 Feb	Completion and start of circulation of 1st product		−30	+30				
12 Feb	Advance of 30	−30	+30					
12 Feb	Balance	0	+30	+30				60
5 Mar	Collection of price of 1st product	+30		−30				
5 Mar	Balance	+30	+30	0				60
26 Mar	Completion and start of circulation of 2nd product		−30		+30			
26 Mar	Advance of 30	−30	+30					
26 Mar	Balance	0	+30	0	+30			60

16 Apr	Collection of price of 2nd product	+30			−30			
16 Apr	Balance	+30	+30	0	0			60
7 May	Completion and start of circulation of 3rd product		−30			+30		
7 May	Advance of 30	−30	+30					
7 May	Balance	0	+30	0	0	+30		60
28 May	Collection of price of 3rd product	+30				−30		
28 May	Balance	+30	+30	0	0	0		60
18 June	Completion and start of circulation of 4th product		−30				+30	
18 June	Advance of 30	−30	+30					
18 June	Balance	0	+30	0	0	0	+30	60

Results again in conformity with Marx's conclusions: there is an intermittent release of money-capital, which is periodically available, between the fifth and twelfth weeks, between the fifteenth and eighteenth, and between the twenty-first and twenty-fourth.

Despite the clumsiness of his calculations, Marx is therefore correct under his assumptions. Contrary to Engels' view, money is not released *under all circumstances*. In cases I and II above, there is no release. The return of each money-capital coincides with the end of a labour-period and the start of the next. This makes it possible to apply it to production immediately. On the other hand in cases III and IV the money returns *between* times. It therefore lies idle between the date of its return and the date of the start of a new cycle of production. In no case is the capitalist 'in the same situation at the end of each turnover as when he established his business', as Engels says.

How was Engels able to make such a remark? It is because, unlike Marx, he assumes the capital is mobilised in weekly sums, probably influenced by the fact that this is the way that wages are paid. So his argument is true on this assumption, but only on this assumption. Let us return to cases I and II above – the only cases in dispute – but with the introduction of weekly payments:

Case I

The circulation period equal to the working period, 3 weeks

Circulating capital needed for each cycle of production: 30

Date	Operation	*Disposable capital (released)*	*Capital employed in production*	*Capital employed in circulation* I	II	III	IV	*Totals*
1 Jan	Initial capital	+60						+60
1 Jan	Advance of 10	−10	+10					
8 Jan	Advance of 10	−10	+10					
15 Jan	Advance of 10	−10	+10					
15 Jan	Balance	+30	+30					60
22 Jan	Completion of 1st product		−30	+30				
22 Jan	Advance of 10	−10	+10					
22 Jan	Balance	+20	+10	+30				60
29 Jan	Advance of 10	−10	+10					
5 Feb	Advance of 10	−10	+10					
5 Feb	Balance	0	+30	+30				60
12 Feb	Completion of 2nd product		−30		+30			
12 Feb	Collection of price of 1st product	+30		−30				
12 Feb	Advance of 10	−10	+10					
12 Feb	Balance	**+20**	+10	0	+30			60
19 Feb	Advance of 10	−10	+10					
26 Feb	Advance of 10	−10	+10					
26 Feb	Balance	0	+30	0	+30			60
5 Mar	Completion of 3rd product		−30			+30		
5 Mar	Collection of price of 2nd product	+30			−30			
5 Mar	Advance of 10	−10	+10					
5 Mar	Balance	**+20**	+10	0	0	+30		60
12 Mar	Advance of 10	−10	+10					
19 Mar	Advance of 10	−10	+10					
19 Mar	Balance	0	+30	0	0	+30		60

26 Mar	Completion of 4th product		−30				+30	
26 Mar	Collection of price of 3rd product	+30				−30		
26 Mar	Advance of 10	−10	+10					
26 Mar	Balance	**+20**	+10	0	0	0	+30	60

Here capital does lie idle between 12 and 26 February, between 5 and 19 March, etc.

Case II
Circulation period longer than, but an integer multiple of, working period
Working period: 3 weeks
Circulation period: 6 weeks

Date	*Operation*	*Disposable capital (released)*	*Capital employed in production*	*Capital employed in circulation* I	II	III	IV	*Totals*
1 Jan	Initial capital	+90						90
1 Jan	Advance of 10	−10	+10					
8 Jan	Advance of 10	−10	+10					
15 Jan	Advance of 10	−10	+10					
15 Jan	Balance	+60	+30					90
22 Jan	Completion of 1st product		−30	+30				
22 Jan	Advance of 10	−10	+10					
22 Jan	Balance	+50	+10	+30				90
29 Jan	Advance of 10	−10	+10					
5 Feb	Advance of 10	−10	+10					
5 Feb	Balance	+30	+30	+30				90
12 Feb	Completion of 2nd product		−30		+30			
12 Feb	Advance of 10	−10	+10					
12 Feb	Balance	+20	+10	+30	+30			90
19 Feb	Advance of 10	−10	+10					
26 Feb	Advance of 10	−10	+10					
26 Feb	Balance	0	+30	+30	+30			90

Continued on following page

26 Feb	Balance	0	+30	+30	+30			90
5 Mar	Completion of 3rd product		−30			+30		
5 Mar	Collection of price of 1st product	+30		−30				
5 Mar	Advance of 10	−10	+10					
5 Mar	Balance	**+20**	+10	0	+30	+30		90
12 Mar	Advance of 10	−10	+10					
19 Mar	Advance of 10	−10	+10					
19 Mar	Balance	0	+30	0	+30	+30		90
26 Mar	Completion of 4th product		−30				+30	
26 Mar	Collection of price of 2nd product	+30			−30			
26 Mar	Advance of 10	−10	+10					
26 Mar	Balance	**+20**	+10	0	0	+30	+30	90

Here again, Engels' hypothesis of staggered payments leads to the emergence of idle money-capital between 5 and 19 March, 26 March and 9 April, etc.

4 Marxist Views on Overproduction Crises

Lenin's analysis

From the outset, in a sweeping schematisation, Lenin distinguishes between two kinds of theory: 'the former explains crises by underconsumption . . ., the latter by the anarchy of production'.[1] Relying on Marx's writings, he naturally rejects the former.

Sismondi is wrong, Lenin says, to attribute crises to the discrepancy between production in general and final consumption, for 'it is precisely in the periods which precede crises that the workers' consumption rises, [and] underconsumption (to which crises are allegedly due) existed under the most diverse economic systems, whereas crises are the distinguishing feature of only one system – the capitalist system'.[2]

Lenin's second argument, that underconsumption exists under the most diverse economic systems, has no meaning at all. Since underconsumption can only be a relative notion, it is difficult to see in relation to what there can be underconsumption in a non-commodity system. In contrast, the first one, borrowed from Marx, is relevant but debatable. Rodbertus, in his letters to Kirchmann, challenged it strongly. He pointed out that what counts is not the level of wages, but their mass as a proportion of the total social product. The period of wage increases that precedes crises is also a period of considerable growth of production. So despite these wage increases, it is quite possible for the sum of wage-earners' incomes to diminish *relative* to the overall value of output.[3]

Of course, one could object that production can only increase during a boom through an increase in employment. It is this increase which makes the mass of wages rise. If wage rates were to remain constant, wages and profits – the two components of value added – would increase, all other things being equal, in the same proportion, and each of them would remain constant relative to production. If wages rise, at the same time as employment grows, the rate of profit

1. 'A characterisation of economic romanticism', *Collected Works*, vol. II, p. 167.
2. *Ibid.*
3. Jean Lescure accepts this thesis and even calls it 'decisive'. *Des Crises générales et périodiques de surproduction*, pp. 483–484.

must fall, which means that in this case, whatever the rise in wage rates, their mass grows more than proportionally to the mass of profits and to that of production.

This seems also to be Marx's position when he himself, making a comparison in the same relative terms as those advocated by Rodbertus, found that in the period before the crisis, 'the working class actually gets a larger share of that part of the annual product which is intended for consumption'.[4]

This, however, rests on the implicit classical assumption of increasing costs. To the extent that the growth of employment is obtained by using idle capacity in the existing units of production rather than by establishing new ones or by adding new equipment to the old ones, unit costs may fall instead of rising following the rise in wages. Furthermore, the increase in turnover can even make a certain rise of unit costs compatible with a rise (instead of a fall) of the rate and mass of profit and end up with the relative under-consumption of the working class noted by Rodbertus, possibly aggravated by the Keynesian law of the increasing propensity to save as income grows. Anyway, reality seems, on this point, to validate Rodbertus' thesis. Not only are the rate and mass of profit at their peak on the eve of crises, despite the rise in wages, but – which is more directly significant for the consumption/production argument – inventories are likewise inflated, as Marx himself notes when examining the immediate causes of the crash.

Be this as it may, after unequivocally rejecting under-consumption, Lenin had to content himself with the second kind of theory, which explains crises by the anarchy of production. Lenin unreservedly accepts this factor as the true expression of the fundamental contradiction between social production and private appropriation. '"Anarchy of production", "unplanned production" – what do these expressions tell us? They tell us about the contradiction between the social character of production and the individual character of appropriation.'[5] The independence of the producers and the autonomous and individual character of their choices are likely to lead to a lack of correspondence between the composition of the social product in terms of use-values and the structure of needs.

> Capitalist production cannot develop otherwise than by leaps and bounds – two steps forward and one step (and sometimes two) back. As we have already said, capitalist production is production for sale, the production of commodities for the market. Production is conducted by individual capitalists, each producing on his own and none of them able to say exactly

4. *Capital*, vol. II, p. 415.
5. 'A characterisation of economic romanticism', *Collected Works*, vol. II, p. 171.

what kind and what amount of commodities will be required on the market. Production is carried on haphazardly; each producer is concerned only in excelling the others. Quite naturally, therefore, the quantity of commodities produced *may* not correspond to the market demand.[6]

I italicised the word 'may' in this quotation. In fact, we are here dealing with a mere possibility, and what is envisaged is an ordinary general disproportion between any kinds of industry. But Lenin did not let mattters rest here. It is not this disproportion, the fruit of anarchy of production and the absence of a plan, which leads to overproduction crises in a necessary way and as a clear tendency. Lenin makes a clear distinction between the possible and the necessary, referring to Engels' pithy saying: 'Crises are possible, because the producer does not know the extent of demand; they are necessary, because the collective character of production comes into contradiction with the individual character of appropriation.'

Crises are inherent in the system, not because of anarchy considered as the absence of something (a plan), but because of a positively disequilibrating factor, engendered by the tendency towards maximisation of the rate of profit, and thus towards relative stagnation of wages, occurring together with extended reproduction as a result of the capitalisation of these same profits; this is not an arbitrary disproportion between industries, occurring because 'the producer does not know the extent of demand'; it is a specific disproportion between accumulation and final consumption.

So in the end, underconsumption does emerge as the basic cause of over-production crises, but in the specific sense of a disproportion between the consumption of Department I goods and the consumption of Department II goods. '[A] definite condition of consumption is one of the elements of proportionality.'[7]

'In actual fact', Lenin continues, 'the analysis of realization showed that the formation of a home market for capitalism owes less to articles of consumption than to means of production. From this it follows that Department I of social production (the production of means of production) can and must develop more rapidly than Department II (the production of articles of consumption). Obviously, it does not follow from this that the production of means of production can develop *in complete independence* of the production of articles of consumption and *outside of all connection with it*.'[8]

6. Lenin, 'The lessons of the crisis', *Collected Works*, vol. V, p. 90.
7. 'A note on the question of the market theory', *Collected Works*, vol. IV, pp. 58–9.
8. *Ibid.*, p. 59.

Increases in the organic composition and the growth of production
The 'connection' in question concerns the organic composition of capital, in the sense that: (i) the relation between the quantities produced in Department I and II also expresses the organic composition of the total social capital; (ii) a rise in the organic composition reflects the application of technical progress to production, which tends to be generalised and affects both Departments; and (iii) this rise, wherever it may occur, leads to an increase of productivity and, for a given quantity of factors, to an increase of production.

Lenin interprets Marx's ideas correctly, but, like him and even more than him (since Marx only considers this question as *one* source of disequilibrium among several, whereas Lenin bases his entire theory of crises on this, to the exclusion of all others), he fails to notice one point: a rise in the organic composition of capital does not necessarily lead to increased output per unit of capital, but rather to increased output per unit of labour. Consequently, as the result of technical progress and growth of the organic composition, it is theoretically possible to use more constant capital than before in a given industry or Department, in order to produce less output than before. Everything depends on the quantity of labour-power used in the industry or Department under consideration before and after the introduction of the new technique. The condition laid down in (iii) above, that the quantity of factors per department is constant, is not satisfied and cannot be so, precisely because of the rise in the organic composition. This condition cannot be abstracted from, on the pretext of isolating the effects of the rise in organic composition, since it itself is affected by this rise.

It is true that exchange between Department I producers cannot continue indefinitely in a closed circuit. They must 'in the end' (Lenin) pass on to Department II, and then they have to confront the 'narrow base' of unproductive consumption which does not keep up with the rate of accumulation. But despite this, we are not entitled to say that these operations are objectively blocked at this point. New Bessemer converters will make more steel, out of which new machine tools will be made, which will be used to produce improved looms. These looms must certainly then be used to make textiles. But it is not true to say that these looms will *necessarily* produce more textiles than was previously produced. It is perfectly possible that the same quantity of textiles is now produced by fewer workers than before, or even that a smaller quantity of textiles is produced by a workforce reduced more than proportionally to the fall in the output of textiles.

What is required from a new technique using relatively more

constant capital than the old one is an increase in output per unit of labour (output–labour ratio), failing which the new technique is not worthwhile from any point of view, whatever the social relations of production. An increase in output per unit of capital (output–capital ratio), while possible under certain circumstances, is not required. On the contrary, experience has shown that this latter ratio generally falls. This continuous fall is one of Marx's own implicit assumptions in his formulation of the law of the tendency of the rate of profit to fall, since otherwise the rate at which existing constant capital decreases in value would be greater than the rate of formation of new capitals, and the rate of profit, in terms of Marx's other assumptions and within the framework of his model, would rise instead of fall.

Let us assume that a bulldozer is equal in value to ten thousand spades. This does not mean that one worker operating this bulldozer can move as much earth as, or more earth than, ten thousand workers each using a spade. He may, and in fact does, move considerably less. The bulldozer is nonetheless economically viable. Tugan Baranovski does not seem to go that far when saying that the capitalist system can reproduce itself without crises by producing more and more iron and coal in order to make more coal and iron. The system can do that of course. But it can do far more than that. To the extent that 'iron and coal' means all intermediate, Department I, goods, the system is, at least technically, capable of using more and more of them in Department II, but still without producing more consumer goods there, thus producing more coal and iron and more power-looms, tractors, concrete-mixers, builders' hoists, etc., without necessarily producing more textiles, wheat or housing, quite simply – by transferring workers from textile mills, farms and building-sites into metallurgy and machine construction. It goes without saying that in cases where the new technique increases not only the output–labour ratio but also the output–capital ratio, what Baranovski suggested may well occur. Since an increase in the organic composition implies relative, not absolute, growth of constant capital, this increase may, even in these cases, be compatible with a fall in Department II's output in absolute terms. For this to occur, as well as certain quantities of labour, certain (smaller) quantities of capital must be transferred from this Department to Department I.[9]

9. We are not venturing any opinion here on whether what is mathematically, materially possible is also possible on the level of investment incentives, i.e. whether it is possible for a capitalist to start producing improved power-looms at a time when textiles consumption is falling or stagnant. In some cases this is not impossible. Thus

Continued on page 150

Transfers of factors between departments

The key to the problem is therefore the possibility of transfers of factors from Department II to Department I. Technical progress and an increase in the organic composition, if generalised – and there is no reason for them not to be – necessarily imply this transfer. For the relative fall in variable capital compared to constant capital in both Departments must necessarily be reflected in a *relative* fall in Department II's output compared to that of Department I.

Unfortunately, Marx did not leave us any scheme showing an increase of the organic composition. In his extended reproduction schemes, the two Departments sometimes have the same organic composition and sometimes different organic compositions, but for each Department taken on its own, and thus for society as a whole, the organic composition remains the same from one period to the next. In the course of successive realizations, the only relations between the Departments are trading exchanges, which are settled accordingly, i.e. on the basis of equivalence. Both Marx and all those who have used his reproduction schemes have always argued as if the two Departments were two shopkeepers who have to settle their mutual accounts without any debit or credit, as if there were some compelling equilibrium to be respected in the balance of inter-departmental transactions – this much I*v* + this much I*s* against that much II*c*, etc. Any unilateral transfer between the Departments is strictly ruled out. The idea that a textiles magnate may use his profits, not to purchase new textiles machinery and expand his mill, but to purchase shares in a chemical, metallurgical or electronics factory, and that this is what he generally does if textiles are saturated, is not allowed to disturb these analyses. Capital and men are immobile; they are prisoners within the frontiers of each Department; they accumulate and multiply on the spot. From year to year, variable capital grows at exactly the same rate as constant capital. On the assumption of constant wages, this implies that the active population grows at exactly the same rate as the accumulation of capital. If wages are allowed to vary, then it is the algebraic product of these two variations – of wages and of the population – that must be equal to the growth of constant capital.

9. *Continued from page 149*
over the last few decades new and heavier technology has been introduced in grain production and coal mining, while in most developed countries the production of both is relatively stagnant. We are not concerned with this question here. What we are trying to show in this chapter is that there is no *material* link, no constraint on the ratio of personal consumption to the production of means of production.

In this respect, the schemes contradict the most fundamental hypothesis of the whole of Marx's works, and this peculiarity can only be explained by seeing that the schemes are an incomplete rough draft, worked out for methodological reasons, to be completed later by a second which would reflect reality, i.e. which would take account of the growth of the organic composition of social capital as a whole. The case Marx dealt with would then be that of extensive extended reproduction; and the case not dealt with, that of intensive extended reproduction.

However this may be, the situation has led to a serious gap in most Marxists' thoughts. It would have been childishly simple to infer the missing scheme from the existing schemes and from Marx's other analyses, and to settle the question once and for all. But the gospel must not be tampered with. The faithful feel a kind of inhibition faced with the sacred text; what Marx did not set out in black and white, no one is allowed to write.[10]

This argument runs as follows: as concerns the theoretical possibility of realization of the social product, it's the accepted schemes or nothing. The schemes certainly show that the product *may* be realized without any problems, but the assumptions of these schemes do not reflect reality. Now if a different scheme, stripped of these assumptions, could have proved this same *possibility*, Marx would surely have written it. Since he did not write it, this must be because it does not exist. Therefore, in reality, the product *cannot* be realized without crises. Since, on the other hand, economic crises do in fact occur, in reality, there is nothing more to be said, and the page can be turned.[11]

10. Apart from the two rather unsatisfactory attempts by Lenin and Tugan Baranovski which we shall examine further on, there are to the best of our knowledge only two Marxist theoreticians who have produced genuinely consistent schemes of *extended intensive reproduction:* Otto Bauer, in his critique of Rosa Luxemburg's theory, which we shall also examine further on, and Charles Bettelheim in his *Problèmes théoriques et pratiques de la planification*.

11. Despite her critical spirit and purpose, it was in essence reasoning of this kind which led Rosa Luxemburg, as we shall see later on, to conlude that it is impossible for surplus-value to be realised in a closed system. But still more characteristic of this approach is the following sentence from Jean Duret: 'It is enough (sic) for us to point out that, *even* in Marx's schemes, where growth of the organic composition of capital is not taken into account, equilibrium presupposes the continual growth of consumption.' (*Le Marxisme et les crises*, p. 109.)

We have italicised the word 'even' because it is in this word that we find a concentrated expression of the error of the Luxemburgist and great Marxist that was Jean Duret. It is *because* the growth of the organic composition is not taken into account that Marx's schemes produce a continuous rise in consumption which does not reflect the reality of capitalism.

Lenin's extended reproduction scheme

However, Lenin saw the gap in Marx's reproduction schemes quite clearly, and even tried to plug it:

> From Marx's scheme . . . the conclusion cannot be drawn that Department I predominates over Department II: both develop on parallel lines. But that scheme does not take technical progress into consideration. As Marx proved in Volume I of *Capital*, technical progress is expressed by the gradual decrease of the ratio of variable capital to constant capital (v/c), whereas in the scheme it is taken as unchanged. It goes without saying that if this change is made in the scheme there will be a relatively more rapid increase in means of production than in articles of consumption.[12]

Lenin takes a step towards intensive extended reproduction by modifying Marx's schemes to allow the organic composition of both Departments to increase from cycle to cycle. This is shown in the table.

	Marx's scheme				*Lenin's scheme*[13]			
	c	*v*	*s*	*V*	*c*	*v*	*s*	*V*
I	4000 +	1000 +	1000 =	6000	4000	+ 1000 +	1000 =	6000
	1500 +	750 +	750 =	3000	1500	+ 750 +	750 =	3000
	5500 +	1750 +	1750 =	9000	5500	+ 1750 +	1750 =	9000
II	4400 +	1100 +	1100 =	6600	4450	+ 1050 +	1050 =	6550
	1600 +	800 +	800 =	3200	1550	+ 760 +	760 =	3070
	6000 +	1900 +	1900 =	9800	6000	+ 1810 +	1810 =	9620
III	4840 +	1210 +	1210 =	7260	4950	+ 1075 +	1075 =	7100
	1760 +	880 +	880 =	3520	1602	+ 766 +	766 =	3134
	6600 +	2090 +	2090 =	10 780	6552	+ 1841 +	1841 =	10 234
IV	5324 +	1331 +	1331 =	7986	5467½	+ 1095 +	1095 =	7657½
	1936 +	968 +	968 =	3872	1634½	+ 769 +	769 =	3172½
	7260 +	2299 +	2299 =	11 858	7102	+ 1864 +	1864 =	10 830[13]

But this scheme of Lenin's is clearly based on completely artificial and arbitrary assumptions. The first period is identical to that of Marx's scheme. The organic compositions (c/v) of the two Departments differ. At the start, this is 4 in Department I and 2 in Department II. Over the following periods, the organic composition of social capital as a whole remains unchanged in Marx's scheme. So does the gap between the two Departments, 4:2. It rises constantly in Lenin's scheme, which is welcome, since this constitutes a step towards intensive extended reproduction which we mentioned above. But, at the same time as the organic composition of the whole economy rises, the gap between the two Departments grows. In the second period, the organic composition of Department I increases by about 6%; that of Department II, by about 2%. In the third period, they increase by over 8% and about 2¼% respectively. In the fourth period, by around 9% for Department I and less than 1% for Department II.

It could just be allowed that this disparity is due to the respective technical conditions of the two Departments. But the way in which it is obtained is unacceptable: the capitalists of Department I regularly save and capitalise exactly half their surplus-value each year; not only do those of Department II save and capitalise a considerably smaller proportion, but this proportion decreases from year to year, and its rate of decrease varies without rhyme or reason. The first year, these capitalists save only 8% of their surplus-value; the second year, around 7.6%; the third year, a mere 4.6%. At the same time, Department I capitalists, all good family men, only consume half their income and make the other half bear fruit, while Department II capitalists are inexplicably prodigal.

Such a distinction in the personal behaviour of capitalists and in their propensity to save according to whether their enterprises belong to Department I or II is absurd. It might be assumed, at least in theory, that the structure of technical progress leads to a higher than average organic composition in the industries producing means of production and one lower than average in all the rest. This is already a very strong assumption, since there is nothing to suggest that this is really the case. But there can be no reason, whether theoretical or

12. *Collected Works*, vol. I, p. 85.

13. In the third and fourth periods, Lenin made a slight error of calculation of 2 units, which does not affect the meaning of his schemes in the least. Here are these two periods with the error removed:

III $4950\ c + 1075\ v + 1075\ s = 7100\ V$
$1600\ c + 766\ v + 766\ s = 3132\ V$
IV $5467\tfrac{1}{2}\ c + 1095\ v + 1095\ s = 7657\tfrac{1}{2}\ V$
$1632\tfrac{1}{2}\ c + 769\ v + 769\ s = 3170\tfrac{1}{2}\ V$

empirical, for the owner of a machine tools company to save five or ten times as much as the owner of a shoe company, given equal incomes.

Marx also resorts to this expedient of residual and irregular saving by Department II capitalists, an expedient which Rosa Luxemburg showed the absurdity of. But Lenin considerably adds to the unlikeliness. The figures for Department II's saving become ridiculously low and, what is more serious, they vary as a decreasing function of income. In Marx, Department II capitalists save 150 the first year, 240 the second, 264 the third, 290 the fourth and 320 the fifth. Hence their savings ratio passes from 20% the first year to around 30% the fifth. These percentages are certainly lower than those of Department I, fixed at 50%, and this cannot be justified, but at least they evolve in a realistic way – as an increasing function of income. In Lenin, for the same income at the start, Department II's saving is only 60, and by the third year has already fallen to 35½! As incomes increase, savings, which are already negligible at the start, instead of increasing, fall markedly and eventually tend to zero!

Why did Lenin resort to such an absurd contrivance? Apparently, because he saw no other way to make the schemes show differing rates of expansion of the two Departments, an indispensable condition for an increase in the organic composition of capital. He tortures the schemes and forces Department II capitalists to adopt residual rates of saving which are improbably low and which vary improbably from one year to the next, in order to bring their accumulation into line with a *predetermined* rate of growth of the organic composition of their own department. Strangely enough, it does not occur to him, any more than it would later occur to Rosa Luxemburg, that Department II capitalists, while saving at the same rate as every one else, could invest their own surplus in other companies and in a different Department than their own, thereby compelling part of their workforce to emigrate in the same way from one Department to the other. Despite their opposite conclusions, Lenin and Rosa Luxemburg were both trapped in the same pointless initial constraint: absence of unilateral transfers between the Departments.

Once this constraint had been imposed, Rosa Luxemburg would take it to its logical conclusion and arrive at the absolute *theoretical* impossibility of realization of the social product. Lenin would formally challenge this *impossibility* and, by means of an artifice, have the schemes say that extended reproduction *is* possible, but the crises which interrupt it are inevitable. Why are they inevitable? Because, however possible it is to suppress – in schemes – the growth of final consumption, and however much one may dissociate the rate of final consumption from that of the expansion of reproduction, final consumption must nevertheless follow accumulation, even if at a great distance, whereas the practice of capitalist exploitation prevents it from doing so.

From this point onwards, it is not clear how Lenin can declare himself an opponent of underconsumptionist theories. Even if his schemes were correct, the only thing that they might demonstrate is that under-consumption is compatible with the normal realization of the product within certain limits and incompatible beyond these limits, which does not seem to constitute so fundamental an opposition to underconsumptionist theories as Lenin believes.

But his schemes are not correct. For if we accept that the saving of Department II capitalists may be determined by their own Department's absorption capacity, and may thus be squeezed down to 4% of their income (while the others are saving 50%), why should it not be squeezed down even further, down to 3, 2, 1, or even 0%. (In fact, it is enough to pick a percentage equal to or lower than that of the growth of the population, to make stagnation or even a reduction of wages compatible, in the framework of these schemes, with realization of the product.)

Lenin does not fail to consider this possibility:

> But perhaps we should take another step forward? Since we have accepted that the ratio of v to $c + v$ diminishes constantly, why not let v [he probably means Δv] decrease to zero, the same number of workers being sufficient for a larger quantity of means of production? In that case, the accumulated part of surplus-value will be added straight to constant capital in Department I, and social production will grow exclusively on account of means of production as means of production, complete stagnation reigning in Department II.[14]

And in a note at the foot of the page, Lenin gives the scheme which illustrates this possibility:

Period	*Department*	*c*	*v*	*s*	*V*
1	I	4000 +	1000 +	1000 =	6000
	II	1500 +	750 +	750 =	3000
2	I	4500 +	1000 +	1000 =	6500
	II	1500 +	750 +	750 =	3000

14. *Ibid.*, pp. 87–8.

Continued on following page

Period	*Department*	*c*		*v*		*s*		*V*
3	I	5000	+	1000	+	1000	=	7000
	II	1500	+	750	+	750	=	3000

and so on.

But he rejects this straight away:

> That would, of course, be a misuse of the schemes, for such a conclusion is based on improbable assumptions and is therefore wrong. Is it conceivable that technical progress, which reduces the proportion of *v* to *c*, will find expression only in Department I and leave Department II in a state of complete stagnation? Is it in conformity with the laws governing capitalist society, laws which *demand* of every capitalist that he enlarge his enterprise on pain of ruin, that no accumulation at all should take place in Department II?[15]

A misuse of the schemes! It is truly difficult to understand why it is a misuse of the schemes to accept that the ratio of *v* to *c* should not decrease at all in Department II, while it is no misuse of the schemes to accept that this ratio decreases at a completely insignificant rate compared to that of Department I, or why it is a misuse of the schemes to accept that Department II capitalists save nothing at all, while it is no misuse of the schemes to accept that they only save a sum of 35 out of their income of 766, at the same time that the others are saving 537½ out of their income of 1075. The misuse of the schemes is the same in both cases: they are manipulated to fit in with the most improbable assumptions, for the sake of the cause.

The idea that proportionality is determined by material conditions of production

Lenin and the vast majority of Marxists after him argue as if there existed technical coefficients that related the production of means of production to that of articles of consumption, independently of the mode and relations of production: 'Any growth in the production of means of production must *necessarily* lead to growth in the production of articles of consumption', J. Duret could write.[16]

More subtly, Bettelheim writes: 'It is true that in the long run demand for means of production will result in a growth of the productive apparatus and, hence, of the supply of articles of

15. *Ibid.*, p. 88.
16. *Le Marxisme et les crises*, p. 89, emphasis added.

consumption and that thus, through a far more complex process than that envisaged by Sismondi, lack of demand for articles of consumption may ultimately decrease employment.'[17]

Samir Amin entirely shares this opinion: 'A certain volume of ultimate production necessitates a certain volume of intermediate production. This latter quantity is merely a way of looking at the volume of investment required to produce the desired volume of ultimate goods.'[18]

This argument presupposes, quite clearly, that the quantity of capital corresponding to each quantity of commodities and services produced is given. We have already had the opportunity to express our disagreement on this point. As technology progresses, more capital is generally required for the same, or even for a smaller, quantity of commodities and services. Further, at each point in time, existing reserves of unutilised advanced technology make it possible to choose in each case a technique that can absorb whatever quantity of capital is available. It is this quantity which is given (and functions as a limit), and not the quantity required per unit of output.

It still remains that, according to this belief, the coefficients in question define a *minimum* rate of growth of consumption, compatible with a given rate of accumulation.[19] Under the capitalist system, this minimum contradicts the tendency towards the maximisation of the rate of profit; whence crises. Under the socialist system, the planner has no reason to reject this *technical* constraint. He happily allows that increase of consumption, or, which comes to the same thing, that reduction in working hours, which corresponds to his rate of accumulation, and in this way crises are avoided.[20]

17. *Le problème de l'emploi*, p. 36.

18. *Accumulation on a World Scale*, p. 498.

19. Keynes, in his *General Theory*, quotes an analogous argument by Hobson and Mummery (*Physiology of Industry*): 'The only use of capital being to aid the production of these utilities and conveniences [consumer goods], the total used will necessarily vary with the total of utilities and conveniences daily or weekly consumed. Now saving, while it increases the existing aggregate of capital, simultaneously reduces the quantity of utilities and conveniences consumed; any undue exercise of this habit must, therefore, cause an accumulation of capital in excess of that which is required for use, and this excess will exist in the form of general overproduction.' Quoted in *General Theory*, p. 367.

20. 'Under socialism', write Baran and Sweezy, 'there is no reason why technological progress, no matter how rapid or of what kind, would be associated with unemployment. In a socialist society technological progress may make possible a continuous reduction in the number of years, weeks and hours worked.' (*Monopoly Capital*, pp. 261–2.)

It is illusory, Bettleheim holds, to rely on capitalist planning to avoid crises, since 'real planning assumes . . . that the society's ability to consume should be increased in parallel with its ability to produce'. (*Le Problème de l'emploi*, p. 73.)

This was the ABC of the catechism of several generations of Marxists.[21] The position adopted by Preobrazhenski on this question on the eve of the five-year plans in the Soviet Union is typical. Considering the condition *sine qua non* of industrialisation to be continuous growth of real wages, and fearing lest the socialist state should neglect this 'law', he went so far as to hope that the working class would exert trade union pressure on their own state, so that this 'fundamental lever' would function to stimulate the growth of production.[22]

The end of NEP and the first five-year plans proved the opposite. Not only does a planned economy have no need of this 'stimulant' to avoid over-production crises while it is accumulating, but it can push its accumulation right up to the level of its economic resources, while at the same time drastically restricting final consumption up to the limit of the politically or socially acceptable. It is not troubled by any *technical minimum.* And it was not *despite* this reduction of consumption, but *thanks* to it and as a function of it, that the Soviet Union was able to carry out particularly accelerated industrialisation.

Acknowledging this does not prejudge the question of whether this policy was the right one, whether the rates chosen were sensible, whether or not the sacrifice imposed on one or several generations of citizens and the resulting very serious political tensions were a necessary and rational price to pay for industrialisation, any more than it guarantees the quality and internal consistency of this planning, or smooths out other disproportions between industries, wastages or losses. But it is certain that nothing which could possibly be called an over-production crisis occurred during this breakneck industrialisation accompanied by compression of final consumption. If there were disequilibria, these came rather in the form of shortages, reflecting errors of calculation and management or natural disasters. And this situation lasted not for the time required for the maturation of investments, or for that needed to pass from Department I to Department II, from the tool to the machine and from the machine to the article of consumption, but far longer. For decades on end, the Soviet Union carried out the exploit which Tugan Baranovski had proclaimed possible in the last century: producing more coal and steel in order to produce even more steel and coal. It even went further. It did what we indicated above to be possible. It

21. However, long before the Marxists, Sismondi had asserted that, in a social organisation without private property, there would be no overproduction because with each technical advance, labour-time would be reduced. (cf "Sur la balance des consommations avec les productions'.)

22. *The New Economics.*

actually produced and installed the new machines in Department II without in the least increasing this Department's output proportionally. And if technical conditions were the only limitation, this could have gone on indefinitely. Or at any rate, easily as long as the capitalist system needs to go through a fine series of big crises. However this may be, when the Soviet state decided, certainly not to suppress this *disproportion* between breakneck investment and regressing or stagnant consumption, but to attenuate it somewhat, it did so not under the pressure of any technical constraint, nor under the threat of any economic crisis, but as master of the situation and for political and social reasons.

As for the reduction of working hours in the socialist system, this is not in the least a *direct* result of technological progress, but of a choice between increasing production with or without an increase in consumption, on the one hand, and increasing leisure on the other. Apart from this choice, there is no necessity under socialism for a reduction of working hours as a result of technological progress.

However, Baranovski was wrong insofar as he believed this dissociation between the two Departments to be already possible in the free enterprise system.[23] It is only possible in a planned economy. But what is possible in a planned economy cannot be taken to be *technically* impossible, as Lenin believed, and as most Marxists still believe. And this is the crux of the matter.

Let us take as an example Paul Sweezy, a Marxist who fully subscribes to the argument of a *technical* correspondence between the expansion of means of production and that of articles of consumption:

> If we [. . .] look upon production as a natural technical process of creating use values, we see that a definite relation must exist between the mass of means of production [. . .] and the output of consumption goods. These relations are ultimately determined by the technical characteristics of production and accordingly can vary with the progressive development of methods of production. Such evidence as we have, however, strongly suggests a remarkably high degree of stability for a reasonably well-developed capitalist economy. On this basis we are justified in making the assumption that the technically determined relation between stock of means of production and output of consumption goods remains constant. [But since capitalists do everything to restrict mass consumption], it follows

23. It does not however appear that Tugan Baranovski saw this as a *real* possibility for the system, as his detractors have argued. It seems rather that for him, this was an abstract extreme case: '. . . it is even possible that, carried away by their passion for accumulation, the capitalists . . .' (*Les Crises industrielles en Angleterre*, n. 1, pp. 216–17.)

that there is an inherent tendency for the growth in consumption to fall behind the growth in the output of consumption goods. [It is therefore incorrect to oppose 'disproportionality' to 'underconsumption', for] under-consumption is precisely a special case of disproportionality.[24]

The author does not justify his assumption. What is more, he refers to 'evidence' about capitalism (and to Carl Snyder's statistics covering a certain period of capitalist practice) to prove the existence of a 'natural technical' law which, according to the author himself, outstrips and contradicts capitalist practice. From the fact that capitalism *cannot* step up accumulation beyond certain limits without a parallel increase of final consumption, it can in no way be deduced that these limits are material and technical.

Further on, he gives an example:

a railroad must be built before it can be used. During the construction period investment proceeds while the provision of actual transportation service is not increased; only when the railroad is finished does the relation between means of production and output of finished product assert itself. So during this period, Department I develops independently of Department II. Once this point has been reached, however, it is generally the case that further additions to means of production (new rolling-stock, double tracking, heavier rails, et cetera) will be closely related to changes in output (ton-miles of transportation).[25]

This example is not convincing. While some additions to means of production certainly do increase production potential, others do not. Improvements in signalling, the introduction of automatic points and automatic timetables in stations, the use of machines and computers in the companies' office work and even the replacement of steam engines by diesels, or the electrification of the line – all these may occur without any increase, or even together with a decrease of railway traffic, purely in order to reduce operating costs by reducing the workforce or intermediate consumption.

Some investments enlarge production, while others deepen it. In order to establish that accumulation is *materially* impossible without an increase of wages (or a shortening of the working week), it must first be proved that the *technically* necessary portion of investments of the first category is such that the resulting growth in the production of articles of final consumption is greater than the natural increase of the population. This proof has never been supplied.[26]

Marxist theoreticians have held that the difference on this point between the two systems is that the socialist system is *capable* of

24. *The Theory of Capitalist Development*, pp. 182–4.
25. *Ibid.*, p. 218.

increasing real wages or reducing working hours in order to avoid overproduction crises, while the capitalist system is incapable of doing this because of the competition between capitalists to obtain profits. This is false. The difference is the other way round. The socialist system is capable of *not* increasing wages, and even reducing them, without thereby raising the danger of any crisis. The capitalist system *is incapable of this.* (Left to itself, without any union or political pressure, it cannot increase wages either, and this is its contradiction. This is also the fine paradox of effective union struggle, which has saved the capitalist system from itself during this century. But this is another question.)

If what is impossible for one system is possible in another, we should not look for the obstacle to realization of the product in the area of the proportions and technical coefficients relating means of production and articles of consumption, but in the area of the motives of those with the power to take decisions. The motivations of capitalist entrepreneurs, or even more generally of independent producers, are such that it is impossible for them to step up their investments at the very moment when final consumption is falling and when the market for articles of consumption is contracting; i.e. it is impossible for them to do something which planners, or even more generally any representatives of an integrated, marketless community, not only can but naturally must do.[27]

26. Sweezy only accepts that the production of means of production can be dissociated from final consumption in an under-industrialized country. But are not all countries under-industrialized, compared to some other existing or possible society?

'It is only when the process of industrialisation is completed [this is the point, it is never completed] that it becomes clear that the capacity to produce consumption goods has been greatly expanded, and the necessary connections between means of production and output of consumption goods comes to the fore again.' (*Ibid.*, p. 219.)

However, the author does not deny that the organic composition rises, but he seems to believe that, for *technical* reasons, it can only increase at a rate slower than that of accumulation. (cf. *ibid.*, p. 254.)

27. A remarkably clear summary of this error is offered to us by Alexander Erlich when he criticises Bukharin's position based on the same hypothesis, namely that the production of means of production, being nothing more than a *preparatory stage* for the production of consumption goods, cannot be dissociated from final consumption:

'Bukharin was on the wrong track when he kept insisting that today's investment cannot mature into anything else but the increased consumption of the future. He did not notice that the crucial issue at stake was not the technological possibility of 'building mills that should make more mills forever' (to borrow J.B. Clark's famous phrase), but the economic rationale of the staggering rate of increase of capital stock which such a policy would entail. In other words, he lacked the notion of declining investment opportunity; just as much as his opponents did. It was therefore not surprising that he did not stop to inquire to what extent planned and unplanned economies differ in this particular respect.' (*The Soviet Industrialisation Debate, 1924–1928*, pp. 11–19.)

Continued on page 162

We will have occasion to return to this crucial question. But in the light of the above, we can already state that it is pointless to try to discover the *necessity* for crises from reproduction schemes. These schemes illustrate the interconnections of Departments apart from investors' motivations, but apart from these motivations there is no necessity for crises. As numerical tables, schemes can only show what is possible. They cannot show what is necessary or what is impossible. But, in the abstract, they show what is possible in itself, independently of the social relations of production. And although their purpose is to illustrate the mechanism of reproduction in the capitalist system, there is nothing paradoxical about the fact that the equilibrium conditions that they define can be attained better in a planned economy than in a market economy.[28]

The scheme for intensive extended reproduction

Lenin's attempt seems more like an anti-scheme. As such, it is not very convincing. First of all, he arbitrarily introduces excessive unlikelihoods, as if this was the only way to combine growth in the organic composition with static production in Department II. He then declares, in the light of these unlikelihoods, that the combination is impossible.

Now, the *theoretical* conditions – and these are what we are concerned with – for equilibrium with this combination do exist, and there is no need to resort to unlikelihoods to schematise them. On the contrary, it suffices for that to eliminate all the unlikelihoods, not just those condemned by Lenin, but also the one which he curiously never thinks of putting in question, despite all the evidence, all Marxism's general teaching and his own writings, i.e. the exclusion of transfers

27. *Continued from page 161*

Although Erlich does not say so explicitly, he seems to mean that, in unplanned economies, the lack of opportunities for investment prevents the means of production sector from becoming independent of consumption, while this obstacle does not exist in planned economies. With this interpretation Erlich's formulation seems perfectly correct to us.

'The growth of output per worker', the author goes on, 'could be completely compatible with a constant or even falling total output of the industry which has adopted the innovation and with the continuous transfer of resources to a capital-goods sector in self-sustaining growth. Here, once more, the only serious attack would have been to question the basic assumption that this sector could always be counted on to continue growing even if consumption fell – but this is exactly what neither Bukharin nor the other Marxist critics of Tugan Baranovski ever attempted.' (*Ibid.*, p. 19.)

28. So it is perhaps not surprising that it should be a specialist in socialist planning, C. Bettelheim, in a work dealing with planning techniques, who systematised the study of extended intensive reproduction (cf. *Problèmes theóriques et pratiques de la planification.*)

of factors of production and, consequently, of unilateral transfers of value from one department to the other. Once this restriction has been abandoned, it is not difficult to construct the correct scheme for intensive extended reproduction. This is shown in the table.

Period	*Department*	*c*	*v*	*s*		*V*
1	I	1000	+ 1000	+ 1000	=	3000
	II	1000	+ 1000	+ 1000	=	3000
		2000	+ 2000	+ 2000	=	6000
2	I	$1714^2/_7$	+ $1142^6/_7$	+ $1142^6/_7$	=	4000
	II	$1285^5/_7$	+ $857^1/_7$	+ $857^1/_7$	=	3000
		3000	+ 2000	+ 2000	=	7000
3	I	2500	+ 1250	+ 1250	=	5000
	II	1500	+ 750	+ 750	=	3000
		4000	+ 2000	+ 2000	=	8000
4	I	$3333^1/_3$	+ $1333^1/_3$	+ $1333^1/_3$	=	6000
	II	$1666^2/_3$	+ $666^2/_3$	+ $666^2/_3$	=	3000
		5000	+ 2000	+ 2000	=	9000
5	I	4200	+ 1400	+ 1400	=	7000
	II	1800	+ 600	+ 600	=	3000
		6000	+ 2000	+ 2000	=	10 000

As can be seen, equilibrium is ensured without the help of any suspect or even strained assumptions. The rate of surplus-value is 100% throughout. Whichever Department they belong to, capitalists save exactly half their income each cycle and spend the other half on their personal consumption. The organic composition increases by exactly the same percentage throughout the economy each cycle, which is the simplest and most realistic assumption possible, since we are concerned with the average organic composition of each Department, and there is no reason for technical progress to favour one Department more than the other, on average and in the long term. According to the law of averages, backward industries and advanced industries should cancel out in each Department as a whole. However, this is not an accommodating assumption.

If the organic composition grew slower in Department II, this would have been more in line with its stationary state, which is the basic constraint of our problem.

Let us recall that what troubled Lenin and those who dealt with the question of markets, was the fact that it seemed impossible to them to confine technological progress within Department I and thus to ensure the realization of the product by means of internal exchanges among capitalists. By 'descending' to Department II, technological progress would end up by increasing the production of articles of consumption and would thus create a specific surplus for which there is no outlet in a situation of wages stagnation. I have therefore taken the most unfavorable case: technological progress is diffused evenly, immediately and at will in both departments. (One could even go further and make the organic composition rise faster in Department II than Department I, and this would not change our equilibrium conditions at all.) Nonetheless, Department II's production does not increase and, though the growth of population and wage-rates remain equally stationary, no disequilibrium is engendered. What does increase as a result of the introduction of technical progress and the rise in the organic composition is *productivity*, not *production*.

This last point is the most important one. By confusing the relative concept of productivity (output per unit of labour) with the absolute concept of value produced, the problem of realisation was rendered insoluble.[29] In our scheme above, productivity rises in the articles of consumption department, as it must. For the same value produced, 2000 units of labour are needed the first year, $1714^2/_7$ the second year, 1500 the third year, $1333\frac{1}{3}$ the fourth and 1200 the fifth. But production, in value terms, remains static, always equal to 3000.

29. Rodbertus had already wrongly identified variations in productivity with those of the production of consumption goods:

'So . . . purchasing-power and productivity are no longer in the correct proportions one to the other. The purchasing-power of the greater part of society falls greatly relative to increasing productivity, and society reaches a point where use-values are being produced which are neither market-values nor purchasing-power, while the needs of the majority are not satisfied.' (Jagetzow Karl Rodbertus, *Zur Beleuchtung der sozialen Frage*, 2nd letter, p. 90.)

This value of 3000 is always equal to the variable capital (2000) plus the half of surplus-value (1000) devoted to capitalists' personal expenditure. On the other hand, the value of the annual product of Department I is equal to both departments' productive consumption the following year ($V_1t_{n-1} = c_1t_n + c_2t_n$). Thus the scheme is entirely consistent internally.

Despite the invariability of value produced, part of the new capitals formed each year in consumption goods industries find a placing in their own Department: $142^6/_7$ the first year, $108^1/_7$ the second, $83^1/_3$ the third and $66^2/_3$ the fourth. The key to the solution is the transfer to Department I of the remainder of these capitals, together with part of the workforce. This is obviously something which happens daily before our eyes. New agricultural machines which multiply the productivity of labour are being invented all the time. Farmers do not refuse to introduce them but the result is not so much an increase in agricultural production, as a decrease in the number of agricultural workers. The textiles capitalist is certainly compelled by competition to replace his semi-automatic looms which require one worker for every two looms with improved fully automatic looms which require one worker for every four looms. But this does not compel him to double the number of his looms while retaining the same workforce and, therefore, to double the scale of his production. If the market is saturated, if wages and therefore the population's purchasing-power are stagnant, he is much more likely to retain the same number of looms, and therefore keep to the same scale of production, while sacking half his wokforce, who will find work upstream in Department I, just like the displaced agricultural workers. As for the farmer's and textiles producer's own savings, clearly there is nothing to make them invest these in their own firms or in their own Department. They can perfectly well use these funds to buy stocks or bonds in chemical or metallurgical enterprises.[30]

It is scarcely credible that Marxists have been able to engage in this age-old discussion about reproduction schemes without taking into account the obvious possibility of transfers of factors from one Department to the other. And yet Tugan Baranovski had already accepted this possibility in his *Theoretical Foundations of Marxism*, where he proposed the scheme shown in the table in three departments, the third being that of products destined for the capitalists' individual consumption.

30. With the development of joint-stock companies and finance capital, capital becomes much more mobile, since the finance capitalist differs from the small boss with his own firm in not having any 'trade', and hence no a priori predilection for one particular firm, industry or department.

		c	*v*	*s*	*V*
	I	1632	+ 544	+ 544	= 2720
1	II	408	+ 136	+ 136	= 680
	III	360	+ 120	+ 120	= 600
		2400	+ 800	+ 800	= 4000
	I	1987.4	+ 496.8	+ 828.1	= 3312.3
2	II	372.6	+ 93.2	+ 155.2	= 621
	III	360	+ 90	+ 150	= 600
		2720	+ 680	+ 1133.3	= 4533.3
	I	2585.4	+ 484.6	+ 1239	= 4309
3	II	366.9	+ 68.9	+ 175.5	= 611.3
	III	360	+ 67.5	+ 172.5	= 600
		3312.3	+ 621	+ 1587	= 5520.3

Period	*Capitalisation*	*Capitalists' consumption*	*Workers' consumption*	*Total unproductive consumption*
1	200	600	800	1400
2	533.3	600	680	1280
3	987	600	621	1221

As can be seen, this scheme is very unusual and rather narrow in its scope. The real organic composition $\frac{c}{v+s}$ remains unchanged from period to period and in all industries at $^3/_2$. If the ratio c/v rises, this is because the value of labour-power falls (or, which comes to the same thing, that the rate of relative surplus-value rises). Capitalists' personal consumption and Department III which supplies them with their specific goods remain static. Workers' consumption and the corresponding production of Department II fall (in value terms) from one period to the next, and all new capitals, as well as some of the old capitals of Departments II and III, flow into Department I. However, the accompanying influx of labour-power into this Department prevents the real organic composition from growing. Finally, growth of the working population at the same rate as aggregate constant capital means that the *overall* real organic composition is also constant.[31]

But despite the anomalous character of this scheme, Tugan-Baranovsky grasped and clarified the problem we are concerned with in the following lines:

> It may seem at first sight that there is no equilibrium between supply and demand in my scheme. Thus, in year 1, means of production worth 2720 million marks are produced. 1987.4 million marks are needed for year 2's means of production. Consequently, a balance of means of production of a value of 2720 − 1987.4 = 732.6 million marks is exchanged for the products of Departments II and III. In the same way, again in Department I, demand for Department II and III goods in year 2 is 904.8 million marks (496 for Department I workers' consumption and 408 for Department I capitalists' consumption, following our assumption that the latter spend only ¾ of their profits on personal consumption). Department I capitalists and workers have therefore spent 172.2 million marks more than they have received (904.8 − 732.6 = 172.2). How can this deficit of 172.2 million marks be covered?
>
> This is only an apparent difficulty. The fall in wages and static consumption of the capitalists result in a reduction in the scale of business for the capitals of Departments II and III, and these therefore move into Department I, which is benefiting from rapid expansion. This explains the fact that, in year 2, Department II's constant and variable capital are together 78.2 million marks lower than the previous year, and Department III's 30 million lower; likewise, the portion of year 1's profits capitalised by the capitalists of Department II (34 million) and Department III (30 million) are transferred to Department I. The sum of these is 78.2 + 30 + 34 + 30 = 172.2: Department I's apparent deficit is therefore covered *by the capitals entering this department from the other two.*[32]

This passage is after all only a simple reminder of an utter commonplace which should go without saying for any economist at all, and especially for a Marxist: the mobility of factors within each capitalist country. Even if this passage did not exist, it would still be

31. This illustrates the inaccuracy of Marx's expression c/v, which we have discussed in the first appendix to Chapter 3. In terms of this definition the organic composition in this illustration of Tugan Baranovsky's rises year by year, which allows its author to believe that he has constructed a scheme of intensive extended reproduction. But the true organic composition, $c/(v + s)$, remains constant at 1.5 units of capital per unit of labour, and this scheme is in fact of extensive extended reproduction.

32. *Theoretische Grunlagen des Marxismus*, pp. 226–7, emphasis added.

difficult to understand how so many Marxist theorists have been able to discuss the question of the realisation of the social product as if relations between the departments of social production were confined to current transactions, one commodity for another of equal value. But this passage does exist. And it alone is enough to invalidate quite a few theories of crisis, which rely essentially on *ignoring* these unilateral transfers. So it is truly dumbfounding to see these theoreticians of supposedly 'scientific' socialism adopt such an unscientific position as completely to ignore this passage, while at the same time expressly rejecting Tugan-Baranovski's arguments and referring to his works.

Rosa Luxemburg is the most striking example of this, as we shall see further on. After spending over two hundred pages building up a proof of the *impossibility* of realisation of the social product, based on the *explicit* postulate of equivalent exchange between Departments, she spends a few sentences directly attacking Baranovski's conclusions, but she gets out of it with a few witticisms, without refuting or even mentioning this premise which contradicts her own postulate.

So far, Tugan-Baranovski has himself not taken the decisive step into intensive extended reproduction. After presenting some statistics which show a faster rise in employment in Department I than Department II, he asks: 'What, then, do these machines do? . . . They are used partly for the production of articles of consumption, but mainly, and in an ever-increasing proportion, to produce more machines. . . .'[33] This is what actually happens, of course. But he is not quite clear about the theoretical possibility of, not 'partly', but completely dissociating the production of articles of consumption from that of means of production, i.e. the possibility of more steel, more coal and more machinery being used in Department II to make *less* textiles or food there, provided that disproportionately less workers than before are employed.

Rosa Luxemburg's theory

Rosa Luxemburg divides the gross social product of a given capitalist system into four parts: the first replaces consumed means of production (constant capital) in value and in kind; the second and third correspond, both in value and in kind, to personal consumption of wage-earners and capitalists respectively; the fourth is to provide the extra means of production and workers' subsistence needed for any expansion of production.

33. *Les Crises industrielles en Angleterre*, p. 225.

In a system composed solely of capitalists and proletarians, realization of the first three parts does not present any particular problems. If we assume that, notwithstanding temporary disproportions of the business cycle, the right use-value composition of these three parts is assured, then this realisation can take place within the system, on its 'home market'. However, realization of the fourth part is completely impossible on the home market, whatever the composition of this residue in terms of use-values, and therefore even if these use-values are exactly what is required by the technical demands of accumulation. It must therefore be realized on 'foreign' markets. A 'foreign' market is defined as any non-capitalist commodity producer, whether found within or outside the geographical frontiers of the system under consideration.

In other words, in a closed system realization is only possible up to the limit of simple reproduction. But since simple reproduction is only an abstraction, created by Marx for analytical purposes, and since capitalism is, by its very nature, inseparable from reproduction on an extended scale, the system itself cannot work. . . . It is compelled to *open* itself to 'foreign' markets as defined above.

The purchasers of this part of the product are therefore in a sense 'third persons' (neither capitalists nor wage-earners), but in an essentially different way from that conceived by Malthus, Chalmers, Struve, etc., in the sense that they do not derive their purchasing power from the alienation of part of the income of the two principal classes of our system, but rather from their own production. They are independent producers, newly constituted from the remains of non-monetary pre-capitalist economies, and going through a stage of simple commodity relations before in turn disappearing into developed capitalism.

It is during this transition period that these strata or communities, depending whether they are within or outside the country in question, ensure the survival of the pure capitalist systems by providing them with a 'foreign' market. Without them the capitalist system is deadlocked and collapses. Objectively, it can only survive so long as the world still contains pre-capitalist zones to be integrated. The real content of imperialism is an attack on and dislocation of these zones. Subjectively, class struggle may make it collapse earlier, but it is continuous contraction of these backward zones which, in the last analysis, fuels these struggles, and it is this material impossibility of living without these zones which underlies the historical inevitability of capitalism's final collapse.

Rosa Luxemburg is not concerned with cyclical disequilibria. 'In order to demonstrate the pure implications of capitalist reproduction', she says, 'we must rather consider it quite apart from the periodical cycles and crises. [. . . This] is the only method . . . scientifically tenable. In order to demonstrate and to solve the problem of pure value, we must leave price fluctuations out of consideration.'[34] Her proof will therefore turn on a fundamental inherent contradiction which blocks the system in its *normal* functioning in the long term, i.e. over and above cycles of depression and expansion. These can at most be effects of this contradiction.

We should say straight away that this distinction between contingencies and basic structure is certainly very welcome, especially as writers too often slide from one to the other very unrigorously, as we have seen above. This apart, however, Rosa Luxemburg's theory seems to us very debatable, in both form and content.

Rosa Luxemburg's method

Rosa Luxemburg's proof is conducted on two fronts: on the one hand that of Marx's schemes of extended reproduction; and on the other hand apart from these schemes. Quite apart from the actual content of this proof, which we shall examine later on in detail, the way in which the author moves between these two areas, and the conclusions that she draws from the two arguments respectively, are completely unacceptable epistemologically.

In order to prove her thesis of the logical *impossibility* of extended reproduction in a pure capitalist system, Rosa Luxemburg would first have to refute Marx's schemes, which for their part show the *possibility* of this reproduction. This is what she sets out to do, and this attempt, whatever its results (which, as we shall see, are completely negative), is exactly what we should expect. But, after devoting a large part of her work to discussion of these schemes, as well as of those which, in her view, might replace them, she concludes that, since all of them are incorrect, extended reproduction, under the conditions laid down, is *impossible*.

This is an astonishing confusion between the possible and the necessary. A numerical scheme can only show what is possible. If it is unsatisfactory, then it proves nothing. But the non-proof that something is possible is not *ipso facto* a proof that it is impossible. Since impossibility is a *necessary* negative, it cannot be shown by schemes or by their deficiencies. But it is from the internal discussion of schemes, or more specifically of *certain* schemes which are particularly deficient in this respect – Marx's two and a third of her own vintage – that Rosa Luxemburg, at the close of this purely

34. *The Accumulation of Capital*, p. 35.

theoretical part of her work, draws the conclusion that realization of the product and, therefore, extended reproduction, are materially, mathematically, impossible.

When she later comes across certain other schemes which are more adequate than those she has just demolished, such as those of Tugan-Baranovski and especially those of Otto Bauer, she takes great care not to examine them from within, as closely as she examined the earlier ones. She changes tack completely, challenging the very principle of the scheme as a form of proof of what is possible, and invites us to abandon these abstract constructs and study reality instead.

She goes too far both times: too abstract the first time, and the second time, not abstract enough. A thousand clumsy schemes cannot prove that something is impossible. One single well picked and well constructed scheme can prove that something is possible, and though reality may actually *give the lie* to it, only an internal theoretical discussion can *refute* it.

Rosa Luxemburg's approach is, to say the least, singular. When schemes are weak, she takes them seriously and devotes some two hundred pages to their refutation. Here she shows an excess of zeal and, on top of their real faults, she discovers a host of others which they do not actually suffer from. When, on the contrary, schemes are strong, at any rate when they claim to remedy the very deficiencies that she believes that she has found in the first, she will not deign to spare even a glance for them; she dismisses them in one short ironic sentence, as exercises which one can enjoy oneself working out '*ad infinitum,* just as long, that is to say, as ink and paper do not run out'.[35] 'The problem of accumulation is itself purely economic and social', she says later, 'it does not have anything to do with mathematical formulae'.[36] One might then wonder what was the point of her long chapters of minutious dissection and internal challenging of mathematical formulae. But this is not very important: it is not only Rosa Luxemburg's method which is unacceptable. She is wrong on the actual point itself. Her reasoning is as invalid when she accepts schemes as when she rejects them out of hand.

The theoretical side of Rosa Luxemburg

I. Critique of Marx's schemes

The two schemes handed down to us by Marx, which Rosa Luxemburg analyses, are schemes of extensive extended reproduction. All

35. *Ibid.*, p. 314.
36. *Anti-critique*, p. 48.

the component parts grow from year to year at a uniform rate – 10% in the first case, 8⅓% in the second – equal to that of the growth of labour employed. Here we are dealing with an economy with unchanging technology, which only grows as a result of demographic expansion, or, more precisely, the expansion of its wage-earning population. Since capitalised surplus-value is divided between constant capital, c, and variable capital, v, in the same proportion as the previous c/v, the organic composition of capital stays the same, both within each Department and in the economy as a whole.

Rosa Luxemburg's first mistake is to take these schemes as the definitive schemes of Marxist extended reproduction. They are nothing of the kind. They only describe an extreme case, which has nothing to do with capitalist reality as explicitly described by Marx. He had already explained, in volume I of *Capital* and in other writings, that with technical progress and the accumulation of capital, growth of the capitalist system is reflected in what he himself called intensive extended reproduction, namely by continuous growth of the organic composition of capital. This implies that the part of capitalised profits which turns into c becomes larger and larger compared to that part which turns into v. Rosa Luxemburg herself, in her discussion with Otto Bauer, notes that for Marx, 'the additional portion of capital must be converted into one *larger part* of constant capital and one *smaller part* of variable capital'.[37] But the situation described by these schemes, taken from Marx's rough notes, implies that v grows at the same rate as c and the gross product. Since the rate of surplus-value also remains constant over time, this implies finally that the working population and employment grow, in these schemes, from one period to the next at the same rate (10% and 8⅓% respectively) as the accumulation of capital, which is not only very different from Marx's ideas, but also seems particularly unrealistic under any assumptions. (Rosa Luxemburg even finds the percentage of 5% assumed by Bauer unrealistic, and refers to statistics from various European countries which suggest that this figure varies between 0.18% and 1.60%.)

We must therefore assume that these schemes of Marx's are a preliminary methodological abstraction, deliberately unrealistic, with a view to further schemes of intensive extended reproduction, which would have come later and which, for one reason or another, are absent from these rough notes. Failing this, Marx's whole teaching on the subject of the continuous rise of the organic composition, the source of so many of capitalism's contradictions and

37. *Ibid.*, p. 127, emphasis added.

the basis of the law of the tendency of the rate of profit to fall, is invalidated. Rosa Luxemburg however takes these schemes as the last word in the schematisation of Marxist theory. Since they are much less than this, and were probably meant to pave the way for other schemes which would have followed, her critique, even if it were well-founded, would miss the mark. But it is not well-founded.

a. *The first scheme*

		c		*v*		*s*		*V*
Previous situation	I	4000	+	1000	+	1000	=	6000
	II	1500	+	750	+	750	=	3000
		5500	+	1750	+	1750	=	9000
1st year	I	4400	+	1100	+	1100	=	6600
	II	1600	+	800	+	800	=	3200
		6000	+	1900	+	1900	=	9800
2nd year	I	4840	+	1210	+	1210	=	7260
	II	1760	+	880	+	880	=	3520
		6600	+	2090	+	2090	=	10 780
3rd year	I	5324	+	1331	+	1331	=	7986
	II	1936	+	968	+	968	=	3872
		7260	+	2299	+	2299	=	11 858
4th year	I	5856	+	1464	+	1464	=	8784
	II	2129	+	1065	+	1065	=	4259
		7985	+	2529	+	2529	=	13 043
5th year	I	6442	+	1610	+	1610	=	9662
	II	2342	+	1172	+	1172	=	4686
		8784	+	2782	+	2782	=	14 348

Rosa Luxemburg's criticism of this scheme is that it subordinates Department II's reproduction to Department I's needs for accumulation. 'A certain increase in the constant capital of Department I always necessitates a certain increase in its variable capital, which predetermines beforehand the extent of the increase in Department II.'[38] Instead of interdependence between the two departments, there is, in Rosa Luxemburg's view, dependence

> of a peculiar kind. Accumulation here originates in Department I, and Department II merely follows suit. Thus it is Department I alone that determines the volume of accumulation. Marx effects accumulation here by allowing Department I to capitalise one-half of its surplus value; Department II, however, may capitalise only as much as is necessary to assure the production and accumulation of Department I. He makes the capitalists of Department II consume 600*s* as against the consumption of only 500*s* by the capitalists of Department I who have twice the amount of value and far more surplus value. In the next year, he assumes the capitalists of Department I again to capitalise half their surplus value, this time making the capitalists of Department II capitalise more than in the previous year – summarily fixing the amount to tally exactly with the needs of Department I. . . .[39]

'Marx', concludes Rosa Luxemburg,

> effects accumulation in Department I at the expense of Department II. In the years that follow, the capitalists of the provisions department get just as rough a deal. Following the same rules, Marx allows them in the third year to accumulate 264*s* – a larger amount this time than in the two preceding years. In the fourth year they are allowed to capitalise 290*s* and to consume 678*s*, and in the fifth year they accumulate 320*s* and consume 745*s*.[40]

Rosa Luxemburg's critique here enters the realm of pure fantasy. There is absolutely no unilateral constraint exercised by Department I on Department II. The scheme under consideration has the peculiarity of a lower organic composition in Department II than Department I. It is 2 in Department II, whereas in Department I it is 4. (Of course, this ratio stays the same from one period to the next.) This combination: $c'/v' = 4$ and $c''/v'' = 2$, taken together with the constraint that surplus-value must be invested in the same department where it is created (a pointless and incorrect constraint, but which has nothing to do with Rosa Luxemburg's objection and which, furthermore, is endorsed by her) *compels* Department I to

38. *The Accumulation of Capital*, p. 122.
39. *Ibid.*, p. 120.
40. *Ibid.*, p. 121.

save 50% of its surplus-value and Department II to save only 30%.[41]

This improbable difference in the propensity to save according to which Department one belongs is not, as Rosa Luxemburg believes, a consequence of the internal logic of the schemes, but derives from the choice of figures for the organic composition of the two Departments, given the ban on transfers from one department to the other. This is the only way for the production of the two Departments to grow at the same rate, actually 10%. In fact, since the rate of surplus-value is 100%,

$$v' = s' \quad \text{and} \quad v'' = s''.$$

Since we also know that

$$c' = 4v' \quad \text{and} \quad c'' = 2v'',$$

it follows that

$$c' + v' = 5s' \text{ and } c'' + v'' = 3s'',$$

$$\text{whence } \frac{c' + v'}{10} = \frac{1}{2}s' \text{ and } \frac{c'' + v''}{10} = \frac{3}{10}s''.$$

Department I *has to* capitalise half its surplus-value; department II, $^3/_{10}$.

One could choose other figures and construct just as coherent a scheme on the basis of Department II. If we take, for example, $c'' = 2000$, $v'' = 1000$, rate of accumulation of capital = 0.2, rate of exploitation = 1 and organic composition of capital = 4, we will have:

	c	*v*	*Surplus-value Consumed capitalised*	
Department II:	2000 +	1000 +	(400 + 600)	= 4000

Since $c' = 4v'$, $v' = s'$ and the rate of accumulation = $^1/_5$, it follows that

$$\frac{c' + v'}{5} = s'.$$

Therefore Department I *must* save (capitalise) all its surplus-value, while Department II only saves $^6/_{10}$. Since

$$v'' = 1000 \text{ and } 1.2(v' + v'') + 400 = 4000,$$

it follows that $v' = 2000$, whence:

41. c', v': constant and variable capital of Department I;
c'', v'': constant and variable capital of Department II.

		c	v	s	
1st period	I	8000 +	2000 +	(2000 cap. + 0 cons.) =	12 000
	II	2000 +	1000 +	(600 cap. + 400 cons.) =	4000
		10 000 +	3000 +	(2600 cap. + 400 cons.) =	16 000
2nd period	I	9600 +	2400 +	(2400 cap. + 0 cons.) =	14 400
	II	2400 +	1200 +	(720 cap. + 480 cons.) =	4800
		12 000 +	3600 +	(3120 cap. + 480 cons.) =	19 200
and so on.					

If we had defined that the two Departments have the same organic composition, equal to 2, we would have had:

$$c' = 2v'$$

$$\text{and } \frac{c' + v'}{5} = \frac{3}{5} s', v' = 1500,$$

whence:

		c	v	s	
1st period	I	3000 +	1500 +	(900 cap. + 600 cons.) =	6000
	II	2000 +	1000 +	(600 cap. + 400 cons.) =	4000
		5000 +	2500 +	(1500 cap. + 1000 cons.) =	10 000
2nd period	I	3600 +	1800 +	(1080 cap. + 720 cons.) =	7200
	II	2400 +	1200 +	(720 cap. + 480 cons.) =	4800
		6000 +	3000 +	(1800 cap. + 1200 cons.) =	12 000
and so on.					

In both cases above, we started with a given structure and propensity to save in Department II, and from this we deduced the corresponding structure and propensity to save in Department I. But it would be just as erroneous to claim that Department II dominates Department I in these schemes as to claim, with Rosa Luxemburg, that Department I dominates Department II in Marx's scheme. Joan Robinson puts it very well: 'The arithmetic is perfectly neutral between the two Departments.'[42]

Both Departments are equally 'dominated' by constraints which we ourselves define by choosing the figures of our schemes and forbidding any transfers between Departments. It is this last constraint which drives us, in the case of differing organic compositions of capital, to adopt the artifice of differing propensities to save between capitalists of the two Departments. To say, as Rosa Luxemburg does, that Department I capitalists *decide* to save 550 out of 1100 and *compel* Department II capitalists to save 240 out of 800 is simply an optical illusion. By the same logic, looking through the telescope from the other end, one might just as well say that the latter *decide* to save 240 out of 800 and thus compel the former to save 550 out of 1100.

But what is even more astonishing is that Rosa Luxemburg could not understand the structure of the figures which she set herself the task of analysing. She asserts that accumulation in Department II, being *subordinated* to that of Department I, becomes residual and fluctuates in an '*erratic*' way. To prove this, she draws up a table of Department II's saving and consumption:[43]

1st year	150 are capitalised,	600 consumed
2nd year	240	560
3rd year	264	616
4th year	290	678
5th year	320	745

This series, she says, proceeds randomly and is not based on any rule.

This is almost unbelievable. Apart from the first pair, which Rosa Luxemburg places in the 'first year', whereas in Marx it belonged to the period *before* the first year (a sort of transition period to pass from arbitrary figures to figures compatible with the chosen structure), the other 'capitalisation–consumption' pairs are neither erratic nor fluctuating; they strictly obey the rule we explained earlier. Actually, each figure in the left-hand column, added to its fellow from the

42. Introduction to *Accumulation of Capital*, p. 19.
43. *Ibid.*, p. 122.

right-hand column, forms a sum of which the former is $^{3}/_{10}$ and the latter $^{7}/_{10}$. Surely, this rule in no way derives from the manipulations of Department I's capitalists, but from the general constraints of the scheme on the one hand, and from those specific to Department II on the other.

One can only be nonplussed in the face of such a gross material error on the part of such an author as Rosa Luxemburg. In the preceding pages where this division was hidden within the aggregated totals, well and good. But here, Rosa Luxemburg herself took the trouble to disaggregate them and set them out in two columns, in such a way that a glance is enough to reveal the 'rule', the existence of which she so categorically denies!

This rule can be generalised as follows: in extensive extended reproduction, under the condition laid down that surplus-value is invested in the Department in which it is produced, the rate of capitalisation of surplus-value in each Department must be equal to the product of the multiplication of two quotients, that of the total capital employed in the Department divided by the Department's variable capital, and that of the rate of growth of the variable capital divided by the rate of surplus-value. Therefore, for Department II, the rate of capitalisation of surplus-value is

$$\frac{c'' + v''}{v''} \cdot \frac{\Delta v/v}{s/v}.$$

This formula, applied to Marx's numerical data, gives us:

$$\frac{1600 + 800}{800} \times \frac{0.1}{1} = 0.3.$$

Consequently, in the case under consideration, the 'rule' defines: capitalisation = 30% and consumption = 70% of the total surplus-value of Department II, and all the figures written in the two columns by Rosa Luxemburg herself obey this, except, of course, those of the 'first year', which are really those of the 'preceding year'.

As can be seen, the above formula contains no variable belonging to Department I. The rate of capitalisation and the rate of saving of Department II capitalists are determined solely by the conditions of their own Department and not in the least, as Rosa Luxemburg claims, by those of Department I.

Applying the same formula, we find that the rate of capitalization of surplus-value in Department I is

$$\frac{4400 + 1100}{1100} \times \frac{0.1}{1} = 0.5.$$

By the same method one can formulate the overall rule for the two Departments:

$$\frac{\text{rate of capitalisation of } s \text{ in I}}{\text{rate of capitalisation of } s \text{ in II}} = \frac{c'/v' + 1}{c''/v'' + 1},$$

whatever the overall rate of growth of production, the organic compositions of each Department and the rate of surplus-value. Naturally, depending on whether one is given the rate of capitalisation in Department I or Department II, one deduces from it the rate in Department II or Department I respectively. This means that there is no unilateral dependence; there is interdependence.

b. Marx's second scheme

		c		*v*		*s*		*V*
Previous situation	I	5000	+	1000	+	1000	=	7000
	II	1430	+	285	+	285	=	2000
		6430	+	1285	+	1285	=	9000
1st year	I	5417	+	1083	+	1083	=	7583
	II	1583	+	316	+	316	=	2215
		7000	+	1399	+	1399	=	9798
2nd year	I	5869	+	1173	+	1173	=	8215
	II	1715	+	342	+	342	=	2399
		7584	+	1515	+	1515	=	10 614
3rd year	I	6358	+	1271	+	1271	=	8900
	II	1858	+	371	+	371	=	2600
		8216	+	1642	+	1642	=	11 500

This second scheme of Marx's is free from the fault that so misled Rosa Luxemburg – different rates of capitalisation of surplus-value (savings ratios) in each Department. It was because the savings ratio in Department II was, in the last scheme, lower than that in Department I, that it seemed to her erratic and residual, and therefore determined by that of Department I. We have seen that this is quite false. This ratio was lower quite simply because the organic composition chosen for Department II was itself lower, and it was neither erratic nor fluctuating, nor residual, but strictly proportional to the organic composition. However this may be, this 'anomaly' disappears in Marx's second scheme, since the organic composition here is the same in both Departments and, consequently, the savings ratios are also the same. Rosa Luxemburg recognizes this: 'Accumulation in both Departments here proceeds uniformly, in marked difference from the first example. From the second year onwards, both Departments capitalise half their surplus value and consume the other half. A bad choice of figures in the first example thus seems to be responsible for its arbitrary appearance.'[44]

As we have seen, this 'arbitrary appearance' was quite imaginary, the product of an incorrect reading of the figures on the part of Rosa Luxemburg. But this is not important. With this new scheme, that mistake has become impossible and, since everything has now sorted itself out, the reader expects Rosa Luxemburg finally to put an end to her nonsense about domination of one Department by the other. This hope is disappointed:

> But we must check up to make sure that it is not only a mathematical manipulation with cleverly chosen figures which this time ensures the smooth progress of accumulation. [Perhaps the writer would like accumulation to progress with badly picked or arbitrary figures?] In the first as well as in the second example, we are continually struck by a seemingly general rule of accumulation: to make any accumulation possible, Department II must always enlarge its constant capital by precisely the amount by which Department I increases (*a*) the proportion of surplus value for consumption and (*b*) its variable capital.[45]

There follows a detailed enumeration of the transactions between the two Departments, which once again attempts to prove that Department II's accumulation depends on Department I, and which can be summed up as follows: if Department I capitalists wish to accumulate 500 and consume 500, they will need 1583 of consumption goods, 1083 for their workers and 500 for themselves, which capitalists of Department II must supply them with and for which, consequently, they must accept 1583 of means of production in exchange. Therefore, if the latter only need 1430 for replacement purposes, they are constrained to accumulate 153. Consequently, Department I commands and Department II obeys.

It is obvious that, following the same logic, one might just as well

44. *Ibid.*, pp. 124–5.
45. *Ibid.*, p. 125.

say: if capitalists of Department II decide to capitalise 184, i.e. 31 in *v* and 153 in *c*, they will need 1583 of means of production (1430 + 153 = 1583), which Department I must supply them with. Consequently, Department I must accept 1583 of consumption goods in exchange, and to make use of them, and of the 5417 means of production which it is left with, it is compelled to consume 500 of them and increase its workforce by 83, since this is the only way to obey the assumption that the organic composition is constant. Consequently, it is Department II which commands and Department I which obeys! It is characteristic that, while working through the series of exchanges between the two Departments, Rosa Luxemburg herself comes to see this dependence in the opposite direction and contradicts her earlier position: 'Here it becomes evident for the second time [?] that accumulation in Department I is dependent upon Department II.'[46]

Finally, the only thing which Rosa Luxemburg 'discovers' is *inter*dependence between the two Departments, which no one ever denied or ignored, and a property of interdependence is alternation between the determinant and the determined, depending which one takes first. Despite all this, she concludes imperturbably, at the end of her laborious analysis, that 'it shows clearly that the accumulation of Department II is completely determined and dominated by the accumulation of Department I', and that it is 'quite obvious that Department I has taken the initiative and actively carries out the whole process of accumulation, while Department II is merely a passive appendage'.[47]

This unidirectional dependence which she bases, in the case of the first scheme, on a simple error of calculation on her part, and which she contents herself, in the case of the second scheme, with asserting without any evidence, is used by her as a bridge to pass, in the subsequent pages, from mathematical formulae to reality, in order to examine 'whether capitalist accumulation does in actual fact conform to this hard and fast rule' of one-way dependence, and naturally to conclude in the negative.[48]

We will later on examine this part of her work referring to 'actual fact', which she interposes between two theoretical analyses of schemes. Up to this point, she has contented herself with criticising Marx's two existing schemes. She sees in them faults which they do not have; she has not yet discussed those which they actually suffer from and which make them unacceptable.

46. *Ibid.*, p. 126.
47. *Ibid.*, p. 127.
48. *Ibid.*

c. The scheme of intensive extended reproduction

Rosa Luxemburg is conscious of the fundamental inadequacy of Marx's schemes. They rule out technical progress, as they are constructed on the basis of an unchanging organic composition of social capital. This implies that the surplus reinvested in each period is always divided in the same proportion between *c* and *v*, either because wages eternally rise at the same rate as the accumulation of capital, or because the wage-earning population and therefore, in the long term, the population as a whole, grows at this rate, or, finally, because the product of these two rates is equal to the rate of accumulation of capital. These implications are not only diametrically opposed to all Marx's most basic teachings, but also quite gratuitous. While Rosa Luxemburg does not notice the second of these implications – at any rate she does not mention it – she is, however, perfectly conscious of the first. She therefore tries to remedy it by changing the figures of Marx's second scheme, in order to take account of a rise in both the organic composition of capital and the rate of surplus-value. She ends up with a scheme as shown in the table.[49]

	c	*v*	*s*		*V*
I	5000	+ 1000	+ 1000	=	7000
II	1430	+ 285	+ 285	=	2000
	6430	+ 1285	+ 1285	=	9000
I	$5428\frac{4}{7}$	+ $1071\frac{3}{7}$	+ 1083	=	7583
II	$1587\frac{5}{7}$	+ $311\frac{2}{7}$	+ 316	=	2215
	$7016\frac{2}{7}$	+ $1382\frac{5}{7}$	+ 1399	=	9798
I	5903	+ 1139	+ 1173	=	8215
II	1726	+ 331	+ 342	=	2399
	7629	+ 1470	+ 1515	=	10 614
I	6424	+ 1205	+ 1271	=	8900
II	1879	+ 350	+ 371	=	2600
	8303	+ 1555	+ 1642	=	11 500

49. *Ibid.*, p. 337.

This scheme attempts to illustrate mixed extended reproduction, extensive and intensive at the same time: extensive, because the quantity of living labour employed increases considerably from one year to the next; intensive, because c/v and even $c/(v + s)$ also increase, although by much less.

Then, Rosa Luxemburg notes, to the extent that c/v does increase, i.e. to the extent that the scheme approaches the reality of capitalist accumulation, equilibrium in use-values between the two portions of output and the two portions of consumption (productive and unproductive) is breached and we reach deadlock. Gross investment between years one and two is $7016^2/_7$, whereas output of means of production is only 7000. Conversely, personal consumption is only $1983^5/_7$, whereas output of consumption goods is 2000. Hence, overproduction of $16^2/_7$ in Department II and equivalent underproduction in Department I. This *over* and *under*production reach 46 between years two and three; and 88 between years three and four.

These findings lead Rosa Luxemburg to conclude that Marx's scheme is not open to improvement; that on the contrary any improvement in the sense of taking account of the rising organic composition reveals the tendency of the system towards increasing *overproduction* of articles of final consumption and, therefore, its *mathematical* incapability of reproducing itself without exchanges with non-capitalist producers. 'If the diagram is amended accordingly, the result . . . will be an increasing annual surplus in the consumer at the expense of producer goods.'[50]

How can the introduction of foreign trade re-equilibrate the system? By absorbing the surplus of consumption goods and supplying the means of production (raw materials) which will make up for the equivalent shortfall in Department I. This is a necessary conclusion of her analysis.[51]

But when she worked out her position, Rosa Luxemburg must have known the realities of international trade, which do not always square with her scheme. In their trade with underdeveloped

50. *Ibid.*, p. 336.

51. This conclusion was put very clearly by a committed Luxemburgist, L. Sartre: 'We should recall that the destruction of equilibrium, inevitably produced by capitalism in its upward march, is caused not only by general overproduction of final consumption goods, but simultaneously by underproduction of means of production. In order to eliminate or at least reduce this disequilibrium, therefore, all capitalist society needs to do is exchange with its non-capitalist hinterland all or part of the consumption goods which it produces too many of, for the means of production it lacks. And it so happens that the agricultural and craft-based environment into which capitalism is born are capable of rendering it this service.' (*Esquisse d'une théorie marxiste des crises périodiques*, p. 108).

countries, developed countries do not always exchange consumer goods for raw materials (textiles for cotton), as she would require that they do. Far from it. They very often exchange means of production for consumer goods – machinery and steel for wheat, coal for tea, etc. There is still stronger evidence that she knew these realities, since a writer with whom she was in dispute, Tugan Baranovski, discussed the case of England – the case of textiles, which is the most favorable to R.L.'s position – and it emerges from the figures published by him that over a period when trade was expanding rapidly, from 1878 to 1890, English exports of iron grew by 73% and those of machinery by 120%, while exports of cotton textiles grew by a mere 17%, woollen fabrics by only 22% and linen not at all. So she changes her tune and completely ignores her own conclusions to declare that overproduction is just as likely to affect Department I, or even both Departments at the same time. 'Conversely', she says, 'capitalist production supplies means of production in excess of its own demand and finds buyers in the non-capitalist countries. . . .'[52] And that is that.

This is a serious inconsistency. But all Rosa Luxemburg's work is like this. Like some litigants in court ('Whereas . . . we deny the existence of the debt for which we are being sued; further, whereas . . . we have already settled the debt; and further, whereas . . . we challenge the amount of the debt. . . .'), the requirements of controversy lead her to switch from one defence to another, without caring in the least whether they are mutually contradictory. 'Each of these cases', she adds, 'differs from Marx's diagram. In one case, the product of Department II exceeds the needs of both departments . . . In the second case, the product of Department I. . . . These two prototypes continually overlap in real life, supplement each other and merge.'[53]

To say the least, this is a most cavalier treatment of the problems involved. Up to this point, Rosa Luxemburg has done her utmost to show that the system has a fundamental tendency to the first kind of inbalance. Nothing in this 'proof' left any room at all for a *reversal* of this tendency. Only her contradiction by reality leads her to envisage the opposite case. So, as if this were a matter of course, she incorporates this contradiction by decreeing without any explanation the 'transformation' of her case into its opposite.

Despite all this, if we ignore this contradiction and confine ourselves to Rosa Luxemburg's theoretical case, we can focus on the central

52. *The Accumulation of Capital*, p. 352.
53. *Ibid.*, p. 353.

point of her theory, the only one compatible with her premises. Here there is no mistake. Given all the assumptions, disequilibrium is inevitable. If (i) the rate of surplus-value is the same everywhere, (ii) capitalists save the same proportion of their profits wherever they may be and (iii) they can only invest these savings in their own Department, the two Departments must expand at the same rate, whereas they produce the material elements of c and v respectively. Since c must grow faster than v, a shortfall in I's output and oversupply of II's output necessarily follows. This much is clear. If there is any error, it must lie in one of the premises themselves.[54]

Exclusively internal financing

Hypotheses (i) and (ii) are necessary, since neither the rate of exploitation nor the propensity to save depend in any way upon the nature of the commodity being produced; but constraint (iii) is, as we have seen several times, not merely gratuitous but absurd. As Joan Robinson points out, '[Rosa Luxemburg's] model is over-determined because of the rule that the increment of capital within each Department at the end of a year must equal saving made within the same Department during the year. If capitalists from Department II were permitted to lend part of their savings to Department I to be invested in its capital, a breakdown would no longer be inevitable.'[55]

Rosa Luxemburg does not just plead ignorance of this possibility of transferring factors from one department to the other: she denies it explicitly on several occasions. Earlier, when studying simple reproduction, she wrote: 'In capitalist society, however, the connections between the two great departments depend upon exchange of commodities, on the exchange of equivalents. The workers and capitalists of Department I can only obtain as many provisions from Department II as they can deliver of their own commodities, the means of production.'[56]

Rosa Luxemburg is forgetting two things: firstly, that equivalence does not operate at the level of Departments, which for their part do not exchange anything, but at the level of individual capitalists, real persons or legal entities; secondly, that the exchange of commodities for stocks and shares is also an exchange of equivalents. There is nothing to stop a capitalist from operating in both Departments at the

54. Leon Sartre expressed this argument formally, giving a complex mathematical proof of it. (*Esquisse*, pp. 6, 28, 29, 30, 31, 33, 34, 41.) We do not consider this worthwhile. Since mathematics is only the shorthand of logic, its use is not justified in cases where clear language is more concise than the use of formulae, as is the case here.

55. Introduction to *The Accumulation of Capital*, p. 25.

56. *Ibid.*, p. 85.

same time, so that after selling his noodles produced in Department II, he uses the funds accruing from these sales to buy machinery and instal it in a metallurgical works belonging to Department I, or even to buy shares in an existing metallurgical works on the stock exchange. In this case he would have settled his accounts without any debit or credit, but exchanges between the Departments would not be equivalent, since Department II would have fed the workers and capitalists of Department I, whereas the counterpart in Department I goods would not have left the Department. This is exactly what some Department II capitalists will necessarily do in the conditions defined by Rosa Luxemburg, with Department II's market overstocked, while that of Department I is expanding. This exit of capitals may lead to a relative fall in the organic composition of Department II, but it is equally compatible with maintenance of the same organic composition in both Departments. In the last case, a proportionate number of workers will also leave Department II for Department I.

In typical fashion, a few pages further on, Rosa Luxemburg herself points out that reality differs from her scheme in several respects, and that one of these divergences is 'the ceaseless flow of capital from one branch of production to another'.[57] It is impossible to tell whether the use of the term 'branch' instead of 'Department' here is deliberate or accidental, but, as Joan Robinson points out, if transfers between Departments are ruled out, then they should also be ruled out between branches and between firms, since a capitalist does not necessarily have closer relations with other capitalists of his own branch or Department than with those of the other Department. Finally, Rosa Luxemburg's model ignores the possibility of outside funding for firms: the financial market and the stock exchange disappear, and we are left with 100% financing from retained earnings.

Rosa Luxemburg reformulates this postulate on many occasions. Thus in Chapter VII, she claims that one of the conditions of capitalist production of commodities is 'the fact . . . that the entrepreneurs of either Department can only obtain the products of the other by an exchange of equivalents'. She goes on: 'Variable capital and surplus value in Department I together represent the demand of this Department for consumer goods. The product of Department II must provide for the satisfaction of this demand, but consumer goods can only be obtained in exchange for an equivalent part of the product of Department I, the means of production. These equivalents, useless to Department II in their natural form if not employed as constant capital in the process of production, will thus

57. *Ibid.*, p. 104.

determine how much constant capital there is to be in Department II.'[58]

This shows how the whole edifice of Rosa Luxemburg's theory comes more and more to rest on this cornerstone of the equivalence of exchanges between the two Departments. The cause of her *impasse* is her unwillingness to challenge this equivalence. This becomes clearer on the following page. It is because of 'the relations of exchange between the two Departments which would in turn necessitate an equivalent transfer of the products of Department I into Department II' that it is 'downright impossible to achieve a faster expansion of Department I as against Department II within the limits of Marx's diagram'.[59]

In Chapter XXV, where Rosa Luxemburg returns to the theoretical examination of the schemes, she again writes: '. . . the technical organisation of expanded reproduction can and must be such as to . . .' etc., but 'in this connection, we must bear in mind also that both departments can obtain their respective elements of production *only* by means of mutual *exchange*'.[60] Later on, in the conclusion to her chapter on protectionism and accumulation, she finds it necessary to recall that the latter 'is confined to the exchange of equivalents and remains within the limits of commodity exchange'.[61]

For Rosa Luxemburg, this need for an equilibrated *balance of trade* between the two Departments is so obvious that she does not even feel the need to discuss it. It was no use for Tugan Baranovski to prove that this is the solution to the problem – Rosa Luxemburg, who had definitely read his work since she devotes a whole chapter to its refutation, does not even mention his argument on this point.

It is only in her second work, the *Anti-critique,* while discussing Otto Bauer's scheme published in *Neue Zeit*, a more consistent scheme than Tugan Baranovski's – and to the best of our knowledge the first true scheme of intensive extended reproduction in Marxist writings – in which equilibrium is maintained by this very transfer of factors from one Department to the other, that Rosa Luxemburg can no longer evade this question. She starts by expressing her bewilderment at such an approach, at which she hurls all the insults in the book – 'bold', 'original', a 'confused contraption which makes one's eyes swim'.[62] But she wants to go further: she tries to prove that

58. *Ibid.*, p. 128.
59. Ibid., p. 341.
60. *Ibid.*, p. 339, emphasis added.
61. *Ibid.*, p. 452.
62. cf. *Ibid.*, pp. 95–6. Leon Sartre's position is more subtle: 'It is true that the scheme only shows a constant relation of the productive forces if we assume that each

Continued on page 189

even if one were to accept this outrageous hypothesis, the process of reproduction would still be mathematically impossible. And here she again displays her astonishing inability to read a scheme properly.

Otto Bauer's scheme
Otto Bauer had proposed the scheme shown in the table.[63]

	c		*v*		*surplus-value*						
					consumed		*invested*				
							in c		*in v*		
I	120 000	+	50 000	+	(37 500	+	10 000	+	2500)	=	220 000
II	80 000	+	50 000	+	(37 500	+	10 000	+	2500)	=	180 000
	200 000	+	100 000	+	(75 000	+	20 000	+	5000)	=	400 000
I	134 666	+	53 667	+	(39 740	+	11 244	+	2683)	=	242 000
II	85 334	+	51 333	+	(38 010	+	10 756	+	2567)	=	188 000
	220 000	+	105 000	+	(77 750	+	22 000	+	5250)	=	430 000
I	151 048	+	57 576	+	(42 070	+	12 638	+	2868)	=	266 200
II	90 952	+	52 674	+	(38 469	+	11 562	+	2643)	=	196 300
	242 000	+	110 250	+	(80 539	+	24 200	+	5511)	=	462 500
I	169 324	+	61 748	+	(44 455	+	14 196	+	3097)	=	292 820
II	96 876	+	54 014	+	(38 899	+	12 424	+	2691)	=	204 904
	266 200	+	115 762	+	(83 354	+	26 620	+	5788)	=	497 724

This scheme satisfies the essential conditions of extended intensive reproduction and all the internal consistencies demanded by the process. The organic composition rises from each period to the next, but slightly faster in Department I. The rate of capitalisation of surplus-value is the same in each Department, but as might be expected it rises along with capitalists' aggregate income. It rises from 25% in the first year to 26%, 27% and 28% in the fourth year. The rate of surplus-value is also the same, at 100%, in both Departments. The total quantity of living labour rises by 5% per year. Department I's annual output is equal to the following year's total constant capital. Department II's annual output is equal to capitalists' personal consumption of that same year plus workers' consumption in the following year.

Realization takes place in the same way each year, and in the first year the breakdown is as shown in the table.

62. *Continued from page 187*
of the two great divisions of industry capitalises its profits within its own group. But this is no gratuitous assumption, it is a condition necessarily realised by capitalist production. The search for profit and competition mean that each capitalist must devote to his own company exclusively all the realised profit which is to be accumulated . . . at least', he adds at the end of the paragraph, 'in the phase when the economy is generally prosperous.' (*op. cit.*, p. 62).

In Sartre's view, 'transfers' are not completely ruled out, but they appear too late, at the wrong time in a sense, after the crisis has broken out. Although it rests on a pure assumption, Sartre's analysis is still more acceptable than Luxemburg's, but this is achieved at the price of depriving the Luxemburgist position of its most striking point, the material *impossibility* of realisation. It then becomes an explanation of the alternation between prosperity and depression, a subject which did not interest Rosa Luxemburg. I would even say that ultimately Sartre's analysis can only become acceptable if it becomes closer to that of Rodbertus, for whom Luxemburg had nothing but contempt. For it was Rodbertus who noticed that technical progress results in the freeing of part of the social capital engaged in the production of consumption goods for the working class; and that this part should move into other branches of production. But this transfer takes time and does not proceed smoothly. . . . The result of this is partial overproduction which, through the play of the interdependencies between all branches of industry, turns into general overproduction.

63. I have corrected the 4th year's figures. Otto Bauer gave:

169 124 + 61 738 + 44 465 + 14 186 + 3087 = 292 600

96 876 + 54 024 + 38 909 + 12 414 + 2701 = 204 924

This seems to be a slip of the pen on Bauer's part, since these figures are not compatible with realisation of the product of the preceding year, or with the extension of future production.

Department II		
Total output		180 000
One portion is realized within the Department:		
Capitalists' consumption	37 500	
1st year's variable capital	50 000	
Additional variable capital for the 2nd year	1 333	88 833
Balance		91 167
Another portion is sold to Department I:		
Department I capitalists' consumption	37 500	
1st year's variable capital	50 000	
Additional variable capital for the 2nd year	2 500	90 000
Unsold balance		1 167
Department I		
Total output		220 000
One portion is realized within the Department:		
Replacement of 1st year's constant capital	120 000	
Additional constant capital for the 2nd year	10 000	130 000
Balance		90 000
Another portion is sold to Department II:		
Replacement of 1st year's constant capital	80 000	
Additional constant capital for the 2nd year	5 334	85 334
Unsold Balance		4 666

It remains to be explained what are the markets for these unsold goods, amounting to 4666 in Department I and 1167 in Department II. According to Bauer Department II capitalists buy these 4666 of means of production, but instead of setting them to work in Department II, they set them to work in Department I, either setting up new firms themselves or buying shares into existing firms. To this they add the 1167 of consumption goods which they have left under the heading of additional variable capital needed to set these additional means of production to work (in the same proportion, 1:4, as the rest of additional capital). So they invest in Department I part of the surplus-value which they realized in Department II. In fact, out of the surplus-value which they extracted in the first year,

amounting to		50 000
they have spent		
on their personal consumption	37 500	
They have invested in their own Department		
in constant capital	5 334	
in variable capital	1 333	44 167
So the sum they still have to invest is		5 833

Or, as above, 4666 + 1167 = 5833.

Rosa Luxemburg is outraged:

So that is the solution, she explains; the first Department sells the indigestible remainder of 4666 to the second Department, which does not make use of it for itself, but 'transfers' it . . . back to the first Department where it is used to further expand constant capital I . . . At this point we are blindly following Bauer through thick and thin [*because it already requires Rosa Luxemburg to be rather conciliatory for her to accept the 'economic fact' of a transfer of surplus-value from one department to the other*]; we just want to notice whether his own freely chosen operations are taking place fairly and cleanly, whether he is abiding by his own assumptions.

Capitalists I 'sell' their commodity-remainder of 4666 to capitalists II who 'buy' it by transferring (. . .etc.) But wait a minute! What do they 'buy' it with? Where is the 'part of the surplus value' which pays for the purchase? There is no trace of it in Bauer's tables! The entire amount of commodities in Department II has already been used up for the consumption of the capitalist class of both Departments as well as for the renewal and enlargement of variable capital . . ., at least except a remainder of 1167. This 1167 . . . is all that is left over from the surplus-value of the second Department. And now Bauer uses this 1167, not as a sort of down payment on the 4666 in means of production, but as variable capital for the additional workers, who were needed for the allegedly 'bought' 4666 in means of production. Whichever way you look at the thing, the capitalists II have used up all their surplus value; they turn out their pockets and cannot find a penny to buy the stored 4666 in means of production.

. . .The fact remains that the manipulations of Bauer's capitalists are sheer swindles. These gentlemen pretend to be buying and selling 4666 in means of production, but in reality there are no means with which to buy them. When capitalists I give the remainder of their commodities to capitalists II it is a lovely birthday present. And, in order not to act shabbily, capitalists II reply to this noble gesture with equal high-mindedness; they give the present straight back to their colleagues and even generously add their own remainder of consumer goods worth 1167 . . .

Bauer uses the following tricks to get himself out of this mess. Firstly, he *fabricates* the 'sale' of the unsaleable remainder of commodities from

Department I to Department II, without a single word about how the latter pays for it. Secondly, after the fabricated 'sale', he lets capitalists II do something even more novel: with the newly acquired means of production they walk out of their own department into the other and invest them there as capital . . . (*Rosa Luxemburg is forgetting that, apart from anything else, there is nothing 'novel' about the solution proposed by Otto Bauer. It had been proposed eight years earlier by Tugan Baranovski in a work which she herself had set out to refute.*[64])

It is certainly a bold idea. Marx was the first in the history of political economy to make the distinction between the two Departments of social production and describe it schematically . . . .

Marx's distinction and his model, however, assume that *only exchange relations* exist between the two Departments, which is precisely the basic form of capitalist or commodity-producing economy. . . . Bauer comes along and casually hurls Marx's entire analysis to the ground by 'transferring' the commodities backwards and forwards from one Department to the other *without exchange* . . . .

Bauer appeals to the fact that, with technological progress, the production of means of production will grow at the expense of the consumer goods production, and the capitalists in the latter Department will thus constantly place a portion of their surplus value in the former Department in some form or other (through banks, share-holding or founding new enterprises). All this is excellent. However, the 'transfer' of accumulated surplus value from one branch of production to another can only occur in the form of money capital. . . . A load of unsaleable wax candles cannot buy shares in copper mines, nor can a warehouse full of unmarketable rubber shoes set up a new machine factory.[65]

We have reproduced this long extract (the passage from which it is taken is about four times as long as our quotation) here for two reasons. Firstly, to show the persistence with which Rosa Luxemburg made use of schemes when she thought they worked in her favour, which totally contradicts her declaration at the start of this second work, that her first volume only used schemes as an 'accessory tool'.[66] And secondly, to show how her extraordinary talent for polemic was wasted in an unworthy cause. For we find it rather difficult to believe that Rosa Luxemburg was incapable of reading figures properly; the only possible explanation is that she was satisfied with a superficial reading of the diagram before launching into a wholehearted attack upon its author.

Of course there is no present from Department I capitalists to those of Department II, nor are there any unmarketable candles. At

64. cf. above, pp. 166–8.
65. *The Accumulation of Capital*, pp. 93–6.
66. *Ibid.*, p. 48.

the point when Department I capitalists still have unsold means of production amounting to 4666 on their hands, Department II capitalists have *already sold* to those of Department I

commodities worth	90 000
but have only bought from them	85 334
So their sales exceed their purchases by	4 666

Precisely because no one ever does give anyone a present, they must have received for this surplus of 4666 either money or something which can serve in the stead of money, such as bills of exchange, IOUs, etc. So this value of 4666 is *already realized* for Department II capitalists and has taken on the form of money-capital, or more precisely of liquid capital ready to be invested. They buy Department I factories with this liquid capital, and not with candles or wellington boots.

What Rosa Luxemburg fails to see is that these 'transfers' take place, not to remedy any existing disequilibrium, but to prevent any such disequilibrium from developing in the following period. With or without 'transfers', equilibrium and realization are assured at the close of the first period. But without these first period 'transfers', equilibrium would be broken and realization would become *materially* impossible at the close of the second period.

This is why:

c		*v*		*s*		*V*
120 000	+	50 000	+	50 000	=	220 000
80 000	+	50 000	+	50 000	=	180 000
200 000	+	100 000	+	100 000	=	400 000
130 000	+	52 500	+	52 500	=	235 000
90 000	+	52 500	+	52 500	=	195 000
220 000	+	105 000	+	105 000	=	430 000
140 500	+	55 125	+	55 125	=	250 750
100 500	+	55 125	+	55 125	=	210 750
241 000	+	110 250	+	110 250	=	461 500

Between the 1st and 2nd periods there is no problem, since

$$\text{Output } I_{t1} = Ic_{t2} + IIc_{t2}$$
$$(220\,000 = 130\,000 + 90\,000)$$

$$\text{Output } II_{t1} = \tfrac{3}{4}Is_{t1} + \tfrac{3}{4}IIs_{t1} + Iv_{t2} + IIv_{t2}$$
$$(180\,000 = 37\,500 + 37\,500 + 52\,500 + 52\,500)$$

But, as could be expected, in the absence of 'transfers' at the close of the 1st period, the following disequilibrium emerges at the close of the 2nd:

$$\text{Output } I_{t2} < Ic_{t3} + IIc_{t3}$$
$$(235\,000 < 140\,500 + 100\,500)$$

and

$$\text{Output } II_{t2} > \tfrac{3}{4}Is_{t2} + \tfrac{3}{4}IIs_{t2} + Iv_{t3} + IIv_{t3}$$
$$(195\,000 > 39\,375 + 39\,375 + 55\,125 + 55\,125)$$

This amounts to overproduction of 6000 consumption goods and underproduction of 6000 means of production.

Once the operation concerning the 4666 means of production has been completed every one has reconstituted his funds, and the only remaining unsold goods are 1167 consumption goods. But as soon as the 4666 have been turned into extra factories employing additional workers, the realization of these 1167 does not present any particular problem. They behave in exactly the same way as the 2500 already added to Department I's variable capital and the 1333 already added to Department II's variable capital, on which subject Rosa Luxemburg had no objections. This is settled by Marx's general assumption under which capitalists' consumption goods are drawn from the current period's output, while those of the workers are drawn from the output of the preceding period, which implies that all the variable capital must be available in its material form, just like the constant capital, by the start of any period. Of course this is a simplification. Capitalists do not use their factories as warehouses for a stock of provisions to feed their workers in the same way that they stock up fuel, any more than they carry these consumption goods in their luggage on the journey from Department II to Department I. Whether these goods are destined for the workers of II or those of I, these goods are sold to the same wholesalers, and the workers later go to buy them from the same shops.

Otto Bauer's scheme is based on the assumption that the wage-earning population in employment grows by 5% annually. Since the rate of surplus-value remains constant the stock of workers' subsistence goods needed for the second year is 105 000. This is the total quantity to be traded, and there is no reason to earmark any part of it, such as the 1167. The overall breakdown can be presented in the table.

Department II	*realizes within its own Department*		
	for capitalists' personal consumption	37 500	
	for the 2nd year's variable capital	51 333	88 833
	sells to Department I		
	for capitalists' personal consumption	37 500	
	for the 2nd year's variable capital	53 667	91 167
	Total sales		180 000
Department I	*realizes within its own Department*		134 666
	sells to Department II		85 334
	Total sales		220 000
Therefore II sells I, as above			91 167
	I sells II commodities worth	85 334	
	stocks and bonds worth	5 833	91 167

Formation of new capital

Department I:	constant capital	14 666	
	variable capital	3 667	18 333
	Financed by:		
	internal financing: Department I surplus-value	12 500	
	external financing: sale of stocks and bonds to Department II capitalists	5 833	18 333
Department II:	constant capital	5 334	
	variable capital	1 333	6 667
	Financed by Department II surplus-value	12 500	
	minus purchase of stocks and bonds from I	5 833	6 667

It is evident that all the accounts are balanced and closed without any 'present' or uncovered balance.

The rate of surplus-value

The question of 'transfers' is not Rosa Luxemburg's only objection. She raises another. She notes that Otto Bauer's scheme assumes a constant rate of surplus-value despite technical progress as expressed by the rising organic composition. In her opinion this is impossible: it would imply that real wages rise in proportion to the growth of productivity, in which case capitalists would have no interest in expanding production. (She must take full responsibility for this last remark, which is not borne out by the facts. Real wages have already been rising continuously for several decades now, but capitalists continue to expand production for all that.) But she also believes that introduction of the assumption that the rate of surplus-value rises would make Otto Bauer's scheme collapse 'like a house of cards',[67] and this claim deserves closer examination.

Both Otto Bauer and Pannekoek had already remarked that the hypothesis of a constant rate of surplus-value is not crucial; that it could perfectly well be dropped and a scheme in equilibrium be constructed without it. Rosa Luxemburg believes the opposite: 'It is a pity that Bauer did not consider it worth his trouble to go on to complete this little detail himself, instead of breaking off his ingenious calculations . . . at the very point where his proof should have begun.' And she adds in a note, 'Pannekoek, also, after calculating his tables with quickly growing capital but with a constant rate of surplus value, says: "As above, a gradual alteration in the rate of exploitation comes into consideration too". . . . But he too leaves that difficulty to the reader.'[68]

The least that can be said is that Rosa Luxemburg is very unwise to take this stand. We do not know if Otto Bauer and Pannekoek took up the challenge and produced the scheme demanded by Rosa Luxemburg. But the scheme is in fact very easy to construct; this is done in the table.

					Surplus-value						
					Consumed		Invested				
c		v					in c		in v		
120 000	+	50 000	+	(	38 019.8	+	10 000	+	1980.2)	=	220 000
80 000	+	50 000	+	(	38 019.8	+	10 000	+	1980.2)	=	180 000
200 000	+	100 000	+	(	76 039.6	+	20 000	+	3960.4)	=	400 000
							100 000				

67. *Ibid.*, p. 109.
68. *Ibid.*, p. 99.

		Surplus-value			
		Consumed	Invested		
c	v		in c	in v	
135 000	+ 52 970.4	+ (40 727.6	+ 11 210	+ 2092)	= 242 000
85 000	+ 50 990	+ (39 205.4	+ 10 790	+ 2014.6)	= 188 000
220 000	+ 103 960.4	+ (79 933	+ 22 000	+ 4106.6)	= 430 000
			106 039.6		
151 741.7	+ 56 096	+ (43 589.4	+ 12 561.9	+ 2211)	= 266 200
90 258.3	+ 51 971	+ (40 385.3	+ 11 638.1	+ 2047.3)	= 196 300
242 000	+ 108 067	+ (83 974.7	+ 24 200	+ 4258.3)	= 462 500
			112 433		
170 334.9	+ 59.424.1	+ (46 642.1	+ 14 083	+ 2335.9)	= 292 820
95 865.1	+ 52 901.2	+ (41 522.1	+ 12 537	+ 2079.6)	= 204 905
266 200	+ 112 325.3	+ (88 164.2	+ 26 620	+ 4415.5)	= 497 725
			119 199.7		

It can be seen that this scheme is based on Otto Bauer's data and assumptions, plus the assumption of growth in the rate of surplus-value, as demanded by Rosa Luxemburg, here assumed to be at 2% per year.

	1st year	*2nd year*	*3rd year*	*4th year*
Wage-earning population ($v + s$) (grows 5% annually)	200 000	210 000	220 500	231 525
Organic composition (c/v) (grows 5.8% annually)	2	2.116	2.239	2.369
Rate of surplus-value (s/v) (grows 2% annually)	1	1.02	1.0404	1.0612
Rate of capitalisation of surplus-value (%)	23.96	24.62	25.31	26.04

So this scheme is internally consistent in terms of realization and the expansion of production from period to period. Yet the collapse forecast by Rosa Luxemburg has not taken place.

II. The real conditions of accumulation

So Rosa Luxemburg tries in vain to deduce the impossibility of accumulation in a *closed* capitalist system from schemes themselves. This approach is intrinsically absurd. It is inconceivable for a numerical scheme to prove the impossibility of anything. It is even more senseless to try to prove this impossibility from supposed weaknesses of certain schemes which were worked out by others in order, on the contrary, to prove the *possibility* of this kind of accumulation. Even if these weaknesses really existed they would prove nothing at all. But when this is added to the fact that these supposed weaknesses, examined so intricately and laboriously, turn out not to exist, it is heart-breaking.

Eventually, despite the decisive conclusions she was able to draw from them, Rosa Luxemburg comes to feel that schemes are not a good ground for her argument, and tries to escape from them. After all, she says, Marx worked out his schemes to show what the necessary conditions of accumulation are. But a necessary condition is not a sufficient condition. It is because Otto Bauer confused these two types of condition that he concluded, on the basis of schemes, that accumulation is possible, etc.

This is another error in formal logic. The necessary conditions of any state define the circumstances in which it is *possible* for it to exist; the sufficient conditions define the circumstances in which it is *certain* to exist. Once the necessary conditions of any state are present, this state is possible. Beyond this, no one has ever claimed that this state is certain, i.e. that expanding capitalism's equilibrium is necessary and indestructible.

However, these two conditions can perfectly well be examined in terms of schemes: if (i) the social product is composed of values in the right proportions and the right composition of use values, and if (ii) capitalists behave in a certain way, i.e. agree to exchange among themselves a portion of the social product equivalent to the capitalised part of their surplus-value; then extended reproduction is assured. In this context the first condition appears as necessary, the second as sufficient. Now the first is no problem for Rosa Luxemburg. She firmly and explicitly condemns any attempt to explain the tendency to overproduction by disproportionality, because it is an effect of Say's influence.[69] So only the second remains: will capitalists

69. Nonetheless, as we have seen, Rosa Luxemburg's analysis also ends up with a plus and a minus, which are strictly equal, in Departments II and I respectively. Foreign trade only redresses the balance. If this is the case, it is hard to see why this disequilibrium is not disproportionality of Say's kind as much as any other.

actually carry out the transactions necessary for the product to be realised and the system reproduced?

If the capitalists 'want', she paraphrases Bauer, to step up production by buying the necessary materials from each other, then the problem is solved. Would they want to? Why should they not want to, she asks, ridiculing her opponent's thinking. This is Rosa Luxemburg's new area of attack, when she leaves that of mathematical abstraction. She goes on to argue that such behaviour on the part of capitalists fundamentally contradicts capitalist rationality and is consequently *materially impossible.*

Rosa Luxemburg does not challenge the actual idea of mutual purchases and sales. Considerable portions of the product are already realized in this way within the limits of simple reproduction – the portion which replaces used-up constant capital and that which is used for capitalists' personal consumption. There is nothing abnormal in this as far as Rosa Luxemburg is concerned. What she denies is that capitalists can continue selling things to each other beyond this point, i.e. when the scale of production is extended.

The value of the social product is composed of three parts, of which the third is further composed of two: *c* + *v* + (*consumed s* + *capitalised s*). The realisation of *c, v* and *consumed s* presents no problem, even though that of *c* and *consumed s* also takes place through sales and purchases among the capitalists themselves. It is the realization of the third part, corresponding to '*capitalised s*', which would be impossible through this kind of transaction.

Why this difference? Because, in the first case, we are dealing with a capitalist who *needs* something – for his personal consumption or to replace an object destroyed in the course of production – and another capitalist who possesses this thing. They do a deal. A 'social need' is the basis of this realization. In the second case this social need is missing. For, to say that these are the same capitalists who now need these extra means of production and consumer goods to expand their production 'implies a previous capitalist incentive to enlarge production'.[70] This means that we are arguing in a circle, since extension of production is used to explain the operations which extend production.

Rosa Luxemburg then poses the question of the purpose of the capitalist system itself.[71] Who would benefit from an extension of production effected by the means suggested by the schemes? She poses the same question in Chapter XXV.[72] On the following page

70. *Ibid.*, p. 133.
71. cf. her description of Bulgakov's theory, *ibid.*, Chapter XXII.
72. *Ibid.*, p. 329.

she wonders explicitly 'who is to benefit by it, who are the new consumers for whose sake production is ever more enlarged'.[73] The same question, several pages further on: 'It cannot be discovered from the assumptions of Marx's diagram for whose sake production is progressively expanded.'[74] Such an extension of production, she concludes, is not accumulation of capital but greater production of machines for the sake of even greater production of machines, without any aim or purpose; it is a merry-go-round running empty, a dog chasing its tail. It is an absurdity. No one produces for the sake of producing.

We should first of all point out that the division of the social product into four slices of use-values corresponding to four aliquot parts of the total value of the gross product, of which only the last cannot be realised within the system, is valid for society as a whole, but not for each industry and each capitalist firm taken separately. When the first three slices of commodities have been sold within the system, as Rosa Luxemburg assumes, a large proportion of the fourth slice, the fraction of surplus-value *destined for capitalisation* will *ipso facto* have been realized in the accounts of certain enterprises, while others will not yet have sold the portion of their product corresponding to the first three slices. The whole branch of luxury goods will at this point, under Rosa Luxemburg's assumptions, have sold the whole of its product and realised all its surplus-value. In the branch of workers' consumption goods, whose yearly growth is quite low, the ratio of unsold goods to sold goods will, at the same point, be so low that, taking into account the uneven rate of sales in different firms, it will be zero for a large number of them. These enterprises will have realized everything; other enterprises in the same industry will, of course, have realized less than the part due to them. To a lesser extent, the same phenomenon takes place in Department I.

When we consider the whole economy, certainly, these leads and lags compensate for each other from the quantitative point of view. But deadlock, considered as a stage, now turns out to be an unacceptable abstraction. For this is not a question of quantity. The concepts 'more' and 'less' do not apply to the notion of deadlock. You are either deadlocked or you are not. The enterprises under consideration will already have passed this abstract stage, and this fact cannot be compensated for by the fact that others lag behind. For

73. *Ibid.*, p. 330.
74. *Ibid.*, p. 334.

in Rosa Luxemburg's own conception, this is a purely qualitative matter, a radical transformation which changes everything. Once this point has been passed, these enterprises change from sellers to purchasers. As such, it is they who supply this motor element which Rosa Luxemburg is searching for so desperately, this 'prime mover', this locomotive which will drag the whole economy into extended reproduction.

In other words these capitalists will already, in Rosa Luxemburg's model, have reconstituted their previous constant and variable capitals and transformed the rest of their product into *clinking coins,* as she likes to demand, or, which comes to the same thing, into liquid assets. Now, at least as far as they are concerned, it is a waste of time to get lost in philosophical speculations on the purpose of capitalism in general. They are not confronted with a multitude of choices: there are only two options open to them – to keep these liquid assets in their vaults or to buy something with them. Since hoarding is ruled out in Rosa Luxemburg's model – to allow it would block extended reproduction, even on the assumption of realization of the surplus through exchange with non-capitalist producers – the first solution is ruled out. Only the second remains: to buy something with them. Now in their situation and under the conditions of the model itself, they can hardly buy anything but extra means of production, and the fact that their behaviour is like a merry-go-round does not alter the issue.

What counts is that by doing this, they release the fourth slice which Rosa Luxemburg believes to be immobilised, but this time on the level of society as a whole. As a result other companies will in turn pass the *critical point* of realization and, by a chain reaction, the whole of output will be realized and extended reproduction accomplished. Does it then have any meaning to ponder on the rationality or aim of this process? A merry-go-round running empty, a dog chasing its tail? Certainly the capitalist system is a bit like that. And so what? How can this be helped? The whole process takes place, as we have seen, without any of the participants having at any point to pose the questions posed by Rosa Luxemburg, or to answer them.

Let us allow that what we have just described is only one possible case among several, the others being the opening of foreign markets, as in Rosa Luxemburg's model, the development of new technology or even simple economies of scale, giving rise to a competitive rush to invest, etc. The final result would be the same: greater production for the sake of even greater production. So if these questions on the purpose of the options open to the capitalists are redundant in one case, then they must be redundant in all of them.

But let us return to Rosa Luxemburg's account. Let us allow that, by the greatest of coincidences, all the runners arrive at the same moment at the fateful stage and prevent any further departure. In each firm there is a 'slice' of unsold goods exactly corresponding in value to the portion of surplus-value destined for capitalisation. Otto Bauer's scheme shows us by means of which exchanges between firms and which transfers of funds between Departments this fourth slice could be mobilised. To sum up, the Marxist theory of reproduction only proves one thing: if capitalists agree to reinvest their surplus right down to the last penny, extended reproduction will actually take place, and the whole social product will find a taker, even if final consumption is kept relatively low. Rosa Luxemburg objects. Why would they do this? Who is to benefit by it? For the sake of whose final consumption?

Quite apart from anything else, reading Rosa Luxemburg's account alone compels us to agree that they have an excellent reason for doing so. Does she not show by elementary logic that the risk of deadlock on the threshold of this fourth slice is a life-and-death matter for capitalism? So capitalists may perhaps find it preferable after all to go round in circles in an absurd capitalist 'merry-go-round' rather than to go in the straight line of a 'rational' career as a proletarian or even as an associated producer in some collectivist system, or, even worse, to go and break stones in a labour camp set up by a soviet republic for its class enemies.

This is especially true since, as Rosa Luxemburg is careful to warn us, what counts here is not the point of view of the individual capitalist, but that of his class. Now whereas it is conceivable for individual capitalists to have a motive in certain circumstances for getting out while the going is good, and for them, in so doing, to endanger their own system, the class, assuming that its point of view constantly determines the actions of its members as Rosa Luxemburg seems to believe, could have no interest in unleashing a crisis upon itself, when all it would have to do to avoid this would be to put together the idle 'slices' of machinery, provisions and workers, and allow them to turn in circles.

The argument is not strengthened but weakened by turning from the independent capitalist to the 'class'. The 'capitalist class' is not a producer cooperative, and Rosa Luxemburg is wrong to treat it as one. But if it were one, Rosa Luxemburg would be doubly wrong. For then there could be no crisis or deadlock. Sale, purchase, realization – everything which causes problems nowadays would disappear under the aegis of this one-capitalist class. It would pass its slaves and its products from one unit of production to another, in the same way as actual factories pass them from one workshop to another or from one branch to another.

Why does Rosa Luxemburg insist on turning from the isolated capitalist to the class? Because at the same time she turns from *investment incentives*, which concern individual capitalists, to the overall purpose of the system. This is perhaps a pity, since otherwise there is a lot to say about the advantages presented by pre-existing foreign markets (H. Denis) over *expected* domestic markets, at the level of the individual capitalist – and it is no coincidence if many commentators (Joan Robinson, Henri Denis, Jacques Vallier for example) try to rescue her theory or soften its rejection by placing it within the modern problematic of investment incentives. But this cannot satisfy Rosa Luxemburg. For she is determined to show, not the difficulties, risks and chances involved in the realization of the product, but its absolute, material, objective impossibility.

No objective law can, however, establish or exlude in any absolute sense the existence of incentives and their effectiveness. Since we have accepted that it is enough for capitalists to wish to invest the whole of their surplus for everything to turn out all right, all we need is an effective incentive for them to do so, and the intrinsic value of this or its share of 'objective' truth or falsity hardly matters.[75]

75. In fact incentives cannot be a priori true or false, real or illusory, since they are verified or refuted to the extent to which they operate or fail to do so. In March 1973 Montagu's of London, specialists in the gold market, published a study forecasting a rise in the price of gold. In the days following its publication, the price of gold rose by around ten dollars an ounce on all the exchanges. In appearance, Montagu's made an accurate prediction of how the market would behave. In reality, the market believed and followed Montagu's.

'A depression', wrote Domar, 'becomes now nothing else but a vast psychological phenomenon. . . . If firms were "somehow" induced to invest a sufficient amount, so that national income rose at the required rate, no disappointments would follow. Suppose now that it were possible for the government (presumably) to guarantee that income would actually grow at this rate for some time to come. Would not this guarantee, if taken seriously by the business public, call forth sufficient investment and thus *make* investment grow at the required rate? This is full employment by magic!' (*Essays on the Theory of Economic Growth*, p. 119.)

'Confidence', Torrens had already written at the start of the nineteenth century, 'like those prophecies which occasion their own fulfilment, creates that increased demand which it anticipates. . . . Now, if a single individual were to be seized with an unusual confidence, [his] expectations of advantage would be disappointed. Very different is the result when the increase of confidence becomes general . . ., each class, having more goods to dispose of, will enlarge the market for the others.' (*An Essay on the Production of Wealth*, pp. 328–9).

'The dominant causal factor', writes Pigou, 'is not on the side of the supply of mobile resources, but on the side of expectations of profit. When these are good, they lead businessmen to increase their borrowings . . . thus . . . bringing purchasing power into

Continued on page 204

It follows that in terms of 'incentives', anything is possible. While foreign markets are, in an open system, very attractive for investors, there is nothing to prevent other catalysts from replacing them more or less effectively in a closed system. Marx had already suggested one such catalyst – the mere existence of competition, which compels individual capitalists to adopt technical advances in order not to be eliminated from the race, despite the fact that the final result is negative, since the mechanisation of each additional enterprise annuls the differential advantage of the last. Otto Bauer refers to the natural growth of the working population which expands the domestic market. It is clear that the same expansion can result from an increase in real wages.

The first incentive, Marx's one, is completely ignored by Rosa Luxemburg. She disputes the other two. A market that expands as a result of extra wages paid by capitalists to extra workers is, for her, an absurdity. Anyway statistics show, she says, that throughout the nineteenth century in all the advanced countries, the rate of demographic growth was insignificant compared to the rate of growth of production. As for any rise in real wages, she declares dogmatically that that is incompatible with the essence of capitalism, and does not trouble herself about it any further.

All this is very weak. Certainly, no capitalist will take on extra workers or increase the wages of those he already employs in order to expand the market for his own products. He will keep the size of his own workforce and his own wage-level as low as he can. But if one can reasonably predict, over the coming ten or twenty years, a certain rate of population growth, and if rises of real wages have become a more or less regular phenomenon, as has been the case in recent years, any market survey, whether undertaken in the context of the launch of a new product or stepping up the production of an existing one, absolutely must take into account the product of these two rates.

75. *Continued from page 203*
circulation, pushing up prices: when they are bad, they have converse effects. Thus, while recognising that . . . expectations . . . may themselves be in part a psychological reflex of good and bad harvests . . . we conclude definitely that they, and not anything else, constitute the immediate and direct causes or antecedents of industrial fluctuations . . . . On the one hand, real causes *may* set going psychological causes . . . On the other hand, psychological causes *must* set going real causes, for an error of expectation made by one group of business men, leading to increased or diminished output on their part, alters the facts with which other groups are confronted.' (*Industrial Fluctuations*, pp. 29, 31, emphasis added).

Aftalion also laid great stress on the psychological factor. Thus in his view, if the holder of money expects a fall in prices, he will abstain from purchasing and prices will fall. In the reverse case, he will flee from money and prices will rise. In both cases what the economic agent expects takes place – because he expects it.

Once they are *anticipated* by economic agents, future markets become no different from those already known. The latter may be more certain and easier; but the former are no less possible. Finally, the comparison of percentages of demographic and economic growth undertaken by Rosa Luxemburg is irrelevant. We are dealing with a catalyst. Its role, by definition, is not to set its own force to work, but to *awaken* a force much greater than itself.

Questions of 'investment incentives' are therefore too tricky for Rosa Luxemburg. She abandons them and adopts a more elevated view of matters. In her work this is the start of a litany of questions on the meaning of capitalist accumulation: What use? For what purpose? For whose benefit? For whose final consumption?

Well now! As far as final consumption is concerned, there are two kinds: workers' and capitalists'. It so happens that, in the incriminated schemes, Marx's as well as Bauer's, they both grow. This is not mathematically essential, but it is part of the structure of the schemes in question. So there are grounds for satisfaction. If the mere increase of some one's final consumption is enough to make it possible for production to grow, it is difficult to see why the consumption of both our classes is not as important as that of some tribes in the Antipodes.

But Rosa Luxemburg has already denied that the growth of workers' consumption can be the aim of extending production. Let us accept this. We are still left with the personal consumption of the capitalists themselves, which also grows from year to year. The merry-go-round does not run entirely empty. Despite everything some of the side-effects are beneficial for some of the actors! Is this not a sufficient motive for letting it continue to run?

'No!', Rosa Luxemburg firmly replies. The capitalist is only a capitalist in so far as he does not consume his surplus-value, but accumulates it![76] About time too! If this is so, then Marx and Otto Bauer's capitalists conform perfectly to the definition. They accumulate as much as any one could desire. Year after year, they acquire extra means of production and take on extra workers; their constant and variable capitals increase, and their output likewise. Why do they not reflect reality? They are stuck in a 'vicious circle' says Rosa Luxemburg. They are producing for the sake of producing. This is an absurdity.

This is the moment at which one is forced to wonder whether it is the capitalists or Rosa Luxemburg herself who is stuck in a vicious circle. One by one she eliminates all the characteristics of a capitalist.

76. cf. *The Accumulation of Capital*, p. 334.

He can neither produce for the sake of producing nor produce in order to consume. So it is not difficult to conclude from these premises that he cannot produce at all, since there is no other purpose in producing. She starts by depriving capitalist production of any purpose to do with consumption, whether that of workers or capitalists themselves. By definition, a capitalists's vocation is exclusively accumulation. But nor does she want a capitalism in which the growth of production becomes an end in itself. She deems it an absurdity. Whence she considers that a pure capitalist system is an impossibility. But, since growth-of-production-becoming-an-end-in-itself is but another name for production which does not take consumption as its aim, what she considers as an impossibility is the phenomenon of capitalism in human history. For a being who accumulates, but who cannot accumulate either in order to consume more in the future, or for the immediate pleasure of accumulating, is not a possible being; it is a mere contradiction in terms.

Accumulation has no need to *become* an end in itself. It is one from the start, by its very nature. The logical circle lies in the content of the concept itself. As soon as one tries to escape from it and use the accumulated object for some purpose other than accumulation itself, accumulation ceases; it becomes its opposite. This lies outside the schemes of Marx and Bauer; it lies outside the capitalist mode of production itself. This applies to Harpagon's hoard, the pharaohs' jewels, Jacob and Esau's flocks.

The capitalists are no exception to this rule. If we can now travel by rail from Paris to Brusssels in 2 hours 20 minutes, for a price roughly equivalent to a dinner in a good restaurant, this is not only because two generations of workers in the nineteenth century spent their lives working 10 and 12 hours a day on starvation wages building our railways, but also because two generations of capitalists embarked on the same adventure endeavoured to obtain profits so devotedly that they forgot to enjoy them.

What does Rosa Luxemburg mean? That such accumulation for the sake of accumulation is insane? Meaningless. The early preachers taught us that long before: *Vanitas vanitatum*! This does not concern political economy. One may discuss the mechanisms of realization and investment incentives. But on the level of ultimate aims a capitalist who accumulates must ultimately go round in circles. Whether he exchanges his products with his next-door neighbour or sends them overseas to be exchanged with the products of a non-capitalist producer at the other end of the world does not affect the matter. The dog will still be chasing its tail, even if a bone tied onto its tail, and hence stuck between its tail and snout, lengthens the circles it describes.

Rosa Luxemburg's explanations of this point vary from chapter to chapter, sometimes from page to page, and are not very clear. When she says on the one hand that the ultimate aim of the capitalists is accumulation of capital, and on the other hand that growth of production cannot be an end in itself, she seems to believe that one does not imply the other, and hence that there is no contradiction.[77] However, in the *Anti-critique* she finally poses the question which has been burning the lips of the reader: '*Then what else is accumulation but extension of capitalist production*?'[78] But we are rapidly disappointed: Rosa Luxemburg does not hesitate to reply in the negative to this question which threatens the collapse of her entire theory. She brings off this masterstroke by introducing a new factor which she had previously formally excluded from her analysis: money.

Money-capital

In Chapter IX of her first work, Rosa Luxemburg quoted in full Marx's famous statement on the question of the quantity of money needed for the realization of surplus-value, which is summed up in the following passage: 'When a mass of commodities . . . has to circulate, it changes absolutely nothing in the quantity of money required for this circulation whether this mass of commodities contains any surplus-value or not, and whether this mass of commodities has been produced capitalistically or not. In other words, *the problem itself does not exist.*'[79] Rosa Luxemburg was in complete agreement with this view and therefore believed that the question is not where the money needed for realization of surplus-value comes from, but where are the purchasers needed for this realization to take place.

She starts off by rejecting the answer supplied by the schemes, that these purchasers are the capitalists themselves. She cannot accept that growth of production is an end in itself for capitalists. But, since other arguments lead her to accept that accumulation *is* an end in itself (and even the sole one) for these same capitalists, she is forced painstakingly to establish a distinction between the accumulation of capital and the growth of production. For this purpose she now needs money as a kind of negative *deus ex machina,* whose function is not to solve the conundrum but, on the contrary, to supply this *impasse* which she has been trying to show us from the start.

So, to the question she posed earlier: 'Then what else is accumulation but an extension of capitalist production?', she replies:

77. cf. ibid., pp. 334–5.
78. *Anti-critique*, p. 57.

'If capitalists each year exchange amongst themselves those commodities corresponding to capitalised saving, that is not capitalist accumulation, i.e. *the amassing of money capital,* but its contrary: producing commodities for the sake of it; from the standpoint of capital an utter absurdity.'[80] The 'aim and goal in life [of capital] is profit in the form of *money and accumulation of money capital.* So the actual historical purpose of [capitalist] production only begins when exploitation aims beyond (a luxurious life for the exploiters . . .) workers are only employed if they produce this profit and if there is the expectation that it can be accumulated *in money-form.*' And again: 'What sort of commodities are they, and who . . . buys them from the capitalists, thus enabling them to turn their profits, for the most part, into *clinking coins*?'[81] And later on, 'for accumulation to take place, it must be possible to sell commodities in increasing quantity in order to convert the profit inherent in them *into money.* Only then is it possible to continue expanding production, therefore to continue accumulation . . . . To accumulate capital does not mean to produce higher and higher mountains of commodities, but to convert more and more commodities into *money capital.*'[82]

So a distinction is to be drawn between accumulation of capital and the growth of production. In Rosa Luxemburg's view, accumulation of capital does indeed lead to growth of production, but not all growth of production is automatically accumulation of capital. For it to be so, money must intervene in this process of extension. This money must come from abroad.

This raises certain questions: at the end of this process, is this money supposed to return to its starting-point, or will it stay permanently in the capitalist country under consideration? Is it equal in quantity to the total surplus-value to be capitalised or does it only represent a portion of this sum, taking into account the turnover time?

Unless it comes from current output of foreign mines, which Rosa Luxemburg rejected as a facile solution in another context (yet another *deus ex machina,* but a positive one this time, and hence unacceptable!), nothing in her model, any more than in reality, leads us to suppose that a permanent deficit in the overall balance of trade of the trading partners of the country under consideration can supply this one-way flow of money. Where would these countries or regions obtain this money?

But quite apart from questions concerning the source of the money, it is contradictory to think that the capitalist country under consideration would retain the money since, to the extent that it retains the money, it deprives itself of the means of acquiring the instruments and materials needed for the growth of production which we have defined as the ultimate aim. We reach the height of absurdity if the country in question has to sell all the commodities corresponding to capitalised surplus-value and buy nothing in return. Extended reproduction would then be materially impossible; the economy would relapse into simple reproduction, while at the same time building up a hoard. This would be a real merry-go-round!

However, this absurdity hardly differs from some of Rosa Luxemburg's statements: '. . . the accumulation of profit as *money profit* is just such a specific and quite essential characteristic of capitalist production and is as valid for the class as it is for the individual employer. Marx . . . returns again and again to the question: how is it possible for the class of capitalists to *accumulate money capital*?' And further down, 'But can new money capital be formed in this way to enrich *A*, *B* and *C*?'[83]

These passages suggest that in Rosa Luxemburg's view, accumulation and the growth of wealth do not occur *with the help of* but *in the form of* money. Foreign money is therefore not merely passing through, it has come to stay. This is so outrageous that, despite the clarity of these formulations, there is a temptation to rely on an earlier passage, in order to allow her the benefit of the doubt: 'Between the accumulation of surplus-value in the form of commodities and the investment of this surplus-value to expand production, there always lies a decisive leap, the *salto mortale* of commodity production, as Marx calls it: selling for money.'[84]

This passage makes sense. Money is only a stage – a decisive, but transitory stage: a catalyst for the qualitative transformation which occurs between 'accumulation of surplus-value in the form of commodities' and 'investment'. Let us then allow that Rosa Luxemburg expressed herself poorly in the other passages; that what counts in her eyes is that money intervenes to validate in some sense the realization of surplus-value, ready subsequently to be re-transformed into means of production so that the process can restart. The aim of capitalist production, she declared right at the start of her second work, is profit. It 'only makes sense if it fills [the capitalist's] pockets

79. *The Accumulation of Capital*, p. 158, emphasis addded.
80. *Anti-critique*, p. 57, emphasis added. For our part, we believe that the capitalist's point of view is the only point of view from which production for its own sake it not a patent absurdity.
81. *Ibid.*, pp. 54–5, emphasis added.
82. *Ibid.*, pp. 70–1, emphasis added.
83. *Ibid.*, pp. 71—2, emphasis added.
84. *Ibid.*, p. 71, emphasis added.

with "pure income", allowing the capitalist 'to recover in money, [his] original expenses as well as the surplus value stolen from the labour forces'.[85]

Let us adopt the interpretation that is the most generous for Rosa Luxemburg. The money is not necessarily hoarded. Whilst this money is indispensable, it is nevertheless only passing through. For some reason capitalists need to finger their money before making new investments. Granted. But do they all need to finger it at the same time and in one go? For in so far as money can circulate between capitalists, the need for initial funds from peripheral markets may shrink dramatically, if not disappear altogether. At this point Rosa Luxemburg, *in extremis*, makes this monumental declaration in black and white:

> But wait: perhaps such questions are putting us on quite the wrong track. Perhaps profit accumulation does take place in this ceaseless wandering from one capitalist's pocket into the other, in the successive realisation of private profits, where the aggregate amount of money capital does not even have to grow . . .
>
> But – oh dear – such an assumption would simply lead us to throw the third volume of Marx's *Capital* into the fire. For the doctrine of *average profit*, one of the most important discoveries of Marx's economic theory, is central to its argument. This alone gives concrete meaning to the theory of value in the first volume – on which are based both the theory of surplus value and the second volume, so these would also have to find their way into the fire. Marx's economic theory stands and falls with the concept of gross social capital as a concrete amount, which finds its tangible expression in aggregate capitalist profit and its distribution, and whose invisible movement initiates all visible movements of individual sums of capital. Gross capitalist profit is, in fact, a much more material economic amount than, for instance, the total sum of paid wages at any given time . . ..
>
> So the problem remains: gross social capital continually realizes an aggregate profit in money-form, which must continually grow for gross accumulation to take place. Now, how can the amount grow if its component parts are always circulating from one pocket to another?[86]

So it now emerges that for Rosa Luxemburg, *aggregate* profit cannot exist without an equal quantity of *aggregate* money. Otherwise, volume III of *Capital* might as well be thrown into the fire! This conclusion is original to say the least. To the best of our knowledge, no Marxist before Rosa Luxemburg had discovered that volume III of *Capital* forbids sums of money from 'wandering from one capitalist's pocket into the other, in the successive realization of

85. *Ibid.*, p. 49.
86. *Ibid.*, pp. 72–3, emphasis original.

private profits'. But it is our belief that, if this discovery had really been made, quite a few Marxists, faced with this dilemma, would react quite differently from Rosa Luxemburg. While not being so coquettish as to charge themselves with heresy, as she did, they would rather throw volume III of *Capital* into the fire than admit that cash can only circulate in one go, as an *aggregate*!

But apart from the authority argument, this passage contains another: that aggregate profit cannot increase 'if its component parts are always circulating from one pocket to another'! As if gold coins were integral, constitutive, so-to-speak physical *parts* of the sum of profit. As if profit was not an abstract magnitude which can be embodied in anything of value, such as gold coins or new means of production, or mere representatives of value, such as fiduciary or bank money, or even simple credit granted by one individual to another; and which can be embodied successively, or even simultaneously, in several of these forms. As if the transitory or ephemeral character of each of these supports could change the abstract aggregate magnitude of profit. This second argument is certainly as unexpected as the first, though more bewildering. But it is with arguments of this calibre that Rosa Luxemburg, to the satisfaction of a certain proportion of her readers, claimed to prove the impossibility of realization of the product in a closed capitalist system.

Conclusion

If we have devoted so much time to analysis and criticism of Rosa Luxemburg's theory, this is because the number of logical dead-ends she reaches illustrates what we have already said: (i) that it is impossible to explain the phenomenon of overproduction as long as one sticks to the fundamental equation between production and income, and (ii) that the more one searches for such an explanation within the confines of this equation – and Rosa Luxemburg has certainly gone as far as any one else in this direction – the more one sinks into the most inextricable contradictions and ultimately the most commonplace absurdities.

Under this assumption one cannot avoid, consciously or unconsciously, formally or informally, explaining overproduction by some kind of hoarding and some kind of disproportion, even if, like Rosa Luxemburg, one has explicitly and formally rejected both these explanations from the outset.

When all is said and done, what are these capitalists, who refuse to exchange their commodities because they cannot see 'who is to benefit by' their investment, doing, if not abstaining from the use of an existing fund of purchasing power? And this money which separates the two transactions of sale and purchase, and makes them 'independent of one another in respect of both time and place', so that 'a further purchase need not follow hard upon a sale',[87] how does it differ from a hoard? Malthus had already said all this in terms which, though less complex and refined, had the virtue of greater clarity: what may be lacking is not purchasing power, but the will to purchase.

On the other hand, it is no use for Rosa Luxemburg to declare her opposition, in the most categorical and even sarcastic terms, to the theory of disproportionality, especially when discussing Tugan Baranovski's position; to those who object (Bulgakov, Lenin, etc.) that 'foreign markets' are not only outlets for certain commodities, but also sources of supply of an equivalent quantity of other commodities, she retorts just as firmly that the re-equilibrating role of these markets is not exercised by reabsorption (destruction) of an overall excess of surplus-value, but precisely by a 'metamorphosis of commodities', which in less fancy terms means locating the problem of equilibrium at the level of use-values and the correct quantitative *proportions* between them.

In this respect Rosa Luxemburg is not a case apart. To the best of our knowledge, all Marxist discussions of this question have ultimately led, directly or indirectly, explicitly or implicitly – and whether the authors wish it or not – to hoarding and disproportionality as ultimate causes of overproduction. Now, the necessity of crises under capitalism cannot be derived from these two factors, since the first depends on the morass of capitalists' subjective motivations, and must fluctuate randomly, hence without any long-term effect, while the second comes down to a technical problem, which as such cannot be considered *materially* insoluble. So, to the extent that these same authors realize this, and also to the extent that they struggle to exorcise these ghosts, which race back at the gallop if the writer relaxes at all, these authors sink into contradictions.

Rosa Luxemburg is an extreme case. She sunk even deeper into contradictions because she saw more clearly than the rest that nothing can be achieved, and Say cannot be refuted at all, if the argument does not go beyond these two causes of crisis, which are both contingent: hoarding and disproportionality. But, appearances notwithstanding, she is also too orthodox a Marxist, and even too classical, to question the postulate that all value is created, not only in its potentiality, but also in its actuality, in the production process,

87. *The Accumulation of Capital*, p. 193.

before any exchanges take place, and therefore to question the equality between production at one point in time and the value of the revenues at that same point in time.

If value is only created in production, realization cannot add anything to the sum of revenues, it can only change their form, i.e. convert non-monetary revenue into strictly equal monetary revenue: whence Rosa Luxemburg's last refuge – money. And this is where the argument becomes totally incoherent; asserting that all real economic magnitudes are already present and in equilibrium, one has oneself, however much one may deny it, relegated money to the role of a technical accessory, which deprives it of any hold on the real workings of the economy. Capitalists are then still masters of their fate. After all the operations engendered by simple reproduction have been completed – initial constant capital rebuilt, stocks of goods destined to feed workers reconstituted, capitalists' luxury consumption satisfied – we are left with capitalist A with a certain purchasing-power (revenue) in the form of machinery required by capitalist B, who himself has strictly equal purchasing power in the form of raw materials required by capitalist A. In these conditions, to say that the system is blocked because A does not have the money to buy B's raw materials until he sells (realizes) his machinery, and B does not have the money to buy A's machinery until he sells (realizes) his raw materials, is quite ridiculous. If A and B have *both* the purchasing power in the form of value already created in production, *and* the will to purchase, they will certainly find some way to unlock their position, even if there were no such thing as barter. A pre-existing money-reserve in the hands of one or the other, who takes the initiative of buying before having sold, Marx would say; bank credit, the moderns would say.

This being so, Say could not be refuted and, to the best of our knowledge, never has been refuted, given that the mere invocation of the phenomenon of crises cannot count as a theoretical refutation, any more than the gibes that have been hurled at him.

Nonetheless, what Rosa Luxemburg was unable to prove, and even managed to obscure, with her debatable science formulated in regular, extensive arguments, she did sometimes stumble upon with her marvellous intuition in barely elaborated remarks. This is the second reason why we have considered it worthwhile to spend so long on the presentation and discussion of this theory.

No one has concentrated more than Rosa Luxemburg on capitalism's fundamental tendency to erect the act of selling to the status of an end in itself. Although purchase and sale can form an uninterrupted chain, Rosa Luxemburg sensed how crucial it is to realize that sale is not the start, but the end of the cycle. One does not sell commodities in order to buy others; one buys them in order to resell them. This means that even if one rushes to spend money the minute one obtains it, one does not sell in order to obtain means of purchasing, one sells in order to get richer.

Rosa Luxemburg sensed this, but her inability to challenge the dogmas of Marxist classicism and explain how one can get richer by exchanging pre-existing equal values prevented her from endowing sales and money with a quantitative meaning. In her analysis sales and money remain qualitative moments in a process of 'metamorphoses'. But the problem which she had to solve – overproduction and the imbalance between supply and demand – is purely quantitative.

It is this contradiction inherent in her position which transformed what, in the final passages of her second work, promised to be a clear explanation of overproduction into a series of imbecilities, such as gold coins which cannot pass from one hand to another, aggregate money which realises aggregate surplus-value, etc.

It remains for us to take this step which leads from quality to quantity and thus provides a theoretical explanation of what seems empirically indisputable: the capitalist system's long-run tendency to overproduction.

For what we are saying in this conclusion about Rosa Luxemburg's theory also applies ultimately, to a greater or lesser extent, to all the theories which we have studied in the first section. The dead-ends appear more clearly in the works of this last author, but remain essentially the same. Everything suggests that the phenomenon of overproduction escapes us because our own premises in some way rule it out. At the end of these long analyses of those who, like the Marxist authors, have searched the most systematically for the causes, it has emerged that we will never get any further unless we start by clearing the ground of what seems, in the end, to block all routes to a solution: the postulate of the equality between production and purchasing power. This is where we must start from.

PART II The Inequality between the Supply Value of Production and the Purchasing Power

5 The Social Recognition of Exchange-Value

Supposing that each part of the social product of goods and services is still unsold in the hands of the capitalist enterprises, we shall call the total price at which the social product must be sold for the sellers to be able to cover their *cost-price* plus their *profit*, the *supply value of production*.

The cost-price is given by the addition of two sums:

1. that of the material and non-material elements bought from other enterprises and consumed in production plus the material and moral depreciation of the enterprise's fixed equipment;

2. that all the revenues that the enterprise has distributed or allocated on account of the production under consideration. The sum of these revenues is independent of the results of sales, and they are acquired by their beneficiaries before sales. This category therefore comprises not only wages but also rents, interest, those royalties that are not proportional to sales, some taxes, etc.

In the category of profit we include all the sums that the enterprise distributes or allocates *after sales* and according to the results of sales: dividends on ordinary and preference shares, transfers to general reserve, retained earnings, etc. This sum total can in theory be worked out for the average enterprise by multiplying the capital employed by the average rate of profit.

Defined in this way, these magnitudes do not coincide with those of Marx's analysis, with the exception of (1), the first component of cost-price, which is identical to the first component of Marx's 'cost of production', i.e. 'constant capital consumed' (c). But the total cost-price as defined above includes, on top of Marx's total cost of production ($c + v$), a part of surplus-value, mainly ground rent and the interest on loan-capital. Finally, profit as defined above is identical to Marx's 'pure profit' or 'enterprise profit', i.e. the remuneration of the enterprise's own funds. The sum of the supply value of social production is likewise identical to $c + v + s$ (constant capital + variable capital + surplus-value), taking into account Marx's simplifying assumption of a speed of rotation of constant capital equal to one.

We can thus establish the correspondences between the above definitions and the Marxist scheme as shown in the table. If we start from a situation of equilibrium, in which our system disposes of a stock of equipment and materials just sufficient to start off its cycle of production and in which, consequently, there are at the start of the cycle no unsold commodities nor any unsatisfied purchasing power, we can at the end of the cycle deduct from the new products which are put on sale the first component of their value, which corresponds to constant capital consumed, since intermediate consumption and the depreciation of equipment destroy exactly as many values as they create. This part does nothing but reconstitute the initial stock which we defined as indispensable for the continuation of production, and which gives rise to no further exchange transactions. It follows that, as far as the equilibrium between supply and demand is concerned, this part of the product may be considered either as zero, or as automatically realized at the end of the cycle by exchanges between capitalists.

We will, then, at this point have an additional product put on sale and offered by its holders at an overall price equal to $v + s$; that is, the 'value added' in the process of production which has just finished. Facing this supply, we have at the same moment an 'effective demand', a purchasing power, but – and this is the crucial point – this purchasing power is by no means constituted by the sum total of revenues corresponding to this production, as the classical economists imagined, but only by the sum of *already* distributed revenues, therefore by the sum of fixed revenues, to the exclusion of all variable revenues, since the defining property of the latter is to be created *after sales* and to depend on sales. Since $v + s =$ fixed revenues + variable revenues, supply exceeds demand by a sum equal to the sum of the variable revenues. In other words, net production is greater than the purchasing power which it itself has created, and this difference is equal to the 'enterprise profit'. It is this disequilibrium which is the source of all the difficulties of realization in the capitalist system, and which manifests itself in reality as a structural tendency to overproduction.

<table>
<tr><td colspan="2">$c + v$</td><td colspan="2">s</td><td>$c + v + s$</td></tr>
<tr><td colspan="2">cost of production</td><td colspan="2" rowspan="2">surplus-value</td><td rowspan="6">value of production</td></tr>
<tr><td>constant capital consumed</td><td>variable capital</td></tr>
<tr><td>raw materials, auxiliary materials, depreciation</td><td>wages + employer's contributions to social security</td><td>ground rent interest</td><td>pure profit</td></tr>
<tr><td rowspan="3">intermediate consumption</td><td colspan="3">Value added</td></tr>
<tr><td colspan="2">revenues distributed before sales</td><td>revenues distributed after sales</td></tr>
<tr><td colspan="2">fixed revenues</td><td>variable revenues</td></tr>
<tr><td colspan="3">Cost price</td><td>profit</td><td>supply price at time of sale</td></tr>
</table>

The mistake of the classical economists lay in their failure to take account of the time factor. Revenues that only exist as revenues after the realization of the product were included by them in the sum of purchasing power which makes this realization possible. They counted what is in fact a result of sales as one of the factors which makes these sales possible. As Sismondi puts it, the mistake lies in their confusion between annual production and revenue. Under this hypothesis, he notes, the most widely attested fact has become inexplicable.'[1]

From the fact that the total value of the net product is equal *ex post* to the remunerations of the factors, it has been falsely deduced that purchasing power *ex ante* is equal to the sales value of this net product. 'The remuneration of the producers assures the co-birth of the products and monetary power'.[2] B. Schmitt was able to write, and this sentence, though written in another context, is a good summary of Say's law, which comes down in the end to a simple failure to notice that the only remunerations which constitute an *ex ante* purchasing power, are those acquired before sales.[3]

Use-values do not appear in the above argument. We are therefore not dealing with a disproportion between branches of production.

1. 'So we end up', continues Sismondi, 'like Mr Ricardo, finding that at the end of circulation, so long as it has proceeded smoothly, production has given rise to its own consumption; but to reach this conclusion we have had to abstract from time and space . . ., we have had to abstract from all the obstacles which may interrupt this circulation.' ('Sur la balance des consommations avec les productions', p. 12.)

But the context of this quotation from Sismondi is weak. In his controversy with Ricardo, Sismondi ignored all productive consumption (purchases of means of production), choosing an example in which the only product is wheat. As the result of a technical innovation farmers are able to increase production with a smaller workforce. The outcome is that 13⅓ labourers are dismissed, while 46 sacks of wheat are left unsold in the hands of the farmer–owners. Soon luxury industries are set up to supply the owners of the wheat with the requisite luxury articles; these new industries take on the dismissed labourers who then consume the wheat. Perfectly true, says Sismondi, but what happens before this new equilibrium is established? Until this new equilibrium is established, Ricardo might have replied, there is a disproportion, with overproduction of wheat and underproduction of luxury goods, so it is not surprising that there is a crisis and unemployment. To get out of this difficulty Sismondi would have had to point out that there is no underproduction of luxury goods, since at this stage there is not yet any effective disposable purchasing power for them, as the 46 sacks of wheat do not constitute a purchasing power or a revenue until they are sold. But Sismondi was not up to formulating this reply. Like Rosa Luxemburg, he produced flashes of brilliance which got lost in a smoky covering of confused ideas.

2. *La Formation du pouvoir d'achat,* p. 147.

3. P. Lambert pinpoints this error of the classics quite accurately when he writes: 'Only those costs which have already been paid for give rise to revenues to start with, since the entrepreneur's profit only comes into existence once all the products have been sold.' ('La Loi des débouchés', pp. 21–2). Strangely enough he attributes this argument to Malthus. There is no trace of this argument in the text of Malthus's *Principles* to which he refers, and to the best of our knowledge, none in any of Malthus' other writings either. So it is Lambert's own argument, but he does not seem to realize its significance.

We are dealing with general overproduction, or, more precisely, an overall excess of the offers to sell at any moment over the purchasing power of the same moment.

This argument also ignores any actual difference between purchasing power and purchasing will. It holds the second to be exactly equal to the first. If this is not so, if in addition to the shortage of purchasing power in relation to the value of production there is also a shortage of purchasing will in relation to purchasing power, i.e. hoarding, this will be added to the first difference and aggravate the disequilibrium. But even if there is no such shortage, even if the bearers of purchasing power rush to the market and make purchases to the value of the sum total of their revenues, the very minute they acquire them, there will nonetheless remain the initial disequilibrium between purchasing power and the total value of the products on sale. For this disequilibrium to be palliated, it is not enough for the will to be equal to the power – it must be greater than it; it is not enough that 'purchases immediately follow sales', as Rosa Luxemburg says referring to Marx – they must precede them; it is not enough for one to spend one's revenues without any delay – one must even spend those that one is anticipating; in other words, the capitalists must spend – productively or unproductively, it makes no difference – their profits *before* they realise them; they must engage in what is commonly called *overtrading*.

Say's law

Money is also absent from the argument above. We have intentionally adopted Marx's theory, which is the most favourable to the realization of the product: the capitalist economy is a special case of the commodity economy, which is the general case. If all other conditions are met, then the exchange of a given quantity of commodities requires a certain quantity of means of circulation – money or credit. Since this quantity is a function of the total value of all commodities, it does not matter what this value is composed of, and whether it contains surplus-value or not; so the passage from a simple commodity economy to a capitalist economy does not alter the laws of monetary circulation at all. There is no special problem about the availability of enough money to realize the surplus-value.

So we assume that these means of circulation do exist, and that a banking system or some other mechanism puts them at the disposal of the economic subjects *up to the limit of their real purchasing power*. Effective demand will nonetheless still not exceed this real purchasing power. If it does, if the economic subjects make purchases beyond this limit, the structural disequilibrium may be palliated, but we will then find ourselves in the special case of *overtrading*, i.e. the use of fictive purchasing power, and the fact that the money or credit necessary to behave in this way can be obtained somehow does not affect the matter at all. What we are saying about the fundamental *inequality* between production and real purchasing-power, i.e. the purchasing power engendered by this same production, still remains rigorously true.

From this point onwards it is better completely to eliminate the question of money from our study as we have done with that of hoarding. If a specific monetary or financial disturbance is added to the basic inequality which we have pointed out, this will be an additional source of tension and disequilibrium. But the disequilibrium exists without this factor. Therefore the monetary form of revenue, a special case, does not concern our study. Its accounting form is enough for us. We consider that as soon as revenue has taken on this form, it constitutes purchasing power ready to be used. We will make our calculations on this assumption.

On this basis, Say can and should be refuted on his own chosen ground. Products are paid for with products. Granted. This obviously does not mean that products are exchanged directly for products as in primitive barter. There is no point in claiming that one's opponents put forward idiocies. Whatever Say's weaknesses may be, he never put forward such an idea, and the fact that a Ricardo could subscribe to his theory should be enough to dissuade us from associating the ludicrous hypothesis of barter with it. Money and credit do exist, and, thereby, sales are separated from purchases. Without this, no disequilibrium would be conceivable, as Marx explained so well. No! What Say and Ricardo abstracted from in the theory of markets was not the very existence of money as an intermediary between sales and purchases, it was the question of whether the quantity of money necessary for the realization of the product is actually available. They maintain that this quantity would become available somehow or other, and this is a legitimate hypothesis which Marx himself adopted explicitly.

Products are paid for with products means only that one and the same quantum of commodities, which we are considering the possibilities for the realization of, constitutes the basis of the purchasing power by which it will be realized. How can one then doubt that purchasing power is equal to the value of these commodities, since this value is the content of both the power and the commodities? Quite simply because, in the real world of capitalism, the same quantum of goods is not worth the same amount on both sides of the barrier which separates supply from purchasing power. Products are paid for with products. But their value considered as means of payment is not the same as the value which these products represent as commodities on sale. For a stock of any kind of commodities, while still in the possession of the seller, is not accounted at its sale price, but at its cost price.

It follows that even if, as we have allowed, the producer is able immediately to mobilise the value of the commodities he has produced without waiting for their sale and without any difficulties of a monetary kind, he will in normal conditions only be able to mobilise their accounting value, their value for him, while the price at which he himself puts them on sale is their total social value, that which society will recognize in them definitively and on average, *after* sales. The difference between these two values is his profit. It is also the difference between the production of one moment and the revenue of the same moment.

By arguing that it is the same collection of commodities which simultaneously constitutes and incorporates both supply and purchasing power and by also arguing that a given commodity may only have one single value, however it is considered and whatever role it is playing, Say and Ricardo explicitly, and Marx implicitly in the reproduction schemes, established the famous equation: production = revenue. On the basis of these arguments this is in fact an identity, since the same thing appears on either side of the equals sign with a different name. The mistake lies in the very arguments which led to this identity, or rather the second of them. For while it is true that it is the same quantum of goods which simultaneously represents aggregate supply and aggregate purchasing power, *it is not at all true that, in capitalist reality, one commodity, whether a means of production or an article of consumption, has the same (recognized) value in its producer's warehouse as it has in that of its purchaser-user.* Any chartered accountant, lawyer, or official receiver summoned to evaluate a stock, any banker invited to finance it, or any tax inspector called on to work out the tax on a capital gain or an inheritance will value the same machine at its cost price, if it is still unsold in the warehouse of the factory which produced it, but at its sale price – i.e. all other things being equal, its total social value – if it is in the inventory of its user. The law itself, directly or indirectly, forbids and penalises taking stock of a commodity at a value higher than its cost price, and settling one's purchases on the basis of this inflated value, since it is explicitly laid down that one of the cases in which an insolvent will be declared bankrupt is when he has spent above his means; since the determination of his 'means' is a question of fact, the court will rely in the matter on the findings of a chartered accountant, who will assess these means by evaluating stocks at their cost price.

So it seems that society recognizes two values in a commodity: the first, lower value at the close of production, not including the producer's profit – a sort of provisional value – and the second, complete value at the close of the sale, including the producer's profit.

The classics could not accept such a doubling of value. The passage in some way from an *ex ante* value to an *ex post* value had no place in their static universe, and this universe was too much directed towards the material conditions and the costs of production for these authors to be prepared to concern themselves with a practice of the business world which seemed to be a pure matter of convention.

Marxism was even less likely to be attracted by such a view of things, not only because of a certain absolutist connotation of value which scarcely lends itself to such manipulations, but also because of a certain a-priorism to be found in Marx himself as well as in the Marxists, but above all in the latter – an a-priorism which gives them a superb disdain for daily reality, under the pretext that the role of science is to know capitalist reality over and above what its protagonists think about it. This is a tiresome confusion between two kinds of 'thought': that which interprets situations and that which leads to action. If a capitalist thinks that his profit is created in circulation, and that it has nothing to do with the labour which his workers have supplied him with or the wages which these workers have received, there is obviously nothing for us to get worried about in that. As for us, we know that nothing can be created by the passage of an object from one hand to another, that there can be no individual profit except on someone else's back, and that there can be no overall profit for the capitalist class except on the backs of the working class. But if the capitalist works out his revenues and evaluates his credit-worthiness on the basis of a certain value of his commodity excluding profit, as if profit had nothing to do with the process of production, this is a completely different matter. For in this case, the capitalist is not just thinking about or interpreting phenomena; he is acting. And, however unreal or irrational his calculations may be, his actions in the light of them may nonetheless lead to a new situation, a quite real one this time, which will prove completely different from the one we deduced from our syllogisms based on the calculation of revenue according to our own concepts.

The objectives of political economy are the laws of the capitalist system. Studying these laws in their objective structure, without worrying about the ideas which men form about them, is one thing. But it is quite a different matter not to take into account those motivations and acts which are *an integral part of these same laws*. This is the difference between the natural and social sciences: in the latter man is at the same time observer and actor. Subjective interpretations of reality on the part of observers must, to be sure, be ignored by scientific analysis, but the subjective motivations of actors are, on the contrary, just as objective as any other motor element.

Sismondi had an inspired intuition of the phenomenon: 'Although revenue is the child of production', he writes, 'revenue' here meaning the classics' 'net revenue', i.e. capitalist profit, 'it is only born after realization. It is then that the producer draws up his accounts, deducts his whole original capital from the exchange, and sees what profits remain; only then does he pay for his personal consumption and restart his operations.'[4]

Classical economics and Marxism have both ignored this argument. It would not square with a certain transcendental rationalism which these theories aspire to. As if there were anything transcendentally rational about a system in which the aim of production is abstract value instead of use-value (and the aim of the producers, in Sweezy's phrase, the enjoyment of accumulation instead of accumulation for the sake of enjoyment)!

The rationality of the cost price

However, the rule of evaluating stocks at their cost price is not such an irrational and gratuitous convention as it seems at first glance. It is founded in the deepest internal logic of the system. In a commodity economy, all values must be recognized by society. It is through their alienation in the process of private exchange, Marx tells us, that the products of private labours come to be recognized as general social labour. But in each private exchange, we have only two persons facing each other: the seller and the purchaser. It is therefore through the confrontation of these two persons with conflicting interests that the social recognition of value expresses itself. It is the individual purchaser who in a way holds the seal of authentic verification. '[T]he product, in order to become capital', says Proudhon, 'needs to have passed through an authentic evaluation, to have been bought or sold, its price debated and fixed by a sort of legal convention. E.g. leather, coming from the slaughterhouse, is the product of the butcher. Is this leather bought by the tanner? The latter then immediately carries it or carries its value into his exploitation fund [*fonds d'exploitation*]. . . .'[5]

4. *Nouveaux principes d'économie politique*, vol. II, chapter 6, p. 121.
5. Quoted by Marx, *Grundrisse*, p. 265.

This is also one of the rare points that Say was able to formulate clearly and correctly: 'In order to constitute riches, the value must be *recognised*, not by the possessor merely, but by other persons. But what more irrefutable proof that its value is recognised can be given than that in order to obtain it other persons are ready to give for it a certain quantity of other things which are valuable.'[6]

So value can only be socially 'recognized' as the outcome of a contradictory debate between seller and purchaser. If this is the case, then one commodity can be recognized at several successive values as it passes from the hands of one re-seller to the next. It is only when it reaches the hands of its consumer (whether productive or unproductive), i.e. at the very moment when it ceases to be a value and becomes a use-value, that it is recognized at its final social value. As long as it remains in the stock of a particular re-seller, the value recognized in it is that fixed by the last contradictory debate over it, i.e. that between its present holder and his supplier.

In this case it can be seen straight away that at any stage, the 'recognized' value of a commodity can be none other than the price it cost the re-seller who presently holds it. It is he who authentically verified this value on behalf of society at the time when he bought the commodity under consideration. Does the same apply to a commodity in its producer's warehouse? Completely. It should in fact be recalled that production is only one moment in the total process of the circulation of capital (Marx): a technical moment, during which there is a change in the form of the use-values which are the basis of value. From this point of view a producer differs in no way from a re-seller. Both of them only buy commodities and resell them, although the latter buys the commodity in the same form in which he resells it, whereas the former buys a collection of items (labour-power, raw materials, machinery, the use of the premises or the land), puts them together and sells their aggregate in a different physical form. The value of these elements has therefore already been authenticated as the outcome of a contradictory debate in which he himself argued for low prices when he was negotiating the wage-rates, the prices of his raw materials and machinery and the ground rent to be paid to the land-owner. As the sum of these values constitutes his cost price, this last is at this stage the only value 'recognized' by society for his unsold products. This practice of the capitalist system is therefore explicable on the level of theory, and is in no way anomalous.

6. *Letters to Robert Malthus*, p. 77, translation corrected.

The socialisation of value

The above analysis should not seem novel, since it was Marx who said that it is through the sale that the social character of the labour which has been expended on the production of a commodity expresses itself. He even dramatised this moment, calling it a 'perilous leap', a 'metamorphosis', a 'trans-substantiation', etc. But does reference to any of Marx's positions provide some kind of warrant for our thesis? We do not think so.

In his works, Marx passes continually between the material and the social conditions of production without ever establishing a clear distinction between them. Value is created in production, but it only becomes social-value, recognized by society, through exchange. For 'on the basis of exchange-values, labour is *posited* as general only through *exchange*'. It is only on the foundation of communal production that 'it would be *posited* as such before exchange'.[7] '[I]ndividual labour must present itself as *abstract, general social* labour only through its alinenation.'[8]

He goes even further than this when he juxtaposes the theses of Ricardo and Sismondi on this point, implying that Sismondi was correct:

> The whole dispute as to whether *overproduction* is possible and necessary in capitalist production revolves around the point whether the process of the realization of capital within production directly posits its realization in circulation; whether its realization posited in the *production process* is its *real* realization. Ricardo himself, of course, has a suspicion that the *exchange-value* of a commodity is not a value apart from exchange, and that it proves itself as a value only in exchange; but he regards the barriers which production thereby encounters as accidental, as barriers which are overcome. He therefore conceives the overcoming of such barriers as being in the essence of capital, although he often becomes absurd in the exposition of that view; while Sismondi, by contrast, emphasises not only the encounter with the barriers, but their creation by capital itself. . . . On the other side, Ricardo and his entire school never understood the really *modern crises*, in which this contradiction of capital discharges itself in great thunderstorms . . . .[9]

In this passage Marx seems to hint at a quantitative-point of view. He speaks of two realizations, the first in production and the second in circulation; and he even poses the question of whether they are equal and of whether that in production is the only true one.

7. *Grundrisse*, p. 171.
8. *Theories of Surplus Value*, vol. II, p. 504, emphasis added.
9. *Grundrisse*, pp. 410–11, emphasis original.

Nonetheless, he does not seem to distinguish, as we do, between an *ex ante* valorisation and an *ex post* valorisation, both occurring in circulation. For Marx there is on the one hand the value *created* by the labour of the producer, which includes surplus-value, and on the other hand, the value finally recognized by society *after* the sale. There may be a difference between the two. But it seems that in Marx's mind, this is the difference between the value or price of production on the one hand and the market price, the price actually realized, on the other. This is not a difference between the price of production and a value already recognized by society before the sale. For Marx, this last variable, which we are introducing into the problem, did not exist. The passage from labour which in a market economy is not directly and immediately social, to labour recognized by society remains therefore, for Marx, a qualitative change. While the unsold commodity is not yet a realized value, it is nonetheless 'self-expanded capital-value . . . because capital-value as such exists here together with the surplus-value.' What we are dealing with 'are merely different forms of self-expanded capital-value, one of them the commodity-form, the other the money-form'.[10]

What is decisive for Marx is that social recognition as expressed in the sale of the product can only change the form of the value and in no way its content, and therefore in no way its quantity, since the content of value is nothing but a certain *quantity* of social labour. A value, he wrote even more explicitly in his polemic against Bailey, 'functions as capital-value or capital only in so far as it remains identical with itself and is compared with itself in the different phases of its circuit. . . .'[11]

Finally, in the *Grundrisse*, in the *Capital* chapter, notebooks 2–7, Marx is clear and categorical: 'Whether or not [capital] posited itself [in the form of hard cash] would again depend not on the quantity of money circulating as medium of circulation, but rather on the exchange of capital for *value as such;* again a *qualitative, not a quantitative moment,* as we shall point out in more detail when we speak of capital as money. (Interest etc.).'[12]

From this point of view, a sum of £1000, whether the product of the owner's own gold-mine or obtained through exchange, is certainly a directly and immediately social value, whilst a commodity with a value of £1000 is not a directly and immediately social value before it is sold. But quantitatively, the two are equal. Trade adds nothing to

10. *Capital,* vol. II, pp. 47–8.
11. *Ibid.*, pp. 109–10.
12. *Grundrisse,* pp. 677–8, emphasis added.

the value of products and these have no more value in the hands of the consumer than they had in those of the producer.[13]

This view implies that Ricardo was right to insist that values are exchanged for equal values, but wrong to let this fact make him underestimate the difficulties of selling. '[T]his false conception . . . is due to the fact that he concentrates exclusively on the *quantitative determination* of exchange-value, namely, that it is equal to a definite quantity of labour-time, forgetting on the other hand the *qualitative* characteristic. . . .'[14]

So Marx rejects Ricardo and his opponents equally. The latter were wrong to maintain that £1000 in money is a greater quantity than a commodity with a value of production (or price of production) of £1000. But Ricardo was equally wrong to think that £1000 was the same thing as a commodity worth that amount. In Marx's view, the former is always preferable to the latter; it is not quantitatively greater, but qualitatively superior.

What does this qualitative superiority consist of? Of the fact that money is the proof of social recognition of the value of a commodity. Anything that can express the same recognition – credit, bills of exchange, an entry in a bank account, etc. – is just as desirable. It is not money which is an end in itself, but selling. It is only as the fruit of the sale that money becomes an end in itself. Money or its substitutes on the one hand, and a particular equivalent commodity on the other, are only two forms of the same value, but the second 'expresses a certain quantity of money in a merely *imperfect* form, since it has to be thrown into circulation in order to be realised. . . .'[15]

If commodity-value were really 'imperfect' compared to an equal quantity of money-value, this 'imperfection' would be quantified by having a price set on it, since capitalism only deals with qualitative differences, even the most impalpable, by finding a quantitative expression for them; so this (qualitative but not quantitative) 'imperfection' turns out to be completely meaningless. It is no more meaningful than all those other qualitative advantages which have been attributed to money to explain the *specific* demand for it, the undeniable existence of which has disturbed every model: indeterminacy, power to choose, etc. which Keynes summed up in the notion of 'liquidity' which is only one more word to add to the list. A

13. cf. his criticism of Condillac and certain 'modern economists' (*Capital*, vol. I, p. 157).
14. *Theories of Surplus Value*, vol. II, p. 504, emphasis original.
15. *Grundrisse*, p. 218, emphasis added.

qualitative difference between two forms of the same value is a pure absurdity. Value is the product *par excellence* of the abstraction from all quality. One value that is qualitatively but not quantitatively different from another is a contradiction in terms.

Let us accept that the whole value of a product is constituted in the process of production, and that the sale *per se* adds nothing to the seller's wealth. Then why is it always more difficult to sell than to buy? Why are there always more sellers than purchasers? Because everyone has a preference for liquidity. Let us accept that. But in the capitalist market every material or non-material element which has economic significance also has a price. Does this 'liquidity' have one? Is it *worth* something? If so, these two values, that of the commodity and that of money, are not equal.

Saying that money is more liquid than commodities is another way of saying that it is easier to buy than to sell. So it is simply tautologous to explain the latter by the former. Money would not be more liquid than commodities if the supply of commodities did not exceed their demand. We must still work out why and by how much.

To answer this question, we should recall that there is always a value at which the commodity does become as liquid as money, i.e. a price at which one can get rid of a commodity roughly as quickly as one can get rid of money. This is, all other things being equal, the value that interests a producer–re-seller, generally its cost price. This is the 'recognized' value of the commodity before its normal sale, while its sale price is its full social value. It is the difference between these two which is expressed by the descriptive notion of liquidity. It is this difference which is equal to the excess of supply over demand.

But it would perhaps be useful to recall that there do in fact exist commodities that, though 'peculiar' in Marx's sense of the term, are immediately social-values, and therefore just as liquid as money.

These include, first of all, certain agricultural products and standardised raw materials traded in the major international commodity exchanges – cocoa, coffee, cotton, rubber, sugar, etc. The very name 'cash-crops', which is the generic term for all these materials, explicitly indicates their recognition as values which are just as liquid and completely constituted as money. As soon as these materials are ready for export, they are valued not at their cost price, but at their sale price as expressed by their quotation at that point in time on the relevant commodity exchange. Even before they are sold, they are considered to represent, for their owner, a purchasing power equal to this price.

These also include commodities made to order, which are immediately recognized by society in the wholeness of their value or price of production. Even if they have not been delivered to their buyer, their producer can value them at their total sale price and, in principle, mobilise up to 100% of the purchasing power which they represent, through credit.[16]

Though our position certainly diverges from the accepted schemes, is it really in contradiction with objective theories of value in general and the Marxist theory in particular? We do not think so. These theories have never maintained that commodities are in fact exchanged (nor, consequently, that they are valued in reality) in the market at their labour-values or prices of production. There is on the one hand an abstract magnitude, the value or price of production, which exists before the circulation of the commodity as a regulating magnitude and the axis of the oscillations of the market-value. On the other hand there is this market-value itself, the actual price, which may vary upwards or downwards according to the vicissitudes of circulation. Now this new value, whose existence we are pointing out, the value provisionally recognised by society at the end of production and before sales, is not another 'value' or another 'price of production'. It is another 'market-value', another concrete value, which, as such, may differ quantitatively – 'quantitatively', this is a pleonasm: a value can scarcely differ from another value other than quantitatively – from the abstract value which is its basis, while at the same time differing from the actual price fixed by the market at the time of the sale. What distinguishes it from this last is that it is not a true exchange-value, but a sort of accounting-value, fixed *before* any exchange. However, the one is just as concrete as the other.

As a social value, a commodity of course remains identical to itself throughout its passage from one hand to another in the course of circulation. It is nonetheless true that as individual wealth of its owner one and the same commodity differs quantitatively from one moment of this same circulation to another.

The inverse dynamic of the planned economy

What is the exception in the capitalist system is the general rule in a planned socialist system. If a plan is directive and if it fixes exactly for each unit of production what kind and what quantity of goods to

16. Tugan Baranovski in his work on industrial crises in England (*Les Crises industrielles en Angleterre*), Pigou in his *Keynes' General Theory*, and more recently Henri Denis have all drawn attention to the existence of certain branches that work partially or entirely to order, as stabilising elements of the system. But only Henri Denis has dealt with this question within the framework of the problematic which is the object of our study: the equality or inequality of production and revenue.

produce, then labour is directly and immediately social. These units of production work in a sense *to order* for the community; everything is sold in advance, and they do not have to worry about markets. As soon as a product is finished, these units of production put it at the disposal of the organ charged with distribution and, considering the whole value as realized, can draw on the state bank and reinvest their whole surplus.[17] By so doing, they ensure the *markets* by their very own act, and thereby the equilibrium between supply and demand which is so cruelly lacking in market economies. The central organ of distribution, through the very fact that it buys everything, can resell everything without difficulty, since in the process of buying everything it distributes revenues strictly equivalent to the product. *Ex post* equality of supply and demand at some or other level of employment of the factors gives way to *ex ante* equality at the highest possible level of employment of the factors.

This is the main advantage of planning, and not some supposed optimisation of the allocation of the factors, the degree of which up to now in the planned countries of the East, given present calculating techniques, does not seem noticeably greater than that attained automatically by the market economies.

It is the economy's basic dynamic which changes. Instead of only investing in what can be sold, in proportion to the previous increase of sales and *after* the results of these last, the whole accumulation-fund is immediately and automatically invested, production is expanded up to the limit of the potential in men and equipment, and then one consumes what one has produced. Sales are assured by the very fact of these maximum productions and investments.

The world is put back on its feet. The community's problem is not how to sell, but how to produce. Instead of being limited by the market, planned production creates its own market. The buyer's market, which is the normal situation under capitalism, is replaced by the seller's market. The effort to sell is replaced by a certain effort to buy. This certainly implies some annoyances for the consumer – deficient packaging of commodities, less concern on the part of the sellers, etc. To a certain extent, a planned economy is an economy of queues. This is the price which must be paid for full employment and maximum returns from the existing productive forces; it is in no way a sign of a low level of development of these forces or any failure to utilise them properly.

17. Of course only if the plan does not dictate a slowdown in the growth of the industry in question and the partial or total transfer of its accumulation-fund to another industry. But this does not alter the fact that this accumulation-fund is disposable as soon as production is completed.

This full employment is reflected in the reabsorption not only of overt, registered unemployment, but also and above all of the latent unemployment of women and the young which exists in capitalist countries. Thus in the USSR (and in other Eastern countries), in 1963, for every 100 men active in the national economy, there were 79 women, while the comparable figures were only 58 in the Federal Republic of Germany, 52 in the US and France and 44 in the UK and Sweden.

But the replacement of the effort to sell by the effort to produce not only leads to this quantitative growth of employment; it changes its structure and improves it qualitatively by leading to a transfer of factors towards directly productive employment. This advantage becomes apparent in the contraction of the tertiary sector in its most parasitic aspects: door-to-door salesmanship, advertising, brokerage, financial operations, etc. Thus commercial workers accounted for 10% of the active population in Czechoslovakia in 1964, in comparison with 14–18% in France, Belgium, the UK and the Federal Republic of Germany and 23% in the US. In the same year the proportion of the active population engaged in the whole of 'services' was 24% in the USSR in contrast to 53% in the US and 46% in Canada.

Conversely, the example of Yugoslavia, with its hundreds of thousands of workers emigrating to Germany and other Western countries because they cannot find work at home, shows that the nationalisation of the means of production does not stop a country from falling back into the disequilibria of the market economy if planning is weakened or disappears.

Yugoslavia is of course an extreme case. The opposite extreme, which does not exist or no longer exists in the Eastern bloc, is completely directive and full planning. Above all after the various reforms introduced since 1964, which we have therefore taken as a reference year, these countries have to varying extents slipped from a planned economy to a market economy. Now to the extent that the enterprises are accorded more autonomy, that a greater and greater power of economic decision-making is conferred on them and the responsibility for production is tied more and more closely to that for sales, the dynamic is reversed. The enterprises must wait for the market's approbation before deciding whether to expand; they must wait for the realization of the product before accounting their profit and reinvesting it. Instead of regulating their investments according to the sum of surplus-value (or surplus-product) created during production, they are obliged to regulate them according to the profits realized in circulation. The value of the product ceases to be an *immediately* social value, it has to be mediated by the market. What starts up is capital accounting, in Max Weber's phrase. The economic subjects have to fight each other for the realization of their produce, to win their place in a market which has suddenly contracted as a result of their own actions, and everything these economic subjects do to cover themselves in case of non-realization makes the market contract even more. Meanwhile, the market becomes a buyer's market in which 'the customer is always right', in the time-honoured expression. As under capitalism, the queues disappear, the shop-windows fill up with products and give the *illusion* of abundance, fancy goods, ties and trinkets are perhaps a bit better quality than before, or at any rate better packaged. But production as a whole is marking time, the rates of growth collapse. The phenomena of deflation, underemployment and finally unemployment inevitably appear. Not only is there a quantitative decrease in the employment of the factors, but as the effort to sell comes to replace the effort to produce, the very structure of employment deteriorates and approaches that of the capitalist model. A larger and larger proportion of the active population, instead of devoting itself to production, wastes its time promoting sales, that is, in a sterile combat in which each tries to increase his market share at the expense of the rest.

These same phenomena, and much more clearly as far as unemployment is concerned, occurred in the USSR when NEP was introduced. The number of registered unemployed rose from 160,000 in 1922 to 641,000 in 1923, 1,240,000 in 1924, 1,241,000 in 1926–7 and 1,289,000 in 1927–8. Conversely, from the second year of the first five-year plan, purely by reversing the system's dynamic and before any effects of rationalising production (assuming they exist) could have made themselves felt, unemployment completely disappeared.[18]

The same reversal of the dynamic can be observed on the level of foreign trade. When the plan is directive and foreign trade is genuinely centralised, a planned economy's basic task is not to

18. It is characteristic that, in order to fight the ideas of Malthus and Sismondi, John Stuart Mill imagines a situation in which everything belongs to the government and concludes from this that the reduction of luxury consumption on the part of the capitalists does not imply that accumulation is pointless because there is no market. He obviously does not see the difference between the state system which he envisages and a competitive system, but his reasoning, according to which if 'everything belonged to the government' accumulation would become independent of the market and of consumption, is correct. (*Principles of Political Economy*, book I, chapter 5, § 3, p. 67.)

export, but to import. Exports are only useful as a means of financing imports.

There exist primary and autonomous needs for a certain minimum of imports. These needs derive from physico–technical constraints and the plan's basic priorities. These are determined in a precise and detailed way. The true objective of the ministries and departments charged with foreign trade is to supply these imports. There is no need in itself to export. Actual exporting is only a secondary and subordinate economic act, in the sense that it is only a means to attain the primary objective on which it depends. Exports are not necessarily laid down in the plan, although they may be *predicted*.

First one tries to assure oneself of the commodities one needs. To pay for these, one *then* chooses which commodities to export as a function of the relation between their domestic costs and their world prices on the one hand, and of unforeseen *relative* elasticities of production and the elasticities of one's trading partners' demand on the other. One tries to give as little as possible for what one has to obtain. For in this context, economic phenomena have their normal meaning. To import is to receive; to export is to give. In a sense, importing is good in itself, while exporting is a necessary evil. If international credit conditions are judged to be advantageous, a planned country will gladly accept a deficit on its trade balance financed by credit. It gladly accepts war reparations in kind, or butter and wheat surpluses from capitalist countries at dumping prices. It can thus profit economically from the economic contradictions of the surrounding capitalist world.

When the plan weakens and the monopoly of foreign trade is relaxed, the functions are reversed again. Exporting again becomes an aim in itself; importing is henceforth the necessary evil. A deficit on the trade balance is unacceptable as such and quite apart from the indebtedness to which it may eventually lead. A permanent surplus on this balance becomes desirable.

The above in no way implies that a genuinely planned country is *ipso facto* socialist, or rather that the socialist character of the social relations of production is a simple increasing function of the degree of reinforcement of the plan. Nor does it mean that the compulsory character of the plan is synonymous with the centralisation of economic decision-making. A democratic process of elaborating the plan is not necessarily incompatible with completely directive and genuine planning. The most centralising plan for the economy may perfectly well be worked out by the most decentralised procedures. Likewise, there is no reason why a weak, indicative and decentralising plan cannot be worked out by the most bureaucratic procedures. Thus, while the present liberalisation of the economies of the countries of the East is the inseparable corollary of the movement in these countries towards the restoration of market, and even capitalist relations, the centralised and authoritarian planning which preceded this was not in itself a sign of socialism. These questions lie outside our field of study; what concern us here are the strictly economic yields of a system.

The mastery of economic calculation and the directness of social labour

Even from the perspective of strictly economic yields, we are not saying that a genuinely planned economy, such as the USSR before the reforms, is free from wastage and losses. Technical errors inevitably occur, leading to disproportions, distortions and even bottlenecks; and these reduce the system's economic yields. But there is no cumulative or blocking effect. The loss is equal to the error committed. It is reflected in the relative scarcity of some article. There is no overproduction or crisis.

In the case of a producer good, this scarcity may have repercussions downstream from the branch under consideration, on branches *technically* dependent on it. The rest of the economy will not be disturbed. It will continue to function at maximum capacity. Because of some mistake or other, a certain quantity of social labour has been expended without an equivalent social need being satisfied. The labour will nonetheless have been directly social, since it was expended *according to the plan*.

It is appropriate here to recall a controversy between Ernest Mandel and Charles Bettelheim. Mandel had affirmed that in a planned economy, labour is always and in all circumstances socially necessary labour. Since there is no possibility of overproduction, none of the labour-time can be wasted. Bettelheim challenged this point. As long as planning is imperfect, he said in substance, as long as social precision is insufficient, as long as society or some parts of it are unable to regulate the whole of social production 'on the basis of a full knowledge of the facts', the labour expended within each unit of production cannot take on a *directly social* character. It can only have this character if it corresponds 'at the very time it is expended, to a social need, the extent of which is really calculated in advance'.[19]

I think that Mandel is wrong to claim that social labour cannot be

19. cf. C. Bettelheim, *The Transition to Socialist Economy*, chapters 4,5 and Ernest Mandel, 'Les Catégories marchandes dans la période de transition' (Commodity Categories in the Transition Period).

wasted in a planned economy. Social labour can be wasted under any circumstances. But this does not stop it from being socially necessary labour, if this waste is inevitable given the means of forecasting and prediction at society's disposal at the moment under consideration. The quantity of *socially* necessary labour must include all *socially* inevitable unforeseen events and accidents.

Mandel's conclusion is therefore formally correct, although it does not seem that this is what he means by 'socially necessary labour' and 'immediately social labour'. What is more, the distinction that he introduces on this subject between articles of consumption and means of production, the first of which can be 'unsaleable' and therefore contain socially unnecessary labour, while the second cannot, is completely inappropriate and shows that Mandel's assertion has an entirely different basis.

Bettelheim is right to criticise this basis. In a planned economy social labour may be wasted in any branch, whether means of production or articles of consumption. Any social product of whatever kind may prove inadequate to the social need which the product was intended to satisfy. But he is wrong to make this adequacy the criterion of the immediately social character of labour. What does 'a *really* calculated social need' mean? If it means *infallibly calculated,* then labour will never be immediately social, since a plan drawn up by fallible men will never be perfect. However much planning techniques improve and the productive forces develop, there will always be inadequacies: a steel complex which cannot deliver all its steel in time because the carrying-capacity of its means of transport have been badly calculated, or a model of boots which does not appeal to the consumers. What then, in Bettelheim's view, is the acceptable percentage of error beyond which labour ceases to be immediately social?

Labour becomes immediately social, independently of the imperfections of the plan, quite simply because society as a whole *assumes* its expenditure in advance, for better or for worse. 'Really calculated' does not mean anything. What is necessary and sufficient, is that labour should be taken over by the plan, in the sense that it should be expended *on behalf of* the community, at the community's own risk, and not at the risk of the individual producer. Labour is or is not immediately social *ex ante*, as a function of the conditions under which it is expended. The word 'immediately' says as much. It would be absurd to await the results of production and the degree of adequacy of the finished product in relation to needs, before deciding *ex post* whether the labour was or was not *immediately* social. When the members of a primitive tribe encircle the forest, no one questions that their labour is immediately social. This does not stop them from sometimes encircling the wrong side of the forest: the game are elsewhere, and by evening it turns out that they have wasted their day. Conversely, in a capitalist country with an indicative plan, if an industrialist starts making a new product on the strength of a very accurate study conducted by the Department of Trade and Industry, his labour is not immediately social even if it turns out *ex post* that this product satisfies a completely genuine social need.

The decisive point is that in a socialist society the loss resulting from the steel that could not be delivered to its destination or the boots that had to be thrown away is not the specific concern of the steel or boot-maker. It concerns the collectivity of producers in proportion to the labour expended by each. It is a social cost. This is what differentiates the dynamic of a planned economy from that of a market economy. Freed from concern about sales and the risks of sales, the units of production produce up to the limit set by their resources. Labour is immediately socialised because the risk inherent in sales is itself socialised.

In exceptional circumstances the economic dynamic may also be reversed in the way described above *even* under capitalist relations (hence without a plan or any authoritarian allocation of resources), resulting in full employment and an extraordinary acceleration of growth. This shows that the leap forward effected by a planned economy as soon as the plan is introduced results from this reversal of the economic dynamic and not from any supposed rationalisation of the distribution of the factors among the different spheres of production. This reversal of the dynamic occurs under capitalism notably in the case of a major war, when the national economy is in effect totally mobilised for the war effort.

Given the total monopolisation by the state of all specifically military expenditure and an appreciable part of the rest, given the acceptance without qualms of an unlimited budget deficit and the resultant inflation, given the general price increases which in turn lead to general overtrading, and given the extreme liberalisation of credit and the speculative flight from money, in fact, if not in theory, everything is sold in advance, and in practice, if not in theory, the enterprises are relieved of the basic financial responsibilities of the capitalist system. So, in the middle of capitalism, the economic machine works in a sense as under socialism, attaining yields which are incomparably better than even the best boom years of peacetime.

To take the example noted by Baran, 'in the years of the war the

United States was not merely able to raise a military establishment comprising over twelve million people, to produce a prodigious quantity of armaments, to supply its allies with large quantities of food and other goods, but to *increase* simultaneously the consumption of its civilian population'.[20]

Marx calls this reversal of the dynamic to mind in the *Grundrisse* when, after discussing the difficulty of realising the product in a market economy, he adds in a note at the bottom of the page: 'Except if one imagines that all capitals produce to order for each other, and that the product is therefore always immediately money, a notion which contradicts the nature of capital and hence also the practice of large-scale industry.'[21]

A product that is 'immediately money' corresponds, in the context of our above analysis, to immediately social labour, and what contradicts the nature of capital, 'production to order for each other', is precisely the property of a society without capital in which the units of production are deemed to work to order for the plan. Under socialism labour is directly and immediately social even if, as the result of errors in calculation, it is badly used.

This was the inspired intuition of some Saint-Simonians, Proudhonists and other cooperative socialists. The realization of the product would present no problem if private exchange was abolished and if a state organ would immediately grant social recognition of the value of the product of each producer. In an impressive multitude of variants – F. Coignet's Direct Credit Bank, Nazel's Exchange Bank, Bonnard's Discount Bank, Lagrue's Universal Exchange Bank, Girardin's Insurance Bank or National Bank – these more or less chimerical projects set up a social organ charged with the authentic verification of value. The basic principle was the same in all of them. All the commodities to be sold were deposited with the bank, which verified how much labour-time was incorporated in them and gave in

20. Paul Baran, *The Political Economy of Growth*, p. 41. J. A. Hobson noted the same phenomenon in the English economy of the First World War: 'The most imposing revelation from the experience of British industry during the war . . . . After nearly two years, during which more than four million men, or nearly one-third of the adult able-bodied male population, had been drafted into the fighting services, while something like a million more had been added for the special requirements of the munitions trades, the ordinary trades of the country were still able to be carried on so as to supply the material requisites of life for the remaining civil population upon a level not appreciably lower than before the war.' (*The Evolution of a Modern Capitalism*, p. 462).

21. *Grundrisse*, p. 549.

exchange a certificate which was freely convertible into any of the other commodities deposited in its warehouses. Since the sum of the certificates was equal to the sum of the certified values of the deposited commodities, there was no danger of an excess of supply over demand. In this way it would become just as easy at any time to sell for money as it is now to buy with money. Production itself would become the uniform and inexhaustable source of demand.

The precious metals would lose their privileged position in comparison with other commodities and 'take their proper place in the market beside butter and eggs, and cloth and calico, and then the value of the precious metals will concern us just as little . . . as the value of the diamond'.[22] The general point was to give all commodities the authentic character of metallic money, to monetise all products and values, to supply the values produced with society's endorsement.[23]

The exchange bank buys commodities in the same way as a central bank buys gold, with its own bank notes. It thus distributes a purchasing power strictly equal to the commodities which it has in stock. If one or other of the acquirers of these certificates wants to hoard these pieces of paper instead of exchanging them for commodities, let him keep them. A central bank would not sell off the gold in its vaults in order to recover its own bank notes; nor will our bank have any cause to sell off the commodities it holds in order to recover its certificates. The producers who have immediately realized their products can reinvest their profits at the time of their own choosing by using their certificates to withdraw the means of production of their choice from the bank's stocks.

In a sense, the bank plays the role of social insurance covering commercial and financial risks, which Girardin saw as the source of all evil. Money becomes useless and production which creates its own market should, according to these authors, rise tremendously.

These projects were partially implemented in the 'labour-bazaars' and 'equitable labour-exchange-bazaars' which saw the light of day in England during the last century, the first being founded by Robert Owen in London in September 1832. The independent producers who formed the membership of these 'bazaars' would bring their products along to exchange them *pro rata* according to the quantity of

22. cf. John Gray, *The Social System. A Treatise on the Principle of Exchange*, quoted by Marx in *Contribution to the Critique of Political Economy*, p. 84.

23. cf. Alfred Darimon, *De la réforme des banques*. Is there not a strange similarity between the 'utopian' projects of one century ago and certain contemporary monetary plans, such for example as that of Mendès-France, of monetising the Third World's agricultural products and raw materials?

labour embodied in them. All these institutions, implanted artificially in a capitalist environment, collapsed in ruins for lack of capital and credit.

Engels made fun of these utopias.[24] But his critique was superficial in the sense that he only saw one aspect of the aim of these associations: the suppression of profit, or its appropriation by the producers themselves. The role that their promoters intended these associations to play in the *realization* of the product at the social level completely escaped him.

However, the idea that the system can be unlocked by the suppression of money alone has never ceased to captivate people's minds.[25] During the great crisis associations were set up in the US to organise the exchange of goods and services among the unemployed: those who had supplied a product of their labour received a certificate which entitled them to buy an equivalent good or service from another unemployed person.

Similar experiments were tried in England. In December 1933, the 'Production for Use League' was set up. The system's limit was encountered in the fact that, without capital or credit, the members could only produce a very limited number of items, in conditions of very low productivity.[26]

In contrast to Engels, who treated this question in most cavalier fashion, Marx was very precise in his critique of Gray in particular and the Saint-Simonians in general. Their mistake does not lie in the principle of the immediate socialisation of productive labour, and thereby the suppression of overproduction crises by the intervention of a central organism setting itself up as the universal buyer–seller; it lies in the desire to implant artificially this institution within a system of *independent* producers, as if it was a simple bourgeois reform. 'On the one hand, society in the shape of the bank makes the individuals independent of the conditions of private exchange, and, on the other hand, it continues to allow them to produce on the basis of private exchange.'[27]

24. cf. his letter of 10 September 1846 to the Brussels Communist Committee and his letter to Marx of 18 September 1846, Marx and Engels, *Werke*, vol. XXVII, pp. 42,50.

25. Is there not, after making due allowances, a bit of this everlasting obsession in the heart of hearts of those who today demand the demonetisation of gold – that lock of trade, in Proudhon's expression – and its replacement by all kinds of 'certificates', SDRs, CRUs, etc.?

26. cf. André Cariven, *La Lutte contre le chomage* (*The Struggle against Unemployment*), pp. 39–41.

27. Marx, *Contribution to the Critique of Political Economy*, p. 85. (Translator's note: corrected according to German original.)

Products are still produced as commodities, but they cease to be exchanged as such. But the bank cannot guarantee the sale of the commodities, while at the same time relying on the good will of independent and isolated producers to determine the choice and conditions of production of these same commodities.

> It would not only have to determine the time in which a certain quantity of products had to be produced, and place the producers in conditions which made their labour equally productive (i.e. it would have to balance and to arrange the distribution of the means of labour), but it would also have to *determine the amounts of labour-time to be employed in the different branches of production*. . . . Precisely seen, then, the bank would be not only the general buyer and seller, but also the general producer.[28]

The mode of production itself would be transformed.

Gray himself is led by the internal logic of his system to make this change. As Marx notes,

> although Gray merely wants 'to reform' the money evolved by commodity exchange, he is compelled by the intrinsic logic of the subject-matter to repudiate one condition of bourgeois production after another. Thus he turns capital into national capital, land into national property and if his bank is examined carefully it will be seen that it not only receives commodities with one hand and issues certificates for labour supplied with the other, but that it directs production itself.[29]

But because he consciously insists on remaining on the level of a mere reform, he sinks into contradictions.

28. *Ibid.*, p. 207, emphasis added.
29. *Ibid.*, p. 341.

6 Prices

The apparent reabsorption of the 'inequality' in the process of realization itself

So far we have established the existence of a structural excess of supply over demand, but we have not shown that this gives rise to any problems for the realization of the social product, still less that this blocks its realization at any stage of the process.

At this point our analysis seems to share all the weaknesses of Rosa Luxemburg's. For surplus value or profit of enterprise are not embodied solely in those commodities which are paid for out of surplus value or profits. They are embodied, in given proportions, in all commodities from means of production and workers' subsistence goods to luxury articles. Consequently, the spending of income acquired during production (fixed revenues) leads straight away to the realization of a portion of profit of enterprise, thus 'giving birth' to a portion of the variable revenues, which its beneficiaries will use in turn to buy luxury products or extra equipment, thereby releasing a further portion of profit of enterprise, and so on till the whole product is realized. So the arguments marshalled above (pp. 200–201) against Rosa Luxemburg's theory could be turned against our own argument, as presented in Chapter 5.

We have assumed that each capitalist replaces his 'constant capital consumed' – raw and auxiliary materials and wear-and-tear of instruments of production – without waiting to sell his own output. But in so doing, these capitalists clearly release the profit of enterprise embodied in these commodities. So once this operation has been completed, the available purchasing power is not solely the sum of fixed revenues – wages, rent and interest, as we described it as a first approximation – but this sum *plus* the variable revenues acquired through the sale of those commodities constituting the constant capital consumed. True, the sum of these two figures still gives purchasing power lower than the aggregate value of the social product still to be realized, or $v + s$, but when this sum of purchasing power is spent, it will free a further slice of profit of enterprise, which will in this way in turn become effective purchasing power which, once spent, will free a further slice, and so on till the process is completed.

Take a given total social product:

				Surplus value				
c		*v*		*Before sales rent and interest*		*After sales profit of enterprise*		*Value of the product*
300	+	50	+	50	+	100	=	500

In this case profit of enterprise is 25% of cost price and 20% of the selling price. Each commodity sold at its normal price (price of production) therefore releases a sum of profit of enterprise equal to one-fifth of this price.

Before any realization takes place, we have an aggregate supply of 500 facing effective purchasing power of 400. Once the 300 *c* have been withdrawn from circulation, we will have on one side a stock of unsold commodities of 200, or $v + s$, but on the other side purchasing power will not be only v + pre-sales s; it will be v + pre-sales s + profit realized from c, or $50 + 50 + \frac{300}{5} = 160$.

When this purchasing power has in turn been spent, supply will have fallen to 40, and the previous purchasing power will have been used up. But new purchasing power of 32 will have been created by the profit realized from these sales of 160, and so on.

A slightly different presentation would perhaps clarify the process better. Under our assumptions – a consistent composition of output in terms of use-values, no hoarding and immediate availability of all 'recognized' purchasing power – the following can purchase immediately upon the close of the cycle of production: (i) capitalist entrepreneurs – 300 means of production; (ii) wage-earners, landed proprietors and loan-capitalists – 100 consumption goods.[1]

1. For the sake of simplicity we are assuming here that neither rent nor interest payments are capitalised; these revenues are used for their owners' personal consumption. In addition we accept that active capitalists' personal consumption is covered by their wages. It is therefore included in *v*. The physical person of the capitalist-entrepreneur is thus counted twice, in his own right when he buys producer goods to restart or expand his output and as a wage-earner when he buys consumer goods. This simplification seems to us to be legitimate these days, now that the host of idle capitalists which haunted Marx's universe and the nineteenth and early twentieth centuries (till the First World War) in general, has practically disappeared, so that total household consumption in a modern capitalist nation is practically equal to the sum of wages, if we include in wages not only those actually paid to wage-workers, but also those allocated to the self-employed.

Since there is no reason to suppose that any of these purchases take place in advance of any others, we can consider them to be simultaneous. The first wave of purchases will be 400, releasing surplus-value of 80.

At this point the market will consist on one side, of a pile of means of production to be sold at a price of 100, and on the other side, of the beneficiaries of the already realized surplus-value, bearing recognized purchasing power of 80. The situation can be described schematically as follows. Capitalist A has a quantity of steel to sell, the price of production of which is 50 and the cost price 40, which capitalist B wants to buy. Capitalist B in turn disposes of a quantity of coal, with the same value and cost price, which capitalist A wants.

Under normal conditions, the value at which banks will accept these stocks as collateral for a loan is their cost-price, or 40 for each capitalist, 80 for both together.[2]

This is a typical case of apparent deadlock. Each of the two capitalists ascribes an accounting value of 40 to his own stock, and it is on this basis that he calculates his own funds, and that he can obtain means of payment from his banker; but he is only putting it on sale at its normal selling price of 50. So neither of them has the means to take the initiative and buy up the other's stock before selling his own. Aggregate supply is 100 and aggregate 'effective' demand is 80. The first exceeds the second by 20.

But once again this only appears to be a deadlock. While it is true that neither capitalist has a purchasing power of 50 with which to buy up the *whole* of the other's stock, there is no reason for him to buy the whole lot in one go. The stock is divisible. Each of them can start by buying some with the 'money' he does have.

So a second wave of purchases follows, equal in value to 40 + 40 = 80, which will pass the inequality on to the 10 of unsold goods on either side while releasing 16 of surplus value. And so on. Despite what Rosa Luxemburg said and what we seemed to be saying in the last chapter, the 'coins' do pass from hand to hand, or more precisely, expenditure of a revenue gives rise to a new revenue. Realization of the social product proceeds without any hindrance.

2. In 'abnormal' conditions – depression, crisis – firms are forced to reduce the value at which their stocks are accounted.

The price-movement engendered by the 'inequality' prevents the reabsorption of the latter

The chain reaction mechanism described above does exist in reality. Otherwise the capitalist system would be mathematically impossible; blockage would be immediate and permanent. Now, the capitalist system is *possible*, not only historically but also theoretically. Always in unstable equilibrium, it survives its strains and stresses while reproducing them at the same time.

However, to use this chain reaction, as described above, in order to conclude that realization takes place without any problems, would be to think in a static way, despite the fact that operations are supposed to take place in a series of stages. It would mean reasoning *ex post*, setting out the effects of a function over time, without taking account of the ways in which time transforms the function itself; it would mean observing this function from the vantage-point of the end of its domain. Appearances notwithstanding, it would mean ignoring the time factor.

This chain reaction lasts for a certain length of time, and over this period the value of commodities on sale constantly exceeds the purchasing power facing them. In the market this means that supply is constantly greater than demand. Although this gap would normally be reabsorbed by the process of realization itself, *while* this gap exists it gives rise to a new factor which interferes with this process and in this way prevents the reabsorption in question. This new factor is the general price level. While it is true that the blocking effects are not *directly* caused by the structural disequilibrium between the value produced and purchasing-power, they do exist. They are mediated by the fall in prices.

Of course we still have to show how the fall in prices itself operates, but if we can accept as a working assumption what is already an experienced fact, that a general fall in prices leads to depression with cumulative effects and gives rise to crisis and deadlock, then we have to conclude that by waiting calmly for the surplus-value to 'thaw' spontaneously through the process of successive disbursements of existing revenues in the order of their creation, we will move further and further away from equilibrium instead of approaching it. The table illustrates the operations in the above numerical example.

We note that supply exceeds demand by the same percentage throughout: 25%. It is true that the quantities supplied and demanded fall in absolute terms, and so the gap between the two tends towards zero. This seems to contradict our above conclusion, since the source of tension withers away and the disequilibrium is reabsorbed. But this is only a result of the separation into successive

	Supply	Demand	Excess of supply over demand	Realized profit
Position at the start	500	400	100	–
First realization Pre-sales ($c + v + s$)	−400	−400		
Enterprise profit from the 1st realization		+ 80		80
Balance	100	80	20	
2nd realization through disbursement of the above profit	−80	−80		
Enterprise profit from the 2nd realization		+16		16
Balance	20	16	4	
3rd realization through disbursement of the above profit	−16	−16		
Enterprise profit from the 3rd realization		+ 3.20		3.20
Balance	4	3.20	0.80	⋮
	⋮	⋮	⋮	⋮
	0	0	0	0
				100

periods which we have made for analytical purposes. In reality production is continuous and, for every lot of commodities sold to its consumer (whether for personal or productive consumption) another lot emerges from the fields and factories to take its place. This new lot is equal in value to the last in the case of simple reproduction, and higher in value in the case of extended reproduction, but in either case it bears within itself the same fundamental inequality and hence stokes up the excess of supply over demand by an equal or greater sum respectively. The source of imbalance never dries up.

The criss-crossing of 'realizations' and the perpetuation of the inequality under simple reproduction
Basing ourselves on the above numerical example, the succession of combined operations and replacements will develop as in the table.

It can be seen from the table that the initial production contains, as before, an excess of supply over demand of 100. The first realization of 400 releases profit of 80, leaving unsold stocks of 100. To this we must add the replacement product of 400 whose composition is the same as that of the initial production, so that its own excess of supply over demand is 80, which, added to the 1st stock's remaining excess of 20, renews the initial excess of 100.

The 1st stock's already realized profit of 80, together with the purchasing power of 320 created before sales by the production of the second lot of goods, give rise to equivalent simultaneous realizations and release profits of 16 and 64 respectively. Since these profits represent new purchasing power, the excess has fallen to 4 and 16 respectively, totalling 20. But at this point the second replacement product arrives and contributes its own excess, so that the aggregate excess returns to its original level of 100. Strictly speaking, the aggregate excess never leaves this level, since production and realization are continuous processes.

Then a third wave of realizations takes place, 16 + 64 + 320 = 400, which releases profits of 3.2, 12.8 and 64 respectively, leaving unsold stocks of 4 + 16 + 80 = 100, which are joined by the third replacement product of 400, and so on.

This scheme is confined to simple reproduction. But a *permanent* excess of supply over demand develops. Naturally, so long as reproduction continues on the same scale, the excess in question always stays at 100, equal to the profit of enterprise still to be realized at each point, a sum which again does not vary from one period to the next.

Variations of the excess under extended reproduction
If production is growing, this excess will grow from period to period at the same rate as the mass of profit of enterprise. Let us assume that the portion of surplus-value corresponding to profit of enterprise is reinvested instead of being consumed unproductively in the form of luxury products, while the two other portions, rent and interest, continue to be consumed unproductively. Let us also assume for the sake of simplicity that the organic composition and the rate of surplus-value remain constant over time, so that we are dealing with extensive extended reproduction. Let us finally assume that surplus-value is always divided between fixed revenues (rent and interest)

S = Supply D = Demand E = Excess	Initial Production			1st Replacement Production			2nd Replacement Production			3rd Replacement Production			Total		
	S	*D*	*E*	*S*	*D*	*E*	*S*	*D*	*E*	*S*	*D*	*E*	*S*	*D*	*E*
	500	400	100										500	400	100
Realization	−400	−400													
Profit on the same		+ 80	− 80												
Balance	100	80	20	400	320	80							500	400	100
Realization	− 80	− 80		−320	−320										
Profit on the same		+ 16	− 16		+ 64	− 64									
Balance	20	16	4	80	64	16	400	320	80				500	400	100
Realization	− 16	− 16		− 64	− 64		−320	−320							
Profit on the same		+ 3.2	− 3.2		+ 12.8	−12.8		+ 64	−64						
Balance	4	3.2	0.8	16	12.8	3.2	80	64	16	400	320	80	500	400	100

and variable revenues in the same proportion of 1:2. It follows from this that after each new production all the magnitudes will grow by the ratio of profit of enterprise (here corresponding to accumulated profit) to the social product, or 20%. The excess of supply over demand is not only reproduced but, in absolute terms, grows at this same rate. In the table is the scheme representing this situation.

The fall in prices transmits and magnifies the disequilibrium

It is immediately and intuitively obvious that the situation described in the last section and illustrated in the two tables, which is the existence of a permanent excess of supply over demand, equal at all times to the sum of profits of enterprise in all the commodities on the market, is a remarkably unstable situation. Prices will start to fall. But when the prices of producer goods begin to fall, not on their own but along with those of finished products, the demand for these goods falls in volume instead of rising.[3] Investment programmes are cut back as a result.

Some firms will make a loss straight away. Others will expect losses and halt their expansion. Yet others will simply anticipate the fall and defer or slow down their purchases in the hope of obtaining a better deal later.

So the structural shortage of purchasing power will be joined by a 'conjunctural' deficit with cumulative effects, since one entrepreneur's abstention from buying will give rise to a failure to sell on the part of another entrepreneur. Another chain reaction starts up, but this time in the opposite direction, triggering off a crisis.

This is the traditional scheme of things, a cliché of economic literature, a scheme which goes round in circles without any support when depicted within the framework of the no less traditional equality between production and revenues, as we have already had occasion to show, but which becomes roughly accurate once the fall in prices is taken as given and independent of the cycle. All the same, this presentation is too simple and 'obvious' not to have left several important questions unanswered, notably the following two, which we must examine more closely:

1. What is the meaning of a uniform variation of *all* prices and how is it possible?
2. How can capitalist profit be influenced by such a variation, which seems at first glance more like a change of scale than a change in real economic magnitudes?

3. In the sense that not only is the product of price multiplied by quantity less than before, but that the quantity demanded is itself less than before.

S = Supply D = Demand E = Excess	*Initial Production*			*1st Replacement Production*			*2nd Replacement Production*			*3rd Replacement Production*			*Total*		
	S	D	E	S	D	E	S	D	E	S	D	E	S	D	E
	500	400	100										500	400	100
Realization	−400	−400													
Profit on the same		+ 80	− 80												
Balance	100	80	20	500	400	100							600	480	120
Realization	− 80	− 80		−400	−400										
Profit on the same		+ 16	− 16		+ 80	− 80									
Balance	20	16	4	100	80	20	600	480	120				720	576	144
Realization	− 16	− 16		− 80	− 80		−480	−480							
Profit on the same		+ 3.2	− 3.2		+ 16	− 16		+ 96	− 96						
Balance	4	3.2	0.8	20	16	4	120	96	24	720	576	144	864	691.2	172.8

But before tackling these two problems, we must answer one question which arises immediately. Up to now we have exluded *disproportionality* and *hoarding* from our search for the cause of crises and deadlock; to this end we have assumed that the composition of the social product in use-values corresponds exactly to the requirements of reproduction, and that the will to purchase arises immediately upon the acquisition of purchasing power. But to pass from the fall in prices to crisis, we have had finally to rely on an *additional* reduction or slowdown of investments, over and above those produced by the structural shortfall of purchasing-power. This *voluntary* restriction of investment – without which there is certainly a disparity between production and purchasing power, but it is not at all clear how this disparity can lead to a crisis – is nothing but a lack of the will to purchase in relation to purchasing power, which is the very definition of hoarding. If this is so, what is the new element in our argument compared to Marx's analysis in Chapter III of volume I of *Capital* and Chapter II of the 1859 *Critique* and notebook XIII of the *Grundrisse,* on which subject we have already expressed our dissatisfaction? (See especially pp. 60–93.)

The place of 'hoarding' in the network of causes of crisis

It is clear that no crisis, or any deadlock of the system, are possible without a *voluntary* abstention from purchasing, over and above temporary involuntary incapacity to do so, that is, over and above the chronic primary shortfall of purchasing power itself.

If despite this shortfall every one decided to play the game to the end, the buyers to buy to the extent that their surplus-value unfreezes, the sellers to be patient while awaiting this thaw, the shortfall embodied in each quantity of commodities would be reabsorbed without any problem, and despite the permanent excess of supply over demand through the constant arrival of new quantities of products on the market, there would be neither any fall in prices, nor any crisis.

In social matters in general, and in matters of economics in particular, causes are always linked to effects by way of actions and therefore, by human motivations. The excess of supply over demand has no 'objective' effect on prices. The latter, let us recall, do not change of themselves. Prices fall *because* sellers compete for buyers by under-selling each other, *because* buyers take advantage of their position and refuse to buy without a reduction. It is also necessary for some one, somewhere to have *agreed* to a reduction, for a lower price actually to come into existence. In the same way, the fall in prices in turn has no *direct* ('objective') effect of restraining investment. It is because potential investors expect this fall and decide to defer their purchases that investments are slowed down or halted.

It is therefore undeniable that the *immediate* cause of any crisis, or even of any stoppage or slowdown in realization compared to its normal rate, is a *voluntary* rupture of the succession of purchases, which can be called *hoarding.* Marx is therefore right on this point, and for our part, we have never denied hoarding its rightful role: an *immediate* cause.

But, precisely because this cause is immediate, it does not get us very far. It leaves us stuck within the business cycle, since it is itself endogenous to the cycle: it is a secondary cause. Now what we need if we are to explain the cycle is a cause exogenous to it, a '*primum movens*' in Marx's expression, for he was perfectly conscious of this limit to his analysis.

All our attempts to escape from it within the framework of Marx's analysis have been fruitless. As soon as we set out, in the course of the long third chapter, to look for the causes of hoarding itself, the ultimate causes of this immediate cause, we unavoidably relapsed into a situation dominated by the *given fact* of the cycle. Whether by means of conjunctural variations in the rate of profit or interest and prices on the stock exchange, or by means of a tightening of credit, or even by means of factors held to be 'objective', such as variations in enterprises' receipts as a result of the criss-crossing between circulation periods and production periods, every theory ended up by explaining hoarding by a present or expected failure to sell, after having explained the problems of selling by hoarding.

All our explanatory tools have presupposed the existence of that which must be explained – overproduction crises. The short-run fall in the rate of profit and rise in the interest rate are not only themselves determined by the business cycle, whose graph they follow faithfully, but they could only have any effect through the intermediary of the fall in prices which accompanies them. This therefore means taking the fall in prices or the expectation of a fall in prices as given. But if there is sufficient purchasing power, the fall in prices is only possible as a result of a lack of the will to purchase. So hoarding again emerges as the cause of its own cause.

Similarly, as we have shown (see above, pp. 70–71), expectation of a considerable rise in the rate of interest is indistinguishable from expectation of a crisis or depression. So, to explain the latter by an abstention from investment motivated by fear of a future rise in the rate of interest amounts to explaining crisis by expectation of a crisis. In the same way, we have seen that any tightening of credit results from a previous build-up of unsold goods. So while, in its own right, it might aggravate the overproduction and failure to sell, it certainly cannot explain them. In turn, the idle assets of enterprises, due to some bad timing between production periods and circulation periods, can never remain idle at the social level unless there is a general tightening of credit; otherwise, they are mobilised by passing from one enterprise to another. The snake bites its own tail.

So we have not challenged Marx's analysis as a study of the cycle and its *internal* mechanisms; we have noted that it does not at any point introduce a prime mover, outside the cycle, which would explain the existence of the cycle itself. What is more, we concluded that this analysis *would become perfectly consistent and immediately acquire irresistible explanatory power* (see above, pp. 84 ff.), if we took the step, which Marx did not wish to take, of abandoning the postulate of the equality of income and output, and if we accepted that there is a basic intrinsic (and permanent) excess of value produced over the purchasing power created by this same production. We have also said that the same lines of reasoning, which always fall short within the framework of the $R = P$ hypothesis, would become extremely fertile and decisive if transposed into the framework of the $R < P$ hypothesis (cf. above, p. 85, note 76).

What is new in our thesis is that the act of hoarding – a voluntary abstention from purchasing – is determined in turn by a certain fall in prices which, for once, is a *long-run tendency,* hence in existence prior to the cycle and, therefore, not due to any earlier voluntary abstention from purchasing; it is independent of the cycle and the trends of hoarding and dishoarding inherent in it. Crises are still the result in the first instance of a lack of the will to purchase, but in my analysis this lack is no longer contingent; it is related by means of prices to a (structural) lack of purchasing *power* and so becomes a theoretical necessity. Hoarding is an inevitable step in the process. But to reach this stage, we must start from a situation in which there is no hoarding. This is what we have done.

It is now time to reply to the two questions which we set ourselves: firstly, what is the meaning of this general collapse of prices which is the origin of the chain of disturbances; secondly, how can such a collapse be anything other than nominal.

The general price level

The idea of a *general* fall or rise of prices implies the existence of *absolute* prices. But economic science does not deal in absolute prices. It is an impossible concept.

There are many statistical price indexes, and in economic literature there is much talk of the general price level, but in pure theory these things do not exist. Ever since Walras, all price systems have been systems of relative prices. In these, prices are only simple ratios, and while these ratios can be normalised by selecting a money commodity, this commodity can be changed without any real change in prices. A general and uniform change in such relative prices, upwards or downwards, is a contradiction in terms.

There can only be one kind of absolute prices, which can all vary simultaneously upwards or downwards, and these are nominal prices expressed in a completely unconvertible currency without any intrinsic value. Real prices can only be relative, and absolute prices must be nominal. Political economy has built theories around the former, but does not deal with the latter.

Marx tried to reconcile the irreconciliable, to construct a price system (prices of production) which is at once real and absolute: real because expressed in a physically given unit, the hour of labour-time, and absolute because this unit is not one of the commodities whose prices must be defined and can thus serve as their common measure. This is the essential cause of his failure to solve the notorious 'transformation problem', a failure which is now generally recognized. We will not renew this long debate which, from von Bortkiewicz up to now, has lasted more than half a century and in which we have ourselves taken part, but it is perhaps worthwhile to recall once more Natalie Moszkowska's sentence which, in our opinion, is a good summary of the logical impasse of 'transformation': 'Individual prices only indicate the exchange ratios of commodities. They are by nature relative and not, like value, absolute. The absolute level of prices can only be defined by choosing a unit of account.'[4]

Of course if all prices, including that of gold, were nominal, expressed in some unit of account, an inconvertible paper franc or paper dollar without any intrinsic value, not only could the ratios between them vary, but so could their general level. In this case, however, this level would have no significance, and it is difficult to see what effect a mere change of scale could have on the exchange of commodities, on capitalists' *real* profits and thus on their investment decisions.

Anyway such a system cannot be formulated mathematically and is therefore theoretically impossible. It must be represented by k commodity equations involving $k + 2$ variables, k prices + wages + the rate of profit and, taking one of the last two as exogenous, there would be $k + 1$ unknowns for k equations.

4. *Das Marxsche System*, p. 21.

Finally, such a system of universal inconvertibility of currencies had never existed in reality, and it can be said that until the 1971 monetary crisis, started by the US gold embargo, which created an entirely new situation which we will have occasion to discuss later, no one even imagined its possibility.

Formerly, while there were inconvertible currencies, these floated in relation to others which were convertible, and the commodities of the areas concerned could still have a real price, expressed in a 'strong' currency. Under these conditions it would have been an academic exercise to worry about what would happen if all the world's currencies became inconvertible and, to the best of our knowledge, no one was ever tempted to carry out this exercise.

Conversely, if our concern is only the rates of exchange between commodities, i.e. relative prices, then for k commodities, the ratios $\frac{a}{b}, \frac{b}{c}, \frac{c}{d}, \ldots, \frac{k-1}{k}$, or, which comes to the same thing, $\frac{a}{k}, \frac{b}{k}, \ldots, \frac{k-1}{k}$, number $k-1$, and if we also include one of the two last variables (wages or the rate of profit), the other being taken as given, we have k unknowns for k equations; our system becomes perfectly determined.

In this case prices are certainly real, since they are nothing but a certain physical quantity of one commodity, the money commodity, and their variations are likely to influence the economy's real economic magnitudes. But here a parallel movement of *all* prices, whether up or down, becomes impossible, since prices are only ratios, and whenever the ratio of a to b falls, the ratio of b to a automatically rises in proportion. A *general level* of ratios is clearly pure gibberish.

By referring to Marx's analysis as set out in Chapter II, in which excess supply of *all* commodities is explained as nothing but the counterpart of excess demand for the money commodity, we find a way out. It can be said analogously that when we speak of the general price level, we include all commodities except one: the general equivalent. Inasmuch as it serves as a physical standard for the rest, it itself has no price.[5]

5. Let us recall that, in relation to a convertible currency, gold has a parity but no price; in relation to an inconvertible currency, it has a price like any other commodity, but no parity. It is the invariability of a parity as opposed to the fluctuations of a price which confers the quality of convertibility.
Continued on page 255

An objection arises here. In a system in which the rates of exchange between commodities depend on the ratios between their respective costs of production, temporary divergences in either direction between market prices and these ratios which serve as their axes of oscillation are perfectly conceivable; but a permanent *tendency* for the prices of all commodities other than gold to fall below the ratio of their costs to that of gold is contradictory and incompatible with the system. If such a tendency were to last, it would give rise to another, just as lasting tendency which would counteract the first: permanent super-profits for the gold mines and a flow of factors away from all other industries into gold mining.

However, this is not a decisive objection. It can be countered in two ways:

1. Gold mines are a prime example of an industry with increasing costs. It follows that any increase in production, far from returning the exchange rate between gold and other commodities to the level prevailing before the increase, will instead consolidate this price

5. Continued from page 254

However E. James did not hold back from writing: 'A currency may be termed convertible as long as it can be freely exchanged against others, even at fluctuating rates.' (*Problèmes monétaires d'aujourd'hui,* p. 286.)

If this were so, then all currencies, however weak, would be convertible, since there is always some rate at which one can exchange them for gold or for other currencies on the international free market.

Perhaps the word 'freely' used by James is meant to imply the condition that transactions should be legal within the issuing country. But this restriction would not have much economic meaning, as it would lead us, for example, to consider today's dollar and the Lebanese pound as convertible currencies, since in both cases there is no legal prohibition of exchange operations.

Let us finally point out the bonds of the Russian loan of 1909, with a nominal value of 500 French francs of the period. These are still, despite their repudiation by the Soviet government, officially quoted on the Paris stock exchange, their current rate being 2.7 new francs. By openly selling some 7000 of these bonds today, one obtains a sum with which one can just as openly, in the same session of the stock exchange, buy a kilo of gold. One should therefore conclude, following James, that tsarist bonds are convertible to gold to this day.

Compare also Marx's forceful critique of Steuart who claimed that the money commodity could also have a price. Gold and silver, says Marx, have no price. What is known as fixing the price of gold 'is, as Locke correctly remarks, only fixing the name of fractional parts of gold'. ... (*Grundrisse,* p. 791).

In conditions of convertibility, which Marx is considering here, to say that an ounce of gold is worth, for example, $35, really means calling one thrity-fifth of an ounce of gold a 'dollar'.

This does not mean that Marx is also correct to deny Steuart's thesis that it would possible to have an ideal standard relative to which gold itself would have a price. We will return to this question when we study the case of universal inconvertibility.

increase at the cost level of the last additional mine brought into operation, while turning the old mines' super-profits into ground rent, or the remuneration of an immobile factor which, as such, is not subject to equalisation. The tendency for prices to fall, resulting from the disequilibrium between supply and demand, will not be counteracted.

2. For currencies to be truly convertible, the size of gold reserves must be disproportionately greater than the volume of current output and current non-monetary consumption of the metal.[6] In this case reserves work as a buffer stock compared to which the supply elasticity resulting from current production is negligible. Monetised metals in general and gold in particular have the same characteristics as non-reproducible commodities. 'A stream', Alfred Marshall noted in this regard, 'makes little difference to the volume of a great lake.'[7] It is therefore pointless to hope for the mines' increase in output to make currency overabundant, discourage demand for currency, reduce the effort to sell and so restore equilibrium between supply and demand of commodities, after this equilibrium has been disturbed by the initial excess of production over purchasing power.

To sum up, this analysis shows that even if the currency in which prices are expressed is completely convertible, or even metallic,

6. Global central banks' gold reserves can be estimated at roughly 45 times annual gold production and 60 times annual non-monetary consumption.

7. *Money, Credit and Commerce*, p. 54.

This independence of the value of monetised metals from their costs of production, resulting from the existence of stocks of a higher order of magnitude than current output, was turned by the classics into a matter of *intrinsic* invariance which predisposed these metals to be adopted as measures of the variations of the value of all other commodities. Thus John Stuart Mill wrote that 'of all commodities, [gold and silver] are among the least influenced by any of the causes which provoke fluctuations of value .... They fluctuate less than almost any other things in their cost of production. And from their durability, the total quantity in existence is at all times so great in proportion to the annual supply, that the effect on value even of a change in the cost of production is not sudden ....' (*Principles*, p. 295).

Quite apart from the relatively non-reproducible nature of monetised metals resulting from their being monetised, economic science has held an ill-defined belief, right from the start and including the classics, about a greater stability of their intrinsic value, as products, compared with all other commodities. It is striking that Marx shared this belief:

'On the economic level, we have seen that gold and silver do not fulfil the conditions required of them as autonomous exchange values and immediately existing money, that is, to be constant in value. In fact, their nature as particular commodities conflicts here with their monetary function, *although their value is more constant than that of the average of other commodities, as Aristotle had already pointed out.*' (Manuscripts of August–November 1858, emphasis added).

prices are still partly nominal, since the currency metal itself, through being monetised, acquires an extra and therefore fictive value, much greater than the value implied by its production cost curves and non-monetary uses. This point applies *a fortiori*, if the currency is inconvertible, if it is only a unit of account.

But as we have already seen, nominal prices can be treated in the same way as absolute prices and, once this is accepted, it is possible to grasp theoretically what is already a matter of experience – variations in their general level.

We still have to show how such uniform price variations in terms of a currency which, even if metallic, is cut off from the world of real values, can have any effect on the real position of economic actors, and thus on their decisions.

The real significance of a general variation of prices

For Ricardo's school, the reply to this question was clear. Money is only an instrument and a measure of exchange, a common denominator. A change in the general price level is only a change of scale; what counts are exchange ratios. If steel costs £1000 per ton while coal costs £500, the steelmaker will sell his hundred tons of steel for £100,000. With this sum he will buy 200 tons of coal. If all prices fall by half, he will only receive £50,000 for his output, but with this sum he will still be able to buy exactly 200 tons of coal. So it makes no difference to him: both before and after he ends up with the same quantity of coal with which to carry on production. It makes no difference to the mine-owner either; if he sells his coal to buy machinery, he will obtain exactly the same quantity and quality of machinery, and so on. It is steel which pays for coal and coal which pays for steel. The 'value' of money is irrelevant, since its intervention is only transitory.

We have already seen in another context how Marx rejects this serene view (see above, p. 69). Money is not merely a medium of circulation, but also a means of payment. Its 'value' is indeed irrelevant when money is used in the former function; it is not irrelevant when money is used in the latter function.

This means that if the steelmaker sells and purchases today, after the price changes, he will obtain his 200 tons of coal and will not have been affected by the fall in prices between production and realization. But if he is unfortunate enough to have bought his coal on credit yesterday, before the price fall, the 100 tons of steel which he owns today are not enough to setttle his debt; he would need twice as much. In this case 100 tons of steel can no longer pay for 200 tons of coal, but only 100, and the fall in the price of steel means a *real* loss for him despite the proportionate fall in the prices of all other commodities.

This brings up the old controversy about the quantity theory of money. The quantity school, and many others after them, deny that purely monetary variations can have any economic effects, since these variations only affect absolute prices, whereas relative prices are what affect the real elements of the economy. They forget that, even if all prices without exception, including that of labour-power, were to vary simultaneously and in the same proportion, at least two or three items would not vary: debts already contracted, taxes already imputed, and the quantity of money in circulation before the price change. They forget the distinction between money as a medium of circulation and money as a means of payment which Marx brought out, or, in other words, the distinction between the *purchasing power* of money as determined by the market and its *debt discharging power* determined by the state, in G. F. Knapp's apt expression.[8]

All this is clearly true, but it does not go far enough. Ricardo would have replied that in this example the steelmaker's loss is the mine-owner's gain, and if the former will have to cut down his purchases after this misfortune, the latter will be able to step up his own. After a general fall in prices, debtors will lose and creditors will gain, but producers as a whole can neither lose nor gain.

Of course there is a danger of secondary effects. The weakening of the steelmaker's position may give rise to insolvencies and job losses which may not be exactly compensated for by the extra expenditure or investments of the mine-owner. These losses may lead to a contraction of outlets for other producers. Creditors, banks and money-lenders may take fright, some distraining their defaulting debtors while others stop supporting them. Interruptions of payments, bankruptcies and even general crisis may follow. But none of these eventualities, however likely they may be, advance us one iota beyond the domain of contingency. All these multiplier effects can just as well result from any accidental disturbance above a certain size, whether as a result of the bankruptcy of a major bank simply through bad management, or a bad harvest of an essential raw material because of a natural disaster.

But what really distances us from the logical necessity we are seeking is the fact that none of these cumulative effects are peculiar to a general fall in prices; the same chain reaction can perfectly well

8. cf. *Staatliche Theorie des Geldes*.

result from the opposite original cause: a general rise in prices. In our example, if prices were to double instead of being halved, the loser would be the mine-owner-debtor and the gainer would be the steel-maker-creditor; but this difference apart, the same chain of events would be just as likely to occur. but we have seen that the system's structural tendency is not to raise but to lower prices. What is more, price rises are generally accompanied by growth and not crises.

This explanation is therefore especially inadequate because it is ambivalent. It is, like all the rest we have examined so far, ultimately based on imperfections in the system's functioning, on its rigidities and imperfect fluidity, its chance happenings, anything that prevents capital from circulating smoothly and interferes with the mutual compensation of gains and losses on the social level. In a theoretically pure system – and this must be our start-point if we wish to establish the theoretical necessity of crises – the mine-owner could, if things seemed likely to turn out so badly, have bought out the steelmaker and taken over his enterprise, or *vice versa*, whichever the case may be, and the gains and losses would have been mutually absorbed without spreading above the level of the individual firm. It can never be repeated too often that we are trying to explain the necessity of crises, not their possibility.

To escape this impasse, we must shatter the classical framework which Marx only partially breached with his distinction between money as medium of circulation and money as means of payment. It is not true that gains and losses can only start from the monetary fixity of debts if purchase and sale are separated in time, while one of these acts takes place before, and the other after, the price change. It is not true that money can only affect the economy in its role as means of payment, as the 'general commodity of contracts' in Bailey's phrase which Marx quotes and adopts, in which case one businessman's loss is necessarily accompanied by an equivalent gain for another. Even if purchase and sale are simultaneous, in the sense that they both take place *after* the price change, and money is therefore functioning solely as medium of circulation, this price change will have a definite effect on the position of those concerned, so that in this case all parties to the exchange can gain or lose at the same time.

For it is incorrect to say that profit can only derive either from the production of a real value, or from an equivalent loss for someone else. In the capitalist system there are profits and losses that do not result either from production or the destruction of real values, or from the transfer of property. These profits and losses may appear illusory from a particular 'scientific' perspective; this does not prevent them from affecting the system's behaviour and, considered properly, they are no more illusory than the rest. By dint of systematically ignoring them, many real phenomena have been made inexplicable.

So, when the prices of iron and coal fall by the same percentage below their prices of production and capitalist A sells capitalist B a quantity of iron and buys back an equivalent quantity of coal, Quesnay, Ricardo and Marx tell us that these men have neither gained nor lost from the exchange, since each has regained in purchasing what he lost in selling. This is a captivating view, but for all practical purposes, in terms of the effects which this operation will have on the economy, in their own view, in that of their bankers, their tax-collectors, their creditors and debtors, their friends and the public at large, in short, in everyone's view apart from a few economists, both these men are losers. For in the real world, it is considered a loss to sell below the price of production, while it is not considered a profit to buy below this price (because all stocks are accounted at their cost price), and from the moment we ruled use-value out of our calculations, profit and loss only exist by convention.

As a matter of fact this is not yet another casual convention; it derives from the system's deepest logic. But this logic is not that of the classics. On the contrary, according to this logic it is as medium of circulation that money has definite effects in a completely determined direction; as means of payment it can only have erratic and unpredictable effects. But the function of circulation does not imply a transitory status. Everything depends on which moment of the circulation of capital we situate money.

The classics had situated money in the middle of the circuit. One sells steel and *re*purchases coal to *re*transform it into steel:

$$\text{coal} \rightarrow \text{steel} - \text{money} - \text{coal}.$$

Since the balance sheet of a circuit can only be drawn up in the terms found at either end, in terms of coal in this case, it is clear that as long as all payments are in cash, the value of money is irrelevant. Money is only the medium of exchange and 'in a changing medium, two different relations to the same thing can always be expressed, just as well as in a constant medium'.[9] In this perspective all that counts is the quantity of coal which returns at the end of the circuit compared to the quantity consumed at the start.

The situation is quite reversed if money is placed at both ends of

9. Marx quotes this sentence by Bailey to say that the proposition is correct if applied to money as medium of circulation. (*Grundrisse*, p. 236).

the circuit, that is, if one does not sell in order to repurchase, but purchases in order to resell:

money – coal → steel – money

Here the balance-sheet is drawn up in terms of money and it is *closed* not when coal refills the depots, but when money refills the coffers. In this case any price variation occurring during the circuit will have a definite effect on its results, even if all payments are in cash and the money does not lie idle in the coffers for an instant, that is, if the money is received with one hand at the end of the circuit and paid out with the other hand to buy new raw material and factors to start the next circuit.

No one has gone further than Marx in deepening the ambiguity of the notion of circuit, no one has shown more clearly the complete reversal of economic behaviour when the form C – M – C (commodity – money – commodity) is changed to the form M – C – M (money – commodity – money) – Chapter III, IV, V of volume I of *Capital* are entirely devoted to this question. In the course of this discussion, Marx goes so far as to call this a 'magic ... change', which in his opinion expresses the move from simple circulation to the circulation of capital.[10] And yet when he studies, in volume II, the process of simple and extended reproduction, he not only returns to the C – M – C form, but even praises Quesnay for being the first to use it in his *Tableau,* while the Mercantilists were satisfied with the M – C – M form.

How can this 'contradiction' be explained? The explanation is that both the reproduction schemes and the *Tableau économique* are national accounts and, of course, a nation can neither lose nor gain from a change in the scale for reducing products to a common denominator. The 'aim of selling' can have no meaning for society as a whole, that is, for a closed system, abstracting from foreign trade, and these are the models of Marx and Quesnay. Such a system does not sell or purchase anything; it consumes coal and steel or wheat and cotton, and produces wheat and cotton or coal and steel. Money can only be a vehicle, a medium, a unit of account. Its position really is in the middle and its role really is transitory. The poles are occupied by *real* values.

The contradiction is not one of reasoning; it is part of capitalist reality itself. For the nation's system of accounting is not the same as capital's system of accounting, even if the nation under consideration is a capitalist nation. In capital's system of accounting, on the

10. cf. *Capital*, vol. I, p. 154; cf. also above, pp. 30–31.

contrary, it is real values that are transitory, and value proper (value as such, therefore money itself, therefore ultimately mere figures) that occupy the poles. How could matters be otherwise, since the very essence of capitalism, or even of commodity production, is that it can only exist *over and above* use-value, although *only* use-value is real and value proper is only an abstraction?

The contradiction consists in the fact that under any mode of production, social wealth can only be concrete, while under the capitalist mode of production, individual wealth is ideal. Independent producers all separately pursue abstract wealth, but in so doing, their own actions prevent the increase of society's concrete wealth, and eventually that of their own wealth, in abstract as well as concrete terms.

The Mercantilists, or at least some of them, were perhaps wrong to apply the microeconomic formula M – C – M to national accounts. But the classics committed a far more serious error: that of applying the sound macroeconomic logic of the whole to the elements which it is composed of but which, at the same time, contradict it, thereby presenting a harmonious world without any problems – a world in which it is quite clear what is really a gain and what is a loss, and in which real things are clearly distinguished from their symbols.

It is extremely difficult to resist the Ricardian siren. Marx himself succumbs to it in several parts of his work, and the drama of some Marxist economists today is that they are simultaneously critics of classicism and its last survivors. In their free time, they supply brilliant proofs that capitalism is an absurd and crazy system, an upside-down world; but in their working hours they try to explain phenomena by arguing as if the world we inhabit were a Cartesian system. Then any phenomenon that does not fit in with this logical organisation is called an 'appearance' and quite simply declared null and void.

Appendix
Simple and Extended Reproduction

Henri Denis, in a paper presented in June 1971 to a seminar on *Imperialism* organised by *L'Homme et la société* in Paris,[1] accepts the existence of an excess of supply over demand in the case of extended reproduction, but denies it in the case of simple reproduction. This is his argument: this year's output, $c_1 + v_1 + s_1$, is paid for out of its cost in materials, c_1, and wages, v_1, of the same year; and the previous year's realized surplus-value, s_0. This makes: $c_1 + v_1 + s_0$. Since its selling price is $c_1 + v_1 + s_1$, everything depends on the variations of s. If $s_1 = s_0$, as in the case of simple reproduction, then

Supply *Demand*

$$c_1 + v_1 + s_1 = c_1 + v_1 + s_0,$$

and there is no disequilibrium. On the other hand, if $s_1 > s_0$, then

Supply *Demand*

$$c_1 + v_1 + s_1 > c_1 + v_1 + s_0,$$

and there is excess supply of $s_1 - s_0$.[2]

If we adopt the same simplification as Henri Denis, by ignoring the distinction between those parts of surplus-value that are distributed before sales and those that are distributed after – which is acceptable as a first approximation – we can juxtapose the two systems as

1. And subsequently published in *L'Homme et la société*, no. 22.

2. Pigou accepted the same distinction: 'When a piece of work is proceeding, the manual wage-earners on it are, for the most part, paid weekly and the salary-earners monthly or quarterly. But the entrepreneurs (or shareholders) do not become possessed of any income for their services until the product they have helped forward is sold. . . . The money income of any period, therefore, . . . cannot be defined as the money value of the real income that comes into being in the same period. ... In stable conditions, however, i.e. so long as what I shall presently call "flow equilibrium" is being maintained, this difficulty is not active, but only latent. For, since successive periods are alike, the money value of the real income received in any one of them is necessarily *equal* to the money value of the income accruing in that period.' (*Employment and Equilibrium*, p. 19).('Flow equilibrium' is Pigou's term for 'simple reproduction'.)

follows:

According to Henri Denis

Supply	*Demand*	*Excess supply*
$(c_1 + v_1 + s_1)$	$-(c_1 + v_1 + s_0)$	$= s_1 - s_0$
$(c_2 + v_2 + s_2)$	$-(c_2 + v_2 + s_1)$	$= s_2 - s_1$
$\vdots$	$\vdots$	$\vdots$
$(c_n + v_n + s_n)$	$-(c_n + v_n + s_{n-1})$	$= s_n - s_{n-1}$

According to our analysis

Supply	*Demand*	*Excess supply*
$(c_1 + v_1 + s_1)$	$-(c_1 + v_1)$	$= s_1$
$(c_2 + v_2 + s_2 + s_1)$	$-(c_2 + v_2 + s_1)$	$= s_2$
$\vdots$	$\vdots$	$\vdots$
$(c_n + v_n + s_n + s_{n-1})$	$-(c_n + v_n + s_{n-1})$	$= s_n$

There is a mistake in Henri Denis's calculations. He draws up the accounts of concluded operations on the assumption that all the goods have been sold, and carries forward, as a positive balance, the purchasing power represented by 'realized' surplus-value. But if all the realization operations of a cycle of production have somehow or other been concluded successfuly, as Henri Denis assumes, then there are no unsold goods nor any purchasing power left over.

Purchasing power, whether created *before* realization, like fixed revenues, or *during* it, like variable revenues, always has a counterpart in an equivalent commodity produced during the same cycle. When all the commodities have been sold, all the commodities have *ipso facto* been bought – this is a tautology – and since, to buy them, the whole of existing purchasing power must be used up, there can in no way be any disposable purchasing power left over.

Henri Denis is confusing the temporal succession of an individual capitalist's operations with the national income accounts. Each capitalist as an individual can only make use of his surplus-value if he has already sold, but, for the nation as a whole, if every one has sold what they *had* to sell, this means that every one had bought what they were *able* to buy, and there cannot be any remaining purchasing power to carry forward. On the social level, realized surplus-value has already, without anything further having taken place, been reinvested, or spent on luxury products, at any rate spent.

If the current period inherits purchasing power created in the previous period, it must also inherit an equivalent stock of unsold commodities. All other things being equal, any reserve of purchasing power must have a counterpart in an overstock from the past, which needs to be realized. Using this purchasing power does not therefore help the realization of current output, but relieves the market of this preceding overstock.

Henri Denis's mistake is very widespread in Marxist literature. It premeates Rosa Luxemburg's analyses. Here are a few examples:

> Realized surplus-value which cannot be capitalised and lies idle in England or Germany, is invested ... in the Argentine, Australia. ...[3]

(The answer is simple: if the surplus-value has been *realized*, capitalisation has *ipso facto* been accomplished, since the product has been sold, and this product includes means of production. Under any circumstances, capitalisation or luxury consumption, if surplus-value has been realized in England or Germany, it no longer exists as a disposable asset to be invested in the Argentine or Australia.)

> There had been no demand for the surplus product within the country, so capital had lain idle without the possibility of accumulating.[4]

(If there is no demand for the surplus-product and if this remains unsold, there is no surplus-value to be accumulated either.)

> So it is really in England that all the material conditions for accumulation exist – a realized surplus value as money capital, a surplus product in productive form, and lastly labour reserves. Yet accumulation cannot proceed here ....[5]

(If the surplus-value is realized 'as money capital', there is no surplus product left in search of a market. Better still: at the social level – and this is the level which Rosa Luxemburg is considering – surplus-value cannot be realized as money capital, for the simple reason that, once 'realized', it does not exist in any form.)

> If part of the surplus value is capitalised, i.e. used to expand production ... where are we to find buyers for the commodity surplus? What will become of the capitalised surplus value? Who will buy the commodities in which it is hidden?[6]

3. *The Accumulation of Capital*, pp. 426–7.
4. *Ibid.*, p. 427.
5. *Ibid.*, p. 428–9.
6. *Ibid.*, p. 196.

(If surplus-value has been 'used to expand production', 'the commodities in which it is hidden' have already been sold. It is those who have decided to capitalise their surplus-value that have bought them.) And so on, and so forth.

Of course Henri Denis may have been making a different point. It may be that his justification for carrying forward the purchasing power represented by the surplus-value of the previous year into the current year, without also carrying forward the stock of commodities which is its counterpart, is the idea that this counterpart has been purchased by the previous year's surplus-value, and so on indefinitely far back in time.

At first glance this seems an acceptable position. It is indeed possible to assume that in the course of its hundreds (if not thousands) of years of existence, capitalism has at least once been in the situation:

Supply	*Demand*
$c_j + v_j + s_j$	$c_j + v_j + s_i$,

if only through the accidental destruction at some point in the past of a group of commodities, whose value, in terms of probability with such a large number of cycles and infinite variations of s, must have at some point been equal to s_i, in which case the following cycle would give us this situation:

Supply	*Demand*
$c_j + v_j + s_j - s_i$	$c_j + v_j$,

which is the same as the above.

The excess supply, in this case, must be $s_j - s_i$, and Henri Denis's first equation would be verified.

But then all subsequent equations would be erroneous. For this reserve of purchasing power (or money-capital), however created in the past, would be carried forward in its totality into future periods, and one has no right to use it, as Henri Denis does, as a kind of catalyst to shift each year's surplus-value forward to the following year.

In this case the correct equations would be:

Supply		*Demand*		*Excess supply*
$(c_1 + v_1 + s_1)$	$-$	$(c_1 + v_1 + s_i)$	$=$	$s_1 - s_i$
$(c_2 + v_2 + s_2 + s_1)$	$-$	$(c_2 + v_2 + s_1 + s_i)$	$=$	$s_2 - s_i$
$(c_3 + v_3 + s_3 + s_2)$	$-$	$(c_3 + v_3 + s_2 + s_i)$	$=$	$s_3 - s_i$
$\vdots$		$\vdots$		$\vdots$
$\vdots$		$\vdots$		$\vdots$
$(c_n + v_n + s_n + s_{n-1})$	$-$	$(c_n + v_n + s_{n-1} + s_i)$	$=$	$s_n - s_i$

Let us examine the excess supply column. In Henri Denis's method (see above p. 264) it was:

$$\begin{array}{ccc} s_1 & - & s_0 \\ s_2 & - & s_1 \\ s_3 & - & s_2 \\ & \vdots & \\ & \vdots & \\ s_n & - & s_{n-1} \end{array}$$

Certainly, the two methods of calculation give the same result, if we imagine an *eternal* system of simple reproduction which, at some point in the past, had the bright idea of throwing into the sea once and for all a group of commodities equivalent to one cycle's surplus-value, since in this case $s_0 = s_1 = s_2 = \ldots = s_i = \ldots = s_n$.[7] But such an academic exercise would be futile. The capitalist system cannot exist without capital, and capital cannot be born without previous accumulation, which means extended reproduction. If we study simple reproduction, this is for two reasons: (i) because simple reproduction exists within extended reproduction itself; and (ii) because the series of extended reproductions may be interrupted by periods of simple reproduction.

It follows that any such pre-existing reserve of purchasing power, which we have assumed equal to s_i, but which may in fact be any sum a, will rapidly become negligible compared with the sum of surplus-value of one cycle, so that the excess supply of any one year j, equal to $s_j - a$, is effectively equal to s_j, whether this particular year is a year of simple or extended reproduction. On the other hand, for Henri Denis, if year j happens to be a year of simple reproduction, the system will be in perfect equilibrium, since the excess supply $s_j - s_i = 0$, even if this year is preceded by a series of years of extended reproduction.

7. Each time we talk of the destruction of a quantity of commodities, we are of course assuming that this occurred in such a way that the corresponding revenues were not affected. However, it is difficult to imagine such conditions. Since all commodities have owners, any 'destruction' would normally be accompanied by the loss of an equivalent income. And if it is impossible to absorb this loss (and there is therefore a bankruptcy), some other economic agent (a creditor of the bankrupt) will absorb it and see his purchasing power reduced by as much. The only source of a pre-existing positive balance of purchasing power, which we can imagine a priori, is a state budget deficit covered by central bank loans, and thus by the creation of money.

Let us introduce this reserve fund into our numerical example:

	Supply	Demand	Excess Supply	Cumulative excess supplies
Previous positive balance: s_0		100	−100	
1st production	500	400	+100	
Balance	500	500	0	($s_1 - s_0 =$ 500/5 − 100 = 0)
1st realization	− 500	−500		
Profit on the same		+100	−100	
1st replacement (500 × 1.2)	+ 600	+480	+120	
Balance	600	580	20	($s_2 - s_0 =$ 600/5 − 100 = 20)
2nd realization	− 580	−580		
Profit on the same		+116	−116	
2nd replacement (580 × 1.2)	+ 696	+557	+139	
Balance	716	673	43	($s_3 - s_0 =$ 716/5 − 100 = 43)
3rd realization	− 673	−673		
Profit on the same		+135	−135	
3rd replacement (673 × 1.2)	+ 808	+646	+162	
Balance	851	781	70	($s_4 - s_0 =$ 851/5 − 100 = 70)
4th realization	− 781	−781		
Profit on the same		+156	−156	
4th replacement (781 × 1.2)	+ 937	+750	+187	
Balance	1007	906	101	($s_5 - s_0 =$ 1007/5 − 100 = 101)

According to Henri Denis's calculations, the respective excess supplies would be:

$$s_1 - s_0 = 100 - 100 = 0$$
$$s_2 - s_1 = 120 - 100 = 20$$
$$s_3 - s_2 = 143 - 120 = 23$$
$$s_4 - s_3 = 170 - 143 = 27$$
$$s_5 - s_4 = 201 - 170 = 31$$

The difference between the two calculations, though substantial, still only seems to be quantitative. It will however become qualitative once the initial sum carried forward of 100 has become a negligible quantity compared with one cycle's surplus-value. From that time onwards, Henri Denis's calculations will continue to indicate excess supply equal to the *growth* of surplus-value alone, while the real excess supply will be equal to its *total*.

But this is not all: assume that these five periods of extended reproduction are followed by a period of simple reproduction. By Henri Denis's formula, the excess supply will disappear, and the system will be re-equilibrated:

$$s_6 - s_5 = 201 - 201 = 0,$$

whereas the correct calculation would give excess supply equal to that of the previous year:

$$s_6 - s_0 = 201 - 100 = 101.$$

The continuation of the above table would give:

	Supply	*Demand*	*Excess supply*	*Cumulative excess supply*
5th year balance	1007	906	101	
5th realization	− 906	−906		
Profit on same		+181	−181	
5th replacement (906 × 1)	+ 906	+725	+181	
Balance	1007	906	101	101
				($s_6 - s_0 = 1007/5 - 100 = 101$)

As can be seen, the excess supply of each period is not the profits of that period minus the profits of the preceding period, but the profits of that period minus the constant sum carried forward from the first period.

Henri Denis's position converges with that of Sismondi when the latter declares:

> Future production is paid for with revenue already received, so this revenue does not grow as fast as production. After all, the whole of current production is simply exchanged for the whole of the previous year's production. Now, if production grows gradually, each year's exchange must entail a small loss, while at the same time ensuring future production. If this loss is slight and spread out, everyone can accept it without any significant fall in revenue. ... But if there is a large disproportion between the latest and the preceding production, firms have to break into their capital, there is suffering, and the nation retreats instead of advancing.[8]

8. *Nouveaux principes*, vol. I, pp. 120–1.

But Sismondi discovers in the course of other arguments that if, in extended reproduction capitalists cannot properly invest their profits without having realized them through the sale of their own products, simple reproduction is not all that different, since there also it is difficult to accept that capitalists can anticipate their profits and purchase luxury goods before having sold their products.

Here Rosa Luxemburg challenges him forcefully, profiting from the fact that Sismondi here invokes an argument which is foreign to his own problematic, the argument that there are physical limits to the capitalists' ability to absorb luxury goods.[9] For her, there is a clear distinction between simple and extended reproduction. With her theory of the four piles of goods, which we looked at earlier, the third being capitalists' consumption and the fourth extra capital goods, the difficulties only start at the foot of this fourth 'pile', thus on the threshold of extended reproduction; there is absolutely no problem in the marketing of the third pile (luxury goods).

In his conclusions, Henri Denis is much closer to Rosa Luxemburg than to Sismondi, although the basis of his problematic – inequality of value of output and purchasing power – are those of Sismondi and have nothing to do with that of Rosa Luxemburg. Despite the vacillations and ambiguities of his formulations, Sismondi had glimpsed the truth: it makes no difference what kind of use-values – luxury goods or means of production – profit is spent on. It can even be said that a situation in which a capitalist anticipates his future profits in order to run up an overdraft on personal luxury expenditure is much more abnormal and has much more harmful consequences than if he anticipates these same profits in order to expand his firm. Besides, it will always be much more difficult to finance such an operation.[10]

9. *The Accumulation of Capital*, pp. 198–9.

10. Here we are of course abstracting from the 'normal' remuneration of the labour which the capitalist supplies to his own firm. This remuneration is an integral part of wages, v, and thus of fixed revenues, distributed before sales, independently of its results. Whether or not this revenue is accounted separately, the active boss has a right to it as long as he is working, and no one will challenge him for withdrawing funds for the sake of personal consumption in conformity with his station, even if his firm is making a loss, or is even in difficulties.

7 Absolute' Prices and Overproduction Crises in Aftalion's Theory

To the best of our knowledge, Aftalion is the only author who considers the general fall in prices, not as a result of disequilibrium and therefore at worse a factor aggravating this disequilibrium in a cumulative process, but as the actual cause of the destruction of equilibrium. He is at any rate alone in making of this point the central argument of a general theory of crises, in a systematic and exhaustive way.

Right from the start, on page one of his very important work, he declares: 'The problem of crises is mainly the problem of the periodic variations of prices.'[1] This means that in order to explain crises without any circular argument it suffices to discover an exogenous factor (exogenous to the business cycle) giving rise to a tendency towards a *general* fall in prices, assuming that this fall is independent of the development of the conditions of production and, thus, of variations in costs; in other words, that we are dealing with market prices and not prices of production.

Hoarding

The only possible immediate cause of such a fall in market prices is an excess of supply over demand in terms of the prices determined by costs (prices of production). But in these terms, the total value of production is, according to standard theory, strictly equal to the sum of the revenues generated by this same production, thus equal to purchasing power. Aftalion does not merely accept this fundamental equation, he forcefully restates it (cf. above, pp. 51–2). It follows that, if demand is in turn equal to purchasing power, this excess of supply is impossible.

But what if demand were not equal to purchasing power? In other words, if disequilibrium were due to a disparity, not between supply and purchasing power, but between supply and the will to purchase? Aftalion reviews and lengthily examines every theory that seems to be attempting to explain overproduction crises by fluctuations in hoarded savings; he rejects them all one by one. In the process he

1. *Les Crises périodiques de surproduction.*

uses arguments of varied quality, which are sometimes very debatable, but he reaches the correct conclusion that these fluctuations cannot be taken as given *prior* to the cycle of prosperity and crisis, but are internal to it; they therefore cannot generate it. We must look for the cause of the break in equilibrium outside of these fluctuations, these balancing movements between hoarding and dishoarding; we must therefore start from equilibrium.

'Marginal utility'

This leads Aftalion to enquire what could make prices fall below their equilibrium values, in a world in which purchasing power always equals the value of output (as calculated in equilibrium prices) and at a point when the will to purchase is itself equal to the power.

He eventually finds this prime cause by making use of marginal utility theory. It is the fall in the utility of each commodity taken separately, which causes all prices to drop when productivity rises in the normal way as a result of technical progress, and when the output of all commodities increases, even if this growth is in correct proportion to the schedule of needs. This is the source of the original movement of prices, starting from equilibrium; all other factors – variations in revenues, fluctuations of savings, speculation, credit mechanisms, monetary disturbances, etc. – only amplify this movement.

What causes the trouble is then neither a lack of purchasing power nor a lack of the will to purchase, but a sort of lack of 'will to pay the price', of the 'will to value'. 'There is no question', Aftalion writes, 'of any lack of purchasing *power*. There is a lack of the *desire* to spend the same sum on each commodity.'[2]

The quantities produced never exceed needs, but they are such that the last unit of each commodity encounters a less intense need.

> The sole innovation in our argument is the extension to the aggregate price index of what is generally accepted in relation to the individual prices which it is composed of. ... Whether one accepts the modern theory of marginal utility or some other theory of value, no one would dream of denying that an increase of the output of a commodity can lower its price. But if this seems obvious for one commodity considered in isolation, why should it become a paradox for several categories of commodities together? Why cannot the overproduction of a series of commodities depress the average price without there necessarily being any compensating rise in the prices of other commodities? Why, quite apart from any monetary effects, cannot such overproduction depreciate the average price index? What stops the acceptance of these possibilities is Say's Law. It would indeed have been

2. *Ibid.*, vol. II, p. 344.

difficult to answer the objections which it suggests, on the basis of the old theories of value. But it is possible to meet these objections on the basis of marginal utility theory or, which comes to the same thing, the modern formulae on the laws of supply and demand. It has already been possible to ascribe a meaning to general overproduction. It is hoped to prove below that this notion becomes conceivable for any one who accepts the new theories of value.[3]

The two elasticities of demand

Aftalion forgets incomes. Demand is not only a function of prices and final utility; it also depends on income. The growth of production gives rise to an equivalent growth of incomes, and all the 'final utilities' must rise proportionally to absorb the increased output. Otherwise there will be unused residual income, hoarded income, which would bring us back to the theory of savings which Aftalion has rejected.

This is the difference between the elasticity of demand 'for one commodity considered in isolation' and 'several categories of commodity', between *one* price and the average price level; this is what stops 'the extension to the aggregate price index of what is generally accepted in relation to the individual prices which it is composed of'. For a given level of income, the price elasticity of demand for an individual commodity can be anything, greater than, equal to, or less than unity; demand may even vary directly with a particular price in 'perverse' cases. Variations in the amount of income left after satisfying this need will sort matters out, by adjusting the marginal utilities of all the other commodities in a compensating direction. But for commodities as a whole (still for a given income, all of which is spent), the price elasticity of demand is always unity since, however prices and quantities may vary, the sum of their respective products is a constant equal to nominal income.

If the level of income is not given, if it in turn varies as an increasing function of the level of output (by virtue of the fundamental equation $R = P$, which Aftalion never questions), then the income elasticity of demand may vary from commodity to commodity and give rise to disproportions (which we do not have to take into account since Aftalion himself abstracted from them), but for commodities as a whole, this elasticity is also strictly unity, in the sense that whatever the apportionment, the inner product of the quantity and price vectors is strictly equal to income. For any level and fluctuations of income, the effect of the income elasticity of demand itself is that as the number of products under consideration increases, the average of the two elasticities of demand must itself tend to unity.

3. *Ibid.*, vol. I, pp. 277–8.

Absolute value

A related question arises here. Assuming that the general fall in values predicted by Aftalion does occur, how can it be measured and in what terms? Aftalion answers this question in the succeeding chapter:

> But behind exchange value, and underlying it, modern science has produced an *absolute* notion of value, which has been ascribed various names, all nonetheless referring to similar things – *final utility, marginal utility, ophelimity, scarcity, subjective utility, use-value.* ... By absolute value is meant a value conceived for each commodity in isolation, without any comparison with other commodities. It expresses a relation between persons and things, and not necessarily any relation between things themselves as well. ... In this way a general fall in final utility, in the subjective value of commodities becomes logically possible.[4]

Aftalion seems to be playing with words here. It does not matter to us if this 'subjective value' falls, whether for several commodities or generally. Our concern is prices. The subjective value attributed to steak by a well-fed person is not the same as that attributed by a hungry person; it is less. This is no reason for the former to offer a lower price for beef steak than that paid by the latter. In proper marginalist logic, while the marginal utility of extra beef steak falls for the well-fed rich person, that of his money or extra income falls just as much compared with that of the hungry pauper. This is the first effect of an increase of wealth: the satisfaction of less and less intense needs, finding it as easy to pay for luxuries now as it was previously to pay for necessities.

'Production', Aftalion writes, 'cannot be excessive in relation to the totality of our needs. But it can be too great for the satisfaction of needs of the same intensity as those which were met before, consequently too great for final utility and the prices of commodities not to drop.'[5] However, if the extra production creates equivalent extra income, once more according to the classical theorem which Aftalion accepts unreservedly, we are now richer than before. In this light it is hard to see why we should refuse to pay the old price to satisfy less intense needs than before. What else can we do with our extra income? And if we refuse to do so and if, by causing prices to drop because of this same refusal, we obtain the increased quantity of goods available for the same sum as we paid out before, what will happen to the extra income in question?

Aftalion misuses 'modern science', whatever its intrinsic merits

4. *Ibid.*, vol. II, p. 283, emphasis original.
5. *Ibid.*, vol. II, p. 398.

and demerits. If there is one thing which marginalist doctrine has rightly or wrongly banished, it is this notion of 'absolute value'. According to this doctrine, value is not in the least a relation between a thing and a person, but a relation between things. The person, with her last need to satisfy or her indifference curves, only intervenes as the common denominator of things, the agent of the reduction from quality to quantity. Marginalists do not determine prices by the 'marginal utility' of the single commodity under consideration, but by the confrontation between the 'marginal utility' of what one receives with the 'marginal utility' of what one gives up.

However absolute prices may be – and we have already accepted that they may be absolute – a uniform movement of all prices has no meaning, in the last analysis, except in relation to income. If, on the one hand, there is no hoarding or sterilising part of income, and if on the other hand the costs of production, defined to include the entrepreneur's profit, are equal to the sum of income created by the same production, as Aftalion's two basic assumptions state, then all production, however great, should be realized at the same prices which served to determine income. Since these prices are on average strictly equal to costs defined in this way, no break in equilibrium can result from a general and correctly proportioned growth of output.

The introduction of income

Aftalion faces up to this objection in Chapter V, where he takes up the question of incomes:

> Any increased production of commodities places in the hands of those who sell them an equally increased sum of resources. ... But this process (which equalises purchasing power) only occurs if prices have not fallen. Use is thus being made against the possibility that prices may fall, of an argument which only applies if prices have not fallen. The circularity is obvious. ... The increased quantities of commodities ... will now satisfy less and less intense needs. ... These are the forces at work to make prices fall. But is the influence of these forces paralysed by an opposite influence deriving from other forces, by an increase in money purchasing power equal to the real growth of production, which can compensate for this growth? There is no reason to think so. There will only be an increase of money purchasing power if prices have not fallen. ... Our two equations were previously:
>
> Production of 100 goods = Income of 100 goods
> Production of 100 × 5 francs = Income of 500 francs,
>
> The crisis arises because there is excess output of twenty articles, which makes prices fall from 5 to 4 francs. This gives us:
>
> Production of 120 goods = Income of 120 goods
> Production of 120 × 4 francs = Income of 480 francs.[6]

6. *Ibid.*, vol. II, pp. 289–93.

This has all the appearances of a mathematical proof. The trouble is that income is not expressed in 'goods' and only later, *after sales* or after a price has been fixed for the goods, in francs. Income is composed from the first, from birth, from *before sales* and *before prices* are ascribed to goods, of francs. Aftalion empties the equation $R = P$ of all its content. It ceases to be an equation *ex ante* and becomes an equation *ex post*. It becomes a pure tautology: $120 \times 4 = 480$.

To establish their equation, $R = P$, the classics converted all income into fixed revenues. To challenge this equation, we have had to point out that a certain part of revenue is variable and depends on the sale of the product. Without challenging this equation, Aftalion turns all income into variable revenues, varying according to the selling price. He argues as if wages (only to mention the most important part of revenue) were only fixed and paid after sales according to the prices obtained for the product on the market. So he concludes that the production of 120 units instead of the previous 100 does not lead to any 'increase of money purchasing power' because prices fall.

To produce these 120 units, his community would, all other things being equal, have had to distribute 20% more than before in wages, interest and rent. What happened to this extra 20%? Aftalion cancels it out *retroactively* through the fall in prices; as if land-owners, usurers and wage-earners were paid as a percentage of the selling-price and *after* the sale.

The transformation of costs into revenues

We said 'as if ...' because this hypothesis that all revenues are paid after output is sold is never made explicit by Aftalion. What is more, as we shall see, he explicitly contradicts it in other formulations. But however distant from reality it may be, this is the only hypothesis which could make the above quotation's reasoning theoretically consistent.

If all revenues were created after sales, their sum could only affect the selling price of the succeeding cycle. So, at the point when production increases from 100 to 120 units, the independent variables of the price function would be the *current* quantities of output and the revenues from the *preceding* cycle. Since the quantities have increased, while revenues have not yet, prices must fall. Then the revenues from the sale of 120 units are created, but since they themselves are affected by the reduced prices of these sales, they do not benefit from the increased quantity and consequently cannot rectify the prices of the following cycle.

In terms of this version, the argument that prices should recover through the growth of revenues, while revenues depend on prices, would indeed seem circular. In fact, it is not at all circular, since those who cherish this hope believe that revenues depend not on selling prices, but on costs of production; and that revenues exist *before* sales as the second independent variable of the price function, the first being the quantities of output.

But this hypothesis, which might seem implicit in Chapter V, is itself rejected in Chapter VIII, when Aftalion attempts to defend his theory on the basis of an *ex ante* equation:

> For industry as a whole, costs amount to the prices of the services of the agents of production – wages, interest and ground rent. On the other hand, there tends to be equality between the prices of commodities and the sum of the prices of the services employed. ... A fall in selling prices should therefore be accompanied by an equivalent fall in costs. ... If such a fall were to occur during crisis and depression, goods produced in greater quantities could find a market without any reduction of profits for the entrepreneurs. The growth of production would not be overproduction. ... But we already know that such a fall in costs equivalent to the fall in prices does not occur either during the months of the crisis or during the depression. . . . The characteristics of capitalist technology and the long duration of production mean that when a crisis develops and lowers selling prices, the entrepreneur has already long been paying for various portions of the cost price at the old, higher rates – plant, raw materials, wages, interest ....[7]

If this is the case, then revenues are already constituted by the time of sales according to the quantity produced, and it is neither apparent why prices should fall, nor (without hoarding) what would happen to the spare revenue if, for some mysterious reasons to do with *subjective* values and judgements (determination of the purchasers not to pay the same price for the extra commodities as they pay for the rest), prices did really fall.

Is Aftalion here introducing, for the first time in his study, a distinction between those elements of the value of production that are transformed into revenues before sales and those that are only transformed after? The words 'various portions of the cost price' might lead us to think so. But this interpretation is in outright contradiction to the start of the passage cited, where he writes explicitly: 'For industry as a whole, costs amount to the prices of the services of the agents of production'; and again: 'The price of commodities and the *total* price of services used tend towards equality.' This shows that Aftalion totally accepts the continental marginalist line that pure profit does not exist on the social scale. But

7. *Ibid.*, vol. II, pp. 333–4.

the only thing that might not be transformed into a revenue before sales is pure profit, profit of enterprise. Does he then consider that it is not the remunerations (of the 'agents of production') generally *acquired* which are transformed into revenues, but only those that are actually 'paid out' – he uses this word – that is, paid in cash? Such an absolute *ex hypothesis* exclusion of credit seems too naive and regressive an idea to be attributed to him, but however this may be, what counts for our calculations is not when these factors are paid, but what price they are paid. Aftalion does not go so far as to imagine that the supplier of raw materials or the worker wait for the final product to be sold before the price of supplies or the wage-rate are fixed respectively. Still, in the passage above, he introduces a strange condition: 'the long duration of production' which results in the entrepreneur paying out these remunerations 'at the old, higher rates'. Should it be concluded from this that in the case of a shorter production period, the rate at which the prices of inputs are fixed depend on the sales of output? That after a certain while the suppliers and employees lose patience and demand to be covered against future fluctuations of these rates? This is a total absurdity. All that can be said on this score is that in such conditions there might be insufficient revenue at any point, and an increase in production is hardly necessary to bring about a crisis.

Or perhaps, in Aftalion's eyes, the cancelling-out of pure profit is not a matter of an immediate balance between plus and minus, as in the 'modern science' which he invokes, but concerns the long-run average? It seems in fact that, in the course of his discussion, Aftalion found the cause of crises in the *fluctuating* relation between cost and selling price: 'the cause of crises is not so much the *low level*, but rather the *lowering* of this price'.[8] Since he includes the remuneration of capital in costs and accepts the eventual tendency to equalisation, he is led to maintain that during depressions the prices of productive services fall proportionately less than the prices of commodities, with the result that costs constantly exceed these prices. But then profit of enterprise, the only variable element of costs, would become negative, and the question of its transformation into revenue before or after sales would not be posed. Whatever the status of profit would be in this case, the other elements of costs would be transformed immediately into revenues, and if their total is already greater than prices, aggregate purchasing power would itself exceed the selling price of production: $R > P$. (Let us point out in this regard that Aftalion had already declared in another context that 'the power of

8. *Ibid.*, vol. II, p. 335.

acquisition may temporarily exceed production' but that 'it cannot be less than production'.[9]) Such a position again makes *both* the fall in prices *and* the destiny of the excess of R over P inexplicable.

His three alternative positions all come to the same thing:

1. Either the whole of costs are transformed into revenues *before* sales; in which case no fall in prices or break in equilibrium are conceivable, even if 'final utility' and the subjectivity of needs are brought into play.
2. Or the whole of costs are transformed into revenues *after* sales; in which case an increase of production can explain crises, but
   a. such an assumption, which turns capitalist firms into co-operatives of associated producers sharing their receipts, is unrealistic;
   b. the ex ante equation $R = P$ loses its meaning, becoming a mere *ex post* identity between the sum of these receipts and the sum of the parts into which they are divided;
   c. it becomes superfluous to refer to 'final utility', since the division of the sum of yesterday's revenues by today's output tells us the new prices directly.
3. Or, finally, some costs are transformed into revenues *before* and some (notably profit of enterprise), *after* sales. In this case
   a. profit of enterprise is, in equilibrium and on average, a positive residue and not zero, as 'modern science' and Aftalion in turn would claim;
   b. 'final utility' is once again superfluous for the reasons given above;
   c. R is less than and not equal to, never mind more than, P.

The last remark is of course the most important in our view. Our aim in spending so long on the critique of Aftalion, was to show that to maintain the framework of the traditional postulate of equality between revenues and production, is to erect a barrier blocking off all possible solutions. This equation is inexorable. The mass of revenues is always there, reappearing after each twist and turn of the search, omnipresent, ready to digest any output; it cannot be evaporated by clever or learned analyses. Consequently the more one insists on trying to obtain an inequality by operating on the equation, the more one sinks into circular arguments; the more detailed one's analysis, the more one contradicts oneself; the more conscious one is of the

9. *Ibid.*, vol. I, p. 311. On the previous page Aftalion had even made it clear that this possibility of $R > P$ only arises during depressions.

need for an 'external' cause, the more one is condemned to remain imprisoned within this space which one has oneself enclosed on all four sides. Finally, if one has the qualities of Aftalion, one will succeed in describing a pretty mechanism for moving from one period to the next of the prosperity-depression cycle, like a delayed-action thermostat, a well-adjusted machine that turns smoothly; by sticking to this, one turns in *circles*.[10]

10. An adumbration of Aftalion's 'innovation' can be found in Malthus:

'The fallacy of Mr Mill's argument depends entirely upon the effect of quantity on price and value. Mr Mill says that the supply and demand of every individual are of necessity equal. But as supply is always estimated by quantity, and demand only by price and value; and as increase of quantity often diminishes price and value, it follows, according to all just theory, that so far from being always equal, they must of necessity be often very unequal, as we find by experience. If it be said that reckoning both the demand and supply of commodities by value, they will then be equal, this may be allowed; but it is obvious that they may then both greatly fall in value compared with money and labour; and the will and power of capitalists to set industry in motion, which is the most general and important of all kinds of demand, may be decidedly diminished at the very time that the quantity of produce, however well proportioned each part may be to the other, is decidedly increased. ('Review of Tooke', *Quarterly Review*, XXIX (1823), quoted in J. Viner, *Studies in the Theory of International Trade*, p. 198).

Much more recently, the essence of this 'innovation' crops up again in J. Duret (*Le Marxisme et les crises*, p. 76). The burden of his argument is that overproduction should not be conceived in relation to the needs of society, or even in relation to the market's purchasing power, but in relation to prices which are profitable for the capitalist, *since demand is elastic*.

By appealing in this way to the elasticity of demand as the determinant, not of a single price, but of all prices, J. Duret implicitly accepts Aftalion's explanation by the 'psychological theory of the value of marginal utility', which he explicitly rejects a bit further on (pp. 88–9).

8 Equality of Savings and Investment, the Latest Incarnation of the Equality of Income and Output

By linking the fundamental classical postulate:

$$\text{Income} = \text{Value of output} \quad (8.1)$$

with this very specific definition of investment:

$$\text{Investment} = \text{Value of output} - \text{Consumption} \quad (8.2)$$

Keynes obtains, substituting (8.1) into the right-hand side of (8.2):

$$\text{Investment} = \text{Income} - \text{Consumption} \quad (8.3)$$

But since

$$\text{Saving} = \text{Income} - \text{Consumption} \quad (8.4)$$

he concludes that

$$\text{Saving} = \text{Investment} \quad (8.5)$$ [1]

Since saving is the same as non-consumed income (equation 8.4) and is equal to investment (equation 8.5) the model rules out the possibility that any revenues may be neither consumed nor invested, i.e. the possibility of net hoarding at the social level, and in this it differs from those of both the classics and Marx. Since, on the other hand, the author agrees with the classics and Marx in retaining the equation between income and the value of output, disequilibrium between supply and demand is impossible. The system is in permanent and unshakeable equilibrium. Only the volume of employment can vary.

Keynes's originality lies in dissociating equilibrium from full employment. Equilibrium is not only possible, but necessary, at all levels of employment. The capitalist system's tendency to overproduction, lambasted by Marxists and classical non-

1. According to John M. Robertson, James Mill was the first to assert the identity of the growth of capital and the sum of savings. '[We] find him formally landed in the extraordinary hallucination that the net amount of annual saving, recorded by the bank totals, always equates exactly with a mass of tangible "saved" materials.' (*The Fallacy of Saving*, p. 74.)

conformists, turns in Keynes into a tendency to unemployment.[2]

Of course this equality at the social level does not exclude inequalities at the individual level. Through the play of money transfers and the creation of credit money, one individual may save without investing (hoard), while another invests without saving (borrows). But overall, the sum of savings must equal the sum of investments.

The transition from '*ex ante*' inequality to '*ex post*' equality

There has been much debate since Keynes on whether this is an *ex post* equation, an equation between *actual* saving and investment, which does not preclude *ex ante* inequality between 'planned' saving and investment. In this case the state of business is determined by the transition from *ex ante* inequality to *ex post* equality. If, *ex ante*, saving exceeds investment, they will actually be equalised at the cost of a fall in prices and a reduction of employment. In the reverse case, *ex post* equalisation would mean a rise in prices and stimulation of economic activity.

A parallel with the stock exchange will perhaps make it easier to grasp this mechanism. It is often said, for example, that funds move out of the stock exchange into property or, conversely, that they flow into the stock exchange under certain conditions, or that money is scarce when tax payments fall due, at the end of each quarter when advance corporation tax must be paid etc.

It is obvious that these explanations do not correspond to reality. The new money which comes onto the stock exchange each day is strictly equal to the sum of brokerages, plus that of new subscriptions, minus that of coupons cashed in. It is impossible for a penny more or less to come onto the stock exchange, since everything else is merely shares changing hands. There is an *ex post* mathematical equality. If there was also *ex ante* equality, the quotations of stocks and bonds could not vary. But there is no *ex ante* equality. One day, more new money than the above sum will *try* to enter, in the shape of an excess of orders to buy over orders to sell;

2. In purely formal terms, this position of Keynes shows the irrelevance of one of the controversies about the 'Law'. It rules out overproduction, but it is compatible with any level of employment. As Hawtrey writes: 'Say's *loi des débouchés* declared that production generated its own demand; but if for any reason production was below capacity and there was unemployment, the demand generated would be no more than sufficient to absorb output at that level.' (*Capital and Employment*, p. 219.)

The validity of this remark is clearly only formal. For if production always and everywhere engendered equivalent demand, there would be no reason, at least tendentially and structurally, to produce less than full capacity.

another day, less than the sum in question will want to enter, the difference being represented by an excess of orders to sell over orders to buy. On the first day, quotations will rise just enough to deter this supplement. On the second day, quotations will fall just enough to encourage other holders of new money. Finally, every day exactly as much money enters as leaves (taking into account the three sums above – brokerages, subscriptions and coupons). Whatever happens, there is complete *ex post* equality, but this equality is sometimes attained by a rise and sometimes by a fall in quotations, depending on the direction of the *ex ante* inequality.[3]

Keynes does not seem to have had this kind of mechanism in mind, in the case of S = I. In his work, the equality between saving and investment appears to be a mere identity, an accounting identity without any effect on price movements. It rests solely on a very special definition of investment: any output which does not enter personal consumption (equation 8.2 above). In this meaning, investment takes place not only when means of production are bought from their producer to be set to work by their user, but also when a lack of investors causes these same means of production to lie unsold in their producer's warehouses, and even when the same depression results in consumer goods similarly staying on the shelves without finding a taker.

If it is considered that purchasing power is already created in production, independently of sales, by the classical postulate which Keynes adopts, it is clear that recalcitrant (hoarded) purchasing power exactly equal to the price of production of these unsold goods must exist somewhere. So by writing these unsold goods on the left and the corresponding hoarding on the right of the double-entry accounts, the accounts are balanced. But it has only been possible to achieve this result by calling 'investment' the very result of an abstention from investing.

It follows that the situation is not the same in both senses of the *ex ante* inequality. If planned investment exceeds planned saving, prices rise and forced saving is added to planned saving up to the sum of actual investment. The analogy with our stock exchange example holds here. But if saving exceeds investment *ex ante*, then no third

3. Ignoring this necessity for *ex post* equality, Lescure counts among the factors leading to depression and crises, the case in which savings prefer to be spent on existing values and refuse to be used in production, by which he means the founding of new firms (cf. *Des Crises générales et périodiques de surproduction*). This does not make sense. No extra savings can enter the markets of existing values, such as the stock exchange, the property market, etc., unless there is a new issue, new construction, or new production of the corresponding kind.

term intervenes. The involuntary inventories created by this situation are decreed to be investments, and the equation S = I applies directly, without any reference to prices.

In this case, the equality is *immediate* and has no relation to any phenomenon developing over time. It can be verified at any point. Of course, though placed in the category of investments, these involuntary inventories still continue to exert a downward pressure on the market, but this is an accompanying effect which plays no role in establishing the equality in question.

The relevance of this distinction between *ex ante* and *ex post* is therefore unclear in relation to the Keynesian equation. It seems more like a timeless equation which follows from several definitions.[4]

In fact it is a pure truism stating only that total saving equals the increase in the quantity of all kinds of material goods in the system.[5] Just as these goods can be divided into two categories of inventories, voluntary and involuntary, the savings which are their counterpart are either capitalised or hoarded. Involuntary inventory fluctuations are the 'negative image' of fluctuations in hoarding. If involuntary inventories are included with voluntary inventories in a so-called 'objective' category of investment in general, then of course the subjective distinction between capitalised savings and hoarded savings loses its *raison d'être*.

If I invest more than the 'capitalised' savings of others permit, I

4. 'If ... we define money investment in such a way that the definition itself compels aggregate money saving and aggregate money investment to be equal, it is nonsense to speak of this equality being "brought about" by equilibrating or any other forces.' (A.-C. Pigou, *Employment and Equilibrium*, p. 39.)

But this point gives rise to the greatest confusion among Keynesians. Thus J. Robinson: 'Saving is equal to investment, because investment leads to a state of affairs in which people want to save. Investment causes incomes to be whatever is required to induce people to save at a rate equal to the rate of investment.' (*Introduction to the Theory of Employment*, p. 10). And even more clearly on p. 13, 'It is through changes in income that the equality of saving and investment is preserved.' This is of course adopting a completely gratuitous interpretation of the *General Theory*. The notion of the equilibrium level of income is absent from the formulae which lead Keynes to $S = I$. The equation holds for any level of income, which is only an intermediate term in the relevant equations.

However Myra Curtis, replying to Lerner, makes the pertinent remark that 'the idea of a process which has to work itself out before the equality of savings and investment is reached is quite foreign to a theory which maintains that they are necessarily and continuously equal. ... A theory which assumed the necessity for such a process would amount to asserting that savings *never* equalled investment except in a position of hypothetical and unattainable equilibrium.' ("Is money saving equal to investment?", p. 613.)

5. Rather like the 'equality' between 'an elephant's trunk and its proboscis', in D. Robertson's phrase. (*Essays in Monetary Theory*, p. 6.)

cause prices to rise and thus impose on other people extra (forced) abstinence – saving. If I 'hoard' my money, I compel someone else to overstock his commodity.

The meaning of an excess of saving over investment

Clearly it suffices to change some of the definitions to obtain an inequality, $S > I$, in place of the equation $S = I$.

Let us return to the series of equations above. Let us start by provisionally accepting the Law of Markets, despite our disagreement:

$$\text{Income} = \text{Value of Output} \tag{8.1}$$

But by defining investment 'properly', equation (8.2) becomes:

$$\text{Investment} = \text{Value of output} - \text{Consumption} - \text{Unsold goods} \tag{8.2a}$$

Substituting (8.1) into the right-hand side of (8.2a) gives:

$$\text{Investment} = \text{Income} - \text{Consumption} - \text{Unsold goods} \tag{8.3a}$$

But since:

$$\text{Saving} = \text{Income} - \text{Consumption} \tag{8.4}$$

(8.3a) and (8.4) together give:

$$\text{Saving} = \text{Investment} + \text{Unsold goods} \tag{8.5a}$$

or

$$\text{Saving} - \text{Investment} = \text{Unsold goods} \tag{8.6}$$

Finally, by introducing the correct definition:

$$\text{Saving} - \text{Investment} = \text{Hoarding}, \tag{8.7}$$

we conclude:

$$\text{Hoarding} = \text{Unsold goods} \tag{8.8}$$

Since, in terms of the equilibrium of the major economic aggregates, there are no grounds for distinguishing between hoards proper and capital which for some reason has not been invested, 'capital lying fallow', equation (8.8) above is only a formal expression of Marx's position that 'overproduction of capital is never anything more than overproduction of means of production – of means of labour and necessities of life – which may serve as capital', that 'furthermore, capital consists of commodities, and therefore over-production of capital implies over-production of commodities'.[6]

6. *Capital,* vol. III, pp. 255, 256.

This position of Marx indirectly confirms his continued adherence to the classical postulate of the equation, P = R. If purchasing power as a whole equals production, the 'stockpiling' of purchasing power on one side must indeed lead to equal 'stockpiling' of unsold goods on the other.

The heterogeneity of the two inventories

Several authors, including Klein, Hawtrey and Harrod,[7] have drawn attention to the artificiality of this inclusion of involuntary inventories in investment, but their attachment to the principle of the Law of Markets (equation 8.1 above) prevented them from stating clearly what is basically unacceptable about this aggregation of the unsold and sold parts of output.

As a result, orthodox Keynesians were not too worried by these objections. For if the two parts of the product – the sold and the unsold – are subject to the same mode of valorisation, why not abstract from their specificity in an aggregate macroeconomic argument? To this way of thinking, restrictive definitions of investment are what would seem 'special'.

Pure sophistry, such as that of B. Schmitt, is then enough to dismiss all criticism: 'Investment includes all kinds of investment, even involuntary. . . . It is contradictory to exclude any involuntary investment from the definition of real investment. . . .'[8]

The reply is of course obvious. It is not a matter of distinguishing between *involuntary* and *voluntary investment*. Voluntary or involuntary, decided on freely or under threat of a pistol, after long reflection or on the spur of the moment, after a fast or a drinking-bout, an investment has exactly the same *objective* effects. The distinction which must be drawn is between an involuntary *inventory* and an investment proper. An unsold Concorde in the hangars of British Aerospace must not be confused with a Concorde bought by British Airways and in service on its routes. Between these two lies the *trans-substantiation*, the *perilous leap* of *realization*, which is the very problem which all these theories are supposed to solve.

The effects differ objectively, not subjectively; they are even diametrically opposed. A hundred buses in a British Leyland yard are a commodity like any other; in a London Transport depot, they are a

7. R. L. Klein, *The Keynesian Revolution*, 1948; R. G. Hawtrey, *Capital and Employment*, 1937; R. F. Harrod, *Towards a Dynamic Economics*, 1948.

8. *La Formation du pouvoir d'achat*, p. 37. This position still does not prevent its author from concluding from other arguments that savings do not always equal investment, even *ex post*, and that hoarding destroys this equality.

means of production. In the former case, they need to be sold, are inflating the aggregate supply and therefore possibly affecting prices, equilibrium, employment, etc.; in the latter case, conversely, the market has been disencumbered of them, and economic activity stimulated by this fact.

This identification is never made in reality: no businessman claims to have made an investment when he simply cannot sell his trash; if theory dares to make this claim, this is essentially due to the unconscious habit of economists of only recognizing a temporal and qualitative difference between a sold and an unsold commodity. Those economists who believe that value is created in the production process cannot accept any quantitative variation between creation and realization. For the rest, who hold that value only exists in exchange, things are even simpler. Realization is itself meaningless. Realization of what? Value does not exist either before or after an exchange.

But, as we have already said, the problems of political economy in general and that of realization in particular are essentially quantitative. If a quantitative difference is recognized between the values of commodities before and after sales, this difference will be ineluctably present throughout the model, and cannot be ignored. Purely qualitative distinctions, even if formally stated at the start, are easily forgotten along the way. This is how, in the problem of 'realization', the barrier of 'realization' itself ends up being defined out of existence. The overstock is put under the heading of investment, although the task is to study the positive effect of investment on economic activity, and the only way for investment to stimulate economic activity is by disencumbering us of the overstock. One has to be pretty unconcerned about the subject of sales to consider sold and unsold goods as homogeneous and add them together indiscriminately.

For a doctrine whose concerns centre on the role of investment as a stimulant of economic activity and thus of the disposal of output, it is a basic flaw to include an actual effect of the difficulty of disposing of output – overstocks – in investment; and this is the source of all the doctrine's eventual impasses.

On this subject we can also say that it does not save the situation to call this pseudo-investment 'passive investment' as Hawtrey does, since the only role of this magnitude is for its variations to preserve equality between savings and investment, turning preservation of this equation into an end in itself.

Yet again – we have pointed this out for other theories – what leads to this deadend is unconditional insistence on the postulate of the equality of income and the value of output and, consequently, the immutability of the latter as it passes from its producer, through the warehouses of various dealers, to its final consumption.

Conversely, such a conflation of overstocks and investment becomes impossible once it is accepted as we suggest that, as installed equipment, each good should be accounted at its selling price, the price at which the factory which produces it sold it to the factory which uses it, whereas, as an unsold stock, the same good should be accounted at its cost price. In the former case, the social value of the good has already been mediated and ratified by the market as including the profit on the producer's capital, while in the second case only a sort of pre-value is recognized, not including any profit on the capital which served to produce the good.[9]

The accounting of unsold goods at their cost-price

If we examine the accounts of any capitalist firm, we see that what counts as income in the real world and is distributed as such is neither the total value-added of the whole of production, nor only that of the sold part. It is the full value-added of the sold part plus that contained in the *cost price* of the unsold part, after this cost price – intermediate consumption plus 'preliminary' income distributed or allotted before sales – has, in some cases, such as depression and crisis, been adjusted downwards for inventory depreciation. Again, in actual business behaviour, involuntary inventories are never considered to be investments.

9. It is possible to arrive at the same equation, S = I, without including unsold goods under investment, but considering them as simply worth nothing. In this case, the excess savings in the hands of hoarder–purchasers, the counterpart of these unsold goods which led to their not being sold, are cancelled out by equivalent dissaving on the part of the owners of these unsold goods, corresponding to the loss they have suffered on account of this failure to sell. Any purchasing power not used productively or unproductively would therefore cancel itself out on the social level. 'Saving is the one thing that cannot be saved', says Robertson.

This version is certainly more consistent with hardline marginalism, according to which value only exists *during* and *through* sales, since all *saleable* output fetches the equilibrium market value, whatever this may be, while any left over is worthless. There are some hints of this interpretation in Keynes. It seems to be present in part II of Chapter VI: 'Income is created by the value in excess of user cost which the producer obtains for the output he has sold; but the whole of this output must obviously have been sold either to a consumer or to another entrepreneur. ... (*General Theory*, p. 64). But in part I of the same chapter, and above all in part II of Chapter XXII, the author treats the growth of stocks (whether voluntary or involuntary) as investment at its full value, and a fall in stocks as disinvestment.

So, by defining:

Product of sales = The selling price of sold output minus the constant capital consumed (Keynes's 'user cost') in the whole of production, sold and unsold; and

Cost price of unsold goods = The value at which, according to the circumstances and financial rules of the time and place, a firm may enter its inventories among its own assets and mobilise it by means of credit, without engaging in overtrading.

we obtain:

Income = Product of sales + Cost-price of unsold goods,
Product of sales = Consumption + Investment
Saving = Income − Consumption

therefore:

Saving = Investment + Cost-price of unsold goods

whence:

Saving − Investment

or:

Excess capital = Cost price of unsold goods

So any uninvested capital has a counterpart in an unrealized commodity. If capital moves abroad to find more lucrative openings for investment, this also leads to a commodity being realized by being exported, since capital can ultimately only move from one country to another in the form of commodities. Whether domestically or internationally, an investment is at the same time, by its own nature, an absorption of capital and an equivalent simultaneous realization of commodities.

There is an example of an excess of saving over investment (*ex post* overproduction of capital) corresponding to a parallel overstock of commodities, in section III of Chapter XXI of vol. II of *Capital*, where Marx is examining the operations of the realization of the product in terms of the scheme:

$$\begin{array}{ll} \text{I} & 5000c + 1000v + 1000s = 7000 \\ \text{II} & 1430c + 285v + 285s = 2000. \end{array}$$

Department I's capitalists accumulate 500*s*, while those of Department II accumulate 70*s*. All the operations take place without any difficulty except for one, the last one, when Departments I and II face each other with 70 means of production and 70 articles of consumption respectively. How can they exchange them? At this point I gets out his money-reserve and buys the 70 articles of consumption from II. But what if II, after taking the money, refuses to buy I's 70 means of production? In that case, says Marx, 'this accumulation of money on the part of II would at the same time express that 70 I*s* in means of production are unsaleable. There would be a relative overproduction in I, corresponding to the simultaneous non-expansion of reproduction on the part of II.

In other words, there is an idle capital in the hands of capitalist II, who is looking for an opening for it, but the only opening available to him, the means of production commodity, which capitalist I offers him on the market, does not suit him. There is therefore excess saving on one side and overproduction of commodities on the other. This is an *ex post* situation.

Of course, here as elsewhere, Marx sticks to the classical line and counts the unsold goods, I*s*, at the full value of 70. By mobilising this value (whether by drawing on his reserves or by a bank loan), the capitalist in Department I has not engaged in overtrading. Consequently, the retention of a purchasing power of 70 by the capitalist in Department II constitutes equivalent hoarding (or excess capital) on the social scale. If, as we suggest, I's unsold goods were valued at their cost price which, in the above example, is 60, capitalist I would have overtraded by 10, because this is the extent to which he would be *anticipating* unrealised surplus-value (or profits). And the fact that he uses his own money to do this changes nothing. This overtrading corresponds to negative saving, and by deducting this sum from capitalist II's saving of 70 we arrive finally at the figure of 60 for net hoarding at the social level, which is equal to the cost-price of the unsold goods.[10]

10. We will return to the subject of overtrading in the special chapter on this subject.

PART III The Specific Effects of General Imbalance

9 Re-equilibrating Factors

The relative consolidation of capitalism since the last world war

At this work's time of writing, we have to recognize that for several decades, since the great crisis of the 1930s or at least since the Second World War, capitalism seems to have been able to overcome a great number of its contradictions. Even if we abstract from the war period and that of 'reconstruction', we are left with a good quarter of a century without any real overproduction crisis. A comparison (see table) between the unemployment rates of the great crisis 1929–33 with those which we are accustomed to today is therefore especially striking.

Unemployed as a percentage of the active population

	1933–4	*1969*	*1970*	*1971*
Germany	20.67	0.7	0.5	0.7
Canada	28.57	4.7	5.9	6.4
United States	36.47	3.5	4.9	5.9
France	13.42	1.6	1.7	2.1
United Kingdom	14.16	2.2	2.3	3.0
Italy	7.00	3.4	3.2	3.2
Japan	15.56	1.1	1.1	1.2
Weighted average of the seven countries covered by the ILO	22.80	2.36	2.84	3.39
Belgium		2.3	1.9	1.9
Netherlands		1.6	1.2	1.7
Australia		1.1	1.0	1.4
Sweden		1.7	1.5	2.1
Weighted average of the 11 countries covered by the OECD for 1969–70		2.30	2.73	3.26

Sources: Number unemployed in 1933–4 quoted by André Cariven, *La Lutte contre le chômage*, cross-checked with ILO statistics; 1969–71 statistics published by the OECD.

Weighted average percentages calculated by ourselves on the basis of the above data and figures for the active civil population; the latter are drawn from various sources for 1930–4 and from OECD publications for 1969–71.

It should be noted that 1969–71 is quite a representative slice of the contemporary period, since it includes the 1970–71 recession. In this way it is possible not only to compare today's 'recessions' with the crises of the past, but also to see the considerable reduction in the divergences between good and bad years, divergences which have also become irregular and erratic considered country by country, if one excludes the US, the UK and Canada.

But these percentages, which are proportions of the active civil population, do not give a full picture of the change in the situation, since the composition of the active civil population has changed between the two periods. The striking fall in the number of those engaged in agriculture as a proportion of the total active population, as well as the fall in the number of unproductive workers – even in 1934, domestic servants were still 11.8% of the active population in Great Britain – and of the idle rich, means that if the unemployed were taken – this would be more meaningful – as a percentage of productive *wage-earners* instead of as a percentage of the total active population, it would emerge even more clearly that today's recessions have nothing in common with the crises of the past. To take but one example, in 1933–4 Japan had only 7 million workers out of an active population of more than 20 million, and of these 7 million workers, 2.8 million or 40% were unemployed.

Moreover, at the time of the great depression, unemployment was only incompletely recorded. We have used ILO figures, which give 31 million unemployed for the seven countries in the table. But according to Sternberg, if partial and 'invisible' unemployment were also counted, the figure would rise to 40 million.[1]

Still, it does not seem worthwhile to adjust the figures: even in this form the above percentages show undeniably that we are dealing with two different orders of magnitude, two qualitatively different situations.

It must also be pointed out that the unemployment rates of the 1930 crisis are not in the least exceptional compared to earlier crises. Matthews, who made a special study of the trade cycle in England, shows that the figures for 1930 are not noticeably different from those for the middle of the last century.[2]

But it is not only during crises and 'recessions' that the two periods differ: long-run averages reveal the same phenomenon. Of course, statistics become very doubtful when we go back earlier than 1900. Nonetheless, all the estimates agree. If we use Kuznets's data to

1. F. Sternberg, *Capitalism and Socialism on Trial*, p. 280.
2. cf. R. C. O. Matthews, *A Study in Trade Cycle History*.

calculate a general average for the period from 1889 to 1928, that is, up to but not including the great depression, we obtain an unemployment rate of 8.5%, although most of this period, the section from 1904 to 1928, was particularly prosperous. If this section is excluded, the average percentage for the rest of the period, 1889–1903, is 11.5%.[3] From 1948 up till now, the average has been well below 3%.

It can be said with little danger of error, that the unemployment rate in the worst recession years since 1948, has been lower than in the best boom years of the nineteenth and first quarter of the twentieth centuries.

In the area of growth, the figures are just as clear. Between 1949–50 and 1970, the Gross National Product of OECD countries grew in real terms by about 4.5% per year on average (at compound interest); that of EEC countries by around 5%. The *per capita* rates were 3.5% and 4% respectively. During the nineteenth century, the average annual rate of growth of the gross product of all the countries which are now developed was, according to Paul Bairoch's calculations, between 2.0 and 2.5%, while the *per capita* rate was between 1.2 and 1.7%.[4]

But a comparison involving all the countries *which are now developed* is not very meaningful, since the average is distorted by the relatively high figures of those among these countries which inaugurated their industrial revolutions during the last century. If we take England alone, its average annual rate of growth, during the nineteenth century, was scarcely over 1%.

We can therefore conclude that the present rate of growth of the advanced capitalist countries is broadly speaking three times greater than during the last century. What is even more surprising is that this was achieved despite a sizeable increase in unproductive consumption following a very substantial rise in wages and phenomenal budgetary expenditure on education and armaments.

These remarks certainly do not prejudge the future. There is nothing to say that the tendency will not be reversed tomorrow, and an overproduction crisis, as severe or even more severe than those of the past, break out before this book reaches publication; however unlikely this may be, it is not impossible. But it is undeniable that, for the moment and for the past twenty-five years, we have been in a situation unprecedented in the history of capitalism: full or almost full employment and rates of growth which are comparable only to those of the planned countries. In the past, the problems of capitalism

3. cf. Simon Kuznets, 'Proportion of Capital Formation to National Product'.
4. *The Economic Development of the Third World since 1900.*

were known as deflation, drops in prices and the slowdown of economic activity; today they are known as inflation, price rises and 'overheating'.

The future is uncertain, and as for ourselves, we are convinced that, by means of some transformations, capitalism has only succeeded in gaining a reprieve and obtaining a new margin of manoeuvre, which will be used up sooner or later like all the rest before. Still, this situation exists and requires an explanation. In this light, while it is important in general to take account of the system's long-run disequilibrium, it is just as important today to search for the causes of its relative stability and present vigour, however fleeting they may be. This is what we shall attempt in this chapter.

The conditions for an improvement in the process of realization

Since, as we have shown in the preceding chapters, the basic cause of trouble is a structural excess of supply over demand, any factor which tends totally or partially to reabsorb this excess will help to eliminate or reduce the disequilibrium.

Since, as we have also shown, this excess derives from the fundamental inequality $P > R$, in which P represents the total value of output, and R a certain fraction of this value, it is clear that it can only be reabsorbed in one of two ways: either by the growth of this fraction compared to the whole, thus by a so-to-speak intrinsic change in various component parts of P and R; or by an extrinsic divergence in the right direction of *effective* supply or demand from their respective supports, P and R. We will examine these two cases in order.

I. Variations of income compared to the total value of production from which it derives its existence

If P equals

> constant capital consumed + variable capital (wages) + the *fixed* part of surplus-value + the variable part of surplus-value,

while R equals the sum of the first three terms, any relative growth of one or several of these elements which is accompanied by a relative fall in the fourth will reduce the inequality of $P > R$, and so have a stabilising effect on the system. A relative reduction of one or several of these three elements will have the opposite effect. So this case can be subdivided into three:

(a) Variations in constant capital consumed

Constant capital consumed is composed of two parts: the depreciation of fixed capital, and the value of circulating constant capital. They require separate examination.

Depreciation The amount of depreciation can vary either through variations in the value of fixed capital, or through variations in its rate.

A relative variation in the value of fixed capital compared to the other components of capital employed, especially compared to wages (a change in the organic composition of capital), can directly affect the rate of profit of enterprise itself. In this case, it is impossible to draw any conclusions about the variation of the ratio profit of enterprise/cost price, without knowing the sign and magnitude of the change in the rate of profit.

On the other hand, if we assume that the rate of profit stays constant, any variation of fixed capital will give rise to an accompanying variation in the same direction of both terms of the fraction,

$$\frac{\text{profit of enterprise}}{\text{cost price}},$$

the numerator through the rate of profit, the denominator through the rate of depreciation.

Let p and R be respectively the profit of enterprise and the cost price before the change under consideration; p' and R', the same terms after this change; C, fixed capital; K, total capital employed; r, the rate of profit; a, the rate of depreciation; c circulating constant capital; v, variable capital and s', the fixed part of surplus-value – rent, interest, etc.

After an increase in depreciation resulting from an increase of C, we will have

$$\frac{p'}{R'} = \frac{p + r\Delta C}{R + a\Delta C}$$

Everything depends on the relation between the ratios $p{:}R$ and $r{:}a$. If we assume that ΔC is positive, then if $r/a > p/R$, the fraction will rise: $\frac{p'}{R'} > \frac{p}{R}$. If $r/a < p/R$, the fraction will fall: $\frac{p'}{R'} < \frac{p}{R}$. Since $r = \frac{p}{K}$, the condition $\frac{r}{a} < \frac{p}{R}$ (the only one we are interested in) can be written: $\frac{p}{Ka} < \frac{p}{R}$

whence: $Ka > R$.

These results are reversed if ΔC is negative.

To put it verbally, if an increase in the sum of depreciation, resulting from the growth of fixed capital, is to have a favourable effect on the realization of the product (a fall in the ratio profit of enterprise: cost price, p/R), the total capital employed multiplied by the rate of depreciation must be greater than the cost price. This condition is impossible, because:

$$R = Ca + c + v + s' \tag{9.1}$$

$$K = C + c + v \tag{9.2}$$

whence

$$Ka = Ca + ca + va, \tag{9.2a}$$

but since a is always less than one,

$$ca < c$$
$$va < v$$

therefore:

$$Ca + ca + va < Ca + c + v + s'$$

and, substituting from (9.1) and (9.2a),

$$Ka < R.$$

It follows that, all other things being equal, an increase in depreciation resulting from the growth of fixed capital alone will have an unfavourable effect on the realization of the product.

Of course, any concomitant fall in the rate of profit itself, if directly related to the assumed growth of fixed capital, will counteract this effect and may even reverse it. But since variations in the rate of profit depend on a second autonomous variable, labour productivity, the effects of growth in the sum of depreciation on the system's general equilibrium are finally unpredictable, and no tendency can be shown a priori.

Things are quite different if it is the rate of depreciation which increases, all other things being equal. In this case, cost price increases without any change in profit of enterprise, so that the part of the social product for which there is no 'prior outlet', in Henri Denis' phrase, falls relatively.

As capitalism develops, is the rate of depreciation bound or likely to increase? Such an increase would reflect a greater rate of physical and/or moral depreciation of machinery, however its value composition, and thus the organic composition of capital, may vary.

There is no reason to believe that the physical life of machinery is decreasing, on the whole and on average, as industrialisation develops and technology advances. On the other hand, some indices suggest that innovations are more frequent and consequently obsolescence more rapid in advanced capitalism than in undeveloped capitalism.

Still, the evidence we have on this subject is not decisive enough to allow us to conclude that any relative increase in cost price deriving from an acceleration of moral wear-and-tear has been reflected in actual fact in a decrease in the ratio of pure profit to cost price, large enough to explain the system's recent vigour.

Consumed material inputs Here we are concerned with the rest of 'constant capital consumed': raw and auxiliary materials. The variations of this part can only stabilise or destabilise the system if they do not give rise to proportionate variations of total capital employed, on which profit of enterprise is calculated.

If the turnover times of the various elements of capital were all equal to unity, this disproportion would be assured by the fact that the whole of fixed capital is included in capital employed, while only part, its depreciation, enters into cost price. It follows that cost price is, in this case, smaller than capital employed and, since the increment of circulating constant capital is added whole to both, it makes cost price grow more than proportionally to the growth of total capital employed and, consequently, more than proportionately to the growth of profits. But turnover times are not all necessarily equal to unity.

Using the symbols of the previous section and introducing q to denote the turnover time of c, we obtain:

$$\frac{p'}{R'} = \frac{p + r\Delta K}{R + \Delta c}$$

but since

$$\frac{\Delta c}{q} = \Delta K$$

we can write

$$\frac{p'}{R'} = \frac{p + r\Delta K}{R + q\Delta K}$$

It follows that

$$\frac{p'}{R'} < \frac{p}{R}$$

if and only if

$$\frac{r}{q} < \frac{p}{R}$$

But $r = p/K$

Therefore, by substitution, the condition becomes:

$$\frac{p}{qK} < \frac{p}{R}$$

or

$$qK > R.$$

Consequently, a relative growth of circulating constant capital (raw and auxiliary materials etc., i.e. all material inputs except depreciation) will only have a favourable effect on the realization of output, that is, will only lower the ratio of pure profit to cost price, p/R, if total capital employed, multiplied by the velocity of the circulating constant capital, is greater than cost price. If not, this increase will have an unfavourable effect. The reverse applies if circulating constant capital *falls* relatively.

Although $qK > R$ is much more likely in practice than $qK < R$, both are possible. Besides, any concomitant variation of the rate of profit, directly related to the variation of total capital employed, would make the number of favourable or unfavourable combinations infinite.

In conclusion, we can say that it is very unlikely that any variations in the material part of the cost price of commodities – depreciation or intermediate consumption – is responsible to any significant extent for the relatively problem-free realization of the social product noted over the last twenty-five years.

The situation changes considerably, as we shall see, and the causal relations become much starker and more decisive, when we turn to the other element of the supply price of output, *value added*.

(b) Variations of variable capital

Rodbertus tried to explain overproduction crises by a decrease in the portion of national income going to wages. Even if these are growing in absolute terms, the fact that they are falling relative to the portion going to capitalists is enough, he claims, to breach equilibrium between production and purchasing-power. Rosa Luxemburg treats this idea with all the irony and contempt which she habitually substitutes for serious criticism when discussing the ideas of others:[5]

5. She is not the first in this. She is adopting an accepted style, unfortunately developed by the great Marxist theoreticians and even, let us admit it, by the founders of a kind of socialism which, in this respect, does not live up to its title of 'scientific'.

In this ingenious theory there are quite a few points to make us wonder. If our commercial crises are entirely due to the fact that the workers' 'wage rate', the variable capital, represents a constantly diminishing portion of the total value of the national product, then this unfortunate law brings with it the cure for the evil it has caused, since it must be an ever smaller part of the aggregate product for which there is overproduction. Although Rodbertus delights in such terms as 'an overwhelming majority', 'the large popular masses of consumers, it is not the number of heads that make up the demand, but the value they represent which is relevant. This value, if Rodbertus is to be believed forms a more and more trifling part of the aggregate product. Crises are thus made to rest on an ever narrowing economic basis, and all that remains to discover is how in spite of it all it can still happen that the crises are universal and increasingly severe besides, as Rodbertus is fully aware'.[6]

It is true that Rodbertus expresses himself with little rigour, but his idea deserved more attention. Whether from intuition or systematic thought, he put his finger on an essential mechanism of realization. But Rosa Luxemburg's reply is infantile – whether or not the position under attack is correct. If it is true that crises are due to the relative decrease of wages, then their basis is not narrowing, but widening, since this basis is not the sum of wages, nor the percentage of the total product which they account for, but the gap between the sum of wages and the whole of national income.

'I know very well', Rodbertus writes, 'that what is taken from the workers' share goes ultimately to swell that of the rentiers [read: recipients of surplus value], and that purchasing power remains constant on the whole and in the long run. But as far as the product on the market is concerned, the crisis always sets in *before* this increase can make itself felt'.[7]

'On the whole', 'in the long run', 'before this increase can make itself felt': these are all clumsy formulations of the same basic idea as Sismondi's: profits cannot compensate for wages as purchasing power, since they only exist after sales. This idea was badly worked out and badly used; it was eventually lost in contradictory arguments, but is essentially correct. Rosa Luxemburg, who herself cites this crucial sentence from Rodbertus, ignores the argument. She only notices a theory of disproportion à la Say or Ricardo, between the different kinds of commodities consumed by workers and by capitalists. However, despite his self-contradictions, it is clear that

6. *The Accumulation of Capital*, pp. 253–4.

7. *Schriften*, vol. I, p. 206. Quoted in Rosa Luxemburg's *The Accumulation of Capital*, p. 254, emphasis added.

Rodbertus meant something quite different here. The difference between the roles of the worker and the capitalist is not that the former represents demand for basic necessities and the latter for luxuries, but that the former represents effective demand *before* sales and the latter only *after* sales.

The theory of disproportion is certainly confusedly mixed up, in some of Rodbertus' arguments, with his correct discovery, and he himself was doubtless unconscious of the implications of this discovery. Like many others, Rosa Luxemburg preferred to shine through facile jokes about this confusion, rather than dealing with its root cause and thus advancing knowledge by herself redressing, if necessary, the weaknesses of presentation which hinder her adversary's theory.

Variations of wages do in fact have a special place in the process of realization of output. In a closed system, there is, in terms of this process, no possibility of any secondary effect which might counteract their influence and complicate analysis, as in the case of material inputs which we studied above.[8] For a given level of national income, wages can only vary inversely with surplus-value and, if the fixed part of surplus-value – rent, interest, etc. – is assumed given, they can only vary inversely with profit of enterprise, i.e. the very part of the value of output for which there is no pre-existing revenue, the part that constitutes the gap between supply and demand. What is more, even if hoarding were accepted as the basic cause of overproduction – which we deny – wages are practically exempt from being hoarded, so their variations are translated directly into variations of aggregate purchasing power.

Of course, Rodbertus was not content with spelling out the functional relation of these variations; he took the risk of formulating a *law*, that is, of predicting the direction of these variations: a constant fall in the proportion of national income accounted for by wages, leading to a worsening of the disequilibrium. We note *a posteriori*: a constant growth in the proportion of national income accounted for by wages, leading to attenuation of the disequilibrium. So reality has refuted his law, but it has verified his theorem.

If this 'verification' is not a mere coincidence between two independent historical facts, if one of these facts explains the other, even partially, then it can be said that one of the paradoxes of capitalism's career is that trade union struggle, with the substantial

8. This kind of effect is possible in an open system, which we shall discuss later, in the context of international trade and payments.

wage increases which it has led to, has had the unexpected result of helping to save the day for the capitalists, in spite of themselves, by contributing to the system's partial stabilisation.

(c) Variations of the fixed part of surplus-value

It goes without saying that, for a given quantity of surplus-value, all other things being equal, the part distributed *before* the sale of output must vary inversely with the part which only becomes income *after* sales. Any increase in the part going to land-owners, usurers, etc. reduces the ratio of profit of enterprise to cost price and thus attenuates the original inequality, $P > R$, by bringing its two terms closer together.

Ground rent and 'third persons' We do not hesitate to state that, just like Sismondi on the general question of realization and Rodbertus on the question of wages, Malthus was correct on the question of rent, when he declared that the expenditure of rentiers facilitates the sale of output, without himself knowing or being able to explain how or why.

Since rent is a deduction from surplus-value, Malthus's detractors could not understand how the transfer of income from one group of economic subjects to another could have any effect on the aggregate sums of purchasing power and commodities produced. They did not see the essential difference, from the point of view of realization, between a fixed and a variable revenue. Rent is an immediate revenue, part of the cost price for the rent-payer; profit is a residual revenue which *does not exist* as such before sales and depends on the results of sales. If part of surplus-value is transferred from the capitalist to the land-owner, future income is turned into current income, indeed a potential income becomes an actual income. However paradoxical this may sound, an industrialist who sells the buildings which contain his factory and continues to occupy them, paying rent to their purchaser, is thereby contributing to the realization of the social product.

On the other hand, the fact that land-owners have themselves become capitalists and invest their rent instead of spending it on luxury consumption does not alter the matter at all, contrary to what Sweezy believes.[9] Since the proportionality of use-values is not in question, the destination of income is irrelevant. Whether it is converted into costly perfumes or into machinery, it frees the market of an equivalent quantity of goods.

9. *The Theory of Capitalist Development*, p. 230.

This question, however, is only of theoretical interest, since no actual increase of rent has been associated historically with the contemporary revival of the capitalist system. On the contrary, in some of the countries under consideration, strong state measures have brought rents down to levels lower than those of the nineteenth century. Certainly one should take into account quasi-rents, industrial rents, especially in the form of royalties. Has the growth of these outweighed the fall in ground rent? It is very difficult to say.

Matters become much clearer when one considers the incomes of 'third persons' other than land-owners. This category was used formerly to include a motley assembly of all who were neither capitalists nor productive workers; for example domestic and civil servants, clergymen and soldiers, the liberal professions and prostitutes. But these groups occupy very different positions in terms of the realization of the product. They must be distinguished.

If we leave aside for the moment those who draw their salaries from the state, whom we will discuss lower down, the remainder can be grouped into two main categories: (i) those who produce something, whether a material commodity or a service, and who, though neither true capitalists nor true proletarians, fit in perfectly with our scheme of the realization of the product. The existence of this category does not affect realization. (ii) those who consume without producing and who are, thus, real 'third persons' in the sense meant by those who refer to this category. Only this second group is in a position to counterbalance general overproduction by its consumption without any counterpart in production.

Nonetheless, the existence of this group still does not change anything. Their consumption has already been counted as the consumption of whoever employs them. If this is a wage-worker, the position is clear: instead of spending his wages himself, he is sharing them with another; on the social level, this changes nothing. If this is a capitalist, he is, as we have seen, entitled as the boss of a company to a certain level of unproductive consumption, whatever the state of his business and without awaiting the company results at the end of the year. It does not matter whether the sum in question appears in the accounts as a salary or as a deduction in advance from profits. Whether he buys a car with this money or hires a servant who, with his wages, buys clothes, this again has no effect on realization.

In the light of the above, it can be said that Rosa Luxemburg's argument when she refutes Struve's theory of 'third persons', an argument which is shared by most Marxist theoreticians, is correct in its conclusions but false in its assumptions: 'These groups can only derive their purchasing power either from the wage of the proletariat or from the surplus value, if not from both; but on the whole, they are to be regarded as joint consumers of the surplus value. It follows that their consumption is already included in the consumption of the capitalist class.'[10]

If Rosa Luxemburg were correct to assume that the consumption of these 'third persons' comes out of capitalist profit, then Struve would be right, since part of profit would thus be turned into purchasing-power before sales, as *anticipated* consumption of profits which, however unproductive it might be, still has the same effect as overtrading, in that it counterbalances the excess. It is only if the consumption of these 'third persons' is taken out of the capitalist's salary (whether earned or allocated) that the theory under attack is refuted.

There is, however, in modern capitalism another very special type of 'third person' or 'third consumption' which would indeed seem to counterbalance the excess of output. This is the marketing and advertising sector, which Baran and Sweezy drew attention to:

> [Since] advertising expenses ... are manifestly unrelated to necessary costs of production and distribution – however broadly defined – they can only be counted as a part of aggregate surplus. ... An even more significant characteristic of the segment of the total surplus which nourishes the sales effort is what might be called its 'self-absorbing' nature. For at the same time that some of this surplus is being extracted from productive workers and an additional amount is being withdrawn from unproductive workers, the whole amount involved is utilised for the maintenance of the sales effort. Unlike the component of surplus which takes the form of net profits, the fraction which takes the form of selling costs calls for no counterpart in capitalists' consumption, no investment outlets. (There is just one qualification to this statement: the profits of advertising agencies and other enterprises engaged in the sales effort obviously enter the general pool of profits and must be offset by capitalists' consumption or investment or both.) The direct impact of the sales effort on the income and output structure of the economy is therefore similar to that of government spending financed by tax revenue.[11]

As can be seen, the authors are arguing on the assumption that the only cause of trouble is hoarding. Workers' incomes (wages) are not likely to be hoarded, capitalists' incomes (profits) are. It follows that, to the extent that expenditure on advertising occurs at the expense of profits (without any increase of selling prices), the part liable to be hoarded decreases and realization is made easier.

We have already given the reasons why hoarding is in our opinion a

10. *The Accumulation of Capital*, p. 295.
11. *Monopoly Capital*, pp. 129–30.

very bad starting-point. We can, in this context, give another simple reason. The problems of realization do not only start when profits, *already realized*, 'must be offset by capitalists' consumption or investment', i.e. when the capitalists, with their profits already in their pockets, have to choose between consumption, investment and hoarding. The problems start before the first morsel of profit leaves the body of the finished commodity, before what is to be consumed, invested or hoarded is even born. These problems must surely exist before the sale of the commodity (from which profits will arise), since it is the problems of this sale that we are concerned with.

Nevertheless, if Baran and Sweezy's argument is transposed into our problematic, which abstracts from hoarding, we reach the same conclusion. The part that these authors believe 'must be offset by capitalists' consumption or investment', i.e. the part of purchasing power which is likely to be hoarded, becomes in our system the part which does not constitute purchasing power at all at the point of time when the two totals are compared. It is clear that any *relative* fall in this part will have the same beneficial effect on realization in either of the two systems.

But this question requires a bit more explanation. Baran and Sweezy rightly consider that the advertising expenses of capitalism are not *necessary* costs of production and distribution. They should therefore not be included in the value of output. In Chamberlin's phrase, which they quote, 'these costs, borne by the consumer, must be counted as selling costs – costs of *altering* his demands, rather than as production costs – costs of satisfying them'.[12] They are 'selling costs' in the sense that capitalists only pay them in order to supplant each other. The output of the advertising sector is not a 'product' on the social level.

If real wages are given, advertising expenses can only come out of profits. There is no reason to suppose that capitalists can succeed in making workers pay part of these costs. If they were not strong enough to reduce real wages without advertising, there is no reason why they should be that strong with advertising.

To sum up, a segment of the social product is destroyed solely in order to be able to sell the rest as quickly as possible. This destruction is direct with respect to the materials consumed by advertising agencies themselves and indirect with respect to the transfer of factors from real production sectors to a sector which only produces sales. P is therefore reduced for an unchanged R. The inequality $P > R$ is attenuated. Both the rate and the mass of profit are reduced.

12. E. Chamberlin, *The Theory of Monopolistic Competition*, quoted in *Monopoly Capital*, p. 127.

If there is unemployment, and if the advertising sector only employs factors that would otherwise lie idle, then P is not affected but R is increased. The inequality $P > R$ is attenuated to the same extent. In this case the mass of profit is unchanged, but its rate falls, since the same mass now has to remunerate those capitals which are employed in the advertising sector and which had no employment without this sector.

Interest

The neoclassical conception This section deals with a crucial point of our position. The dominant economic theory teaches that in equilibrium, the rate of interest covers all the returns to the capital-factor and that 'pure profit' or 'profit of enterprise' is only a conjunctural excess remuneration to individual firms in the short run. It must be compensated for by equally conjunctural under-remunerations, so that there is nothing left over on the social level and in the long run.

If this were so, it would have great implications for our argument. Only interest on a firm's internal funds could then be counted as a revenue not realized before the sale of output, in the framework of our system. Whether only at the rate of interest or at the slightly higher rate of profit, these funds, as collateral to third parties for the successful conclusion of operations, are not entitled to any remuneration until these operations are concluded.

If we take a step further and accept the notion of the 'entrepreneur without capital', then the whole of the returns to capital employed in production would be an integral part of the costs of this production, since they would be owed to the lenders of funds, and would be fixed before sales. In this case, prices would equal costs, P would equal R, and general overproduction would once again be mathematically impossible.

Let us add that this is the most consistent version of neoclassical theory. It is pointless to counter it with the empirical observation that, in practice, there are no entrepreneurs without capital, because we are dealing with social functions, not physical persons.[13]

13. Many Marxists are happy with this 'refutation'. It is ironic that the very same thinkers who are so intransigent on the absolute distinction between the theoretical and empirical levels do not themselves hesitate to reject opposed theories on the basis of a reference to 'facts'. When they are shown tables and statistics that, for example, throw doubt on Marx's law of the tendency of the rate of profit to fall, they turn aside haughtily. Theories cannot be refuted by tables. Fine! But when they are presented with a proof, by strict logic, that the rate of profit tends to be equal to the rate of interest, or that general overproduction crises are impossible, they invoke facts of
Continued on page 306

The question is not whether entrepreneurs without capital exist, but whether one can and should distinguish between the functions of the capitalist, the rentier, the wage-earner, etc., even if they are united in the physical entity of a single individual. Functions are characterised by the nature of what has to function, not by the nature of whoever carries out the functions. If the nature of capital is unaffected by the characteristics of its juridical owner, then one individual can perfectly well encompass three functions, that of *salaried manager without capital*, that of capitalist and that of rentier, while two different individuals, one of whom invests his capital in some one else's firm, and the other of whom invests his in his own firm, will have exactly the same function, that of capitalist.

Finally, if this nature of capital is still unchanged when it passes from one form to another, from that of loanable funds to that of funds employed in production and *vice versa*, and if there are no obstacles to this transfer, which are both assumptions which Marxists have never denied, then it is inconceivable, in equilibrium, for capital to receive different levels of remuneration, depending on which of these two forms it adopts. As J. Robinson says, if the returns to the capital goods form (rate of profit) were greater than those to the loanable funds form (rate of interest), then entrepreneurs would transfer more and more loanable funds into capital goods; if these returns were lower, they would transfer less and less – and this would go on until the two rates were equalised.

In these terms Walras is correct to state that, in rational accounting, the entrepreneur should allocate to himself his salary, the interest on his own capital and the rent on his own land and buildings. Once he has received these, he should be happy to make neither profit nor loss.

In this perspective, there is no danger of any excess of supply price over purchasing power. If one has paid 50 for material inputs, 100 for wages, credited oneself with 50 for various reasons, and if one is then content to sell the product for 200, one will have distributed pur-

13. Continued from page 305
daily experience, tables, the mountains of unsold commodities, the millions of unemployed, and block all theoretical discussion. They are clearly wrong in both respects. In the first because, while facts cannot refute a theory, they can do something even more important: cast such doubt on it that some one is led to develop a theory to refute it. One should therefore not despise facts, even in the form of capitalist tables. In the second respect, because however great the apparent contradiction between the facts and this or that theory, so long as one has not found a new theory to refute the existing theory, one has not advanced one single step. One should therefore not underestimate one's enemy's theories.

chasing power equal to the sum of costs, which is itself equal to the selling price: 50 + 100 + 50 = 200.

The neoclassical argument can be summed up by saying that the rate of interest either is a sufficient remuneration for capital, or it is not. If it is, there is nothing that any extra pure profit could be remunerating. If it is not, there is no reason for pure capitalists to agree to supply capital at this rate.

Profit of enterprise in Marx Marx did not solve the problem. He notes that the total rate of profit sets an upper limit to the rate of interest. He does not point out any lower limit, nor does he set forth any rule for fixing this rate at some point below its upper limit. As opposed to the prices of commodities and labour-power, where competition between sellers and buyers only determines divergences, while a law determines the centre of balance of these divergences, here competition between financial and industrial capitalists is the sole determinant. 'There is rather no law of division except that enforced by competition, because ... no such thing as a "natural" rate of interest exists.'[14]

If the rate of interest is undetermined, the rate of profit of enterprise must also be undetermined, since the latter is nothing but the rate of profit minus the rate of interest. This means that, in Marx's formulation, there is nothing to stop the equilibrium rate of interest from standing at its upper limit, the overall rate of profit, and the equilibrium rate of pure profit from being zero, once the managing director's salary for his real labour of *necessary technical direction* has of course been deducted.

This conclusion hardly conflicts with neoclassical doctrine, and it becomes difficult to see why Marx describes as a 'joke' Proudhon's position that 'the pure economic affirmation of capital is interest' and that what is called 'profit is nothing but a special kind of salary'.[15]

If it is true, as Marx declares categorically, that 'the rate of interest may be defined to be that proportional sum which the lender is content to receive, and the borrower to pay ... for the use of a certain amount of moneyed capital',[16] then it is not only possible for the rate of interest to equal the overall rate of profit, but they must necessarily be equal or tend to become equal. For the elasticity of supply of the

14. *Capital*, vol. III, p. 356. And on p. 362, Marx adds '... there is no such thing as a natural rate of interest [prevailing average rate in a country] in the sense in which economists speak of a natural rate of profit and a natural rate of wages'.

15. Letter to Engels, 14 August 1851, Marx and Engels, *Werke*, vol. XXVII, p. 312.

16. *Capital*, vol. III, p. 370.

lenders is positive as the rate of interest increases, while the borrowers' demand is unlimited compared to supply, for any rate of interest lower than the overall rate of profit. Consequently, profit of enterprise, as the difference between the two rates, disappears.

Marx talks of a division of total profits which is qualitative rather than quantitative:

> This qualitative distinction is by no means merely a subjective notion of the money-capitalist, on the one hand, and the industrial capitalist, on the other. It rests upon an objective fact, for interest flows to the money-capitalist, to the lender, who is the mere owner of capital, hence represents only ownership of capital before the production process and outside of it; while the profit of enterprise flows to the functioning capitalist alone, who is non-owner of the capital.[17]

But what entitles him to this 'profit of enterprise', if not the ownership of capital nor labour supplied?

> One portion of the profit appears now as fruit due as such to capital in *one* form, as interest; the other portion appears as a specific fruit of capital in an oppositie form, and thus as profit of enterprise. One appears exclusively as the fruit of operating with the capital, the fruit of performing capital, or of the functions performed by the active capitalist.[18]

It is one thing to say that this part of profit is 'the fruit' of these functions; it is quite another to say that it must necessarily be paid to the exerciser of these functions, as a result of the way the system operates. The first statement is not a sufficient condition for the second. Under the capitalist system, no one receives 'the fruit' of his functions. Why should the manager of capital be an exception? What is it that makes him capable of appropriating the fruit of his function (profit of enterprise) instead of being satisfied, like all other workers, with a mere salary?

Marx does not answer this question. Throughout the obscure and clearly unfinished Chapter XXIII of volume III, 'Interest and Profit of Enterprise', he often talks of differing rights, of differing 'claims', of the active capitalist's special 'right' to profit of enterprise, whether he himself is or is not an owner of capital, a right which does not derive from the *ownership* of capital. What then can it derive from?

> The profit of enterprise springs from the function of capital in the reproduction process, hence as a result of the operations, the acts by which the functioning capitalist promotes this function of industrial and commercial capital. But to represent functioning capital is not a sinecure,

17. *Ibid.*, p. 374.
18. *Ibid.*, p. 375.

> like representing interest-bearing capital. On the basis of capitalist production, the capitalist directs the process of production and circulation. Exploiting productive labour entails exertion, whether he exploits it himself or has it exploited by someone else on his behalf.[19]

Is it then a matter of a special wage for administration and supervision, and is Marx here abjuring his previous ideas, which, fourteen years earlier, had inspired his bitter criticism of Proudhon?

The dual nature of the personal labour of the entrepreneur At some points in reading this chapter of *Capital*, an interpretation seems to surface, which would eliminate the contradictions in Marx's position; the personal activity of the entrepreneur should be divided into two parts: (i) the *technically* necessary labour of management and the coordination of different parts of the productive process; (ii) the labour of supervision and defence of the interests of capital in its relations with the workers and in opposition to them.

The former is 'a productive job, which must be performed in every combined mode of production'.[20] The latter is a job which is only necessary in modes of production based on the antagonism between the immediate producer and the owner of the means of production. The role of the former is to maximise production, that of the latter is to maximise exploitation.

In this respect, the former produces value and surplus-value, and it is paid like any other kind of labour, according to the law that governs wages, and has nothing to do with capitalist profit. The latter produces neither value nor surplus-value; it serves to extort as much surplus-value as possible from the rest of the workers. It can therefore only be paid for by the transfer of some of the surplus-value created by productive workers. This part of surplus-value can only be overall profits, minus the interest on capital employed – both that borrowed from idle capitalists and his own – minus the wages due to himself or someone else for the real labour of technical management. This is the profit of enterprise.

In so far as this interpretation of the text in question reflects Marx's thinking, this thinking becomes much clearer and more coherent, but is still debatable. The fact that the active capitalist's labour includes a part which produces neither value nor surplus-value, and has therefore to be paid out of the surplus-value extracted from others' labour, is not a sufficient reason for paying him *all* the surplus-value which is left after all the other 'rightful claimants' have been remunerated.

19. *Ibid.*, p. 380.
20. *Ibid.*, p. 383.

The active capitalist is not alone in this respect. All unproductive workers, from mere domestics to the employees of advertising agencies which we have already discussed, together with various commercial employees, brokers, sellers, etc., whose parasitic function Marx analyses elsewhere, are in exactly the same position: they do not produce value or surplus-value and are paid out of the surplus-value produced by productive workers. But they are not paid on the basis of a 'sharing-out' of the surplus-value, but at the same rate as productive workers of comparable skill, according to the rules which set the price of labour-power in general, with no regard to 'function'.

One of the most important of these rules is that labour-power is not valued according to what it produces, its use-value, but according to the conditions of its own reproduction. Thus the slave supervisor in ancient Rome – Marx himself, in the text in question, draws an analogy between him and the modern businessman – received less food than the other slaves because his work was lighter, despite the fact that the greater opposition between exploiter and exploited, which Marx himself notes, meant that his role as the slave-owner's lieutenant was more important than that of the active capitalist as the capital-owner's lieutenant.

With respect to the determination of what the active capitalist should receive beyond the pure remuneration of his capital, for his personal labour, the distinction between the two functions of this labour, productive and unproductive, is irrelevant. As far as its remuneration is concerned, this labour is a homogeneous and undifferentiated whole, the expenditure of labour-power of given complexity. It is reproducible at will by means of education and training; it is therefore 'mobile', subject to the general competition between workers, and to equalisation. Its price is a wage no different from other wages. In these terms, this price cannot depend on the profit of enterprise, still less be equal to it, since the latter depends on overall profits and it is overall profits which depend on wage-rates and not the other way round.

One could certainly assume that the entrepreneur's effort is proportional to the amount of capital he looks after; and that it is appropriate for him to be paid at some percentage of the sum of these capitals or their returns. This would not save the situation. This would only be a special way of calculating wages which would not affect their nature. This would be a kind of piece-rate, which, as Marx tells us elsewhere, is only a time-rate in a deceptive disguise.

What counts is that even in this form, this wage would still be *predetermined*, at least on average, and would have nothing to do with the pure remuneration of capital, whether loan-capital or self-owned capital. This chain of thought only ends up confirming the neoclassical theory that the rate of interest is strictly equal to the marginal 'productivity' of capital, once it has been made clear that what counts is net productivity, with all charges deducted including the supervisor's remuneration.

Marxist views on profit of enterprise Marx posited the existence of profit of enterprise without ever justifying it theoretically. Marxist theoreticians have not gone any further. They doubtless felt that since profit of enterprise is both a fact of experience and formally recognized by Marx, that was enough.

It is characteristic that Hilferding, dealing with joint-stock limited companies, devotes many pages to the search for the recipient of this profit of enterprise, a recipient who is not immediately visible, and he eventually discovers this recipient in the person of the firm's founder, without ever posing the prior question of whether this profit of enterprise exists or not. Now, it so happens that Marx, who Hilferding quotes as authority, saw limited companies as an exception, saying that in this type of firm, capital is satisfied with a dividend calculated according to the rate of interest, and that there is no profit of enterprise in this case.

This becomes even clearer when Marx describes the spread of joint-stock companies as the sixth factor counteracting the tendency of the rate of profit to fall, since 'these capitals, although invested in large productive enterprises, yield only large or small amounts of interest, so-called dividends, after all costs have been deducted. ... These do not therefore go into levelling the general rate of profit, because they yield a lower than average rate of profit.'[21]

This prevents the general rate of profit from falling because these firms, Marx explains, are precisely those with the greatest ratio of constant to variable capital, so that their withdrawal from the pool of firms subject to equalisation lowers the average organic composition in relative terms.[22]

21. *Ibid.*, p. 240.

22. *Ibid.*, p. 437. In this respect we should point out that when Marx discusses equalisation of the rate of profit, he always argues as if every industry were 'non-basic' in Sraffa's sense. Otherwise he would have found an additional factor raising the average rate of profit, over and above the unequal distribution of constant capital: a fall in the prices of production of limited companies.

While we are on this subject, it is worth pointing out that this is one of Marx's 'forgotten' ideas, and with good reason. In diametrical opposition to this idea, today's Marxists speak of monopoly 'superprofits' as an undeniable 'well-known fact' which

Continued on page 312

Profit of enterprise in Keynes Keynes differs fundamentally from the neoclassical position. Like Marx, he firmly insists on the existence of profit of enterprise in equilibrium. But he does not explain its existence any more satisfactorily than Marx. In fact, neither of them could have done so without establishing the determinants of the rate of interest independently of the determinants of the overall rate of profit. This has not been done.

Marx pointed out that the upper limit of the rate of interest is the overall rate of profit. It must be said that this is as undeniable as it is trite. Below this limit the actual rate is abandoned to the play of a supply and a demand whose parameters we do not know. Keynes believes that he has defined these parameters, but in fact he has only defined those of supply. This means that instead of explaining the determinants of the interest rate, he in fact only shows its lower limit.

'The rate of interest', he writes, 'serves to equate the demand and supply of hoards – i.e. it must be sufficiently high to offset an increased propensity to hoard relatively to the supply of idle balances available.'[23] In his *General Theory*, these two determinants of the rate of interest are called, more precisely, liquidity-preference and the quantity of money. But the conjunction of these two factors only gives us the supply curve, since both only affect the motivations of the lender. This conjunction solves the problem of knowing, for a given quantity of money, how much, at each rate of interest, will be turned into bonds and how much will be kept in liquid form. It does not give us any indication of the level of this rate itself. As can be seen from the graph in Figure 9.1, an infinite number of rates of interest are compatible with each pair of values for the quantity of money and liquidity-preference.

At rate i, the quantity lent out will be OQ' and the quantity retained in liquid form will be QQ'; at rate i', these will be respectively OQ'' and QQ''; at rate i'' all the money available will be lent out to entrepreneurs. It follows that through changes in the ratio of funds loaned out to liquid funds, any rate of interest between O and i'' is acceptable to lenders. But the actual rate is still undetermined: the demand curve is missing.

22. *Continued from page 311*
does not need proving. Now this category of monopoly is quite simply defined as all firms above a certain size, i.e. the most anonymous and impersonal companies there are, whose shares are the most widely dispersed: therefore those which represent *par excellence* the case pointed out by Marx, firms with the ability to obtain capital 'cheap' and find shareholders who are happy with dividends scarcely equal to the rate of interest.

23. 'Alternative theories of the rate of interest', pp. 248–52.

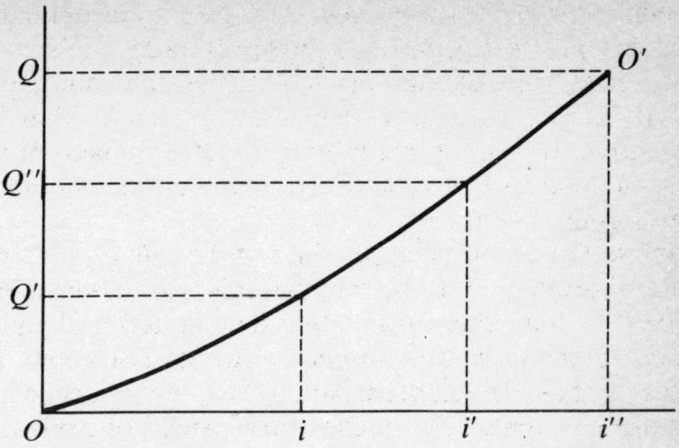

Q: total quantity of money

Figure 9.1

We find a very clear formulation of what this complement might be in the first of the two following propositions of Henri Denis:

1. As a function of the rate of profit which they can reasonably expect, those entrepreneurs who are borrowing on the capital market demand a particular quantity of funds for each particular rate of interest.
2. For their part, the holders of capital who do not wish to run the risk of direct investment supply greater or lesser fractions of their available funds at each different rate of interest.[24]

The second determinant is correct. There is no reason to deny that the interest-rate elasticity of the supply of capital behaves like the price elasticity of any commodity: the supply of capital is an increasing function of price. But the first determinant does not correspond to reality. Entrepreneurs who borrow on the capital market should not demand a particular quantity of funds, but *unlimited* funds, as long as the interest rate is the slightest bit below the rate of profit 'which they can reasonably expect': they should demand no funds at all as soon as the interest rate reaches or exceeds the rate of profit.

We have chosen this passage from Henri Denis because it brings out clearly the error which many economists commit in a confused way: by applying to the capital market the same law of supply and

24. *La Formation de la science économique*, p. 49.

demand which regulates the goods market, they do not take into account the special nature of the capital-commodity. Even accepting that loan capital is just as perfectly available as any other commodity – which we do not accept, as we shall see later, but without which the law of supply and demand cannot apply at all – the elasticity of demand of the capital-commodity is not the same as that of any ordinary commodity.

The use-value of an ordinary commodity is to satisfy a need, to procure enjoyment, or, in the case of means of production, to produce the goods that will satisfy this need and procure this enjoyment. The use-value of money-capital is purely to produce value. It follows that, leaving aside 'perverse' cases and all other things being equal, the utility of an additional unit of an ordinary commodity is less than its average utility. The utility of an additional unit of loan capital is always equal to its average utility, which is itself always equal to the difference between the rate of profit and the interest rate. However cheap an ordinary commodity may be, its price must still be paid, and this can pose a problem for potential buyers and limit their demand. If capital is cheap, i.e. below the rate of profit 'which can reasonably be expected', one does not have to pay any price, one simply receives a present and, under the stated conditions (perfect availability), there is no limit to demand, except that the borrower may fear that his own additional borrowing, whether invested in an existing unit of production or an additional unit created by this borrowing, may lower the marginal efficiency of capital, and thus the rate of profit 'which can reasonably be expected'. But, apart from the fact that this consideration contradicts the assumption of perfect competition within which this discussion takes place, this only confirms the tendency towards the equalisation of the rate of interest and the marginal efficiency of capital proposed by the neoclassics, and thus confirms the nullification of 'profit of enterprise'.

Either the marginal efficiency of capital is the second variable of the function, or the overall rate of profit is taken as given. In the former case, since the marginal efficiency of capital is a decreasing function of the quantity of capital employed, and the rate of interest is an increasing function of this same quantity, they will end up equal with no margin for 'profit of enterprise'. In the latter case, since the millionth unit of borrowed capital brings in exactly as much as the first, borrowers will bid up the charges, and equilibrium will only be attained when borrowing brings in nothing, i.e. when the rate of interest equals the overall rate of profit, again leaving profit of enterprise at zero.

Let us try to illustrate these two alternatives in two diagrams. If the overall rate of profit, r, is taken as given, the demand curve DD' will have an unusual shape (Figure 9.2). It is totally inelastic as long as the rate of interest varies between O and r, and is thus parallel to the X-axis up to this point; after this point, it instantly collapses to zero and falls down to the X-axis as soon as the rate of interest equals the rate of profit, $i = r$. As for the supply curve, OO', it must necessarily be asymptotic to the line QQ', since liquidity preference can never fall to zero. However attractive the interest rate may be, those involved will always keep some money in liquid form.

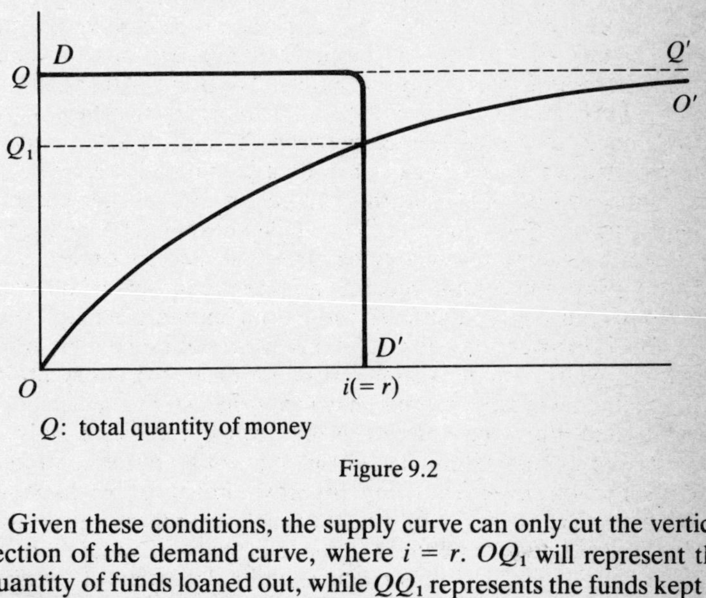

Q: total quantity of money

Figure 9.2

Given these conditions, the supply curve can only cut the vertical section of the demand curve, where $i = r$. OQ_1 will represent the quantity of funds loaned out, while QQ_1 represents the funds kept in liquid form.

If, on the other hand, we take the total rate of profit itself (the marginal efficiency or profitability of capital) to be a decreasing function of the quantity of capital invested, then the curve DD' will represent both variations of the rate of profit and of the demand for capital, and will have the shape shown in Figure 9.3 which repeats the same supply curve. As in the first case, in equilibrium $i = r$. Profit of enterprise, as the difference between r and i, has still not been explained theoretically.

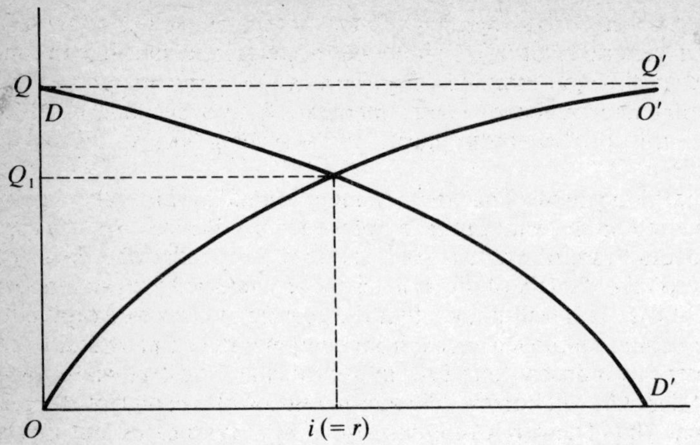

Q: total quantity of money

Figure 9.3

The 'risk premium' The explanation of profit of enterprise by identifying it with a 'risk premium' is a very old idea: it is already to be found in Adam Smith. Among contemporaries who adopt this justification are counted Henri Denis, who we have already referred to on this subject in Chapter 3, F. H. Knight[25] and P. Samuelson.[26]

This justification does not seem to us to be satisfactory. By talking of a 'rate of profit which can reasonably be expected', one has already deducted any risk premium of any kind, or else the expectation is not reasonable. We are being asked to explain a long-run revenue on the social level. A properly calculated risk premium cannot constitute a revenue in any way; it should be just sufficient to compensate for those losses which are statistically inevitable. Running costs and remuneration of insurance companies' own capital apart, insurance business is, in itself, a zero sum game.

The neoclassics do not deny that after subtracting interest, whether actually paid out or retained, some firms will make profits and others will make a loss. It goes without saying that these profits could only be made if firms added something to their costs when working out their

25. *Risk, Uncertainty and Profit*, pp. 310–11: profit is the remuneration of a risk of a special kind, 'a unique uncertainty resulting from an exercise of ultimate responsibility which in its very nature cannot be insured nor capitalised nor salaried'.

26. 'Understanding the Marxian notion of exploitation', p. 405: profit is the same thing as interest when uncertainty is not knowable.

selling prices. This something is in fact nothing but a 'risk premium', called 'general reserve' in commercial accounts and 'unforeseen contingencies' in the estimates of government contractors, etc. In the overall balance-sheet of a large number of firms over a long length of time, this provision disappears by absorbing losses; this is its function.

But this is not all. This 'risk premium' should by any reckoning be calculated on the total capital employed in production. Assume that the overall rate of profit is 10% and that a capitalist who does not want to take the risk of direct investment is satisfied with an interest rate of 8%. It is well-known that the gearing of borrowed capital to total capital employed varies from company to company and from industry to industry: one firm in a particular industry, whose own capital is 500, will borrow 100; another firm with a capital of 200 will borrow 400. The profit of enterprise is 12 in both cases, but this is 2.4% of the first firm's own capital while it is 6% of the second firm's. If we consider the total revenue of the active capitalist – interest on his own contribution plus profit of enterprise on the whole capital – we find it to be 52 or 10.4% of his own capital for the first capitalist, and 28 or 14% of his own capital for the second capitalist. This is not an equilibrium position: capital will flow from the first company to the second. For if profit of enterprise really does exist, then only it – or at a pinch the active capitalist's total income – can be the object of equalisation, since these are the only relevant magnitudes for the agents of this equalisation, those who effect the arbitrage between different industries, i.e. the active capitalists who do not know the overall rate of profit and do not care about it. It follows that the existence of profit of enterprise in equilibrium would prevent equalisation and, thus, prevent any equilibrium.

'Profit of enterprise' as a statistical category It is however undeniable that after all financial costs have been subtracted, there remains in firms' accounts, *on average,* a profit balance which, if taken as a proportion of equity capital, is clearly higher than the going rate of interest, so that if all the funds at the firm's disposal had been borrowed from others and, consequently, had to have interest paid on them, there would still be a sum left over, corresponding to the definition of profit of enterprise.

A brief overview of the various statistics and estimates available, from the start of the nineteenth century up to the present day, shows that the ratio of this sum left over to total pre-tax profits or, another way of looking at the same thing, the ratio of long-term interest rates to the overall rate of profit (before interest payments and taxes), has stayed remarkably constant. Broadly speaking, the former has varied between 0.4 and 0.5, the latter between 0.7 and 1.0.

From the mid-nineteenth century up to the First World War, a period of almost complete monetary stability, the overall rate of profit generally considered normal varied between 7 and 8%. The rate of interest was spread between 2.5 and 5%. The lower rate is the Bank of England's Minimum Lending Rate; the higher rate is that of high-interest bonds issued by the most dubious foreign states, i.e. those who did not have any special guarantee in the leading financial centres where they were issued.[27]

Gilt-edged bonds issued by domestic borrowers, public or private, generally only yielded 4%, while long-term secured loans cost not more than 5%.[28] Similarly, in the same period, all writers used a rate of interest between 4 and 5% to capitalise rents and calculate the 'natural price' of land.

After the First World War a new factor emerged, which must be taken into account in calculating the yield of capital; the erosion of money's purchasing power. This tendency has accelerated considerably since the Second World War.

By deducting a certain average percentage, depending on the period, corresponding to the average rate of depreciation of the currency, it can be shown that the overall rate of profit and the interest rate have certainly not changed in their relative positions, and probably very little in absolute terms.[29]

Paul Bairoch, who devoted his time to detailed and exhaustive estimates, concluded that in the inter-war period (not counting the crisis of the 1930s), the general rate of profit was between 9 and 11%, and in the period following the Second World War, between 12 and

27. The Russian 'unguaranteed' loans, issued in the 1890s in the London and Paris centres, brought in a rate of interest slightly above 4%; those of 1900, around 5%. But a Greek loan guaranteed by the great powers, issued in the 1890s, yielded only 2.5%. Despite this, it was fully subscribed. Finally, despite the post-1900 rise, the German empire issued a large loan in 1908 at 4%.

28. Cairncross estimates that in France, over the last years of the nineteenth century and the first years of the twentieth, the average yield of domestic bonds varied between 4.28 and 3.84%, and that of foreign issues between 3.85 and 3.23%.

Keynes estimates that 'for a period of almost one hundred and fifty years the long-run typical rate of interest in the leading financial centres was about 5%, and the gilt-edged rate between 3 and 3½%. ...'(*General Theory*, pp. 307–08).

29. Typical example: nowadays when the value of the principal is made as stable as in the past by tying the repayment value to that of gold or a gold coin (the Napoléon), as in the case of the Pinay loan of 1958 and the Giscard d'Estaing loan of 1973, rates of interest identical to those of the past, 3.5% in the first case and 4.5% in the second, are enough to make these investments very attractive.

14%, 14% from 1946 to 1950 and 12% from 1951 to 1955. It should still be pointed out that these ratios of Bairoch's express the ratio of *net* pre-tax profits to total assets, while to obtain the overall rate of profit one must either take the ratio of net pre-tax profits (after interest payments) to net assets (equity capital) or even better, the ratio of pre-tax profits *before* interest payments on total assets. Insofar as the interest paid to creditors is lower than the firm's overall profit margin, this last, more accurate ratio is higher than Bairoch's ratio.

Thus figures published by the *Financial Times,* taken from an analysis of the results of 993 British firms over the last few years, show that the ratio of pre-tax profits before interest payments to total capital assets (having deducted depreciation and short-term debts) is around 15%. For the two accounting years ending between 15 October and 14 January 1971/2 and 1972/3, the average general rate for all industries was 14.2 and 15.9% respectively.

With regard to the overall profitability of capital employed, the long-term interest rate since the Second World War has moved from 6 to around 10%.[30] It follows that the overall rate of profit, on average and in the very long run, has been of the order of one and a half times the long-term interest rate, without any great changes over time once cyclical variations have been abstracted from. The rate of 'profit of enterprise' is then about half the interest rate. In absolute terms, if we deflate the rates of the current period by the prevailing rate of inflation, we find that the *net* rates, roughly calculated, are not far from those of the earlier period of monetary stability, that is, an interest rate of 4 to 5% and a rate of profit of 7 to 8%.[31]

30. The inter-war years are less significant: firstly because the great crisis and subsequent depression introduced extraordinarily large cyclical variations; secondly because the erosion of the value of currency, a relatively new phenomenon, had not yet acquired the permanent character which alone makes it possible to take it into account in expectations and thus, to add it to the rate of interest. Thus for example, the African colonial loans of 1913 to 1935 were issued in the Paris and London centres at rates between 3.24 and 5.09%, which only shows a slight increase over those of before 1897.

31. Keynes does not agree. He disputes the distinction introduced by Irving Fisher between the nominal and real rates of interest, the latter equalling the former as corrected to take into account variations in the value of money. 'It is difficult', he writes, 'to make sense of this theory as stated, because it is not clear whether the change in the value of money is or is not assumed to be foreseen ... if it is not foreseen, there will be no effect on current affairs; whilst, if it is foreseen, the prices of existing goods will be forthwith so adjusted that the advantages of holding money and of holding goods are again equalised, and it will be too late for holders of money to gain or to suffer a change in the rate of interest which will offset the prospective change during

Continued on page 320

'Profit of enterprise' as a scientific category Profit of enterprise is one of the scandals of political economy. The dominant theory has taken the option of purely and simply denying its existence as a remuneration of capital. The precursor of neoclassicism, J.–B. Say, only regarded profit of enterprise as the entrepreneur's wage, a conclusion which is quite inevitable once it is accepted that capital is fully remunerated by interest. For the distinction between 'active' and 'inactive' introduced by Marxism to explain the existence of two different 'claims' to the yield of the same funds is irrelevant. It concerns capitalists, not capitals. Capital is active by definition, otherwise it is a hoard. Since no one borrows in order to hoard, a sum of money borrowed by an entrepreneur must always be active capital. Capital cannot even start to produce interest without in actual fact being employed in production. It is clear that capital can only receive any remuneration, whether interest or profit, in so far as it produces surplus-value; an 'inactive' capital, whatever this term might denote, would not receive any. In these conditions, if profit of enterprise exists, as a special remuneration, this cannot be related to a particular state of capital, that of being engaged in production, since this state is already required for interest. It can then only be related to a particular kind of rightful claimants.

But the capitalist system does not have categories of citizen, orders of society, like the *ancien régime*; it remunerates impersonal factors – labour-power, capital, monopoly of the land, etc. – while the owners of these factors – workers, capitalists, rentiers – are anonymous and

31. *Continued from page 319*
the period of the loan in the value of the money lent. For the dilemma is not successfully escaped by Professor Pigou's expedient of supposing that the prospective change in the value of money is foreseen by one set of people but not foreseen by another.' (*General Theory*, p. 142).

It is true that the devaluation of the currency must be foreseen by those involved, otherwise it can have no effect on the rate of interest. But we cannot see any 'dilemma'. The fact that a devaluation of the currency is expected and foreseen does not in any way influence the *current* price of any commodity bought for cash. It only influences the price of a commodity in two cases: (i) if the commodity is sold on credit, in which case we are in fact dealing with a rise in the rate of interest disguised as a rise in the price; (ii) if the commodity is to be delivered in the future and paid for on delivery, in which case it is sold at the price expected to prevail at the time of completion of the contract, without any increase. On the other hand, for an immediate cash sale, if a commodity is worth 10 francs today, it will still be worth only 10 francs even after both parties have become certain that in six months' time it will be worth 12, for the simple reason that 10 francs today are equivalent to 12 in six months' time. But the lender for his part, will only agree to defer his purchases for six months and lend his money out for this period if he is granted, over and above the normal rate of interest, 2 extra francs for every 10 to compensate for the expected rise in prices.

irrelevant. It is therefore difficult to see in what capacity these 'active capitalists' demand and obtain a portion of the social product over and above that due to 'active' capital itself. In their capacity of capitalists, they supply something completely identical to that supplied by inactive capitalists. In their capacity of being active, they only supply labour-power, however complex it may be and whatever use the system may make of it. These two capacities taken together can in no way give more than the sum of their respective fruits.

Profit of enterprise has thus remained a challenge to the basic logic of competition, the uniqueness of the price of each commodity, and general equilibrium. The neoclassics judged it most sensible purely and simply to ignore it, that is, to count any surplus for a company above normal financial costs as the entrepreneur's wage, as 'the normal supply price of the ability and energy required for managing the business', in Marshall's definition.[32]

This is a position that produces certain contortions and problems. For it is difficult to ignore the fact that above a certain size of firm, the surplus in question is of an order of magnitude completely incompatible with any kind of remuneration for labour, however able and energetic it may be.

So the attempt was made to drown the problem in words. Any positive balance after the remuneration of management and deduction of the risk premium, is 'not a normal thing, but a specific element of the individual business ... often the outcome of sheer accident', Cassel tells us.[33] This kind of balance, Hawtrey declares, is tied up with the level of turnover. A normal level of turnover will, according to this writer, produce a profit equal to the corresponding salary, thus excluding pure profit. But, for various reasons, an entrepreneur's level of turnover may be higher than normal. The basis of profit would then be exceptional 'selling power', the firm's good reputation, an established clientèle, a sort of 'quasi-monopolistic advantage ..., an exception to the general principle of the equalisation of rates of remuneration through the labour market ..., a congenital malformation of the individualist capitalist system'.[34]

Special cases, monopolistic situations, the result of accidental distortions, the dominant theory always ends up by attributing profit

32. *Principles*, pp. 605–06.

33. *The Theory of Social Economy*, vol. I, pp. 175–6.

34. R. G. Hawtrey, *Capital and Employment*, 1952 edition, p. 33. In the first edition of his book, Hawtrey includes actual profits in marginal efficiency, which means that normal profits are zero. In the second edition, he treats normal profit 'however defined' as a cost. But in both cases he considers profit as the normal remuneration of the entrepreneur.

to imperfections of competition, whether this is stated explicitly, as in R. F. Harrod for example, or in a more sophisticated way, as in Dieterlen's definition: 'a discontinuous disequilibrium income paid to innovatory ventures'.[35]

The real theoretical status of profit of enterprise in relation to interest
In one sense, this is correct: we are dealing with an imperfection of competition, but this description is nothing more than a word. It is not a matter of accidental realities compared to a model of pure capitalism; it is fairly and squarely an *essential* difference between the capital market and the goods market, a difference which the reference model unwarrantedly conceals. To be more precise, it is not a matter of imperfections, but of special features of competition inherent in the very nature of capital. The error lies in treating the act of borrowing capital in the same way as the act of buying some good or service. In the latter case, all relations between purchaser and seller are over after a simple act of purchase-sale. If it is pure purchase-sale, i.e. cash down, not accompanied by a loan, then the operation is completed as soon as it takes place. Once the quality of the good or service has been checked, in order to obtain the quantity desired it is enough to pay the corresponding price. No other conditions must be met, and the individual characteristics of the purchaser are irrelevant.

Not so with a loan of capital. This is not a purchase of capital, but a purchase of the use of capital. Consequently, the two parties stay linked throughout the period of this use. Since this capital can only be used by passing into the possession of its non-owner, its use necessarily endangers to some extent something which the borrower has not bought and has not paid for, namely the value of the capital itself. To obtain the desired quantity of loan capital, it is not enough to pay the price (the rate of interest). It is also necessary to assure the lender that the principal will be repaid upon maturity. The ability to purchase an ordinary commodity is limited by its price; the ability to borrow is limited prior to the price, by something other than the price. It is limited by the borrower's 'creditworthiness', i.e. not only, and even not mainly, by the guarantees he can offer, his general solvency, but above all by a predetermined proportion to the equity capital employed in the particular enterprise which is seeking finance for its activities.

This is generally forgotten. Capital is not on open sale; it is rationed. We are not referring to the rationing that results from a

35. Pierre Dieterlen, *Au-delà du capitalisme*, p. 225.

tightening of credit or a credit squeeze; that is only extra conjunctural rationing in the business cycle, related to imperfections of competition. We are referring to permanent structural rationing which exists even in the most liberal conditions imaginable. This kind is no anomaly or imperfection of competition; it is an inherent aspect of the nature of capital and its laws of circulation. And even more importantly, the ration is a function of the borrower's own outlay in the business concerned, involving proportions which vary from case to case, but which do *not* depend on the rate of interest. It is as if butter or some other produce were to be rationed according to how much each consumer already possessed, and, what is more, not as a decreasing but as an increasing function of this quantity!

These proportions are defined by precise and strict rules, which are generally respected by the financial authorities, form part of the traditions, customs and principles of the business world, are often reinforced by central bank controls and even, in some countries, by legislative sanctions.[36]

The neoclassics argue as if the capital-factor were available to the highest bidder. They naturally conclude that its price will be bid up until it equals its yield. Marxists reject this conclusion but accept its premises, so their refutation is flawed. The conclusion follows directly from the premises. If capital were really a commodity like any other, the uniqueness of price *should* apply. One hundred pounds lent out and one hundred pounds invested should have exactly the same use-value. Under perfect competition, they must have the same price. The mistake does not lie here. It lies in the premises themselves. Capital is not available to the highest bidder, even in ideal conditions of competition. In this light, there are no grounds for saying that if the rate of interest were lower than the overall rate of profit, entrepreneurs would demand more loan-capital and bid up the interest rate until the two rates were equal. All other things being equal, entrepreneurs can only demand and obtain more loan-capital within limits determined by the size of their own capital and by their general solvency. Depending on cyclical fluctuations and their own investment programmes, they may or may not exhaust these limits. They cannot exceed them. At the point where this

36. In the US, banks are forbidden by law from lending a customer more than 10% of his capital. Following the dramatic bankruptcy of Penn Central in 1970, First National City Bank had to publish energetic denials of certain allegations which appeared in the press, including the suggestion that Penn Central owed it $396 million. Its spokesman declared on several occasions that the sum of its loans was well below the legal limit of $90 million. The Morgan Guaranty Trust, in reply to the same charge, defended itself in the same way.

ceiling is reached, there is nothing to stop the rate of interest from still being considerably below the overall rate of profit, just as there is nothing to prevent ration-coupon butter from costing less than the same butter on the free market. Despite the identity of quality, of use-value, rationing splits up the two forms and creates two distinct commodities, so the rule of the uniqueness of price no longer applies.

Entrepreneurs have no interest in bidding up a given interest rate. They would not obtain any more loan capital than that to which they are entitled, and this much they can have without any extra charge. For this to hold, it is enough that the banks should be able to create extra capital and that the cost of this creation should be lower than the overall rate of profit. Everything suggests that capitalist reality has up to now fulfilled these two conditions.

The above is clearly only a general theoretical framework. It goes without saying that in practice this rigidity is softened by deviations of all kinds. A host of special cases overflows the rules of the proportions between different kinds of asset and different means of finance. There are margins which make interpretation and calculation more flexible. Businessmen in trouble or sharpers pure and simple may break the rules by offering abnormal rates of interest, thus interesting speculators and outsiders in a sort of capital black market. But it remains true that the basic characteristics of the financial market are that it is *oligopsonistic*; and that it is run on a quota system.

It is not because there are, in practice, no entrepreneurs without capital, that the abstraction of the neoclassical school is fallacious; it is because an entrepreneur can only borrow because he has his own capital, and in a fixed proportion to this capital. Since the sum of capital belonging to entrepreneurs is given at any one point in time, the sum of capital which can be borrowed is also given, and does not depend on the rate of interest. This rate is therefore indeterminate in relation to demand.

Each entrepreneur knows in advance that, in the industry he intends to invest in, he can, all other things being equal, count on credit equal to a certain fraction or multiple of his own capital, at the prevailing rate of interest. Therefore, to calculate the profitability of investing in the industry in question, he adds the profit of enterprise (the excess of overall profit over the rate of interest) on the capital loaned to him to the overall profit on his own capital, and compares the sum of these two magnitudes with his own capital. It is on this basis that he chooses between different industries and that he makes equalisation occur.

Suppose that in manufacturing industry, the debt-equity ratio is 0.5, overall profit is 14% and the rate of interest is 8%. He can expect a profit for himself of

$$0.14 + \frac{0.14 - 0.08}{2} = 0.17,$$

that is 17% on his own capital.

If, instead of manufacturing industry, he were considering, for example, real estate, where the debt-equity ratio is far greater, say 2, he might well find that with a lower overall rate of profit the profitability of directly invested capital was higher than in manufacturing. Suppose, for example, that the overall rate of profit in real estate was 12% instead of 14%; then he could expect his profitability to be

$$0.12 + [2 \times (0.12 - 0.08)] = 0.20,$$

or 20% on his own capital.

In these conditions, therefore, there will be a transfer of capital from processing into real estate, until the price of production of this sector falls enough to bring its overall rate of profit down from 12% to x%, such that the profitability of the directly invested should be

$$\frac{17}{100} = \frac{x}{100} + \frac{2(x - 8)}{100}, \text{ whence } x = 11.$$

Finally, to take another extreme example, that of running a petrol tanker, in which just recently Japanese and Spanish shipyards were granting credits of 80% of the ship's value over 15 years, giving a debt-equity ratio of 4, and retaining the same rate of interest, we find that the equilibrium rate of profit of this industry is 9.8%, since

$$9.8 + [4 \times (9.8 - 8)] = 17.$$

General equilibrium for the three industries we have examined would be expressed by these equations:

$$14 + [0.5 \times (14 - 8)] = 11 + [2 \times (11 - 8)] =$$
$$9.8 + [4 \times (9.8 - 8)] = 17.$$

On the borrowers' side there is nothing to stop the interest rate from being lower than the overall rate of profit. Contrary to Joan Robinson's position (cf. above, p. 306), the borrower-entrepreneurs' demand is not active in fixing the rate of interest. This can be considerably below the rate of profit without leading to any 'over-investment'. The 'natural' rate of profit, the only rate which can determine investment, is defined by profit on equity capital, plus the difference between profit and interest on borrowed funds, with these two taken as a proportion of the entrepreneur's equity stake. Then why does the borrower not increase his borrowings to infinity, in order to raise the rate of profit as calculated on his own unchanged stake, that is, in order to maximise 'leverage'? Because this option is not open to him. Because he can only borrow on condition that he respects a certain proportion between borrowed capital, which has priority in remuneration, and his own funds, which can only be remunerated after sales, as a remainder. This is why the interest rate is not a determinant of the propensity to invest. Its only effect is to change the timing of investments according to expectations of its future variations.[37] As we have seen, equilibrium is attainable, not through the equalisation of the interest rate and the rate of profit, but through differentiation between the individual rates of profit so that, taking into account the different gearing ratios of loans to equity capital, the overall return on capital is equalised between different industries.

But what happens on the lenders' side? If directly invested capital yields more than the interest rate – over and above a risk premium and the manager's salary – why do long-term lenders not opt for direct investment? If they did so, the resultant diminution of the supply of loanable funds would re-establish equilibrium through the equalisation of the two rates, despite the above-mentioned inelasticity of demand.

This objection would be valid if, on the one hand, the supply of loan capital were equal to or lower than the portion of savings that savers are willing to immobilise for a long period and if, on the other hand, any individual savings were likely to be loaned out or directly invested. Neither of these two conditions is satisfied in reality. The former is not satisfied because banks do not produce long-term loans from long-term deposits only, but also from medium-term deposits, short-term deposits and above all current accounts, and even from nothing at all, by creating their own bank money.

The latter condition is not satisfied because, first of all, the nature of loan capital is not the same as that of risk capital; and it is here that the notion of 'risk' makes sense. It is a qualitative notion, with the same meaning here as in Henri Denis: '... the holders of capital who do not wish to run the risk of direct investment. . . .' (p. 313 above.)

37. The opposite belief is so deeply rooted with economists that the Radcliffe Report *On the Working of the Monetary System* caused a sensation by revealing that the entrepreneurs interviewed stated on the whole that the rate of interest had scarcely any influence on their decisions about investment in fixed capital.

On the other hand, it seems erroneous to us to equate (quantitatively) profit of enterprise to a so-called 'risk premium'. The distinction between a lender and a direct investor is precisely that the former does not wish to incur the risk incurred by the latter, even if the yield on direct investment exceeds the rate of interest by as much or more than a mathematically established 'risk premium'.

To be sure, in this qualitative sense, the 'risk' exists on the side of the borrowers too, since the equity capital serves as a collateral for borrowed capital. This is, however, only another word for the counterpart of the *borrowing-power* which is bestowed on active capitalists by the financial community and which we have already dealt with.

Another reason why the saver is not always in a position to choose between lending and direct investment is that the latter involves a minimum size for each operation, and this size is rarely attained by individual savings.

Of course investment can be financed through the stock exchange, where bonds and shares are near enough equally liquid and divisible. In this sector there is free arbitrage, and as we have seen there is a tendency towards the equalisation of yields, if not by raising the interest rate to the level of the rate of profit, then at least by a fall in the latter to the level of the former. But except for this case, the composition of savings is incompatible with direct investment, because of the dimensions of its basic components and the length of time for which they are available.

The sum lent to firms are not 'primary', unprocessed funds, as supplied by savers. They are 'secondary' funds, 'produced' by specialised financial institutions, the banking system, insurance companies, various savings banks, etc., through 'transformation' of the funds with which they are entrusted and the *ex nihilo* creation of bank money, while this creation is in turn limited by direct restrictive measures by higher authorities – the central bank, the state, etc.; and by requirements for reserve assets engendered by the division of the producers of bank money and competition between them.

Let us imagine a closed system with one single private bank. Every economic subject must hold an account with this bank. This bank could, if not prevented by official measures, create unlimited quantities of bank money without any risk, and lend out as much money as its clients required without being limited by its own capital and without a single depositor having brought in any currency (issued by the central bank). Since everyone is a client of this establishment, all payments can be effected by transfers from one account to another, that is to say by means of its own bank money.

Now imagine a private bank with one single client. It is obvious that any sum lent to the client must be instantly available, in money valid outside the bank in question. It is only in this form that the client can use his credit to pay money to others, since these others are, according to our assumptions, clients of other banks, and balances between banks are settled in national money, while a bank's 'private' money (bank money) is only valid between its own clients.

Between these two extremes there lies the whole range of intermediate real situations, i.e. a certain number of private banks, each of which has a greater or lesser market share, so that each one can create its own (bank) money *ex nihilo* to cover any payment whose drawer and payee are both its customers, but must use outside money (gold or a claim on the central bank) for any payment in which the drawer is one of its customers but the payee is not, and which is not compensated for by another payment in which the payee is one of its customers while the drawer is not.

It emerges that the larger its number of customers, the smaller is the portion of a bank's advances that must be covered by outside money from its capital or its depositors, and thus the smaller is the part which has, so to speak, a cost to the bank, and the larger is the free part. This is why private banks have an interest in acquiring as many customers as possible.

However, the regulatory intervention of the central bank attenuates the inequality between the different banks' ability to create bank money, because the various proportions which it lays down between deposits and advance, deposits and reserves, etc. prevent the largest private banks from pushing their potential for bank money creation to the limit.

Still, whatever the number of customers of each bank separately, the system as a whole is automatically able to create bank money – therefore money *ex nihilo* – in inverse proportion to the reserve requirements laid down by the central bank or by each banker's prudence. The number of customers of each individual bank helps determine this fraction, also taking into account regulatory measures from on high. But once this rate is fixed, the sum of bank money that the whole system will be able to *create* will be equal to the 'primary' deposits in national money (metallic or fiduciary), multiplied by the reciprocal of this fraction.

Assume that the liquid reserves which French banks are required to hold (in the form of notes on the Bank of France and/or sight accounts with this bank) are fixed at 20% of the sum of their deposits. If the 'real' money (issued by the central bank) injected into the system is 1,000,000 francs, the sum of bank money which the system will tend to create will be $1{,}000{,}000 \times \frac{100}{20} = 5{,}000{,}000$ francs. The coefficient $\frac{100}{20}$, which is the reciprocal of the reserve requirement $\frac{20}{100}$, is known as the credit multiplier.

To prove this, let us assume as a simplification that there are only two private banks, the BNP and the CIC, which start with their accounts at zero, with no capital or deposits. An entrepreneur, Dupont, delivers a section of motorway to the Ministry of Public Works and is paid with 1,000,000 francs in bank notes or in a cheque drawn on the Bank of France. He deposits this sum with the BNP. This bank credits its deposits account (Dupont sub-account) in its books and, if paid in cash, it debits the 'cash' account; if paid by cheque, it debits the Bank of France's account. This comes to the same thing – an account in the black with the Bank of France is just as liquid as till money – but, to explain the multiplier process more clearly, we shall assume that this 'primary' payment is made in cash and that the Bank of France, after giving the Ministry of Public Works a packet of 1000 notes of 1000 francs each, which have just arrived from the mint, and having debited the Exchequer and credited the 'notes in circulation' account, does not intervene further in the chain of events, so it will be quite clear that any extra money can now only come from the operations of the private banks.

Respecting the 20% reserve ratio, the BNP keeps 200,000 francs in liquid form and advances 800,000, lending them to M. Durand, who needs them to settle with his supplier M. Petit. M. Petit is a customer of the CIC, and deposits this sum there. The CIC uses $800{,}000 \times 0.2 = 160{,}000$ francs of this as reserve, and lends the remaining 640,000 to M. Dufour, who pays off his creditor M. Legrand with this sum. M. Legrand in turn deposits it with the BNP. The BNP works out its accounts. Its liquid assets are now 200,000 from the earlier operation, plus 640,000 from the new deposit, totalling 840,000 francs, while its deposits are 1,000,000 by M. Dupont + 640,000 by M. Legrand = 1,640,000, giving a reserve ratio of over 50%. This is too high. By bringing it down to the established requirement of 20%, or $1{,}640{,}000 \times 0.2 = 328{,}000$ francs, the bank releases $840{,}000 - 328{,}000 = 512{,}000$ francs, which it lends to M. Lacroix, and so on.

By amalgamating the separate accounts of the BNP and the CIC, we have the accounts shown.

Cash				*Deposits*		
Receipts from		*Payments to*		*Debit*	*Credit*	
Dupont	1 000 000	Durand	800 000		Dupont	1 000 000
Petit	800 000	Dufour	640 000		Petit	800 000
Legrand	640 000	Lacroix	512 000		Legrand	640 000
			⋮			
X	512 000		⋮		X	512 000
	⋮					⋮
	⋮					⋮
	5 000 000		4 000 000			5 000 000
Balance	1 000 000					

Debit Account			*Balance-sheet*			
Debit		*Credit*	*Assets*		*Liabilities*	
Durand	800 000		Reserves	1 000 000	Deposits	5 000 000
Dufour	640 000		Loans	4 000 000		
Lacroix	512 000			5 000 000		5 000 000
	⋮					
	⋮					
	4 000 000					

As can be seen, from an original contribution of 1,000,000 francs, the private banks' deposits payable on sight (what is known as bank money, which is just as liquid as cash) have risen to

$$1 + 1(1-0.2) + 1(1-0.2)^2 + 1(1-0.2)^3 + \ldots = 1 \times \frac{1}{0.2} = 5$$

The remarkable thing is that for each private bank taken separately, all the deposits are 'primary' and the cash brought in by M. Dupont is no different from that brought in by M. Petit or M. Legrand. Beside this, neither of the two banks have at any point lent any one the smallest sum without having previously received from another customer a deposit in real money of a greater sum, the difference having very prudently and in the prescribed manner been left sterile in its safe.

Neither banker feels that he has *created* money and each of them can proclaim loudly and clearly and quite legitimately from their experience, that he only transmits funds from savers to investors. 'Deposits make loans'.

This is of course both true and false at the same time. True, because it reflects part of reality – the act of banking proper; false, because the overall truth is the opposite. Only economic analysis can reconstitute this total reality by elucidating its other half, in which it is loans which make deposits.[38]

The following points can now be clarified.

1. The role of financial institutions is not that of a mere broker, confined to making contact between lenders and borrowers. They themselves produce the commodity that they sell: loan money-capital. The fact that in this production they partially or entirely use the funds entrusted to them by individuals does not alter the matter: these funds are not the same thing as the finished product which these institutions supply to their borrower-clients. The former are in a sense the latter's raw material.

A deposit payable on sight is certainly not the same commodity as a three-month deposit, which is in turn different from a one-year deposit etc., and all these deposits, while differing from each other, are also different from the finished product, which is a loan to a firm.

2. This finished product, banking finance for enterprises, is in a way a service like the telephone or advertising and, as such, has a cost and

38. It is worth pointing out that in this case it was neoclassical theory which dispelled the illusion that banks only play a passive role, whereas those Marxist economists who have lately found it appropriate to claim for themselves exclusively the distinction *in abstracto* between essences and phenomena and who, in the name of this distinction, have even gone so far as to deny the scientific nature of political economy in general, have confined themselves in this concrete case, as unfortunately in so many others, to the 'common sense' of the protagonists. Marx himself had not failed, more than a century ago, to note this power of banks to create money, though, it is true, without developing it further. Those who oppose the neoclassics on this point today in Marx's name, are for their part quite simply too palaeo-classical to admit that something real can emerge from a pure convention, in a sense from nothing. Their position is well summarised by this sentence from Suzanne de Brunhoff, referring to Gurley and Shaw: 'Loanable funds ... are created by firms with surplus funds and not by financial intermediaries. The latter only act as transmission mechanisms, offering the firms with surplus funds their own form of debt. ... Banks do not constitute a separate group because of their ability to create loanable funds, since these last have already been created by firms with surplus funds; banks only substitute a particular form of indirect debt for direct debt. ...' (*L'Offre de monnaie*).

There could be no better description of what happens at the level of a banker's consciousness (or perhaps only that of his cashier), which we have just shown to be illusory. Transposed into theoretical thought, this is something which Marx would happily include in the category of Vulgar Economy. It is ironic that this should be what the sublime Anti-Economics of our period should often be reduced to at the end of the day.

a price of production. The latter is the interest rate. This must be such as to assure its producers – banks, insurance companies, etc. – of a rate of profit, or rather a rate of return on their own funds, equal to that of non-financial enterprises.

The cost of production, or cost price, of this *service* is constituted by the operating costs of financial institutions, plus the price of their *raw material*, that is the interest paid on the various classes of their customers' deposits.

3. The basic standard of these classes – and by far the largest class – is the current account, which offers its holder the same liquidity as a note or a coin, while giving him greater security. Since it is no sacrifice for the depositor to open such an account, compared to holding his money in cash, and is even more convenient than cash, there is no need to remunerate this kind of deposit with any positive interest rate, and a small negative interest rate may even be charged on it, in the form of a commission or *bank charges.* This negative interest is actually charged in some circumstances and in some countries. If it is low enough, it does not result in any fall in deposits.

It goes without saying that in the most frequent case, where these accounts are neither credited with interest nor have bank charges raised on them, the funds they provide to the bank, the raw material of banking production, are not entirely free. They cost the bank the operating costs of these accounts in personnel, office materials, premises, etc.

4. On this basis, it is easy to determine the price of the deposit one rung higher, that is to say the most short-term deposit possible, say a three-month deposit. The interest rate paid on these accounts must on the one hand be sufficient to prompt a section of depositors to give up the absolute liquidity of current accounts; on the other hand it should not exceed the difference in *productivity* for the bank between these short-term deposits and current account deposits in terms of the total quantity of bank money which the bank can produce from each of these raw materials, taking into account the different liquid reserve requirements which the bank must abide by from its own rules of prudence and those imposed on it by the higher authorities.

Thus, one by one, the interest rates paid on different categories of account are perfectly determinate.

5. Once the different prices of the different categories of *raw material* are fixed in this way, the average total cost of the final product, i.e. the quantity of bank money offered to firms, depends on the proportion voluntarily or involuntarily *frozen* by the banks; and

on the relation between the sum of deposits created by the introduction of outside money and the sum of deposits created by the extension of bank money credit by the bank itself. It of course also depends on the cost of managing the bank.

In general, a credit squeeze policy, which makes banks' turnover fall and therefore increase the unit cost of their output, also forces the interest rate to rise and, conversely, an easy money policy lowers the interest rate. The change in the interest rate compensates for government policy in its effect on the profitability of the bank itself. Equilibrium can be attained at an infinite number of rates of interest, all lower than the overall rate of profit.

6. The sharing of risks ensured by the intervention of the central bank places the private banks as a whole in the same position as that of the imaginary single bank, which we examined. To the extent to which private banks, thanks to the backing of central bank policy, become responsible for each other, and abstracting from any extraordinary economic catastrophe or generalised panic, the advantage of fixed-term deposits over sight deposits will tend to disappear. Because of this, the interest rates paid on term deposits can be reduced. If one assumes complete joint responsibility, which amounts to a total monopoly of the banking system, they could even be abolished. The resulting conversion of term deposits to sight deposits would not in the least reduce the ability to produce bank money, whereas the unit cost of this money would be considerably reduced, allowing a fall in the equilibrium rate of interest paid by firms.

7. Another question may arise. However low the cost of production of their money-capital, what is to compel the banks to lend at interest and thus forfeit to the borrower the profit of enterprise it produces? Why do they not invest directly so that they themselves could earn the difference between the overall rate of profit and the interest rate? While the original savers are not, as we have seen, in a position to take this option and are compelled to go through the banks, what prevents the banks themselves from taking it and thus effecting the equalisation of the two rates?

The reply is simple. If banks were to invest directly, set up companies, run them, etc., they would no longer be banks – at any rate, not deposit banks; they would become, depending on the case, commercial and industrial firms, holding companies, or, at the very least, merchant banks. They would lose their access as deposit banks to the raw material at cheap rates, to rediscounting business and in general to the help and backing of the central bank, so that the profitability of their own capital would not be improved.

In this line of argument, one might just as well wonder why Peugeot or Michelin borrow money from the banks at 7, 8 or 10% instead of themselves opening cheque accounts payable on sight to depositors in order to obtain money for nothing, or, for example, why coffee importers do not do their own roasting or set up retail shops. Each activity has its own organisation, tie-up of capital, running costs and charges.

To sum up, it seems to us not only empirically undeniable, but also perfectly clear theoretically that the equilibrium rate of interest is lower than the overall rate of profit, leaving a margin for a profit of enterprise or pure profit.

We can also say that the most characteristic remuneration of the capital-factor is not interest, but profit of enterprise in the broad sense, that is to say the whole of profit on equity capital plus profit of enterprise in the strict sense on borrowed funds, or, what comes to the same thing, the whole overall profit on capital invested minus the interest paid out on borrowed funds.

'Profit of enterprise', as an excess of total profit over interest, is neither a wage nor a risk premium, although being the *specific* remuneration of risk capital.

To return to our particular concern: distinguishing revenues constituted *before* sales from those constituted *after*, it is really only the interest actually paid to creditors which can be included in the first category, to the exclusion of the interest which can be allocated to the owners themselves on their share of the capital. To allocate to oneself the interest on one's own capital employed in one's own business, as Walras recommended, may be an excellent accounting method, which can give the boss a realistic view of the profitability of his firm. The trouble is that according to the most basic rules of the system, rules which are backed up by law, this can only be done after the close of operations and to the extent that the results of concluded business permit, that is to say after the sale of output and to the extent that a positive balance is left after all bills have been paid and the remunerations of all the other factors have been settled, thus after the real interest has been paid to creditors who are not part of the business.[39]

39. Maurice Allais also considers that the market rate of interest should be allocated on net assets. He proposes the term 'net gain' for what is left over after this allocation, and suggests that this balance alone should be taxable. (*Les Fondements comptables de la macro-économie*, pp. 19–20.)
Continued on page 335

It follows from this that, as opposed to real interest actually owed to creditors, this 'interest' calculated on the entrepreneur's equity capital, which is a matter of internal bookkeeping, does not constitute 'prior' purchasing power, helping in the realization of the product, but second-wave purchasing power, purchasing power which depends on sales. Consequently, even when the overall rate of profit is brought down to the level of the rate of interest, as is the case with the yields of shares quoted on the stock exchange, the whole of this profit, while included in the supply price of the social product, is missing from the aggregate demand engendered by the same product and facing it.

It remains the case that any relative fall in the proportion of surplus-value remunerating equity capital, compared to that remunerating borrowed funds, whether resulting, on the social level, from a relative fall in direct investment including new share issues and a relative rise in the volume of loans including new issues of bonds; or from the spread of large corporations whose shareholders are satisfied with remuneration roughly equal to that obtained by bond-holders; or, finally, simply from a rise in the rate of interest, will have a positive effect on the realization of the social product and on the equilibrium between the supply and demand of commodities. It seems very likely that this has been the tendency in reality in the course of the last few decades, in the advanced capitalist countries.

(d) Variations of a 'quasi-fixed' part of surplus-value. Duties and taxes

The question of whether the state's revenue is or is not an integral part of surplus-value is a controversial one. If we postulate that what is really at stake in negotiations between wage-earners and employers is a real net wage, that is to say a bundle of goods, then any tax, direct or indirect, whoever is liable to pay it or wherever it is levied in the first instance, ultimately must come out of surplus-value. If one assumes subsistence wages, or, more generally, the determination of the value of labour-power by its costs of reproduction, this position follows automatically. This is not so if the negotiation of wage contracts is about nominal wages, that is to say, a particular quantity of one single good, the money-commodity or, in the case of

39. Continued from page 334
But does this 'net gain' exist at the social level? On p. 37, the answer is an unqualified yes. He also introduces the term 'national gain' to refer to the excess of the sum of profits of enterprise over the sum of interest. But on p. 72, he makes the existence of this excess conditional upon growth. In a stationary economy, he writes, there could be neither gains nor losses.

an inconvertible currency, a nominal quantity of units of account.

But this controversy does not concern our study. What matters here is whether state revenue, as a secondary revenue, whatever the primary revenue which it derives from, should be considered a fixed or a variable revenue. In this perspective, while one part of fiscal revenue seems to be a fixed revenue, by the very fact that it is levied on fixed primary revenues, another part which is certainly the greater – various taxes on the net income of companies and physical persons, indirect taxes on consumption, etc. – depends directly or indirectly on the realization of the product and thus corresponds to our definition of a variable revenue, that is a revenue which cannot be included in the sum of effective demand which serves to realize the production which it derives from.

But this conclusion is only true at first glance. Deeper examination shows that from the point of view of the realization of the social product, state revenues, whatever their source, should be counted as fixed revenues, and so should be considered as acquired and *normally* mobilisable before their actual acquisition.

For the state *believes* in its revenues and can legitimately anticipate them. This is the real meaning of the budget. At this level of aggregation, microeconomic ups and downs disappear. The state behaves as if its planned expenditure were independent of its revenue. It places orders with and extends advances to suppliers, without waiting for an exactly equivalent sum of revenue to materialise. In this way it intervenes positively in the realization of the product, and one result of this is that it helps ensure the conditions for the materialisation of its own revenue. For this result to be obtained, the budget must constitute at least a certain proportion of the national economy. Quantity becomes quality. Even if balanced, a large budget is active through its very absolute size.

In this perspective, it goes without saying that an increase in taxes, resulting directly or indirectly in a fall in firms' net profits as a proportion of national income, will have a beneficial effect on the overall equilibrium between supply and demand.[40]

40. There is a certain diffuse consensus about the idea we are formulating in the text. Thus Baran and Sweezy clearly explain that government expenditure can create extra demand and help the realization of the product, even with a balanced budget. The influence of the government on effective demand, they write, is a function not only of the size of the deficit, but also of the absolute level of expenditure (*Monopoly Capital*, pp. 136–7). But on the basis of the fundamental postulate $P = R$, which these writers accept, their explanations necessarily fall short. The difference between the state with a balanced budget and any other income-owner, is that for the former,

Continued on page 337

We should add that this effect of a balanced budget is entirely different in nature from that of a budget in deficit which we will discuss lower down.

II. Variations in supply and demand without any change in the composition of the value of the social product

Up to now we have studied those factors that affect the different components of the value of output in relation to each other, and we have examined in turn:

1. The effect of relative variations of the two basic components of the gross value of output: intermediate consumption and value-added;
2. The effect of relative variations of the sub-components of value-added: wages and surplus-value; and
3. The effect of relative variations of the sub-components of surplus-value itself: rent, interest and taxes on one side, profit of enterprise on the other.

By their very nature none of these variations can do more than merely attenuate the disequilibrium. This attenuation is ultimately expressed by a relative fall in profit of enterprise compared to the value of the product, thus by a fall in $\frac{P-R}{P}$. But $P - R$ is still greater than zero. So these variations can never entirely reabsorb the initial disequilibrium between supply and demand, still less reverse it.

We must now study those factors that have a direct effect on the two elements of equilibrium, P and R. These differ from the earlier factors in that they are unlimited. By making P and R vary directly, they can make $P - R$ equal to or even less than zero. They can therefore lead, depending on the case, to perfect equilibrium between supply and demand, or even provoke the opposite disequilibrium, that of a demand greater than supply.

If P is considered to express the value of the aggregate mass of the social product, as supplied by the units of production, whatever may be its destination, and R to express the cost of this production (apart from pure profit), then it is clear that once the composition of P is given, nothing can change the ratio of P to R. This is a mere tautology

40. Continued from page 336
purchasing power is always matched by the will to purchase, whereas for the latter, this may not be the case if there is a lack of investment opportunities. Taxes only pass purchasing power from one hand to another; its only advantage is then, if our understanding of these author's position is correct, that it passes the purchasing power from a hand that hoards to another that does not.

since *R* is part of the composition of *P* itself. In this case the factors that we are going to discuss – unable to affect *P* and *R*, but only effective supply and effective demand – will unhitch the former from *P* and the latter from *R*.

However, if *P* is considered to express the effective supply of commodities on a given market, wherever these commodities are produced, and *R* to express effective purchasing power on the same market, whatever its source, then it can be said that these factors directly modify the relative values of *P* and *R*.

This is a matter of terminology and therefore secondary. Whichever definition is chosen, what matters is that there are factors which tend towards equilibration, or the partial or total reabsorption of the disequilibrium, without affecting the composition of the value of output. These factors are (i) a surplus balance of trade; (ii) a budget deficit; and (iii) overtrading in all its forms.

We will study the possible effects of each of these factors in turn.

(a) Surplus in the trade balance

This section returns to this lasting preoccupation of politicians in charge of state economic policy and that unreserved conviction of policy-makers and the public at large of all times that a surplus in foreign trade is beneficial, which we discussed in the Introduction and which seemed at first glance to lack any theoretical justification.

We should start by saying that a surplus in the trade balance can only affect the major aggregates that determine equilibrium in the domestic market, if it leads to a surplus in the balance of payments. If, on the other hand, this surplus only compensates for the remuneration of a factor belonging to non-residents, the same sum is withdrawn from both sides of the inequality, $P > R$, and the initial situation is not affected.

Suppose that our firms owe the rest of the world interest on loans, dividends on their shares, royalties on their patents, etc. A surplus in the balance of trade supplies our exporting firms with a sum of foreign currency which these firms then send back abroad to settle their debts mentioned above. This is just as if this or that resident, a worker, rentier or usurer, etc., having received a revenue created by current production, were to use it to acquire part of this production and, then, instead of consuming these goods on the spot, were to take them away and consume them abroad. The determinants of equilibrium would not be affected by this. Since the same sum is simultaneously deducted from *P* and from *R*, the initial excess, $P - R$, will still equal

(P – surplus on the trade balance) –
(R – revenues of non-residents).

It follows that a positive trade balance only interests us if the variations of invisibles and financial operations are covered by *ceteris paribus*. This seems to be the implicit assumption behind the assertion that an export surplus has a beneficial effect, an effect consisting of the reduction of the number of commodities on sale on the home market without any reduction of the purchasing power facing them. The question is whether this effect is necessary without any further conditions.

Contrary to the belief of many Keynesians on this point, the answer is no. The effect of this surplus depends on how the nation's foreign accounts are settled. To discover this, one must go beyond the balance of payments and examine the official settlements balance.

If this surplus is finally settled by the acquisition by residents, other than the central bank, of an equivalent sum of foreign holdings payable at sight or on term (currency or securities), all other things being equal, the relation between supply and demand on the home market, and the original disequilibrium will not be affected at all. Part of the commodities flow off abroad, but an equal part of disposable purchasing power is sterilised by its conversion into claims that can now not be used as means of purchase at home.

On the other hand, if this surplus has been settled (i) by inflow into the central bank's reserve of gold or of international fiat money,[41] (ii) by the inflow as payment to exporters of cash which is universally acceptable in its own form, without being converted, then the initial gap, $P - R$, is reduced to the extent of this inflow. In this case, the initial disequilibrium may, depending on the size of the export surplus, be reduced, completely reabsorbed, or even reversed, with overproduction and the failure to sell being replaced by an inflationary excess of demand over supply.

Foreign trade only changes the physical form of commodities. If it is balanced, the equivalent imported commodities replace the exported commodities in the shops. The market situation is not helped. But if there is an export surplus, a part of the exported commodities is not replaced by imported commodities, or, to put it

41. Settlement in international bank money, which is accepted and entered in the reserves by the central bank, thus making it possible to balance accounts between the surplus country and the rest of the world, is a very recent method, whose acceptance in principle and occasional use date from the 1922 Gênes Conference, but which has only been used regularly and generally since the 1944 Bretton Woods agreement.

another way, it is replaced, but by commodities of a special kind – gold or foreign currency – which do not go into the shops, but into the vaults of the central bank. The place on the shelves that was occupied by the exported commodities stays empty. The commodities imported in return, gold and foreign currency, are recovered by an institutional buyer, the central bank, for its own notes. It is as if part of production were purchased by a bearer of purchasing power not created by this same production.

The situation is exactly the same when the rest of the world, in return for its purchases, directly sends us cash which is legal tender here or which can be recoined by the mint into other coins which are legal tender.[42]

In both cases, the excess on our balance of trade reduces P or increases R – this is merely a matter of words – which explains the extremely positive role attributed to it with respect to the realization of the product and the reabsorption of chronic overproduction.

Since neither the mint nor the central bank buy or sell any part of the output whose realization we are studying, their intervention is added on, in a way external to our system, and what happens in this system is, in the last analysis, that monetary signs (equal to the surplus balance) flow in from a source that is not fed by revenues created by the production in question. Our producing consumers are joined by a kind of non-producing consumers, a sort of 'third party', the bearer of purchasing power which does not derive from the redistribution of one or more primary revenues.

Writing e for the export surplus as defined above, the improvement of the situation can be represented by

$$(P - e) - R < P - R$$

or equivalently by

$$P - (R + e) < P - R.$$

Opposite effects will of course result from a deficit balance. If, in order to pay for imported commodities or for any other reason, one sends abroad reserves obtained from the central bank in exchange for domestic money, R is reduced by this much without P being affected (or equivalently, P is increased by this much while R is left unchanged). Part of the income generated by current production is used to buy something that is not part of current production – gold or foreign currency in the vaults and coffers of the central bank.

42. Since there is no conceivable functional relation between export surpluses and the propensity to save, this factor can legitimately be relegated to the *ceteris paribus*.

Writing m for the import surplus, the aggravation of the disequilibrium can be represented by

$$(P + m) - R > P - R$$

or equivalently by

$$P - (R - m) > P - R$$

On the other hand, if this import surplus is the counterpart of a financial transfer from abroad – debt-servicing, purchase of securities, etc. – there should not, in principle, be any deflationary effect. The part of R that pays for this import surplus is made good by the new revenues flowing into the hands of the domestic beneficiaries of the corresponding financial operations, e.g. the owners of foreign debt, the sellers of securities, etc.

It still needs to be made clear that this only accounts for the *direct*, so-to-speak *material* quantitative effect of disequilibrium in the balance of trade on the supply price of social output, on the one hand, and on aggregate income on the other. But, as we shall see later, in relation both to the question of the opening up of new markets and to that of wage increases, the direct effects on the two components of the value of output are one thing; their *indirect* effects on subjective incentives to over/under-trade are quite another matter.

A sheikh who uses his oil revenue to purchase the Grand Hôtel in Paris injects as much income into the French economy as he withdraws as the counterpart of his oil. Realization of French output is, mathematically speaking, made neither easier nor more difficult by the whole process. Nevertheless, it is not at all clear that the Grand Hôtel's seller's propensity to spend (whether on consumption or investment) is as great and as fast-acting as the equivalent propensity of the purchasers of the oil, in the way shown earlier. There is indeed every chance that is is not nearly so great or fast-acting.

Mutatis mutandis, the same point applies to an export surplus counterbalanced by a financial operation.

Finally, taking account both of objective means and of the protagonists' motivations, it emerges that a surplus (deficit) on the trade balance

1. if covered by a change in central bank reserves, has an unambiguously positive (negative) effect on the realization of output, since it has a positive (negative) effect both on the means and on motivations;
2. if counterbalanced by a financial operation, *often* has the same effect, since it affects motivations in the same direction, notwithstanding its neutral effect on the means.

As might reasonably be expected, the age-old conviction of trading humanity that a surplus trade balance has a beneficial effect and a deficit a detrimental one, and the corresponding Mercantilist doctrine, are not without foundation.

Disequilibrium on the world scale and gold mines As a surplus in the balance of one or several countries must correspond to a deficit for the rest of the world, it follows from the above that the equilibration and resulting stimulation of the economies of the surplus countries correspond exactly to an aggravation of the initial disequilibrium and, consequently, even greater depression in the deficit countries. In the whole closed system composed of several countries, the structural disequilibrium, $P > R$, must therefore be unchanged.

Still, if the international currency is purely metallic, as in the case of the pure gold standard (as opposed to the gold-exchange standard), there is one important exception to this overall invariance of the inequality, $P > R$, at least in theory. To the extent that some of this metal exported by the producer countries is to be monetised and thus add to the money circulation, whether by circulating directly or by entering banks' reserves, the reabsorption of disequilibrium in the exporting countries is not accompanied by any aggravation of disequilibrium in the importing country, because, to this same extent, the export surplus of the former is not accompanied by any real equivalent deficit for the latter. This is because precious metals are an ordinary commodity, which must be included in the producer country's exports, whatever their destination, industrial or monetary, while they should only be included in other countries' imports to the extent that they are to be used for industrial purposes.

Marx did not ignore this question; he even devoted so much attention to it that Rosa Luxemburg accused him of using gold-mines as a *deus ex machina* of realization. These are the most typical passages:

> The capitalists producing gold possess their entire product in gold – that portion which replaces constant capital as well as that which replaces variable capital, and also that consisting of surplus-value. A portion of the social surplus-value therefore consists of gold, and not of a product which is turned into gold only in the process of circulation. It consists from the outset of gold and is thrown into circulation in order to draw products out of it. The same applies here to wages, to variable capital, and to the replacement of the advanced constant capital. Hence, whereas one part of the capitalist class throws into circulation commodities greater in value (greater by the amount of the surplus-value) than the money-capital

advanced by them, another part of the capitalists throws into circulation money of greater value (greater by the amount of the surplus-value) than that of the commodities which they constantly withdraw from circulation for the production of gold. Whereas one part of the capitalists constantly pumps more money out of the circulation than it pours into it, the part that produces gold constantly pumps more money into it than it takes out in means of production.

We see surplus-value incorporated in products thrown into circulation without the money required for their conversion into money, on the one hand, and on the other surplus-value in the form of gold without previous transformation of products into money. The additional commodities to be converted into money find the necessary amount of money at hand, because on the other side additional gold (and silver) intended for conversion into commodities is thrown into circulation, not by means of exchange, but by production itself.[43]

While the other capitalists, aside from the investment in fixed capital, draw more money out of the circulation than they threw into it on purchasing the labour-power and the circulating elements, the gold and silver-producing capitalists throw only money into the circulation ... while they withdraw only commodities from it.[44]

Marx had previously declared that the problem of the quantity of money needed for the realization of surplus-value simply does not exist. A definite quantity of money is needed for commodities to circulate, whether or not they contain surplus-value. It is also significant that the chapter that contains these quotations (except the last) is entitled the 'circulation' and not the 'realization' of surplus-value. It is true that Marx here seems to go a bit beyond the *technical* side of the question. He deals with the movements of gold in terms of *realization*, not of *circulation*, despite the title of the chapter. His analysis sheds light on the compensatory phenomena which we have noted above, even if he himself was still not prepared to question the basic equation, $P = R$. But it is equally certain that neither Marx nor Bulgakov (who is accused of the same sin by Rosa Luxemburg) had the least intention of presenting gold production as the *deus ex machina* of realization: firstly, because both considered 'realization' to be possible by less miraculous means, and secondly, because gold production alone could only affect the realization of surplus-value on a world scale if it were equal in value to the sum-total of the surplus-value produced in all other industries of all capitalist countries,

43. *Capital*, vol. II, pp. 340, 348.
44. *Ibid.*, p. 481.

which, according to the same Marx and Bulgakov, would be an absurd hypothesis.[45]

It remains true that, for each country taken separately, the values, gold or paper-money, which it receives from abroad for its export surplus, have, to the extent that they can be monetised, a beneficial effect on the equilibrium between supply and demand and the realization of that country's output, and thus stimulate economic activity in that country.

The effect of the 'multiplier' The conclusion above is quite different from that drawn by most Keynesians on this question. By including the surplus on foreign trade in investment, these writers, prisoners of their own definitions, apply the theory of the multiplier to it.

In the framework of this theory, only the surplus left over after monetary transfers have been taken into account can stimulate domestic effective demand, since this alone brings into existence a long-term claim on the rest of the world which can be included in investment. In our opinion, on the contrary, it is precisely the part of the surplus paid for in money, and to the extent to which it gives rise to the creation of national money, which has the most definite beneficial effect on the trade-surplus country.

Joan Robinson has written a good summary of the neo-Keynesian position. She includes gold flows in the imports and exports of commodities, so she is only considering those surpluses that are not paid for with 'short-term transfers' (gold or currency), when she writes that

> when, over any period, the inhabitants of a country have collectively a surplus of receipts from exports over payments for imports (or *positive* balance of trade) they must, over the same period, on balance be lending (in the broad sense) to the inhabitants of foreign countries an exactly equal sum. Similarly a surplus of imports (or *negative* balance of trade) must be matched by an equal amount of borrowing. ... A positive balance of trade is equivalent to investment, ... and it has the same influence as investment upon the level of effective demand. ... It represents a certain volume of demand for current home output without representing a supply of goods coming into the home market (for the trade balance represents the home incomes earned by selling to foreigners *minus* that part of home incomes

45. A very rough calculation on today's data shows that the sum of annual non-labour incomes in capitalist countries represents a multiple of the order of one hundred times the value of annual gold output calculated at the free market price. The latter quantity is therefore negligible with respect to realization of surplus-value on a world scale.

which is expended upon foreigners) and so gives rise to secondary employment.[46]

This passage from Joan Robinson is a good example of the impasses created by the ill-considered application of Keynesian formulae. Both halves of the thesis are incorrect.

1. We have no right to treat gold as an ordinary commodity when we are dealing with a problem of realization, for the simple reason that gold is a directly 'realized' commodity without any problem. Besides, the central bank's purchasing power which realizes gold is not, like the rest of purchasing power, derived from the remuneration of a factor of production. It is a kind of 'self-generating' purchasing power, outside production, unlimited, and coupled – this is crucial – with an equally unlimited *obligation to purchase,* laid down by law. It follows that any purchase by the central bank of gold not produced in the country leads to an inflationary growth of demand, which helps compensate for any previous excess of supply.

2. Conversely, when our commodities are bought by the rest of the world with securities, total supply on our market certainly falls, but this is reflected in a net export of capital, therefore an equivalent removal of purchasing power and reduction of demand. The 'home incomes earned by selling to foreigners' are not added to demand on the home market, as Joan Robinson states, for the simple reason that they are not disposable. They have precisely been lent or invested abroad.

Let us examine a very simple example. One of our citizens has sold a service to a foreign tourist by working for him for a few hours on a Sunday. The tourist, not having any local money on him, gives him in exchange an IOU which our citizen locks away in a cupboard. If the rest of our trade is in balance, this operation fulfils all the conditions of what Joan Robinson calls an export surplus counterbalanced by 'lending ... to the inhabitants of foreign countries' and functioning in exactly the same way as investment. But it is clear that this operation, closed in on itself, has no connection with, and no effect, positive or negative, on the level of aggregate supply and demand of commodities confronting each other on our home market.

Taking the question another way, one can agree with Joan Robinson that any export surplus is in fact really a loan. If it is paid for in gold, it is a loan to our own central bank; otherwise it is a loan to the rest of the world. Either way, one receives an IOU: notes from

46. *Essays in the Theory of Employment*, p. 136.

our central bank in the first case, foreign currency or securities in the second. But there is an essential difference between the two, which Joan Robinson ignores: debts of the first kind are monetised, the others are not. Depending whether they are monetised or not, they are or are not added to the sum of disposable purchasing power.

The investment 'multiplier' has nothing to do with export surpluses, especially as this surplus works to best effect when it is least plausible to consider it as investment, i.e. when the rest of the world pays us out of its gold and currency reserves.

It cannot even be said that at least the effects of this surplus are, in this case, the same as those of investment in general. These effects are the same as those of one kind of investment, that which is financed by credit without any corresponding *ex ante* savings. They are the same, not because there is also investment in this case – there is not – but because there is also a creation of purchasing power by the banking system, independently of and above existing revenues. A growth in consumer credit effected by the same means would have exactly the same effect.

The balance of trade and the terms of trade At first glance there is an obvious contradiction between a 'favourable' development of the balance of trade and an improvement in the terms of trade. The former implies an effort to increase the volume of sales, making concessions on prices if necessary; the latter implies an effort to increase one's own prices at the risk of allowing the volume of one's sales to decrease. Depending whether there is stagnation and unemployment or growth and high employment, the former or the latter of these aims should inspire the economic policies of capitalist states.

Since the first situation – relative stagnation, overproduction crises and unemployment of the factors – is much more common than the second, the quest for markets has played a far greater historical role than the struggle for favourable terms of trade. Indeed it is only recently, since the Second World War, and in the context of the study of flows between underdeveloped countries and developed countries, that the question of terms of trade has come into the forefront of economic reality. This has happened in a period of economic growth and exceptionally high levels of employment. It seems as if the luxury of optimising the terms of trade can only be afforded once the maximisation of exports in particular and the marketing of the social product in general have been more or less achieved. If this is not so, the main aim is to undersell competitors.

But, while they are not equal priorities, these objectives are not so irreconcilable as is generally believed. What makes them opposites in theory is the assumption that the elasticity of demand is always greater than unity. It is assumed that any price variation will give rise to a more than proportional inverse variation of demand. By making revenue from sales, or the counter-value of purchases, a decreasing function of price, the maximisation or minimisation of both at the same time becomes a priori impossible. A choice must be made between them.

This assumption is in general a myth. As with all myths, its tenacity rivals its ill-foundedness. It is so firmly entrenched in the way people think that it is sometimes confused with a different, correct, proposition, namely that except in 'perverse' cases (which are so rare that they are not worth discussing), the *volume* of sales or purchases is indeed a decreasing function of price. But what we need to know is not whether volume varies inversely with price – this is not in dispute – but whether it varies more or less than proportionally to price variations. If it turned out to vary less than proportionally to price, the trade balance and the terms of trade would improve or deteriorate together as a result of the same price variation, and all ideas about this matter would stand in need of revision. Devaluation, for example, might, because of particular elasticities of demand, lead not to an improvement but to a deterioration of the balance of trade. The present complete certainty that it necessarily leads to an improvement has no basis, unless it be the fear, if this certainty were destroyed, of having to revise too many painstakingly constructed theories. As for statistical verification, not only is there no evidence behind this certainty, but, as J. Viner admits, 'all or nearly all statistical investigations of the price elasticity of demand for particular commodities have found such elasticities to be low, usually substantially less than unity'.[47]

It should still not be forgotten that the elasticity of demand for this or that particular commodity is not the same thing as the elasticity of demand for the exports of a particular country. In the latter case, one must take account of the elasticity of (competing) supply of other countries producing the same products or substitutes. And this is why, in the short run, price variations are in most cases indeed followed by inverse variations of the balance of trade.

47. *International Trade and Economic Development*, p. 23. After referring to certain faults and unclear points in the statistics, the author typically eventually rejects their result and sticks to the dogma of a price elasticity greater than unity, as if the weakness of the statistical proof of a proposition could constitute *per se* a proof of the correctness of the opposite proposition, for which we have no statistical backing, whether weak or strong.

To put it another way, if a rise in the price of English textiles or machine-tools leads to a fall in exports, not only in volume, but also in value, this is not because foreign purchasers of these products cut back their consumption more than proportionally to this price rise (case of price elasticity of demand greater than unity) but because some of them will now obtain their supplies from Sweden and Germany. And if a devaluation of the French franc actually leads to an improvement of the French balance of trade, this is not because the world will increase its consumption of champagne more than proportionally to the fall in its price, but because some customers of Fiat or Volkswagen will opt for Citroën or Renault instead.

This is not very important in terms of definitions, since the price elasticity of international demand for the exports of a particular country can perfectly well be understood to mean the overall elasticity of demand for the products under consideration, whatever their origin, as modified by the possibility of substituting products of different origin. A price elasticity of demand lower than unity, for a product in general, can then become greater than unity, for the same product exported by a particular country.

But in real terms, matters are quite different. For the contradiction between the need for markets and concern for the terms of trade, which is insoluble in the short run, on the level of an individual country, is resolved in the long run, on the level of the group of countries faced with the problem of markets, the developed capitalist countries.

The number of these countries is not large enough for the supply of each to be considered as negligible and for the elasticity of supply of the other countries to be taken as unlimited. If, as the result of an *accord de Grenelle*,* some of Renault's foreign customers turn to

47. *Continued from page 347*

On the other hand, Joan Robinson is one of the rare writers who accept the possibility of a price elasticity of demand lower than unity. Following a devaluation of the currency, 'if the physical volume of exports increases their home price cannot fall, therefore the value of exports in terms of home currency must increase. But the effect on imports is more complicated. Foreign goods are now dearer at home, and while the physical volume of imports purchased out of a given income will decline, total expenditure upon them may increase. Thus a fall in the rate of exchange of our currency will not necessarily improve our balance of trade.' (*Essays in the Theory of Employment*, p. 138).

The conclusion is correct, but the argument is peculiar. It is carried out in terms of local currency instead of foreign, international currency. It should properly be reversed: the value of imports in terms of international currency cannot increase in any circumstance, but the value of exports in the same terms may fall as the result of a devaluation, if the elasticity of foreign demand is lower than unity.

* Translator's note: Grenelle Agreement – general wage increase in France, following the events of May 1968.

Austin or Fiat, the price of these will rise in turn, though perhaps by less than that of Renault. Consequently, France, while losing on the balance of trade, will gain on the terms of trade, while Britain and Italy will gain relatively little, but on both counts. The same applies to the industrialised countries as a whole. If, despite this, troubles persist in France, and France is forced to take counter-measures (for example, a currency devaluation) to make its prices competitive, a *partial* readjustment will generally be enough to re-equilibrate its balance and win back its clients without losing the whole terms-of-trade bonus.

Sometimes, if the initial rise was not too abrupt, the country in question will not even need to make this readjustment. It can wait for the various tendencies to equalisation to operate on its competitors. Between the highly industrialised countries, a mechanism of communicating vessels spreads out any disturbance. The least competitive factors on a world scale, like labour-power, become so within these limits, not through mobility, but by a sort of institutional solidarity. By the very fact that these countries produce roughly the same articles, their competition in the search for markets in less developed countries reacts back on their factors of production and gives rise to an equalising tendency. Fluctuations become contagious. The French *Grenelle*, through the very fact that it reduces the pressure of French competition on German prices, weakens the resistance of German employers and improves the position of the German working class in negotiation and struggle. In this case, the country in the lead may pull the rest of the group all the way up with it, instead of meeting them half-way back down again.

In all these cases, the whole group attains a new price level and since, for the producers of an article as a whole, only the pure price elasticity of demand counts (i.e. the elasticity of the article in general, whatever its origin), if this is, as we said above, lower than unity, this group of countries can, after a few internal readjustments, improve its overall terms of trade and safeguard its overall trade balance with the rest of the world. Of course the internal competition for markets continues between the group members, but it now restarts on a higher level, on the basis of the previous cumulative gains in price.

In the course of the debate which followed the publication of my *Unequal Exchange*, one argument formulated by several of my opponents was the balance of payments constraint. In various ways, it was argued against me that wages cannot be an independent variable of the system, since, if an exogenous increase in wage-rates is incompatible with the other economic variables of the system, it will lead to a deficit in foreign trade and, thus, to a devaluation of the currency which will cancel out the increase in real terms.

The answer is that, while the balance of payments does set a limit for wage variations, it does not make the wages variable *dependent* on the balance of payments. Any independent variable of a system inevitably comes up against constraints of compatibility with the system's endogenous variables. But, within the margin allowed by these constraints, fluctuations of such a variable are still exogenous.

The fact that, for almost a century, the terms of trade of the developed countries as a whole have been improving spectacularly, while the overall balance of payments of the same group has not been in deficit, proves that the two phenomena are perfectly compatible. Perhaps this compatibility stands in need of explanation – the assumption of a price elasticity of demand lower than unity explains it – but it cannot by itself establish a causal link between the two phenomena.

Consequently, this compatibility does not prevent the first phenomenon, the improvement in the terms of trade, from being a result of the rise in wages any more than it prevents this rise from being exogenous.[48]

Despite this, the main aim of developed capitalism has always been to increase sales, not to raise their price. It only worries about good terms of trade in the rare periods of full or near-full employment. But other forces, especially trade-union struggle, shoulder the task of providing it with these into the bargain.

This should not be surprising. As we have already had occasion to remark elsewhere, capitalists, whether as individuals or as a class, have nothing to gain from an improvement in the terms of trade. The factor they own, capital, is the most mobile and competitive of all, while, by their very nature, the terms of trade can only benefit those incomes that are least subject to international equalisation. So, while they try to get rid of their surplus stocks by squeezing today's prices, these prices, for reasons outside their control, are higher than those of yesterday.

(b) Budget deficits

As in the preceding case, part of the social product is, again, realized by purchasing power which has not been created by this same production. The only, purely formal, difference between the two cases, is

48. For a fuller treatment of this subject, see my discussion with E. Somaini, L. Boggio and M. Salvati, *Un Débat sur l'échange inégal*.

that in the case of a trade surplus, the extra purchasing power and corresponding domestic money are created in exchange for the central bank's reserves, while in the case of a budget deficit, they are created in exchange for claims on the Exchequer which cannot properly be included in central bank reserves. It must also be added that just as a trade surplus is all the more favourable where it does not result in the acquisition of foreign non-monetary claims, a budget deficit can likewise only stimulate economic activity to the extent to which it is not covered by the sale of securities (Treasury bills or bond issues), but is financed solely from current central bank advances.

Finally, just as in the case of a surplus trade balance, we can look at the situation in two ways: we can look at *the moment* of surplus government consumption and consider the fact that it takes place without any corresponding fiscal revenue, thus without the utilisation of any secondary purchasing power derived from the redistribution of primary incomes, or we can look at *the moment* of the Exchequer's overdraft with the central bank and consider the fact that purchasing power is created in this way (in the hands of the state) without there being any corresponding production of goods.

Writing b for the budget deficit, the two expressions for the improvement of the situation compared to the initial disequilibrium are:

$$(P - b) - R < P - R$$

or equivalently:

$$P - (R + b) < P - R.$$

Since $P - R$ has been defined as equal to the sum of profit of enterprise, the budget deficit, depending whether it is smaller than, equal to, or greater than this sum, will have the effect of palliating, completely reabsorbing, or reversing the disequilibrium with, in the last case, a reversal of the situation and the replacement of deflation by inflation.

In this respect, it is completely irrelevant whether the budget deficit represents wages of government employees, and thus a redistribution of the purchasing power created by the central bank, or direct consumption of commodities by the public services, provided of course that saving by government employees, like all saving, is relegated to the *ceteris paribus*.

Since we are also abstracting from disproportions between industries, it is also irrelevant what kind of commodities are acquired by the public services, whether they form productive or unproductive consumption. Whether they are weapons and munitions which turn into scrap-iron and smoke, the construction of nurseries and parks, or productive investment, the effect is just the same. What matters is whether the consumption under consideration is financed by part of the revenues created by current production (including the object of this consumption itself) or by external revenues added on to this production. A hydroelectric dam or post offices built by merely printing money are more or less stimulating for economic activity, or more or less inflationary, depending on the relation of the magnitudes in question, while a war totally financed by taxes or domestic borrowing is not at all stimulating or inflationary.

It can now be seen much more clearly what we meant earlier, when we said that stimulation of activity by a balanced budget is completely different from stimulation by a budget deficit. The difference is not quantitative but qualitative. The former replaces a variable revenue by a fixed or quasi-fixed revenue, an *ex post* revenue by an *ex ante* revenue, a revenue resulting from realization by a 'prior' revenue; the latter creates an extrinsic revenue over and above the revenues created by production, whether 'second-wave' or 'prior'.

(c) Overtrading

This third and last factor – the most important of all – for the re-equilibration of the system (without any change in the composition of the value of output) belongs to this category of revenues created extrinsically to production.

In Chapter 5 we sketched out its definition: to spend a virtual revenue by anticipating its realization. We broached the same subject at the end of Chapter 8, in the course of our critique of the Keynesian equation, S = I. In both places we stressed that this is a question of realization, not of circulation.

Because Marx retained the classical premise that the value of output is equal to incomes, his vision is different. In the analyses of volume II of *Capital* – simple and extended reproduction – the *acknowledged* problem is the circulation of capital, while the question of realization is so-to-speak entangled in the mechanisms of this circulation and only appears as an after-effect of this process. Nonetheless, here and there, as we shall see from the following quotations, he seems to slip into a problematic within which the realization of the product is a special and more or less autonomous problem.

While the capitalist awaits the realization of surplus-value, Marx writes, 'for all that he does not suspend his consumption for a single moment. He advances to himself (immaterial whether out of his own pocket or by means of credit from the pocket of somebody else[49]) money in *anticipation* of surplus-value still to be snatched by him; but in doing so he also advances a circulating medium for the realization of surplus-value to be realized later.'

This is of course in simple reproduction. In this framework, spending an anticipated revenue can only mean personal (unproductive) expenditure, which does not exactly correspond to the literal meaning of overtrading. But this does not affect the principle, and our definition above is purposely broad enough to encompass the capitalist's personal expenditure. This should not make us lose sight of the fact that, in contemporary reality, this consumption is covered by his salary which, like all other wages, is an integral part of the cost-price of output and a 'prior' revenue, and does not require any 'anticipation', while it is investment, expanding production, which usually gives rise to overtrading proper.[50]

As a general rule, the personal consumption of the capitalist–entrepreneur is entered in the accounts in the same way as all the other costs of production and this is a practice accepted both by the Inland Revenue and banks who, even when following the most conservative and orthodox rules of credit, have no objection in principle to mobilising the value of stocks on the basis of cost-price including the manager's salary. There is no need for any special financing outside the firm's ordinary circuits. 'He who works in the temple shall eat in the temple. ...' When calculating the capital needed for this or that undertaking (equity capital plus credit), the manager's wage is counted along with the other expenses. Given this, it would not even be legitimate to speak of anticipated consumption of surplus-value. This consumption should be included in variable capital instead.

Nonetheless, for this to be so, we must be dealing with a genuine wage, that is to say, certain quantitative limits must not be exceeded. Beyond these limits, we have a case of overtrading like any other. This is expressed clearly by Marx in the rest of the passage in question.

> Payments and receipts are distributed over different terms throughout the year. But one thing continues uninterruptedly, namely the consumption of

49. Or from the pocket of nobody, from nothing, we would say today. but entirely fictive (scriptural) money is not always present in Marx's conception, although he sometimes envisages this possibility, as we have already had occasion to point out.

50. It is rather curious that Marx only refers to this need for anticipation in the context of simple reproduction. In the chapter on extended reproduction he manages to make investment occur without mentioning any anticipation of surplus-value.

> the capitalist, which *anticipates*, and whose volume is computed on a definite proportion of the customary or estimated revenue. With every portion of commodities sold, a portion of the surplus-value to be produced annually is also realized. But if during the entire year only as much of the produced commodities is sold as is required to replace the constant and variable capital-values contained in them, or if prices were to fall to such an extent that only the advanced capital-value contained in the entire annual commodity-product should be realized on its sale, then the *anticipatory* character of the expenditure of money in expectation of future surplus-value would be clearly revealed. If our capitalist fails, his creditors and the court investigate whether *anticipated* private expenditures were in proper proportion to the volume of his business and to the receipt of surplus-value usually or normally corresponding to it.[51]

In theory, there is then no reason why capitalists' luxury expenditure should not also be covered by overtrading.[52] But in practice, what is in question is overtrading in the strict sense, in relation to investment.

However – and this is the heart of the matter – we are not concerned with it as *investment*, but as *overtrading*.

This is a crucial distinction: it will enable us to avoid the trap of the fetishisation of *investment*, which Keynesians generally fall into and which, for example, leads Joan Robinson, as we have seen, to attribute a 'multiplier' effect to the export of capital – investment abroad –, whereas, all other things being equal, this exit of funds has an opposite (deflationary) effect.

Abstracting from any disproportion between industries, what makes it possible to correct a situation in which aggregate purchasing-power is lower in value terms than the aggregate supply of commodities, is not the use of part of *existing* purchasing-power to buy capital goods rather than consumer goods, but the *creation ex nihilo* of extra purchasing-power to buy capital and/or consumer goods, it does not matter which. The determining factor is the anticipation of revenue and not the way in which this revenue is used, even if, in reality, this anticipation is, for the most part, engaged in by

51. *Capital*, volume II, pp. 424–5, emphasis added.

52. This expenditure and, in general, purchases of articles of consumption by the capitalists, is the only case of overtrading systematically analysed by Marx in his study of reproduction in volume II. The 'anticipations' which he mentions on numerous occasions sometimes also include the mere replacement of constant capital consumed, but this case can scarcely be considered as overtrading, since it is not an expenditure of revenue. This is a purely technical problem of the circulation of money, and this is how Marx sees it (cf. *Capital*, vol. II, pp. 404–05, 421, 422).

capitalists, and is usually accompanied by investment.[53] It is not *qua* investment that this outlay stimulates economic activity, but *qua* purchasing.

Nor is the kind of use-values purchased what counts, but the way in which these purchases are financed. It is perhaps immaterial, as Marx says, whether the money used for the purchases of a particular capitalist is advanced 'from his own pocket or by means of credit from the pocket of somebody else' – and, especially when the problem is considered as one of circulation, it is certainly pointless to introduce a third party. But it is not immaterial whether the money is advanced from *the pocket* of somebody or of nobody – in other words, whether payment is made with pre-existing money or with bank money specially created for the occasion; and when the problem is one of realization, it is this second alternative which is relevant. Between the first and second parts of the alternative, there is all the difference between individual overtrading compensated for by equally individual undertrading, and net social overtrading.

It is only where Marx deals with realization as a specific structural problem of capitalism, where he is concerned, not with equilibrium conditions as in the reproduction schemes of volume II, but with the system's disequilibrium and structural problems, especially in Chapter XV of part III of volume III (pp. 207–337) and in part V (pp. 338–613), that he envisages this overtrading as being financed by mere money-creating credit.

We have discussed this at length in Chapter 3, where, for the third time, we broached this phenomenon and used this term (following Engels' usage). But yet again, on the basis of the fundamental equation between the value of production and purchasing power, overtrading, in these analyses by Marx, instead of being an anticipation of revenue which equilibrates the economy, appears as frenzied 'overspeculation' which disturbs this equilibrium; instead of making good the original time lag between supply and demand, it destroys their supposed equivalence; instead of bringing about full employment, it gives rise to a useless overheating of activity.

This is a matter of different starting-points. If the starting-point is the inequality $P > R$, overtrading must lessen the gap; if the starting-point is the equation $P = R$, it can only destroy equilibrium.

53. Although nowadays consumer credit – hire-purchase – for wage-workers is growing at a headlong rate. But for there to be overtrading on the social level, of the kind required by our problematic, the sum total of these sales for any given period must exceed the sum total of saving by wage-earners as a whole, over the same period, which is not at all clear.

Depending on the starting-point, it is equilibrating or disequilibrating.

Means of overtrading (the two types of credit) We have said that overtrading depends on the creation of exogenous purchasing power, but it must be understood that this purchasing power is only exogenous in relation to current production. In the long run, it is certainly not exogenous, since it depends upon expected future production.

Overtrading rests on credit but – this is the crucial point – on a qualitatively different kind of credit from that of the classics, which, in all its forms, could only displace purchasing power in space, transferring it from one person to another, from a saver to an investor or consumer, whether directly from the lender to the borrower, or indirectly, through a specialised institution acting as intermediary. The type of credit which makes overtrading possible is quite different, in that it displaces purchasing power in time, from the future to the present.

This kind of credit is not new. It has existed since the dawn of capitalism, in various more or less developed forms. Still, the classics on the whole chose to ignore it. When they could not ignore it, they condemned it. In the harmonious universe of the $P = R$ equation, credit which autonomously generates purchasing power was an intolerable disturbing factor.

Typical in this respect is the intransigent position, a model of extreme classicism, adopted by Ricardo in his evidence to the House of Lords' Committee set up to examine the feasibility of restoring the pound's convertibility.

'Do you not know', he was asked, 'that when the Demand for Our Manufacturers is great in this Country, the very Credit which that Circumstance creates enables the Manufacturer to make more extended Use of his Capital in the Production of Manufactures?'

Ricardo's reply in the negative:

> I have no Notion of Credit being at all effectual in the Production of Commodities; Commodities can only be produced by Labour, Machinery, and raw Materials; and if these are supplied in one Place they must necessarily be withdrawn from another. ... Credit, I think, is the Means, which is alternately transferred from one to another, to make use of Capital already existing; it does not create Capital; it determines only by whom that Capital should be employed: the removing Capital from one Employment to another may often be very advantageous, and it may also be very injurious.[54]

54. *Works and Correspondence*, p. 436.

This is the quintessence of the classical doctrine. Ricardo does not believe that there can be any unemployed capital or labour, so that credit could withdraw them not from other employment – which anyway is never the effect of credit – but from unemployment.

'May not a Man', the Committee insisted, 'get Credit from a Bank of Credit on the Security of his Capital ... and may he not by means of that Credit purchase or create an additional Quantity of Machinery and raw Materials, and pay an additional Number of Labourers, without dislodging Capital from any existing Employment in the Country?'

'Impossible' is Ricardo's peremptory reply; 'he can purchase Machinery, etc. with Credit, he can never create them. If he purchases, it is always at the Expence of some other Person, and he displaces some other from the Employment of Capital.'[55]

How can this reply be explained? Did Ricardo not know that before machinery becomes active capital, it is an ordinary commodity? Of course he did, but he was unshakeably convinced that the production of commodities is strictly equal to the purchasing power distributed at the same time and, consequently, that the existence of any stock of machinery on sale implies the existence of equivalent purchasing power as counterpart in someone's hands. This machinery will therefore get sold one way or another. Credit can only change the identity of the purchaser. Did Ricardo not also know that unemployed workers are available and that these can be taken on without withdrawing them from another employer? He certainly knew this, but he also knew that, for these workers to be employed, they would have to be fed, and to feed them, subsistence goods would be needed. Either these subsistence goods do not exist, in which case credit cannot create them; or they do exist, in which case, once more, equivalent purchasing power must also exist somewhere else. Credit can therefore only substitute a different entrepreneur for the original bearer of this purchasing power.[56]

The classical web is seamless. Credit cannot alter its essential functions. It can only mobilise funds which are already available. Even if these funds are transferred from consuming classes to investors, as Professor Pigou notes, neither the general level of employment nor the overall equilibrium value will be affected. Only the rate of growth of production could possibly be affected.

55. *Ibid.*, p. 437.

56. cf. MacCulloch, *The Principles of Political Economy*, pp. 123–4: 'all that the highest degree of credit or confidence can do, is merely to change the distribution of capital'.

While some, like Juglar, do analyse the two types of credit and recognise that the second has an acceleratory effect, they do not conclude that the latter gets rid of unemployment, but that it precipitates a crisis.[57]

Until the Keynesians, only a few isolated economists considered that credit, as a creator of purchasing power, has a positive effect on the level of economic activity.

Special mention should be made of Schumpeter. He drew a clear distinction between credit coming from savings, which represents a transfer of purchasing power from one agent to another, and the *creation* of money by banks.

> Here we are always dealing not with a transformation of purchasing power which would have existed anyway in someone's hands, but with a creation of *new* purchasing power, which is added to that already in circulation; this is a creation *ex nihilo*, even if the loan contract, in compliance with which the new purchasing power has been created, is based on real guarantees, which are not themselves means of circulation.[58]

But, still faithful to the Law of Markets and its basic equation, he does not consider these loans as a claim on current production in anticipation of future revenues, but as an anticipation of future *production* which will result from 'new projects'.

57. Clement Juglar, *Des Crises commerciales et de leur retour périodique*. The cause of crises is a speculative growth of production, because of the availability of credit and general euphoria: 'Excessive growth of domestic and foreign trade, at prices inflated by speculation and not at the natural prices, this is the main cause of all the trouble.' (p. 7). The same picture is presented by Ch. Dupin, *La Crise commerciale de 1839:* Alexis Rostand, *La Crise 1870–71 et les sociétés de crédit à Marseille*. Also Camille Heurtier, *La Crise monétaire*. Carried away by the boom, entrepreneurs produce excessively – speculation, pyramiding of credit and discounting. Then the banks put on the brakes, causing foreclosure on loans, bankruptcies, etc. After this, a tightening of credit through fear, going too far in the opposite direction. This picture, which is not entirely absent from the analysis of Marx himself (cf. above, Chapter 3), collapses as soon as one asks the simple question: 'produce excessively', in what sense and compared to what? But as soon as it is explained, as we are endeavoring to do, how this initial excess arises, the same picture becomes perfectly valid to explain the cyclical character of this 'excess'.

A good example of a naive exponent of this line of thought is Jacques Rueff: 'But there is', he writes, 'another way to maintain economic equilibrium: monetary policy. Its basic principle is the refusal to create money which is not the counterpart of a supply of an equal quantity of real values. To put it another way, it forbids the discounting of fictive debts.' (*A l'âge de l'inflation*, p. 44).

It goes without saying that, if our analysis is correct, this 'refusal' does not establish equilibrium between supply and demand; it sanctions and consolidates their initial disequilibrium (the initial 'excess').

58. *Theory of Economic Development*, p. 328.

> This is the *normal* source of finance for new projects .... These means created in order to extend credit ... are certainly claims with which one can directly obtain consumer goods. But they are not claims on previous production. This condition, which is usually attached to any access to the reservoir of consumer goods, is of course not yet fulfilled in this case. It is only met after succesful completion of the new projects under consideration. As a result this kind of extension of credit has a special influence on the general price level.[59]

This is where we see what makes his position compatible with that of Keynes – which is also what differentiates our position from theirs.

Since the commodities on the market are, according to both Keynes and Schumpeter, always equivalent to the purchasing power *already* created, any creation by credit of extra purchasing power, in excess of planned savings, can only make prices rise and thus cause forced savings. In our opinion, on the contrary, although the credit in question is in excess of planned savings, up to a certain limit it only makes good the shortfall in *previously* distributed purchasing power and, as long as it stays within these limits, it does not make prices rise by depleting normal stocks, but ensures that they do not fall, by liquidating the overstocks.

As we have seen, Marx did not entirely neglect credit of the second kind, the type which is not confined to making existing purchasing power liquid, but which brings future purchasing power into the present. But it is only in Chapter XXXIII of volume III ('The Medium of Circulation in the Credit System') that one can say with certainty that he sees the matter clearly: 'Thus we see here how banks *create credit and capital*. ...'[60] The enumeration of these means which follows, shows that Marx did have in mind actual artificial *generation* of what is nowadays known as 'bank money'. Everywhere else, mainly in volumes I and, above all, II, Marx is either ambiguous or he explicitly specifies that he is referring to the first, classical type of credit: the type which only displaces purchasing power from one subject to another. Thus, for example, 'with capitalist production an altogether new force comes into play – the credit system, which ... is finally transformed into an enormous social mechanism for the *centralisation* of capitals'.[61] 'The so-called credit economy is merely a form of the money-economy, since both terms express functions or modes of exchange *among the producers themselves*.'[62] 'With the

59. *Ibid.*, p. 329.
60. *Capital*, vol. III, p. 542, emphasis added.
61. *Ibid.*, vol. I, p. 587, emphasis added.
62. *Ibid.*, vol. II, p. 119, emphasis added.

development of the credit-system ... this money no longer serves as a hoard but as capital; however not in the hands of its owner but of other capitalists at whose disposal it has been placed.'[63]

Marxists, most of whom feel more at home with the static-classical side of Marx than with his more dynamic side, have generally stuck to this concrete and palpable credit: the kind which makes a real value, preferably metallic, pass from hand to hand. In this way Hilferding, who carries his analysis very far with many subtle sub-divisions – circulation credit, capital credit, etc. – only ever subdivides one type of credit, the first type: the type which transfers purchasing power from one economic subject to another.[64]

Incentives to overtrade Credit, as we have studied it, even if it does generate and not merely redistribute money, is a necessary condition of overtrading. It is not a sufficient condition. The possibility of obtaining finance is not enough to make a businessman undertake a particular project; he must also have an interest in doing so. It takes two to engage in overtrading: a banker prepared to finance it, and a capitalist prepared to go ahead with it.

Generally speaking, financiers and industrialists are both subject to the same influences, the same euphorias and depressions which affect the business world during booms and slumps. All other things being equal, if a project is worthwhile in itself, it will be 'bankable'. What we mean here is that the existence of the mechanism for creating bank money is not sufficient on its own: there must also be opportunities for profitable projects.

63. *Ibid.*, vol. II, p. 185.

64. *Finance Capital*, pp. 82–98. An extreme example is Suzanne de Brunhoff, in her *L'Offre de monnaie*. she is not content with ignoring credit's ability to *create* money; she does her utmost to prove its non-existence: 'Let us assume', she writes, 'that the banks, for some reason, buy extra nominal securities and create extra nominal money. The increase in the latter will raise the price of current output, money wage rates and the nominal prices of securities, all of which are purely nominal rises which do not affect real magnitudes. As a result, banks' nominal profits will rise in the same proportion, giving unchanged real profits (which makes even more mysterious the initial act of creating extra money which no one requires and which does not earn anything for the banks!).' (p. 74).

Suzanne de Brunhoff's argument may be correct for the banking sector – private and central – as a whole, but not for private banks alone, still less for each private bank considered separately. This is rather like trying to discourage forgers by explaining to them that, if every one in their syndicate, plus the mint, increased their issues of currency in the same proportion, no one would gain. The position of the money created by private banks in relation to the national fiduciary currency is exactly the same as that of forgeries in relation to genuine money.

These 'opportunities' must be considered subjectively rather than objectively. Given that economic reality does not exist outside and apart from economic subjects, but is itself the result of their own acts, their optimistic or pessimistic forecasts come true to the extent that they determine behaviour, and to the extent that they are widely believed.

These incentives to overtrade fall into two categories: some are recurrent, following a permanent overall law; others are the product of specific and individual circumstances. The first will be studied in Chapter 10, which deals with the business cycle. The second, which we will discuss here, depend on four main factors: (i) innovations; (ii) the opening up of foreign markets; (iii) exogenous growth of wages; (iv) depreciation of the currency.

(i) Innovations A distinction should perhaps be drawn between technological and commercial innovations. The former concern the introduction of new techniques in the production of the same articles; the latter concern the introduction of new articles, produced more or less on the basis of existing techniques. The two types may of course be combined.

We shall not study this factor in great detail: it is a subject on which, since Schumpeter, there has grown up an extensive literature; we shall confine ourselves to warning against a very common mistake in calculating the effect of this factor. It is generally believed that the new units of production, or extensions of existing units of production, will eventually result in the partial or complete removal from the market of other producers, and that the only increase in activity at the social level will be that resulting from the setting-up operations (investment) proper. This is of course false. Except in the case of full employment, the new output will, in its own right, distribute additional revenues and expand the market.

When a particular entrepreneur starts plastic bottle production for the first time, he calculates *ex ante* his chances and future profitability on the basis of the potential of the *pre-existing* market, in which he hopes to supplant glass bottles. But once it is set up, this new industry distributes new revenues and creates *ex post* an additional market for all industries, including the bottle industry. So his output is added on top of the former total social product, and any eventual contraction of the former glass bottle industry is compensated for by equivalent expansion in other industries.

(2) Foreign markets

It is in this area that our last remark has the widest ramifications.

Rosa Luxemburg saw foreign markets as an outlet for excess production (sometimes localised in Department II, sometimes undifferentiated). It was objected that if these exports were not to be given to the rest of the world as a present, and if the kind of use-values exchanged did not matter, then the equivalent imports would weigh on the home market, just as much as the exported goods had done. In reply to this, Rosa Luxemburg argued vaguely that 'realization' consists in the actual process of exchange, and got bogged down as we have already seen, in a confused and incoherent argument about a 'global' money-capital which realizes a 'global' surplus-value.

Several of her partisans now try to extricate her from this difficulty by transposing her theory onto the level of investment incentives alone. We have already dealt with this question (see above, p. 202) and given the reasons why it seems to us impossible to credit Rosa Luxemburg with this version of her theory. But what are its intrinsic merits? The answer is that it can only be valid if it is taken out of Rosa Luxemburg's problematic and put on its own terrain – that of a psychological catalyst.

In this sense foreign markets act, not as a function of their own capacity to absorb a surplus, which is anyway illusory, but as the catalyst of a process of interaction between internal factors of the economy under consideration.

If this is so, then it does not matter theoretically whether this new market is a pre-capitalist or capitalist region, or whether the commodities one hopes to sell there belong to Department II or Department I, and Rosa Luxemburg's analysis, which is entirely based on these considerations, becomes irrelevant.

Of course, in practical and historical terms, it has always been a matter of an underdeveloped region which has just been opened up to foreign trade by an expanding capitalist country. This is bound to be the case, since only this case would provide investors with the factors that convince them – political domination or even the mere fact of being first in the penetration process. But the practical results have been a function of this conviction and the resulting investment, rather than a function of the volume and nature of actual resulting exchanges.

What we are concretely maintaining here is that, given the *objective* condition of underemployment of the factors, the *subjective* expectations and incentives which are engendered by the opening-up of a foreign market, and the resulting *practical* behaviour, *can* be factors for the reabsorption of the excess product, even if the real conditions are the opposite of Rosa Luxemburg's assumptions, while the objective conditions defined by these assumptions would have no effect if the subjective expectations and incentives were lacking.

It is clear that this position not only differs from that of Rosa Luxemburg but, if it is correct, is a refutation of her theory, even if it were the case – as it is indeed the case – that adequate incentives are more likely to arise in the case of a *pre-capitalist* region than in any other case. For, as we have already said above, what reinforces the incentives in the first case is not the fact that the structure of the new region is able to absorb what more developed structures are unable to absorb, but that, in practice, the *opening-up* of an underdeveloped region is usually accompanied by a privileged position, whether this is the result of the beginning of political domination by the advanced country or of the end of domination by a competitor, provided in this last case that it coincides with the emergence of marked economic superiority for the country in question.

What determines whether these incentives are *adequate*? In essence, a particular order of events in time. To illustrate the point, it is helpful to return to our plastic bottles example. If one examines it more closely, it becomes apparent that there is an implicit assumption that the new industry was set up and on line *before* any negative reaction on the part of the old producers. In this way, the resulting revenues make it unnecessary *ex post* for the old factories to contract in compensation, whereas this is what the new factories were meant *ex ante* to provoke.

If, on the other hand, we were to assume that before or simultaneously with the inauguration of the new industry, the managers of the old bottle factories, anticipating its effects, closed their factories and disinvested to the extent of the expected output of plastic bottles, there would be no overall rise in the level of employment.

In the same way, in the sphere of foreign trade, if, after contact is made with a new market, foreign sellers arrive here to sell their wares at the very moment that our commercial travellers arrive in their country to sell our products, or if, in any case, rightly or wrongly, the negative reactions of those of our industries that are susceptible to foreign competition are just as rapid and strong as the positive reactions of our exporting industries, they will cancel each other out, and no general improvement in our business climate can be expected.

This is in danger of occurring (although not necessarily) when France liberalises its trade with Italy; it is much less likely, or impossible, when France secures the market of Equatorial Africa or of Indochina, although in both cases, *ex post,* in the long run and on average, our exports are paid for with equivalent imports.

The explanation of this phenomenon lies in the variations of incomes. The expansion of our export sector means the mobilisation of hitherto unemployed factors, and therefore the creation of extra revenues. Henceforth the total home market, expanded in this way, can absorb the extra imports, without any general contraction of our traditional industries producing for the home market.

It is because he abstracts from revenues that Henri Denis, in his article quoted earlier, reaches different conclusions.[65] According to these conclusions, in both cases, the expansion of exporting industries will be accompanied by equivalent contraction in industries affected by competition from imported goods. But in the case of Italy, this contraction will hit French manufacturing industry, which is just as vital for the national economy as export industries, while in the case of Africa or Indochina, the contraction will hit the French agricultural or mining sectors, which are less important, since the accumulation of capital is based on the development of manufacturing industry.[66]

This argument is original and sometimes valid but, as a general picture, it does not seem to us to be very convincing. With respect to the market's general equilibrium in value terms, all the different industries and sectors are equally important. Overproduction cannot be localised and circumscribed. If the agricultural and mining sectors are unable to sell their output, their factors will see their revenues fall and will therefore purchase less manufactured goods for productive and unproductive consumption. Except in special cases, overproduction will extend over the whole front.

It is the very idea of the necessity of compensation which is, in our view, false. It is based on the relegation of revenues to the *ceteris paribus*, whereas their variations are tied to those of production.[67]

65. *L'Homme et la Société*, December 1971, no. 22.

66. Denis considers his presentation to be related to that of Luxemburg, but it seems to us to differ considerably. According to Rosa Luxemburg, there is no overall excess of supply over demand. There is, in capitalist countries, an excess in Department II and a deficit in Department I. Foreign trade brings the two into line, and no industry need suffer from this. According to Henri Denis, there is an excess in Department II and equilibrium in Department I (this Department produces to order). Foreign trade tends to reabsorb the excess in processing industries while causing an excess in the rest. The general excess remains, though less damaging now because the industries suffering from it are less important than the rest.

67. Economists' habit of taking incomes as given is as tiresome as it is irresistible. It derives perhaps from Marshall, who took the marginal utility of money to be constant, and therefore believed that a consumer's demand for any particular good is independent of his income.

As J. D. Domarchi points out, 'Income has no place in traditional thought, it is implicitly considered (along with the value of output) as a constant.' (*La Pensée économique de Keynes*, p. 172).

Continued on page 365

If we take into account revenues as an endogenous variable, we will see that, depending on circumstances, the growth of export industries may or may not be accompanied by a contraction in industries affected by foreign competition.

If actual exports, for one reason or another, *precede* the imports which pay for them, or even if only the sanguine investing actions and reactions of exporters precede or exceed in intensity the defensive, disinvesting reactions of others, it is highly possible that the extra trade, though balanced, will give rise to growth in exporting industries without any contraction of other industries, with the value of imports being realized against extra revenues, instead of against a fall in national output.

This remarkable result merely of priority in the internal phases of a single phenomenon, that of trade relations with a new partner, should not surprise us if we turn to the analyses of the preceding chapters. In fact, we have been able to conclude that, to solve the problem of realization, we do not need to find some one who buys *without* selling; it is enough to find some one who buys *before* selling, or to whom *we* can sell *before* buying, or even to whom we *believe* we can sell *before* buying.

67. *Continued from page 364*
Thus after the First World War, it was said to be materially impossible for Germany to pay its reparations: according to these predictions, any attempt to do so would have made this country enter a vicious circle of export drives leading to a fall in prices, with this fall in prices necessitating a new export drive, the cumulative effects of which would have eventually required a level of exports out of all proportion to the German economy's ability. A variable that was generally left out of the calculation was the acquisition of credits (income) by the countries receiving reparations, whose disbursement could, on the contrary, only lead to a rise in German prices and thus reduce the real burden of the reparations.

Exactly the same error is committed today in calculations of the effects of the rise in the price of oil. OECD 'experts' have just (May 1974) estimated the deficit on the balance of trade for a certain number of countries in 1974. They took the imports of petroleum-based products of each of the countries under consideration, corrected to take into account a fall in consumption, and multiplied this figure by the difference between the new and old prices of oil. And that was that! This calculation is based, fairly and squarely, on the astonishing assumption that the oil-producing countries will not spend one single dollar out of this mass of billions of extra income which will flow to them.

It is true that a large part of these billions will stay in the form of overseas balances wandering from one bank to the next. This part will therefore stay fictive and will not really be *paid* by the consuming countries. It is also true that countries such as Saudi Arabia and Kuwait, because of lack of reception structures (i.e., either sufficient domestic income in the case of market economies or centralised management in the case of more or less planned countries), are not in a position to *materialise* these enormous holdings, and it is this kind of country which accounts for the proportion which will never be *paid* in real terms.

Continued on page 366

In Chapter XXI of volume II of *Capital*,[68] we find a good illustration of the above. Marx examines in turn the operations of realization of the product on the basis of the following scheme:

$$\begin{array}{ll} \text{I} & 5000c + 1000v + 1000s = 7000 \\ \text{II} & 1430c + 285v + 285s = 2000 \end{array}$$

In the course of this analysis, the two Departments are personified, and all the operations are settled without any difficulty, except for the last one, in which Department I with 70 producer goods faces Department II with 70 consumer goods. How can they exchange them? It is at this point that I gets out his money-reserve and buys the 70 consumer goods. The situation is unlocked.

This 'money-reserve', this pre-existing hoard, is of course quite an assumption. In the course of studying a similar problem in a different passage, Marx tells us that it is immaterial whether the capitalist in question advances this money to himself out of his own pocket or

67. *Continued from page 365*
But to move from this to the assumption that countries such as Algeria, Iraq and even Libya and Iran will not spend a single cent of these formidable extra receipts on equipment, arms, or anything else, and that even the princes and emirs of the other countries in question will not be led by this windfall revenue to spend some extra money, however small relatively, on luxury or prestige goods, on personal or national consumption – that not one extra bottle of champagne, not one Rolls-Royce, not one tanker, not one refinery, not one Mirage more than last year, will take the road to the Middle East – this is an astonishing step to take, especially when this part of the super-price for oil, even if the least important relatively, accounts for billions of dollars.

As in the case of the Germany of 1918, each country is today calculating the 'export drive' it needs to plug the gap caused by the rise in the price of oil. Giscard d'Estaing has evaluated this effort, for France, as a thirteenth month of exports. OECD experts consider that this is not enough. But the basis of all these calculations is entirely false. Even without any special effort at exporting, part of the disbursements on oil will automatically return to the consuming countries through additional purchases for which the producing countries will themselves, inevitably, take the initiative. Only for what is left over after this will the consuming countries actually have to make an autonomous effort at exporting.

Of course the consuming countries may go mad and launch this competitive 'effort' starting with the first dollar, each fearing that they may not obtain their share of the purchases induced in the oil countries. But this is not objectively necessary in any of these countries. For, not only does the law of probability make it very likely that these purchases will be spread more or less evenly, but this is inevitable. The sums involved are so large that any discriminating concentration of orders would give rise to such problems with delivery dates, prices and other conditions of sale, that the oil countries would have no choice but to switch from suppliers who are saturated in this way to substitute suppliers, and, from substitute to substitute, to spread their purchases over the whole zone of industrialised countries.

68. pp. 418–22.

from the pocket of somebody else (by means of credit).[69] The point is that this capitalist, by *anticipating* his own sales, purchases. However he obtains the money, he is engaging in overtrading.

While theoretically possible, this overtrading is, however, in the concrete circumstances laid down, very unlikely. The supply price of all the commodities on sale is 2 × 70 = 140. On the other side, the purchasing power of the holders of these stocks is equal to the value that society already recognizes in them, that is to say their cost-price, which, in Marx's example, is 2 × 60 = 120. There is therefore conspicuous overproduction of 20, with all the risks of cumulative effects which this entails. This is therefore not really the time for industrialists to engage in overtrading, still less for the banks to encourage them to do so. For we are dealing with a competitive system, and each industrial capitalist, as well as each of their bankers, is in a position where he has no guarantee that the one facing him will play the game, rather than profiting from this injection of funds to attain a liquid position and withdraw from the market.

At this point, to put this market (France) in contact with another similar market (Britain) would be to introduce two more holders of stocks who are also trying to sell before buying or, to put it another way, who refuse to buy *before* selling. Except in special circumstances, this would not solve our problem.

The situation changes dramatically if the region put in contact with France is an undeveloped, pre-capitalist society, for example West Africa. In this case several possibilities arise.

One possibility is that France begins by buying coffee and palm oil, but these are goods which she does not herself produce. These purchases therefore only replace those she made before from, say, the British Commonwealth. Consequently these purchases, at whichever stage they occur, do not affect France's domestic equilibrium or disequilibrium at that point in time. But French exporters keep in step with the coffee and oil purchasers. The same import–export

69. It is of course very unlikely that he should advance it out of his own pocket, especially since he is not consuming his surplus-value unproductively, but productively. For if he has so much faith in his company that he expands it before realizing his first profits, whereas he already had the necessary money in reserve, why would he not have invested it from the start? Besides, such a sum of money can only come from a previous unspent revenue, from hoarding. All other things being equal, this reserve of purchasing power must, therefore, have its counterpart in a pre-existing overstock which needs to be realized. The effect of using it is thus not to initiate the realization of current output, but to disencumber the market of this previous overstock.

agencies, which will receive the first wads of bank notes to be distributed to the inhabitants for coffee and oil, will also take delivery of the first shipments of French commodities by means of which they will recover these notes. And this sale of commodities will unlock the situation in France.

Another possibility is that before anything else, France will send steel, cement, machinery and engineers to West Africa to build railways and roads, install mining equipment, etc., in order subsequently to produce and send to France agricultural and mining products which France was previously producing on its own soil or did not produce at all. There is an odds-on-chance that the assumed business stagnation in France on the eve of this event will not prevent the banks from financing such a promising venture (which is also a kind of overtrading).

If France manages in some way, through one of these types of operation – through one or other of the possibilities or their combinations – to export *before* importing, the mechanism for the expansion of French production, which we have already examined, is set to work, and there is nothing more to add.

But in the sense that this operation involves the partial or total elimination from the French market of the products of a third country (the British Commonwealth), Marx and Lenin would say that this only displaces the problem of realization from one country to another, or from a lower level to a higher level.

But this objection would miss the point. The French market has done more than find a new supplier for certain products; it has itself grown by the full amount of the revenues created by the new production sent out as the counterpart of these products. Its purchasing power, domestic and foreign (for all kinds of goods, including coffee and palm oil), has grown by exactly the same sum and, if this were the end of the matter, its trade balance would now be in surplus by this same sum. But this is not the end of the matter. This surplus now allows France to maintain its former level of imports from the Commonwealth, with or without some diversification of their composition, or if these imports have to be reduced, then the residual surplus will enable France to compensate for this shortfall with imports from other countries, which can in turn use their resulting surplus to buy goods from still others, and so on, until equilibrium is reached by some one's purchases from the Commonwealth equivalent to this shortfall.

The problem really was displaced. But it turns out that the very process of displacement is the key to its solution. It is the intention to solve it on someone else's back which enables it to be solved at no one's expense.[70]

It should be understood that in this context 'no one' means 'none of the advanced capitalist countries in search of markets'; in our example, France and Britain. Nevertheless, even at this level, this is still only a general theoretical possibility. In historical reality, this process of the system's long-run re-equilibration is punctuated by crises and explosions which put in doubt the trend towards the regular diffusion of domestic expansion and the growth of markets.

As far as the underdeveloped countries are concerned, the countries whose conquest supplies this catalyst for the extended reproduction of capital, their role was not long confined to that of a transmission belt in the circuit of realization of the social product and surplus-value created within developed countries. They rapidly became sources of surplus-value themselves, a reserve of wealth draining towards the developed countries. For these nominally equivalent exchanges, whose mechanism we have just described, still turned out actually to be very lucrative, with the end result that, to the extent that the advanced capitalist country secured new markets, the two apparently contradictory aims of high rates of domestic extended reproduction and good terms of trade were attained together.

We also believe that this second role is the most important for capitalism in the advanced countries. For quite some time already, no *new* pre-capitalist region has been opened up to the world capitalist system, and the old ones' integration – however flexible this term may be made in terms of duration – must either be considered to be definitively completed, or to be suspended, frozen, since the structures have not been significantly transformed for a long time, with the two worlds firmly installed in fixed bipolar relations. Nevertheless, despite the absence, for a long time, of this catalyst, the realization of the social product in industrial countries is no more difficult – quite the contrary – than at the time when 'integrations' were going on, while the accumulation of capital is developing at incomparably greater rates than during the preceding period, that of the so-to-speak horizontal extension of the system.[71]

70. This is the real dynamic. Not a confrontation between the two situations: before and after the *displacement*, on the basis of the same initial facts, but a change in the facts themselves, caused by the *displacement* as such.

71. Henri Denis, in the article quoted above, sees 'decolonisation' as a new wave of opening up new markets. Elsewhere, he explains that in the case of the United States in the nineteenth century, the 'new market' derived from distribution of the land to the immigrants and the development of this land. This argument inspires two comments:

Continued on page 370

It seems that the extensive expansion of production by integration of the periphery and diffusion of growth was, over a certain length of time, bit by bit replaced by intensive expansion within the centre by segregation of the periphery and extraction of its substance.

The centre then seems quite capable, at least provisionally, of resolving its problems both directly, because the exploitation of the periphery affords it a level of well-being that stabilises it politically, and indirectly, because the continuous growth of wages and resultant expansion of the home market, made possible by this foreign exploitation, is an incentive to overtrading, and thus an economically equilibrating stimulant, and apparently a much more effective one than the previous overseas expansion.

(3) The exogenous growth of wages

We have already studied the effect of wage variations on the realisation of the product in the first part of this chapter. This was in the context of our analysis of the effects on the equilibrium between supply and demand of changes in the relative weight of each of the components of the value of output. There we were dealing with a direct and objective effect; a simple mathematical relationship. Since wages represent a fixed revenue, *prior* to the sale of output, any relative increase in their size compared to and at the expense of profit of enterprise must reduce the gap between the selling price of output of one period and the purchasing power created during this period, and have a positive effect on realization.

But this effect – like any modification of the composition of the value of output – is limited by the fact that profit of enterprise can never fall to zero. In this context, then, a residual disequilibrium is unavoidable.

This does not apply to this new approach to the question. Here we are concerned with the *indirect* effect of wage-increases on realization, through their effects on the subjective motivations and the overtrading which they may encourage. This effect is less automatic and perhaps less certain. But it is unlimited. Depending on circumstances, overdraft investments may even overcompensate for the excess of supply. There is nothing materially preventing this.

71. Continued from page 369

(i) there was no major shift in the trade balance between developed and underdeveloped countries at the time of decolonisation, which could express a renewal of the process of 'integration': (ii) decolonisation is a relatively recent event, whereas occupation of the land in America was completed more than a century ago. It is hard to imagine that, over this long interval, American capitalism was only digesting the effects of the immigrants' 'long march'.

There is a second difference between the two mechanisms: while the first is set in motion by any variations in wages, however unintentional or accidental they may be, the second can only work if the variation can be foreseen. It is only those variations which result from a more or less long-run pre-determined tendency – notably the semi-institutionalised rises which have already been occurring in the most advanced capitalist countries for quite a while, especially since the Second World War – which can be taken into account when calculating the profitability of investment projects.

The same can be said of all other variations of supply and demand – with or without any change in the composition of the value of the product – which we studied before tackling *overtrading*. Each of these variations has a direct effect under any circumstance; it only acts as an *incentive* to overtrading under special circumstances, mainly when it is sufficiently clear and predictable as to be anticipated by businessmen.

In this way, a surplus on the trade balance or a budget deficit, whether forecast or not, have a direct effect on equilibrium; here their effect is strictly proportional to their volume. But if, on top of this, they were predicted and taken into account by entrepreneurs, they also have an effect in this way, and on this level a multiplier comes into play which can make the secondary effect considerably exceed the primary effect in magnitude.

But nothing is so important as the variations of wages, in both theory and practice.

1. On the level of theory, this relates to the main contradiction of capitalism, which derives from the fundamental contradiction between social production and private appropriation. Though capitalism is the system which relies exclusively on the market in a way in which no other system does, and though all its working parts take their cue from the market, its dynamic tends to contract this market by compressing wages.

If one could ever manage to withdraw from it and examine it from outside, capitalism really would look like a world stood on its head. In all the other modes of production, the upstream determines the downstream. First of all production takes place according to the productive forces available. Then the product is consumed according to the rules laid down for its distribution. Consumption depends on previous production. In the system of commodity relations, this dynamic is reversed. Production can only take place as a function of prior real or expected markets. Here everything is determined from downstream. Instead of the growth of production making growth of consumption possible, it is the previous growth of consumption which acts as a catalyst to production. Instead of it being the upper waters of the river which feed the lower reaches, it is – however absurd this may seem – the river-mouth which sets the flow of its source and tributaries. And what is more, the system's own peculiar laws of motion prevent any expansion of this mouth, so that the system continually tends to choke itself. Left to its own devices, capitalism starts to eat away its own support, to cut off the branch it is standing on.

The system's endogenous forces tend to reduce wages, at least relatively,[72] and any reduction of this kind endangers and blocks its growth. This blockage, in turn, destroys any future chance of raising wages.

In these conditions it is quite understandable why a wage-increase caused by exogenous factors, such as an increase resulting from institutional negotiations over the division of the fruits of foreign exploitation, should be able to break this 'vicious circle' and free the system from its own inhibitions. The effect of this on its equilibrium and growth will then be immeasurably greater than that of any other stimulant.

2. This is what has actually occurred in history. A capitalism so old and tired that it gave Lenin the impression of 'putrefaction' has begun to grow green again, and once more to develop the productive forces at rates which it had never previously attained in its first flush of youth, at the very point when real wages began to rise not only absolutely, but also relatively. To crown it all, it goes through a period of almost half a century without any real crisis.[73]

72. The number of Marxists who believe that Marx never spoke of absolute impoverishment, but only of relative impoverishment, is astonishingly large. But the texts in which this position is set out are among the most well-known. It is to be found in the *Manifesto of the Communist Party* (*Collected Works*, vol. 6, pp. 491–2), *Wage Labour and Capital* (*Selected Works*, pp. 91–2) and especially in the *Manuscript* for the Brussels conference of December 1847, on wages (*Collected Works*, vol. 6, p. 426), where Marx writes unambiguously: 'In the course of development, there is a double fall in wages:

'Firstly: relative, in proportion to the development of general wealth.

'Secondly: absolute, since the quantity of commodities which the worker receives in exchange becomes less and less.'

It is also found in Lenin, in 'Impoverishment in Capitalist Society', (*Collected Works*, vol. XVIII, p. 435), and Plekhanov in *Socialism and the Political Struggle* (*Selected Philosophical Works*, vol. I, p. 95), as well as *A Critique of our Critiques* (*Ibid.*, vol. II, pp. 549–51).

73. But long before this exceptional situation, historical reality had belied the thesis of impoverishment in its version in *absolute terms*. Despite this, Marx was not wrong,

Continued on page 373

If the term *consumer society* has any meaning, which is doubtful, it can only refer to the state of affairs which has just been described, both in its earlier negative phase – when capitalism, unable to produce without the existence of *previous consumption* and likewise unable to create the ability for such consumption without *previous production*, sinks into contradictions – as in its present phase when, putting the cart before the horse, capitalism succeeds in solving its problems by this unwonted means, if only provisionally and precariously.[74]

In the situation created since the last rises in the price of oil, there is a good contemporary illustration of the key role of wages in the dynamic of the capitalist system. For it is now apparent that these increases and the resulting fantastic gains will be illusory and turn into mere games of banking entries in Zurich, London and New York, for lack of the structures to absorb – therefore to consume – the goods and services that could be imported by the producing countries. These absorptive structures are nothing but domestic revenues, and especially an adequate level of wages, since, even if it is producer goods which are to be imported, these are in the free enterprise system related to the production of consumer goods, so that no entrepreneur will invest upstream in an industry unless there is already a pre-existing market downstream for the corresponding final product.

On the basis of the *present* incomes of the Bedouins, no businessman would import new products into the deserts of Arabia or set up factories to produce them. But without new means of production, the Bedouins' revenues cannot be raised. A socialist country, or any centrally planned country, does not share this problem. If tens of billions of dollars fell from the sky one day, it would have no difficulty in converting them into real values. On the contrary, it would profit from the frugality of its Bedouins to accelerate its accumulation by devoting as much as possible of its extra revenue to

73. *Continued from page 372*
since this really would be the system's endogenous tendency, if the exogenous factors which we have mentioned – exploitation of the periphery and trade union struggle – did not exist. Kautsky put this question very clearly: 'Socialists are all agreed that the capitalist manner of production when unhindered has as a result an increase of physical misery. They are also agreed that in present society the organisation of the laboring class and the capture of governmental powers has attained a height where it is able to somewhat ameliorate this misery.' (*The Social Revolution*, p. 38.)

74. It was Henri Denis who coined the expression 'prior outlets', which I have used several times in this work, in a sense which does not, I believe, differ greatly from his.

purchasing and installing capital goods: importing machinery to construct blast furnaces, with which to produce iron, from which to manufacture sheet steel, with which to produce refrigerators or washing machines in ten or twenty years' time.

Over this period these intermediate operations would have turned the Bedouins into industrial wage workers, with sufficient revenues to consume these refrigerators or washing machines.

Rosa Luxemburg called this closed-circuit expansion of Department I a merry-go-round running empty. Following her, Samir Amin called it a 'carousel'. In his eyes capitalists are too sensible to behave in such a way. They would prefer to increase wages.[75] But the fact that the USSR behaved in exactly this way to build up the industrial base of its economy proves that this 'carousel' does not necessarily run empty. If under capitalism this process appears like a merry-go-round running empty, this is because each capital is taken separately and has no interest in joining in. But if an external force, some kind of incentive – these have arisen in certain historical circumstances – forced them all to join in, then each would find himself better off at the end of the day than before.

In the case of the oil-producing countries, as we have described it above, this is obvious. If something could force the few Arab capitalists to do on their own account what a planned state would have done in the same circumstances, everything would turn out all

75. cf. *L'Echange Inégal et la Loi de la Valeur*. The writer believes that he is being original, but is only reformulating an old Marxist position which we have already examined in Chapters 3 and 4, when we studied the positions of Lenin, Rosa Luxemburg, etc., on the question. This is the contradiction between a rising organic composition of capital and the stagnation of final consumption. It can be summarised as follows: The increasing productivity of labour in the course of extended reproduction goes along with a rising organic composition of capital, in relation to which it is defined and measured. A rise in the organic composition means an increase in the quantity of means of production set to work by a given quantity of living labour.

So there are two alternatives; either the consumption of these living workers stays constant, or it increases at the same rate as the growth of means of production. In the first case, Department I – production of means of production – must develop in a closed circuit alongside a stagnant Department II – production of means of consumption. This would be Tugan Baranovski's merry-go-round, and is therefore ruled out. (The writer does not tell us why. He doubtless considers that the combined force of such a striking image as a merry-go-round and such a heterodox man as Tugan Baranovski is enough.)

So we are only left with the second possibility (and here the writer differs from orthodox Marxism, which denied capitalism's ability to take this path) to allow the system to work: a parallel growth of consumption, and therefore wage-increases.

Thus, the growth of productivity determines the growth of wages, and the latter are not exogenous. Q.E.D.

right and in twenty or thirty years' time they would find themselves a lot better off, as capitalists, and without any planning, than if they had merely let their petrodollars wander from one financial centre to the next.[76]

But though this is possible in theory it is improbable (though not impossible) in practice, and it is infinitely easier to make capitalism work by means of a 'previous' extension of the market resulting from a rise in wages. This still does not allow us to conclude with Samir Amin that this rise is 'endogenous'[77]

For while a capitalist is incapable of investing without a rise in wages, he is even less capable of increasing wages with the sole aim of making his investments rational. To show, as Samir Amin does, that without these increases the industrial countries would not have been able to increase their growth and surmount their contradictions does not prove that these increases flowed automatically from the system's internal logic. This logic also contains the end of the system's career, and in this light the system could just as well have perished. Consequently these increases can perfectly well be exogenous and adventitious, the conjunction of trade union struggle which in a sense saved the system from itself, as we have already had occasion to remark, and of a transposition of its contradictions from the national level to the world level.[78]

76. Which is what some of the oil-producing countries – precisely those that are the least planned – seem to have done, with the result that the price rise will most probably remain merely formal and cost nothing to the consuming countries as a whole, nor benefit the Arab countries in question. The latter will continue to receive in real terms only the extraction costs – some 10 to 20 cents per barrel – plus a tiny extra proportion of the selling price, received in the form of arms or a few petrol tankers, and maybe some refineries set up here and there. They will never receive the rest of the price, for lack of the ability to consume it.

So we see that these countries, after having long been too poor to be able to sell their oil at a proper price, now that they have had the good fortune to manage to unite to impose this price nominally, are too poor to collect it in real terms.

Of course not all Arab countries are in the same position. Here we are mainly thinking of countries like Saudi Arabia and Kuwait. On the other hand, countries such as Algeria, Iraq and even Libya are in a position to *materialise* at least a greater or lesser part of their receipts.

77. Unless the meaning of the term is broadened to include the industrial and political organisation of the working class in the countries of the centre, state intervention, imperialist transfers, etc. – but then everything is endogenous, since everything is ultimately based on a socio-economic infrastructure.

78. By endowing the system with this 'endogenous' unblocking factor, Samir Amin does not realize that he is making the capitalist system immortal.

Faced with the same dilemma – deadlock of the system or a rise in wages – classical

Continued on page 376

It is in this way that the *reprieve* of this apparent second childhood of capitalism in the metropolis reaches it limit. Otherwise if we isolate the centre by basing its prodigious development of these last few decades on its own dynamic, and if we are to believe Marx that 'no social order is ever destroyed before all the productive forces for which it is sufficient have been developed', we would envisage neither decline nor any limit.

It is only if we agree to see the organic unity of the world system with its class-nations in the centre and its nations divided into classes on the periphery that the appearance of wealth and growth is dissipated – and decline and limits of the whole become visible.

(4) Depreciation of the currency

A historical summary It is often said that devaluations are a relatively modern phenomenon, inaugurated during and above all after the First World War. It is true that 1914 sealed a period of almost a century of monetary stability, which is a comparatively long period, but that is all. If one goes back before the nineteenth century, monetary manipulations re-emerge.

Although the English pound, after the Napoleonic Wars and their accompanying inconvertibility, returned to its former 1552 parity, on which basis it had only lost two-thirds of its original value, the Germinal franc of 1803 was only one-hundredth of the corresponding unit of Charlemagne's time.[79]

It is nonetheless true that the rates of devaluation were very different before and after this nineteenth century interval. In fourteen years, 1914–28, the Germinal franc developed into the

78. *Continued from page 375*
Marxism expected deadlock. Capitalism can neither develop independently of the market for consumer goods, nor expand this market by increasing wages. It was on this *insurmountable* contradiction that Marxism ultimately based the inevitability of its destruction. If this analysis were false, if, as Samir Amin states, there were such a direct, structural, endogenous and positive link between rises in productivity and wage increases, it would be Beaulieu, Bastiat, Carey and all the proponents of pre-established harmonies and of the convergence of class interests in the long run who would be right, not Marx, who for his part believed that rises in productivity and the growth of the productive forces tended to lower wages.

79. 4.5 grams of pure silver instead of a pound of 436 grams, or 0.29033 grams of pure gold instead of ± 29 grams.

On the basis of a parity calculated at the free market price of gold, and ignoring a mere change of denomination in 1959, it turns out that the ratio of the value of the French currency today to that of 794 is approximately 1:80,000. The ratio of the current British pound to the original pre-1300 unit is 1:66. Over time the French currency has lost value about 1200 times as quickly as the British.

Poincaré franc, which was worth only one-fifth as much as the former; and in 46 years this became the centime of today's new franc. This 'centime' represents only 1/160th of the Poincaré and 1/800th of the Germinal franc. For the sake of comparison, it took ten centuries for Charlemagne's Livre to become the Germinal franc which was worth one-hundredth as much.

Though of a different order of magnitude, the English rates also accelerated after the First World War. After Peel's Act of 1821, the pound returned to its sixteenth century parity, i.e. £3 2*s* for 11 oz, 2 dwt of fine silver or about 8 grams of gold per £1 – a third of its original parity. This rate was maintained until the 1931 devaluation. Today on the free market for gold, only 43 years later, £1 is worth rather less than half a gram of gold, or 16 times less.

But apart from the comparison of average rates, there are other differences between the two periods. In the earlier period devaluations, or what took their place in the system of metallic currencies of the period, that is to say increases in the proportion of alloys or 'revaluation' of the coins in relation to the unit of account, only interrupted periods of stability long enough to prevent the phenomenon of depreciation from being imprinted in society's collective memory, and becoming something to be expected.

It took three centuries before Philip I touched Charlemagne's Livre, calling a weight of eight ounces a 'livre'; another century for this 'livre' to change to 84 grams; and a further century and a half for it to fall from 84 to 60. In ten centuries there were perhaps 10 'devaluations' in France. Between 1928 and 1974, there have been 12.[80]

Since a modification in the rate of exchange between money and other commodities is not such a sudden and instantaneous phenomenon as a modification in its parity with the metal standard, such frequent changes in the latter make the former almost perfectly continuous.

Whereas in the earlier period several generations might pass before there was any talk of changing the value of money, nowadays these changes have become one of its normal characteristics, something which goes without saying and features in all forecasts, even the most short-term.

80. William Lowndes gives a longer series of monetary manipulations in England since the time of Edward III, but there cannot have been more than ten or so real major devaluations (*A Report containing an Essay for the Amendments of the Silver Coins*, pp. 56–7.)

This characteristic of continuity increases once the currency ceases to be convertible and, with the fixed parity abolished, the metal is allowed to float. It is quite clear that the market fluctuations which determine the value of money are by their very nature continuous, whereas the princely manipulations of the old coinage were necessarily discontinuous.

The only case in which there could be continuous variations in the earlier period, was when the conditions of production of the precious metals themselves changed, especially through the discovery of new geological veins. But the effects of such changes, however spread out they might be, only lasted for a definite length of time.

Finally, what prevents us from taking this pre-nineteenth century period as a precedent, is the fact that capitalist relations of production were not developed at that time, and even simple commodity relations were not dominant. But the problem that we are studying – the realization of the product – and which has as one of its variables the intrinsic value of money, is a problem of commodity economies in general and capitalist economies in particular.[81]

The mobilising effect These pre-capitalist manipulations of the currency had as their main aim to procure resources for the prince. However, several authors had already pointed out a second effect, beneficial for economic activity.[82] There were even some cases – over relatively short periods and without the systematic character which the same phenomenon has today – in which one could speak of a real flight from money. This occurred especially after several periods of short-lived introduction of an inconvertible paper currency, with a headlong growth of circulation.

This was the case with the paper-money of Law's bank, and with the French *assignâts*.[83] This was also the case in the United States in the 1810s, on which Thomas Jefferson wrote:

81. If this were not the case, it would be possible, in the matter of devaluations, to go much further back. To refer, for example, to Solon, who increased the nominal value of metal coins, or the devaluation of 663 in Rome, where Livius Drufus not only increased the nominal value of metal coins by one-eighth, but at the same time reduced the grade of the alloy by as much; or even that of the Punic wars (referred to by Adam Smith), when the grade of the Roman copper *as* was successively reduced from twelve ounces to half an ounce, or that of the Egyptian drachma under the Ptolemys etc.

82. cf., for example, David Hume, *Writings on Economics*, pp. 92ff.

83. For the case of Law, cf. an excellent account in J. Steuart, *An Inquiry into the Principles of Political Economy*, vol. II, pp. 266ff.

We are encumbered with banknotes whose depreciation is raising the nominal price of everything ... and there are now, in all likelihood, around one hundred banks with capital amounting to $100 million, authorised by law to issue up to three times this value in notes. ... Since our resources have been used up by the war ... [the banks] have all suspended cash payments, while promising to resume them later .... In the meantime, since we have no other means of exchange, we must needs accept these notes, but we keep them in our hands for as short a time as possible.[84]

It is remarkable that such a man as Say, whose system was entirely based on the idea of inevitable full employment and a structural equilibrium between supply and demand, was still able to accept the existence of a phenomenon so against his principles as stimulation of production and employment by deterioration of the currency. In passages that would not be disavowed by Malthus, Sismondi, Proudhon, or Silvio Gesell, he explains to us that, just as one will use any means to sell perishable produce,

if the national money be deteriorated, it becomes an object to get rid of it in any way, and exchange it for commodities. This was one of the causes of the prodigious depreciation of the French *assignâts*. Everybody was anxious to find some employment for a paper currency, whose value was hourly evaporating; it was only taken to be re-invested immediately, and one might have supposed it burnt the fingers it passed through. On that occasion, men plunged into commerce, of which they were utterly ignorant, manufactures were estasblished, homes repaired and furnished ....[85]

In an attempt at generalisation, he passed the same judgement on Law's issues, and even on the inconvertibility of the British pound during the Napoleonic wars:

It has also been possible to observe, in the early period of all the paper currencies, a rapidity of circulation which was very favourable to industrial activity. The start of Law's system, during the Regency, was scintillating; the same could be said of the first period of *assignâts* in the French revolution; and agriculture, manufacturing and trade developed very rapidly during the years following the suspension of convertibility to gold by the Bank of England.[86].

For the author of the Law of Markets to sing the praises of such a phenomenon, it really must have been difficult to challenge or deny.

84. Letter to J.-B. Say, 1815.
85. *Treatise on Political Economy*, vol. I, p. 187.
86. Translated from the French. cf. *Ibid.*, vol. I, p. 482. During the period of inconvertibility, the pound had fallen from 24 to 16–17 francs.

Nonetheless, Ricardo succeeded in remaining faithful right to the end to the sacrosanct principles of classicism by denying the evidence. When the restoration of the convertibility of the pound at the old rate made prices collapse catastrophically from an index number of 100 in 1814 to 47 in 1830, and plunged England into a deep depression, Ricardo was unshakeable and continued as almost the only defender of monetary orthodoxy.

To find a repeat performance of such obstinacy nowadays, one has to consider extreme cases: Jacques Rueff for example, who goes around repeating incessantly that, since excess consumption is an obstacle to saving and investment, the inflation corresponding to this excess consumption is likewise an obstacle to investment; or Giscard d'Estaing, who, asked on 15 November 1970, 'Is growth possible without inflation?', expressed the greatest astonishment that such a question could be asked. For his part, he had never imagined that any one could conceive inflation to be a growth factor to the slightest extent.[87]

Nevertheless, judging by the internal consistency of their theories, it must be admitted that Ricardo and Rueff are on stronger ground than J.–B. Say. For it is illegitimate to maintain simultaneously that capitalism is a rational system and to state that it can only be made to work by smashing windows to provide work for glaziers.[88]

But alongside those who prefer price stability (because in their eyes it promotes more growth than does inflation) and those who accept inflation as a necessary evil, the price of growth in other words, there are some who reject inflation, even if it is the only road to growth. Thus Wormser, the Governor of the Bank of France, in an astonishing statement in May 1974, dramatically invites us to choose between well-being and price stability.[89]

It is difficult to find anything more absurd: (i) since alternatives must exist on the same level, price stability, in Wormser's view, must be as much of an end in itself as well-being; (ii) considered in this way as the second part of an alternative, whose first part is well-being, price stability must necessarily be associated with the opposite of

87. Reading this interview, one expects the journalist at any moment to ask him whether he has ever heard of a certain Keynes and his supporters.

To be fair we should point out that Keynes himself depicted the effects of inflation in the most dismal terms in *The Economic Consequences of the Peace*. But this was in 1920.

88. Or burying old bottles filled with bank notes at suitable depths to create opportunities for investment by mining firms, as Keynes suggested to make fun of the 'well-tried principles of *laissez-faire*' (*General Theory*, p. 129).

89. See *Figaro*, 25–26 May 1974.

well-being. What he is really offering is a choice between well-being with inflation, or price stability without well-being; (iii) he seems convinced that, if it is proven that well-being and price stability are incompatible, we would unhesitatingly choose price stability, even without well-being: poor and sober-minded, rather than rich and dissipated.

This would still be comprehensible if Wormser meant short-lived and illusory well-being, or well-being for a minority, following the harmful redistribution of revenues which inflation can engender. But he speaks of well-being without any restrictions, and must therefore be referring to real, general and lasting well-being. Given these conditions, and since it is not a question of the salvation of our souls, it would be a vice to choose non-well-being solely in order to have price stability.[90]

If money, as Proudhon says, is not the key, but the 'lock' of trade, it should be quite easy to see how and why its depreciation frees trade and tends to prevent crises. If money, as Marx says, is a kind of anti-commodity, it is not surprising that the process of its annihilation has a positive effect as the negation of a negation. If the passage from commodity to money is an elevation from the particular to the general, a 'trans-substantiation' of capitalist wealth, it is natural that putting money in question, desanctifying it, should amount to an elevation of the profane world of commodities. If the demand for money is nothing other than the supply of commodities, a reduction in the former amounts necessarily to a reabsorption of the latter. If, as Silvio Gesell says, money has too many qualities to serve as a vehicle of circulation, its debasement can precisely enable it to fulfil its role. If bad money chases out the good, as stated by Gresham's Law, money even worse than the worst commodity can realize all the commodities and disencumber our markets and warehouses.

90. What possible mysterious reason could there be for a man who was earning 100 per month last year, and who would earn 118 today if prices went up by 15%, to feel worse off than if he received 102 today with prices at their original level? This purely *aesthetic* attitude of bankers to their beautiful monetary mechanism, without any consideration of real economic effects, is somewhat disturbing.

All the same, 132 years ago, Sir Robert Peel, who was as unconditional a defender of orthodoxy as Wormser, introduced at least a note of rationality when he distinguished the short-term from the long-term: 'I admit that there are modes by which a temporary prosperity might be created ... by the issue of £1 notes, and by encouraging the Bank to make large issues of paper; but such a prosperity would be wholly delusive. It is much wiser in my opinion to abstain from the application of the stimulus.' (Quoted by T. Tooke, *An Inquiry into the Currency Principle*, p. 64).

Everything that degrades money revalues the real productive process. Just as a flight from commodities gives rise to hoarding and recession, so a flight from money accelerates realization and induces expansion. This is true not only through its direct effect on the purchases of consumer goods, but also through the dishoarding caused by its expectation. Fear of inflation compels businessmen to invest *without delay* all their liquid assets – cash and bank deposits – *even if there are signs that the market is contracting.*

For, as we have already had occasion to say, variations in the value of capital itself have much greater effects than variations in its yield. What sense is there in deferring the choice between different investments so as to choose between yields with only 1, 2, or 3% between them, or in refusing to invest for fear of not making enough profits, or indeed of not making any, if, by holding back and keeping one's money liquid, one is sure to lose 5 or 10% of its value in a few months?

But the effect of such a situation is not only to accelerate the mobilisation of liquid assets, whether directly by their owners or indirectly by borrowers in the framework of normal credit, which is restricted to transferring liquid assets (in space) from one agent to another. (We have already seen that this kind of mobilisation of already created purchasing power is not sufficient.) Such a situation also mobilises the other kind of credit, the kind that *creates* purchasing power or, equivalently, transfers purchasing power in time and thus anticipates it; it encourages overtrading.

This kind of overtrading, while only being limited like the others by full employment, is more strongly motivated than the other kinds. The other incentives to overtrade are all based on the hope of a new market, whether this be a new article, a foreign outlet, or a wage-increase. Consequently, they all involve a considerable degree of uncertainty. For it is not enough to predict overall expansion; it is also necessary to predict its specific incidence on the products of the industry in which one is involved. On the other hand, depreciation of the currency creates a universal bonus for investing, and the only thing to predict is its rate.

But there is an even more decisive difference in favour of this last factor compared with the rest. This relates to their respective limits.

Innovations, to the extent that they build up and that the production process broadens and becomes diversified, become by their very nature more localised, and their field of application contracts relatively. In the exceptional period of growth of the last 40 years, with no crises and with effective full employment, nothing in this area can compare, in its effects upon the economy as a whole, with, for example, railway construction in the last century.

As for the 'opening-up' of new pre-capitalist markets and wage-increases, these two factors, though not limited in their effects, have a limited possibility of arising. Their common source is the periphery and this source is not inexhaustible. Already the first of them, 'opening-up', can be considered as belonging to the past.

On the other hand inflation, as an *internal* cause of overtrading, and as soon as the introduction of index-linking for fixed incomes redresses distributional distortions and saves the system from resultant socio-political dangers, seems to have no limit, either in its effects or in its future. At first sight this would seem to be capitalism's ultimate weapon.

But this is only true in appearance and the limit emerges under closer examination: it is to be found in the effects of inflation on the relative positions of the metropolitan capitalist countries in international trade. This is the other side of the coin. For while there is an interest in stimulating a flight from money at home, this must at all costs not be greater than that affecting one's neighbour's currency. This flight is meant to operate in favour of one's own country's commodities; it is not meant to operate in favour of one's competitors' commodities and currencies.

On the one hand allowing prices to rise in order to stimulate domestic activity, on the other hand clamping down on price increases to preserve the overseas competitiveness of one's industries; on the one hand stoking up inflation to annul *ex post* the wage increases which one has had to concede, on the other hand fighting inflation to cut off the exodus of capital and outflow of foreign exchange; these are the two pairs of contradictory objectives between which all the capitalist countries are now separately floundering.

This outflow of capital is a result of fear of devaluation – whether officially decided upon or as a result of the introduction of exchange controls. This outflow is therefore an effect of inflation in that domestic price rises make it likely that the government will adopt one or other of these measures – devaluation or exchange controls, or even both.

The contradiction here is that devaluation itself promotes an inflow of foreign exchange, but the expectation of devaluation promotes their outflow. But regular recourse to devaluation ends up by making its use objectively probable as soon as the slightest deficit balance appears. The resulting outflow of capital will increase the deficit and eventually verify the predictions by making a devaluation unavoidable.[91]

It should be noted that when there is a flight from the domestic currency, foreign currencies are a much safer refuge than domestic commodities. The 'over-value' of foreign currencies immediately covers the whole 'under-value' of domestic currency, while this coverage is slower and less certain in the case of conversion of wealth into domestic commodities. Once again the two effects of inflation are contradictory. Conversion into commodities is desirable; conversion into foreign currency is disastrous. One is constantly buffeted between what one hopes for and what one fears, both of which are simultaneous effects of the same cause or of the same measure taken to combat this cause.

Cost-push inflation In the situation described above, that of modern capitalism, it can be seen that the two last causes of overtrading, wage increases and the devaluation of currencies, are closely intermeshed. In this respect it is true that inflation generally follows wage increases, if only in part. But it does not follow from this that inflation is the *inevitable* result of these increases. On the contrary, with metallic or convertible money, this is an *impossible* result, and Marx, working on these assumptions, had good reason to stress this point in his refutation of Proudhon.

Under these assumptions, it is indeed impossible for a truly general rise in wages, which therefore also applies to the gold mines, to make *all* prices rise, since it will also have made their standard measure rise.

91. This is what happened after May 1968 in France. The expectation of a devaluation of the franc, reinforced at that particular time by expectation of a revaluation of the Deutschmark, led to an outflow of liquid capital which eventually made devaluation necessary, although the wage increases ceded in the Grenelle agreement were far from having caused a deficit on the foreign balance serious enough to require such a measure.

'Fear of currency depreciation and exchange restrictions often indeed tend to stimulate private capital flows from deficit countries to surplus countries, and to aggravate, rather than cushion, the impact of current account imbalance.' (Triffin, *Gold and the Dollar Crisis*, p. 33).

The fear which Triffin refers to is not accidental. It is based to a great extent on precedent. Thus in France, if this fear is so to speak endemic, this is because, for reasons relating to a degree of backwardness in industrial development, strictly monetarist views (a sort of 'money-box syndrome') inform the traditions of the highest financial authorities – the Ministry of Finance and the Bank of France. It seems as if these authorities, conditioned by the fear of a loss of reserves, will devalue at the drop of a hat. Dealers take this into account and, at the slightest fall in reserves, even if their new, lower level is in absolute terms more than ample, they speculate on a devaluation. By speculating on it, they create the conditions which justify it.

Consequently, in the conditions assumed by Marx and Ricardo, a general rise in wages comes out of profits, while individual prices will vary in both directions according to the organic compositions of each industry, and the general price index will not rise.

Since Marx's time, two new conditions, which fundamentally change the theorem's data, have been introduced by historical reality:

1. Since gold mines are generally located in underdeveloped countries, they have not been hit by the general rise in wages in advanced countries. By also turning a national paper currency – first the pound, then later the dollar – into international money and linking it to gold, it has been possible to restrict the monetary 'consumption' of gold, by enough to avoid the creation of a rent in the gold-mining sector, which would have cancelled out the effect of its low wages. In this way, the increased productivity of the mines remaining in use has been able to compensate for the rise in the price of their material inputs and maintain a low cost of production corresponding to their wages.

2. Unofficially before 1971, and officially since that date, the capitalist world has seen the introduction, for the first time in its history, of a system of universal inconvertibility. Before 1971 this was the result of a more or less voluntary abstention by the central banks of the major industrial countries from converting their dollars – initially because they still needed to fill up with dollars, later on because they gave in to political pressure from the United States, and because it was against their own interests to destabilise their debtor. After August 1971, this system was imposed by the open proclamation of an embargo which made all currencies nominal at a stroke. These two facts, the first partially and the second completely, have made possible what was unthinkable for Marx and Ricardo: a simultaneous rise in wages and profits, or rather a rise in wages without any fall in profits. This possibility can best be illustrated by the traditional system of Sraffa's industry-equations:

$$
\begin{aligned}
(A_a p_a + B_a p_b + \ldots + K_a)\,(1 + r) + L_a w_a &= A p_a \\
(A_b p_a + B_b p_b + \ldots + K_b)\,(1 + r) + L_b w_b &= B p_b \\
&\vdots \\
(A_k p_a + B_k p_b + \ldots + K_k)\,(1 + r) + L_k w_k &= K
\end{aligned}
$$

A_a, $A_b, \ldots, A_k$ represent the quantities of A consumed in the production of the industries $a, b, \ldots, k$; B_a, $B_b, \ldots, B_k$ represent the quantities of B consumed in the production of the same industries, etc. $A, B, \ldots, K$ are the total quantities produced in industries $a, b, \ldots, k$; $L_a, L_b, \ldots, L_k$ represent the quantities of labour expended in $a, b, \ldots, k$; $w_a, w_b, \ldots, w_k$ represent the wages of one unit of L in $a, b, \ldots, k$; $p_a, p_b, \ldots, p_j$ represent the prices of one unit of $A, B, \ldots, J$.

K is the money-commodity. Consequently, all the *w*s and all the *p*s represent a certain quantity of physical units of K; r is the general rate of profit.

We know that, when the currency is convertible, and when all wages vary together in the same direction, there is no problem. Wages being given, we have k equations and k unknowns ($k - 1$ prices, plus r). Our system is perfectly determined, and any variation of wages will give rise to an inverse variation of the rate of profit, r.

If either one of these two conditions is not fulfilled, that is to say in either one of the two cases mentioned above, matters change considerably, and wages and profits cease to be decreasing functions of each other.

First case. Convertible currency, but production costs of gold kept low by the means indicated above

What has to be proved is that an increase of any w except w_k is compatible with an increase of r, or, *a fortiori*, a constant r.

If the productivity of industry k increases exactly fast enough to compensate for the increased cost of its inputs due to wage rises in other industries, then K becomes an endogenous (dependent) variable, and joins the other unknowns. As a result we will have, in this case, $k + 1$ unknowns for k equations.

This can be put another way. The effect of the extra-economic manipulations which we have introduced will be completely to dissociate the costs of industry k from prices and from the costs of other branches. In this case the production conditions of this branch become immaterial, and the corresponding equation becomes superfluous. Our system will now only have j equations:

$$\begin{aligned}(A_a p_a + B_a p_b + \ldots + K_a)\,(1 + r) + L_a w_a &= A p_a \\ (A_b p_a + B_b p_b + \ldots + K_b)\,(1 + r) + L_b w_b &= B p_b \\ &\vdots \\ (A_j p_a + B_j p_b + \ldots + K_j)\,(1 + r) + L_j w_j &= J p_j\end{aligned}$$

Here we have one less equation ($j = k - 1$) for the same number of unknowns ($j + 1 = k$). The result is the same: in both cases, we are obliged to take one of the unknowns as given, and this therefore allows us to take the rate of profit, r, as given.

In other words, this makes it possible to fix r *prior* to prices, which makes r just as exogenous as wages, and consequently independent of wages.

Second case. Universal inconvertibility
Here we have to show that a rise in any w, *including* w_k, is compatible with a rise in r or a constant r.

Since all prices are nominal, gold itself becomes an ordinary commodity in this system, and has a price. In other words, $p_a, p_b, \ldots,$ etc., cease to represent a certain number of units of k, and now represent arbitrary external objects, francs, dollars, or pounds. They thus become abstract numbers. It follows that a new unknown, p_k, has been introduced:

$$\begin{aligned}
(A_a p_a + B_a p_b + \ldots + K_a p_k)\ (1 + r) + L_a w_a &= A p_a \\
(A_b p_a + B_b p_b + \ldots + K_b p_k)\ (1 + r) + L_b w_b &= B p_b \\
&\vdots \\
(A_k p_a + B_k p_b + \ldots + K_k p_k)\ (1 + r) + L_k w_k &= K p_k
\end{aligned}$$

and with wages still taken as given, we have $k + 1$ unknowns for k equations.

As in the first case, the only way to escape from this is to make r independent of prices and exogenous, thus independent of wages also.

In both cases this means that (i) relative prices – relations between commodities within the system – become absolute prices – relations of the system's commodities to something determined outside the system – gold itself in the first case, an arbitrary denomination in the second; (ii) capitalists are free to 'mark up', that is to add on to their production costs, as affected by wage increases which they have had to concede, their normal rate of profit, or any rate of profit, and determine prices in this way; thus they can pass any wage increase, at least the part of this increase which exceeds any accompanying rise in productivity, on to *absolute* prices (the general price level).

This is what happens today in reality, where we have archetypal cost-push inflation. It is pointless to deny that wage increases lie at the bottom of the process, but it is important to stress that these rises do not *per se* lead inevitably to inflation. What does lead to it is the fact that capitalists have granted themselves the power to make these rises wholly or partly nominal *post factum*, therefore cancelling them out in real terms. It is only to the extent that these rises turn from real into nominal, that they lead to inflation. To the extent to which they stay real, they are taken either out of growth of productivity or out of the rate of profit or both.

However this may be, in this way also the contemporary capitalist system creates a double stimulant of economic activity: firstly, an expansion of the market for consumer goods due to the residual increase in real wages (after subtraction of the rate of inflation), secondly an expansion of the market for producer goods through overtrading, itself a result of this inflation.

This second, very important effect, results in a tendency for the system's resistance to wage claims to weaken. This tendency in turn promotes the restarting of the process.[92]

However all this, once again, finds its own limit in that of the product of foreign exploitation and its vicissitudes. Thus examination of variations in the price index and wage rates in France shows that between January 1969 and January 1973, the former was growing at 5.5 to 6.5% annually, and the latter at 8 to 12% annually. This represents a gain in real wages of 2.5 to 5% per year. In 1973 this gain was 6.8%.

But, in 1974, the rate of growth of real wages slowed down markedly. The curves of prices and wages began to rise almost parallel to each other.[93] Everything suggests that this slowdown was due to the considerable increase in the prices of imported raw materials during 1973 and the first three months of 1974, taking into account the time-lag between rises in the fob prices of raw materials and the manufacture and retail sale of the finished product.

With the recent rise in the price of oil, continued growth of nominal wages at a rate faster than that of the retail price index (or even growth at the same rate to preserve the *status quo*) has been put in doubt. But if wages do not grow faster than prices, extensive extended reproduction – the only kind compatible with the motivations of overtrading, and thus relatively easier for the system – cannot be maintained. This is a critical limit. Since the system is incapable of going further and moving into intensive extended reproduction (growth of Department I in a closed circuit, on the basis of a stagnant

92. It is this second effect which appears to inspire Samir Amin's thesis which we discussed earlier. Over the last period, capitalism actually has raised wages, and this has allowed it to resolve its contradictions and develop intensively. Samir Amin does not see that this has only been possible at the centre because particular, conjunctural, 'exogenous' circumstances have allowed this increase to take place without any fall in the rate of profit.

For an interpretation different from our own of the same phenomenon, the simultaneous growth of wages and profits, see the important article by Paul Fabra, 'L'Inflation et la société de consommation', which appeared in *Le Monde* on 26 June 1969.

93. See the statistics and graph published in *Le Monde* on 25 June 1974.

Department II), which would contradict its own rationality, there is collapse and crisis.

This has been well captured by the Americans in their description of the situation resulting from the recent oil price increases: 'unmanageable'.

All the system's contradictions which we have seen above are reflected in attempts by economists to analyse inflation and in the measures adopted by those in charge of fighting it.

They are happy to talk of cost-push inflation in order to make the workers responsible for it, but they take refuge in neoclassical dogmas about the determination of prices by the level of demand, as soon as non-wage costs are in question. On the pretext of reducing the pressure of demand by draining off part of the money supply, they take measures which increase these costs even further: for example, rises in the interest rate, the price of energy, the prices of public services, transport, etc.

These last increases are the ultimate absurdity; prices are increased in order to combat price increases. Still, this is an inevitable logical consequence. If consumption is to be squeezed, prices must be increased, not decreased. Thus when the old rate of VAT was restored in France – it had been reduced in 1973 on certain basic necessities – it was explained that the fall in prices resulting from the reduction of VAT was stimulating demand and feeding inflation!

In fact, 'cost-push inflation' can only have any meaning if an effect is taken to be a cause. Inflation was originally defined as a situation in which the creation of fictive purchasing power meant that demand exceeded supply at the existing prices of production (prices which remunerate the factors at the prevailing rates). Price increases are only a result of inflation; they re-establish equilibrium by annulling the inflation. It follows that if prices rise for a different reason, deriving from production conditions – a fall in productivity, a rise in the cost of energy, raw materials, etc., i.e. in general a fall in output for the same level of input or, to put it another way, a rise in the cost of inputs for the same level of output – demand and thus inflation are irrelevant. 'Cost-push inflation' is, strictly speaking, a contradiction in terms.

The attempt to *de*flate demand, although it is recognized that it is costs which have *in*flated, is the height of absurdity. It can be explained objectively by the fact that the system's contradictions are made more serious by the attempt to retain the market's basic determining role while 'overdetermining' the market by additional governmental measures; subjectively, by the basic marginalist principle of downstream price formation by variations in demand, a principle which still underlies official economic thinking and which has the result that when an autonomous cause of price rises appears upstream, such as the unilaterally-fixed price of oil – as accepted and even invoked by the same economists – one is trapped in the antinomy which separates these two kinds of determination.

The government then has recourse to measures dictated by the most simplistic quantitativism, which have the opposite effect to that required, not only on costs but also, indirectly, on demand itself. Haunted by the fear of a mass of money which must be reduced whatever the cost, the government decides for example to levy emergency supertaxes on firms, in order to pump out part of their liquid assets, or decrees a ceiling on dividends in order not to let more liquid assets be thrown into circulation. Then the stock exchange collapses, with savers turning away and businesses unable to make any new issues, and in this way one method of immobilising part of disposable money is lost.

The government increases the rate of interest charged to companies, still in the hope of making prices fall by reducing the supply of (bank) money. Companies quickly pass this surcharge on in prices. The result is that these rise instead of falling.

The government also refuses to increase the rate paid on saving-bank deposits on the same pretext as the one used to limit dividends, that is, to reduce the circulation of money, and here the policies become totally absurd. For – by interest or by principal – circulation can only be increased through the workings of savings-banks if withdrawals exceed deposits. But a rise in the interest rate is of course an incentive to deposit money, not to withdraw it!

Thus the holders of liquid assets, put off by these variations in prices on the stock exchange, limitations on dividends and rates of interest below even the rate of erosion of money, are left with only one way to use their money — to spend it, if not on immediate consumption goods, then at least on durable goods. This increases effective demand instead of squeezing it, if the source of the problem is indeed excessive demand.

But apart from all our other arguments above, which show that 'cost-push inflation' has nothing to do with the state of demand, there can never be excess demand except compared to the supply facing it. This means that insufficient supply, or, equivalently, insufficient output, is exactly the same thing as excess demand and, consequently, equilibrium can be reestablished equally well by squeezing demand or by stepping up supply.

But the measures we have mentioned – credit squeezes, high

interest rates, restrictions on dividend payments – together with their immediate effect, which is that firms' sources of finance dry up, lead ultimately to a fall in production, which is exactly equivalent to a relative rise in demand and leads to an aggravation of the assumed disequilibrium.

There is however no hesitation in declaring that a certain fall in the rate of growth would be acceptable, or even desirable, as the price of the struggle against inflation. Thus, in making this struggle the first priority, the French prime minister did not hesitate recently to declare that it would be fought to the finish, even if some problems should arise on the employment side. Since the level of employment makes the level of production vary directly, and with it the potential for consumption and general well-being, while prices are really only units of account, distribution vectors, there is no greater condemnation of the system than to say that one is compelled to reduce its overall yield for want of the ability to master its internal mechanisms, that social wealth has to be held back for want of the ability to carry on the accountancy of its distribution, reducing the size of the cake for want of a suitable knife to divide it properly.

But apart from these considerations, even if one accepts the official picture that purchasing power is dangerously outstripping the value of commodities produced, there is still some difficulty in grasping how it is hoped to reduce the gap between the two by cutting production back even further or reducing its rate of growth; how equilibrium can be re-established by replacing the purchasing power distributed in the form of wages to people who are in work and producing, by purchasing power distributed in the form of benefits to the unemployed who produce nothing.

It is clear that, to pay for the considerable increase in the price of imported oil, *more* work and production is needed, not less – a thirteenth month, in the phrase of a French government spokesman. Is it surprising that, in a 'topsy-turvy world', a series of measures intended to make the French work one month extra should end up making them work one month less than before?

When he was only the Minister of the Economy and Finance, in 1973, Giscard d'Estaing declared, in a televised discussion, that there is one thing the government will never do – instigate deflation; except, he added after a pause for thought, in the case of a grave imbalance in the nation's foreign accounts.

It must be accepted that this major imbalance, caused by the steep rise in the price of oil, is what caused this drastic turn-around. This brings us back to the constant aim which, as we have seen on several occasions in the course of this work, determines the behaviour of firms and nations in the capitalist mode of production: to sell more than one buys, to export more than one imports. Anything can be accepted, except a deficit on international transactions. The point is not so much the overall settlements balance, which has been far from bad for OECD countries as a whole. On 30 June 1974, the reserves of the US, the Federal Republic of Germany, Switzerland, Canada, Spain and Portugal were slightly higher than on 30 June 1973 and, for some of these countries, substantially higher than at the end of 1970. The reserves of Italy, the UK and Australia fell very slightly between 1973 and 1974, while Italy's were around the 1970 level and those of the other two were very substantially higher. Finally, the reserves of Japan and France have fallen more substantially since the introduction of the new oil prices, but they are still, respectively, two-and-a-half and one-and-a-half times the level at the end of 1970. French reserves rose to $8.2 billion by 30 June 1974. Today, at the end of September, there has been no marked change, while by way of comparison the UK and Italy, with roughly the same population, have respectively only $6.7 billion and $5.3 billion, and the United States, with four times the French population, has barely $15 billion. So, in terms of the overall balance, the position is far from worrying.

But what really matters is the balance on current account, which is a real obsession for capitalist states. These are of course in deficit as a result of the rise in the cost of oil imports.[94] This is what cannot be tolerated. This is where the main contradictions of the system interlink, and where efforts to overcome the permanent over-production crisis through institutionalised inflation come up against the insurmountable barrier of international competition for the conquest of markets. In so far as inflationary measures favour the domestic realization of the product, they reduce the competitive ability of the country under consideration in foreign markets. The ideal would be to induce sufficient inflation to revitalise domestic activity, but at the same time to keep it at a lower rate than that of foreign competitors. Since all the countries in the same area of competition are trying to do the same thing, this is an objectively unattainable combination.[95]

94. The maintenance of the reserves of the oil-consuming countries at a satisfactory level, despite the deficit on their trade balances, is explained by a kind of natural 'recycling' of the receipts of the producer countries. The free funds, incapable of being materialised in real goods, are, at present and for the most part, either invested or in temporary accounts in the major industrial countries. However, nothing will change in terms of reserves even when these funds are turned into commodities. What will grow are the industrial countries' receipts on their trade balances.

95. Let us recall what Marx wrote in his 1859 'Plan for the *Economics*' on the subject of the world market 'in which production is posited as a totality ... but within which ... all contradictions come into play'. (*Grundrisse*, p. 227.)

In the other direction, if inflation is combated in order to restore the balance of trade, one enters another network of contradictions. Any extra foreign sale which is not settled by the use of funds already deposited with us by the purchaser, but instead results in a net inflow of currency, involves an equivalent creation of domestic currency through the sale of the foreign currency to the central bank. In this respect it should be recalled that economic functions are not reversible. An autonomous deflationary measure will cause an increase in exports, but an autonomous increase in exports will, on the contrary, have an inflationary effect. When all the 'counter-inflationary' measures – credit squeeze, high interest rates, etc. – are designed to promote exports and impede sales on the home market, there is a classic dumping situation in which all these preferential policies result in the formation of an over-price on the home market to compensate for the various export premiums, and firms determine their overall profitability on an average between these two prices. Finally, this promotion of exports causes price rises at home and counteracts the 'counter-inflationary' policy.

Then, thanks to an inorganic whole of *ad hoc* and contradictory measures, one actually ends up by causing a collapse of demand and, consequently, discouraging investment and reducing employment. But prices still do not fall. The result is the *aberrant* phenomenon of inflation together with unemployment, which is known as 'stagflation'. Aberrant, because inflation in the neoclassical sense – demand exceeding supply at the equilibrium prices, causing these prices to rise – is inconceivable at any level below full employment.[96]

This result should cause an awakening and a change of course. But no! It is immediately concluded that the measures adopted were too weak and they are redoubled.

Reality will obviously end up by validating this approach. Whatever the cause of the rise in prices, even if they are caused exclusively by exogenous material conditions of production – for example, the rise in the cost of imported energy – it is still possible to make them fall by acting on demand. It is sufficient to go as far in this same

96. It could be replied that even if there is less than full employment, and it is still possible to satisfy extra demand by additional production, prices may rise, indirectly if not directly because of the effect of decreasing returns (increasing costs).

But, quite apart from the fact that the predominance of decreasing returns is yet another neoclassical assumption which has never been verified, this would anyway not be an inflationary rise in prices, something unhealthy, an effect of shortage, but a normal rise, something healthy, a side-effect of abundance. At any rate, this would not then be stagflation, since in stagflation production is not growing, and so the effects of decreasing returns cannot apply.

direction as is necessary. If it is made so difficult to sell that most firms are having serious problems in meeting their payment obligations, with the result that some are compelled to sell at a loss to avoid bankruptcy, one will eventually secure a fall in prices. In the last analysis this is what crises are. Equilibration downwards.

10 The Business Cycle

Investment as an increasing function of consumption

Imagine a primitive fishing community. Only consumer good: fish. Only productive activity: fishing. The tribe decides to reduce its consumption in order to release a surplus to improve its instruments of labour and, thereby, its productivity, with the aim of producing more fish later. To do this it withdraws a certain number of men from fishing and sets them to work making dug-outs. This means a fall in consumption and a rise in investment, a fall in the production of consumer goods and a simultaneous rise in the production of means of production.

Some time later, the tribe finds that dug-outs are not being produced at the expected rate, while it is still possible to make do with a bit less fish. Result: another contingent of workers leave the fishing industry and join their fellows in the dug-out yards. This means a further growth of investment (output of Department I), accompanied by a further fall in consumption (output of Department II).

Later on, it may perhaps be decided that the tribe has gone too far in sacrificing the present to the future, and the operation may be reversed: some men leave the dug-out yards and return to fishing. Investment falls, consumption rises. Investment, always and under all circumstances, varies inversely with unproductive consumption. *This is in conformity with the nature of these two magnitudes, since they are the only two components of a given total magnitude, social production capacity, and hence must vary inversely with each other.* And the economy of our tribe is in permanent and unshakeable equilibrium. Department I does not grow independently of Department II, but it does something even more astonishing: it grows in proportion to the latter's contraction. Our community not only *can*, but *must* make the two Departments vary as decreasing functions of each other; this is the necessary condition for equilibrium.

Now imagine that private entrepreneurs arrive, invade the tribe and take over and privatise all its economic activities. The fundamental function is now reversed: no private entrepreneur will step up dug-out production at the very moment when fish consumption is falling, nor cut back dug-out production just when fish consumption is rising. In the incentives which motivate those now in charge of economic decisions, investment is directly proportional to consumption, which is materially impossible, since the two magnitudes are the components of a fixed magnitude and cannot, in the short run, rise or fall simultaneously. They can do so in the long run, since an increase in investment at time t_0 may lead to an increase in final consumption at time t_n, but in the timespan over which our entrepreneurs' decisions are taken, the two magnitudes, objectively, vary inversely with each other. Subjectively, however, independent producers can only treat them as if they varied directly.

Capitalists are obliged, in a sense, to act at the wrong moment: to invest when – because of absorption of a greater part of the social product by final consumption – the means of investment are becoming scarce, to disinvest, or slow down investment, when – because of a fall in final consumption – means of investment are overabundant. This is the way in which the fundamental contradiction between social production and private appropriation of the product acts, on the level of realization of the product. It is this contradiction which underlies the structural disequilibrium of the capitalist mode of production, or even the market economy in general.[1] But what is the explanation for the fact that, despite this disequilibrium, despite this fundamental contradiction between the private interests of entrepreneurs and the objective conditions of social production, the free enterprise system is not immediately deadlocked for ever? The explanation is that in this system, the sum total of the two magnitudes – what we earlier called production capacity – is itself elastic and *reflects*, in the short term, the joint variations of its two components instead of defining the limit of these variations.

In other words, in the private enterprise system, the productive forces set to work are not equal to production capacity; they are only

1. Keynes pinpointed the essential character of this contrast between the two dynamics clearly when he declared that 'apart from the necessity of central controls to bring about an adjustment between the propensity to consume and the inducement to invest, there is no more reason to socialise economic life than there was before' (*General Theory*, p. 379). 'The weak point of traditional theory', writes A. Paquet, 'lies in its assertion that a growth of capital goods is possible at the same time that demand for consumer goods is falling' (*Le Conflit historique*, p. 322.)

'The profitability of capital goods', wrote Joan Robinson, 'depends upon the demand for the consumption goods which they produce. Thus if individuals decide to save, that is, not to spend on immediate consumption, they reduce rather than increase the motive of the entrepreneurs for acquiring new capital goods, and the decision to save reduces the demand for consumption goods without increasing the demand for capital goods.' (*Introduction to the Theory of Employment*, p. 4).

a part of it, and this part can vary quantitatively in its own right, before and apart from any quantitative change in overall production capacity. It is these variations, this *cycle* between higher and lower levels of *under-employment* of the capacity, which permit simultaneous variations in the same direction of the two components and which, in a closed free enterprise system, ensure conjunctural and temporary equilibrium on the very basis of structural and permanent disequilibrium. Construction of dug-outs and production–consumption of fish can indeed increase or decrease simultaneously, but on one condition: that the tribe has a reserve of unemployed workers and/or instruments of labour, which can be activated and de-activated at different times.

If the system is open, then on top of this internal reserve of productive forces, we have a supply of foreign productive forces in the form of capital and men.[2] This supply gives extra elasticity to the *effective* production capacity, i.e. the sum of productive forces actually set to work at each particular point in time.

It is this domestic and foreign reserve of human and material production capacity, and thus the system's own tendency to underemployment – the existence of which we have shown in the course of this work – which allows capitalism to function according to its own nature, which is in a way the reverse of every other human society: instead of consuming as an increasing function of production capacity and as a decreasing function of investment, capitalism produces and invests as an increasing function of unproductive consumption.[3]

The rationality of the cyclical form

This parallel movement of the two kinds of consumption, productive and unproductive, whether they are increasing or decreasing, must necessarily be 'cyclical' (or more literally, oscillatory, recurrent).

2. This is how one should interpret the recent phenomenon of massive immigration of foreign workers into the industrial countries of Western Europe.

3. It is for this reason that a rise in this unproductive consumption, at a given level of development of the productive forces, may in certain conditions not only not make a community poorer, but even enrich it. This is the great paradox of capitalist reality. Thus Paul Fabra pointed out: 'Despite a rapid growth in unit wage costs, US firms succeeded in 1968 in increasing their net income after tax by 10%, the First National City Bank reported in astonishment. ... In France, following the 16% rise of the Grenelle agreement, profits rose sharply in 1968. ... These forecasting errors are nothing new. Thus in Italy in 1963, in Holland in 1964, workers' incomes grew suddenly by around 20% in the space of a few months, and each time the experts predicted catastrophes which did not occur ....' ('L'Inflation et la société de consommation', *Le Monde*, 26 June 1969).

Since it occurs between two unbreachable limits, it can only continue, once it has reached the neighbourhood of these limits, by changing its direction.

What are these limits? The upper limit is clearly full employment – here, the existence of a ceiling is immediately apparent. It is also clear that there is a theoretical lower limit at zero, but it is obvious that, in practice, the worst depressions are still well above this limit. How far above depends on a combination of factors, the most important of which are these:

1. The law of *increasing returns* (or *decreasing costs*) generally applies to industry, with the effect that the unit cost of output increases as the volume of production decreases. What is more, the rate of increasse of unit costs is itself increasing as the break-even point is approached from above.[4] This is already a substantial factor reducing the incentive to cut back production in response to falling prices.

2. As long as prices are even marginally above *variable costs alone*, the firm loses less by producing and selling below total cost (fixed costs plus variable costs), than if it paid out fixed costs alone without producing anything.

In modern capitalist states, with complex up-to-date technology, fixed costs (cost independent of the level of output) are relatively very high: firstly, because of the maintenance costs of equipment; secondly, because of legislative measures aimed at ensuring relatively stable employment, for example restrictions on sacking, compensation, staff status for administrative personnel and for a relatively large proportion of manual workers, etc. Today, abandonment of Concorde would cost more than completion of the project.[5]

3. Why cannot prices fall below unit variable costs? Because below this level all production ceases. But, and this is perhaps ultimately the true limit, a complete stoppage of production is impossible because of the existence, in all circumstances, of an absolute minimum of social consumption. Even in a model of pure capitalism in which the

4. The break-even point is the minimum quantity that must be produced and sold so that, on top of the variable costs proportional to this quantity, the firm's fixed costs can be covered. This quantity is equal to $e_x/p - e_v$, where e_x stands for total fixed costs; e_v for variable costs per unit of output; and p for the prevailing price of a unit of output.

5. According to Matthews, as early as 1840 in the English cotton industry a fall in demand did not lead to a fall in production because overhead costs were high in relation to prime costs (*A Study in Trade Cycle History*).

unemployed are left to die of hunger, there is still the minimum unproductive consumption of the state itself and its agents, of the administrative staff of firms and of those workers who are indispensable to maintain equipment (which is kept in working order even in the case of bankruptcy), i.e. consumption which roughly corresponds to the *fixed costs* which were mentioned above. And finally the consumption of those among the self-employed, liberal professions, capitalists, land-owners, etc., who despite lack of incomes, or even with negative incomes, will not hesitate to dig into their reserves of liquid assets (dishoarding) or to exhaust their lines of credit, ultimately by mortgaging unsaleable assets, in order to keep up their consumption.

The demand represented by all these minimum levels of consumption will keep prices sufficiently above the limit of variable costs so that – taking into account differing individual productivities and costs – a sufficient number of enterprises to satisfy these kinds of consumption should remain in operation.

On the basis of the above, we can present the following summary of our results.

1. The system can only reproduce itself if it is impelled by a combination of impulses which we cover under the category of overtrading.
2. It can only invest as an increasing function of final consumption, therefore – the supreme paradox – as a decreasing function of saving.[6]

For a given level of employment, this is mathematically impossible. It reflects the contradiction between the incentive to invest which is directly proportional to consumption and the material means of this investment which vary inversely with this same consumption. The system cannot resolve this contradiction and enlarge or contract its reproduction except by changing the level of employment in the same direction.

6. This is ultimately the deepest meaning of the *General Theory*, which Keynes and the Keynesians do not, in our judgement, explain clearly enough. Investment is *ex post* equal to actual saving, but since the latter is the sum of planned saving and forced saving, investment is at its highest when the propensity to save is at its lowest. In other words, for investment to take place it is ultimately necessary that someone should save in one way or another, but to promote investment, it is not desirable that people should save by choice; it is necessary that they should be forced, in real terms, to save, through a rise in prices.

3. Since all the magnitudes in question, acting on each other, vary in the same direction, this is a perfect example of unstable equilibrium, in which the effects of primary impulses engender secondary forces which multiply the original impulses. This reflects its contradictory mode of existence.
4. This cumulative process can only stop at the ceiling of full employment and at the lower limit of the greatest possible unemployment. It makes the system traverse the space between these two extremes, in each direction alternately.

In other words, the system is prevented by its own contradictions from moving along the path dictated by its own rationality – raising the organic composition of capital – since this path implies a change in Department I more than proportional to that in Department II, and thus a certain independence for Department I, which contradicts the rationality of each individual capitalist. So, incapable of expanding in depth, it expands in breadth – parallel variation of the two Departments – and it is only, so to speak, through the vibrations of this movement, in a manner of speaking through the furrows which it plows in the impetuosity of ascent, and above all at the moment when the system starts to move back upwards at the end of a depression, that deepening occurs all the same and that the organic composition rises and the productive forces are developed, as an outcome of this perpetual to-and-fro motion.

To complete the explanation of the cycle on this basis, it remains to show what mechanisms make the movement reverse when it reaches either of the two limits. To show, on the one hand, how once full employment is reached, or once the period of growth has somehow or other been started, collapse becomes possible; and on the other hand, what are the forces which, in the trough of the wave, act as a stimulus and enable the system to recover. In other words, it must be explained why the system does not stick at the level of one or other of these two limits. For the fact that it can only move in a certain way does not *per se* prove that it must necessarily move.

Taking into account the general impossibility of realization of the product without some anticipation of this realization by the bearers of variable revenues – which we refer to as 'overtrading' – to pose this question is in effect to ask: (i) why overtrading, which has propelled the system up the slope of employment, should leave it becalmed on the approaches to the summit; (ii) why the conditions of this recurrent overtrading should once more be reunited in the depths of the valley, that is to say, at the objective lower limit of the collapse.

We believe it is necessary to make an excursus here. The various elements of the answers to these two questions have already been given in the course of this work, mainly when we were reviewing former descriptions of the cycle, above all those of Marx in Chapter 3, and those of certain Marxist theoreticians in Chapter 4. As a result the reader will probably get the impression that after having expressed our dissatisfaction with their proposals we are now adopting a substantial part of their analysis as our own.

However, it is inevitable that these elements should be reformulated here, since these *descriptions* generally provide a good account of the sequence of the various phases of the cycle, once the cycle itself is taken as given. These descriptions become insufficient and lead the argument into a dead-end as soon as one recalls that the cycle is only the form in which our problem appears, and that the task is not to explain the structural tendency by conjunctural fluctuations, but to explain the conjunctural fluctuations by a structural tendency.

Many of these descriptions, therefore, suddenly become lucid and perfectly valid as soon as one sees the object of description – the cycle – as a combination of the concrete effects in time and space of a previously recognized and explained fundamental disequilibrium, instead of looking within the cycle for this disequilibrium which transcends and determines the cycle.

If, on the contrary, one consciously or unconsciously denies the existence of this disequilibrium and argues on the basis of the fundamental equality of production and purchasing power, then one is obliged to deal with the cycle as a disruption of equilibrium instead of accepting it for what it really is: a means available to the system to reproduce itself and advance *despite* disequilibrium. Consequently, overtrading in all its forms comes to be seen as the only cause of this disruption of equilibrium, instead of being, as in our analysis, the only way to restore this equilibrium, at all costs, in the framework of the disequilibrium (its opposite, undertrading, coming after the crash and crisis as a reaction to extreme overtrading).

It is clear that there is nothing a priori to say whether overtrading will play a disequilibrating or an equilibrating role. It all depends on the point of departure. If, at this point, demand is less than supply, as we believe, overtrading will attenuate the gap; if demand is *already* equal to supply, according to the classical postulate, it will, on the contrary, aggravate the gap in the other direction.

However, if overtrading were a disequilibrating factor, the point at which equilibrium is disturbed would have to be located well below full employment in order to allow the effects of overtrading to develop in the margin left for the improvement of employment. This would put everything in doubt, since such an unemployment situation would itself stand in need of explanation.

We have already seen how Marxism left this problem unsolved.

Keynes and the Keynesians have attempted to show that equilibrium at various levels of employment does not contradict the fundamental equation of the Law of Markets. In a formal and static sense, it does indeed not contradict it. But liquidity-preference – another term for Marx's 'hoarding' – presented as the generator of underemployment, presupposes what it should explain. For it could only be a characteristic of capitalists, and could therefore only concern investment. But any abstention from investing implies a previous failure to sell, which is precisely what must be explained and which is in outright contradiction, substantially and dynamically, with the Law of Markets and its fundamental equation.

As for the pre or anti-Keynesian neoclassics, they have generally, more or less openly, tended to elaborate a rationale for unemployment as a normal feature of the system's harmonious functioning, while any lowering of unemployment below its normal level is called 'overheating', an unhealthy state of affairs which is the source of all kinds of ills. Crises, disturbances, tensions and disequilibria are, according to this view, only backlashes of artificial and untoward measures aimed at improving the level of employment. To avoid falling, one must give up climbing; to stabilise the economy, one must cut off its peaks.

We can now reply to the two questions that we set ourselves.

The barrier of full employment and crises

To wonder why, in normal conditions of *laissez-faire*, the recurrent overtrading which has brought the system in sight of full employment cannot keep it there means, basically, to wonder why it cannot make the system pass from extensive extended reproduction to intensive extended reproduction. In reality there is always a combination of the two, with the vital qualification that extensiveness is predominant in the former, while intensiveness is only a by-product; in the latter the order is reversed.

On this topic it must be recalled that only three types of reproduction are possible: (i) simple reproduction, in which neither Department varies; (ii) extensive extended reproduction, in which both Departments grow together at the same rate; and (iii) intensive extended reproduction, in which Department I grows, while Department II stays constant. The last two types may be combined – growth of both Departments together, but not at the same rate – but the first cannot of course combine with either of the others.

It is immediately apparent that the first type, simple reproduction, is completely ruled out. It is materially almost impossible, in developed capitalism, for all the recipients of surplus-value to spend the whole of it on their personal consumption.

Given that the rate of profit considerably exceeds the normal rate of population growth, the second type, extensive extended reproduction, is materially just as impossible, except in conjunction with growth of one or more of the following three variables: (i) wages; (ii) the level of employment; (iii) immigration of foreign workers.

This type of reproduction is therefore quite possible while unemployment is being reabsorbed: firstly because there is nothing to stop the rate of growth of employment alone from equalling or even exceeding the rate of capitalisation; and also because wages also increase to some extent during this period.

On the other hand, when the domestic reserve of unemployed workers runs out and the conjunctural rise in wages slows down or is insufficient, extensive extended reproduction becomes impossible again, if these missing factors are not relieved either by factor (iii), immigration of foreign workers, or by an *institutionalised* rise in wages.

In the absence of these factors, the only *objectively* possible alternative left is intensive extended reproduction, but this is *subjectively* impossible for the reason we have already set out, that it implies increased investment in Department I, producing means of production, just when the market for consumer goods suddenly stops expanding or even contracts.

This is the most critical phase of the process; the passage from extensive to intensive. This represents an essential transformation for the agents of capitalist reproduction. It is the nodal point of all the contradictions.

Up to this point, through the whole course of the rise, the expectations of capitalists and the bankers behind them have been realized for the simple reason that they were acted upon. For in the framework of extensive extended reproduction, these actions meant, among other things, the creation of jobs and the hiring of those previously unemployed. With each capitalist expanding the market for the others, each one's forecasts were confirmed *a posteriori*, and the related financial operations were concluded to the satisfaction of the most orthodox lenders.

Competition between investors eventually made wages rise somewhat, which accelerated the market's rate of expansion. Success in realization retrospectively blurred the intrinsic boldness of projects.

But when unemployment begins to level out and the rate of growth of final consumption begins to flag, the incentives weaken. Some investors, mainly those whose industries are most affected by this falling-off, begin to hesitate. There is still no real reversal of the tendency, but a slight shortfall below the expected rate of expansion. This is enough to lead some to revise their projects downwards or spread them out over time, or even quit while the going is good. This withdrawal by some compromises several other projects – more or less related, already being carried out. The outcome no longer automatically and infallibly verifies all the forecasts. Bankers, who have already reached the limit of their ability to create money, begin to be worried. The mechanism of crisis swings into motion.

To see the *necessity* of this process, it is enough to wonder what would happen if, once arrived at the summit, capitalists persevered in ignoring this stoppage of expansion of the consumer market and continued to behave as if nothing had happened. Then the phenomenon which Rosa Luxemburg indicated – this is one of the grains of truth in her theory – would emerge for a while: relative overproduction in Department II, relative underproduction in Department I.

This is what actually happens to some extent, on the eve of collapse, thanks to the swelling of stocks in the hands of dealers. For a certain while, the elasticity of these stocks masks the slow-down in sales to final consumers, and both Departments enjoy the same apparent demand, despite the real disproportion.

But, whereas overtrading by producers is beneficial as a real generator *ex post* of the revenues it anticipates, overtrading by dealers is inherently sterile – Hawtrey's 'passive investment' – and is the last thing for the banks to finance. By becoming worried and trying to secure their own positions at each other's expense, by trying to overtake each other, they cause the crash.

In this way, at the moment of full employment, the recurrent overtrading has exhausted its powers and is no longer capable of ensuring the system's reproduction. To overcome this barrier, a different kind of overtrading must take its place. This is the institutional overtrading of contemporary capitalist economies which, as we have said earlier, have not known anything worthy of the name of crisis for about 40 years. Institutional, because it is based on three factors that have themselves been institutionalised: (i) generally, a rise in wages, effected independently of the level of employment; (ii) sometimes, imports of foreign workers; (iii) chronic inflation.

The first two factors tend towards equilibrium quite simply by taking over from growth of domestic employment, which hitherto ensured the market's growth. These two new factors allow *extensive* (or predominantly extensive) extended reproduction to continue, despite the relative stability of the level of employment and the lack of population growth.

The third factor acts in part directly, as an autonomous cause of overtrading, as we have explained at length in our earlier arguments, and in part indirectly, in conjunction with the resources coming from exploitation of the periphery, as a condition allowing wages to increase *without any fall in the rate of profit*, which constantly reinforces the stimulating effect of the first factor. The precarious nature of these three factors reflects the limits of the apparent resolution of present-day capitalism's contradictions.

The way out of depression

At the other end of the course, we have to apply the same argument. If, as we have already made clear, simple reproduction is ruled out under all circumstances, and if the bottom of the depression is a barrier to the continuation of the *negative* extended reproduction by means of which the economy has gone down the slope, the only possible kind of behaviour left to the system, at this point, is *positive* extended reproduction, whether extensive or intensive is of little importance here.

At this end, matters are much clearer than at the other end. Firstly, because we do not have to choose between extensive and intensive, which frees us of a particularly delicate problem of the capitalist mode of production. All we have to show here is that the system will start off again forwards and, in this respect, the two kinds of extended reproduction are equally good. Secondly, because the opposition between the two fundamental postulates – equality or inequality between production and revenues – does not affect the mechanisms and direction of overtrading. In either framework this will, from the moment it starts up, be a re-equilibrating factor, in line with the very depth of the depression and extent of unemployment. As for the specific mechanisms of this boost, Marx and the theoreticians of Marxism have left us the richest analyses.

In this section of the cycle, we are in a situation where the fall in consumption has over a certain period been slowed down, and finally halted. No negative forecasts can be made any more. The most pessimistic expectation is the *status quo*. The same course has been charted by the rate of interest, which is now at its lowest. In borrowing long or medium-term, there is practically no risk of a further fall, and there is every chance of an actual rise. Also, in this depressed business climate, there are not many firms in whom the banks still have confidence. All the more reason to take advantage of this kind of *situational rent*, if one belongs to the select few.

Material inputs, especially fixed equipment, are undervalued and are being sold far below their replacement costs because of liquidations and bankruptcies.

Therefore, on the cost side, the most favourable conditions are united. But this is still perhaps not sufficient to induce optimistic expectations, the kind which outstrip demand instead of following it, and which alone can propel the whole machinery upwards. We know that the number one problem for capitalism is not to produce, but to sell.

However, the decisive factor, which will cause a preparation for growth of the market, is not long in arriving, if not in overall, absolute terms, then in partial, relative terms for certain individual firms. For in this difficult situation, in which the margins of survival are narrow, and the most needed credit is both so selective and so cheap, the differentiation in competitiveness between firms is extremely accentuated, and a not very costly effort by the most powerful units is enough to eliminate their weakest competitors. At any rate, now or never is the time to take some risks of this kind. The decision to take these risks is overtrading of a special type, which anticipates, not expansion of the overall market nor of the market of certain industries or sectors, but of the market share of one firm at the expense of another firm.

It is at this point that, in the classical model of capitalism, the process of concentration of capital intensifies. But the very effort which these large corporations make to absorb others and obtain their share of the market, expands the market as a whole, since it is done by employing factors and creating revenues, in such a way that once this phase of major regroupings is over, classic overtrading based on overall anticipations, which we have already analysed, comes into play – and everything restarts.

Bibliography

AFTALION, A., *Les Crises périodiques de surproduction*, Paris, 1913.

ALLAIS, M., *Les Fondements comptables de la macro-économie*, Paris, 1955.

AMIN, S., *Accumulation on a World Scale*, Hassocks, 1974.

AMIN, S., *L'Echange inégal et la loi de la valeur*, Paris, 1973.

BAGEHOT, W., *Lombard Street: A Description of the Money Market*, London, 1888.

BAIROCH, P., *The Economic Development of the Third World since 1900*, London, 1975.

BARAN, P., *The Political Economy of Growth*, London, 1973.

BARAN, P.A. and SWEEZY, P.M., *Monopoly Capital*, London, 1968.

BAREL, Y., 'Des Contradictions du capitalisme contemporain' *Politique aujourd'hui*, nos. 8–9,10,11.

BASTIAT, F., *Oeuvres complètes*, Paris, 1855.

BETTELHEIM, C., *Le Problème de l'emploi et du chômage dans les théories économiques*, Paris, 1952.

BETTELHEIM, C., *Problèmes théoriques et pratiques de la planification*, Paris, 1951.

BETTELHEIM, C., *Studies in the Theory of Planning*, London and Bombay, 1960.

BETTELHEIM, C., *The Transition to Socialist Economy*, Hassocks, 1975.

BETTELHEIM, C., 'Variations du taux de profit et accroissement de la productivité de travail', *Economie appliquée*, October 1959.

BODIN, J., *The Response of Jean Bodin to the Paradoxes of Malestroit, and the Paradoxes*, Washington D.C., 1946.

BOTERO, G., *The Reason of State*, London, 1956.

BOURGUIN, M., *Les systèmes socialistes et l'évolution économique* . . ., Paris, 1906.

BRUNHOFF, S. de, *L'Offre de monnaie. Critique d'un concept*, Paris, 1971.

BURET, E., *De la misère des classes laborieuses en Angleterre et en France*, Paris, 1840.

CARIVEN, A., *La Lutte contre le chômage*, Toulouse, 1935.

CASSEL, G., *The Theory of Social Economy*, London, 1932.

CHILD, Joseph, *A new Discourse of Trade ...*, London, 1693.
CLARK, C., *The Conditions of Economic Progress*, London, 1957.
COLQUHON, P., *A Treatise on the Wealth, Power and Resources of the British Empire*, London, 1814.
COURNOT, A., *Researches into the Mathematical Principles of the Theory of Wealth*, N.Y., 1897.
CURTIS, M., 'Is money saving equal to investment?' *Quarterly Journal of Economics*, August 1937.
DAIRE, L.F.E., *Economistes-financiers du XVIIIe siècle*, Paris, 1843.
DANJOU, Fr., 'Sur la baisse tendancielle du taux de profit', *Cahiers*, no. 3 (October 1972). Published by CEREL of Lille.
DARIMON, A., *De la réforme des banques*, Paris, 1856.
DAVENANT, C., *Discourse on the Publick Revenues, and on the Trade of England*, London, 1698.
DAVENANT, C., *An Essay upon the Probable Methods of Making a People Gainers in the Balance of Trade*, London, 1699.
DENIS, H., *La Formation de la science économique*, Paris, 1973.
DENIS, H., *Histoire de la pensée économique*, Paris, 1971.
DENIS, H., 'Marchés nouveaux et accumulation du capital', *L'Homme et la Société*, no. 22.
DENIS, H., 'Remarques sur l'Etude de F. Danjou ...', *Cahiers*, no. 5. Published by CEREL of Lille.
DENIZET, J., *Monnaie et financement*, Paris, 1967.
DIETERLEN, P., *Au-delà du capitalisme : théorie des débouchés*, Paris, 1946.
DMITRIEV, V.K., *Economic Essays on Value, Competition and Utility*, London, 1974.
DOMAR, Evsey A., *Essays on the Theory of Economic Growth*, New York, 1960.
DOMARCHI, J.D., *La Pensée économique de Keynes*, Paris, 1943.
DUPIN, F.P.C., *La Crise commerciale de 1839*, Paris, 1832.
DURET, J., *Le Marxisme et les crises*, Paris, 1933.
ELLIS, Howard S., 'Bilateralism and the Future of International Trade', *Essays in International Finance*, no. 5, Summer 1945.
EMMANUEL, A., *Un Débat sur l'échange inégal*, Paris, 1975.
EMMANUEL, A., *Unequal Exchange: A Study of the Imperialism of Trade*, London, 1972.
ERLICH, A., *The Soviet Industrialisation Debate, 1924–1928*, Harvard, 1960.
FABRA, P., 'L'Inflation et la société de consommation', *Le Monde*, 26 June 1969.
FERRIER, F.L.A., *Du Gouvernement considéré dans ses rapports avec le commerce*, Paris, 1805.

FORBONNAIS, Veron de, *Eléments du commerce*, Paris, 1754.
GESELL, S., *The Natural Economic Order*, Berlin, 1929.
GRAHAM, Frank D. 'Some aspects of protection further considered', *Quarterly Journal of Economics*, February 1923.
HARROD, R.F., *Towards a Dynamic Economics*, London, 1948.
HAWTREY, R.G., *Capital and Employment*, London, 1952.
HEEREN, A.H.L., *Historical Researches into the Politics, Intercourse and Trade of the Principal Nations of Antiquity*, Oxford, 1833.
HEURTIER, C., *La Crise monétaire et le taux de l'escompte*, Paris, 1861.
HICKS, J.R., *A Contribution to the Theory of the Trade Cycle*, Oxford, 1950.
HILFERDING, R., *Finance Capital*, London, 1981.
HOBSON, J.A., *The Evolution of a Modern Capitalism. A Study of Machine Production*, London, 1917.
HOBSON, J.A. and MUMMERY, A.F., *Physiology of Industry*, London, 1889.
HUME, D., *Writings on Economics*, Edinburgh, 1955.
JAMES, E., *Problèmes monétaires d'aujourd'hui*, Paris, 1963.
JEVONS, W.S., *Theory of Political Economy*, London, 1879.
JUGLAR, C., *Des Crises commerciales et de leur retour périodique*, Paris, 1889.
KAUTSKY, K., *The Social Revolution*, Chicago, 1902.
KEYNES, J.M., 'Alternative theories of the rate of interest'. *The Economic Journal*, 1937.
KEYNES, J.M., *The Economic Consequences of the Peace*, London, 1919.
KEYNES, J.M., *The General Theory of Employment, Interest and Money*, Cambridge, 1973.
KLEIN, R.L., *The Keynesian Revolution*, New York, 1948.
KNAPP, G.F., *Staatliche Theorie des Geldes*, Munich, 1905.
KNIGHT, F.H., *Risk, Uncertainty and Profit*, Boston, 1921.
KUZNETS, S., 'Proportion of capital formation to national product', *The American Economic Review*, May 1952.
LAMBERT, P., 'La Loi des débouchés', *Revue d'économie politique*, 1952.
LATOUCHE, S., 'À propos de la baisse tendancielle du taux de profit', *Revue économique*, January 1973.
LATOUCHE, S., Article in *Documents*, no. 2, published by IREP of Grenoble.
LAW, J., *Money and Trade Considered, with a Proposal for Supplying the Nation with Money*, London, 1720.
LEMONTEY, P.E., *Oeuvres*, Paris, 1829.
LENIN, V.I., *Collected Works*, Moscow, 1972.

LESCURE, J., *Des Crises générales et périodiques de surproduction*, Bordeaux, 1906.
LOWNDES, W., *A Report Containing an Essay for the Amendments of the Silver Coins*, London, 1695.
LUXEMBURG, R., *The Accumulation of Capital*, London, 1951.
LUXEMBURG, R., *The Accumulation of Capital: An Anti-Critique* in Rosa Luxemburg and Nikolai Bukharin, *Imperialism and the Accumulation of Capital*, London, 1972.
MacCULLOCH, J.R., *The Principles of Political Economy*, London, 1843.
MALTHUS, T.R., *Principles of Political Economy*, Edinburgh, 1843.
MALTHUS, T.R., 'Review of Tooke', *Quarterly Review*, XXIX, 1823.
MANDEL, E., 'Les Catégories marchandes dans la période de transition', *Economica*, June 1964.
MANDEVILLE, B. de, *The Fable of the Bees: or, Private Vices Publick Benefits*, Oxford, 1924.
MARCHAND, J., *La Renaissance du mercantilisme à l'époque contemporaine*, Paris, 1937.
MARSHALL, A., *The Economics of Industry*, London, 1879.
MARSHALL, A., *Money, Credit and Commerce*, London, 1923.
MARSHALL, A., *Principles of Economics*, London, 1922.
MARX, K., *Capital*, London, 1974.
MARX, K., *Le Capital*. Paris, 1963–1968.
MARX, K., *A Contribution to the Critique of Political Economy*, Moscow, 1970.
MARX, K., *Grundrisse: Foundations of the Critique of Political Economy*, London, 1973.
MARX, K., *Selected Correspondence*, London, 1956.
MARX, K., *Theories of Surplus Value*, London, 1972.
MARX, K. and ENGELS, F., *Collected Works*, London.
MARX, K. and ENGELS, F., *Werke*, Berlin, 1965–8.
MATTHEWS, R.C.O., *A Study in Trade Cycle History*, Cambridge, 1954.
MILL, James, *Elements of Political Economy*, London, 1844.
MILL, John Stuart, *Essays on some Unsettled Questions of Political Economy*, London, 1948.
MILL, John Stuart, *Principles of Political Economy*, London, 1867.
MOLINARI, G. de, *Etudes économiques*, Paris, 1846.
MONTCHRETIEN, A. de, *Traicté de l'oeconomie politique*, Paris, 1889.
MOSZKOWSKA, N., *Das Marxsche System*, Berlin, 1929.
MUN, T., *England's Treasure by Forraign Trade*, London, 1644.

NOGARO, B., *Le rôle de la monnaie dans le commerce international et la théorie quantitative*, Paris, 1904.
PAQUET, A., *Le Conflit historique entre la loi des débouchés et le principe de la demande effective*, Paris, 1953.
PETTY, W., *The Economic Writings of Sir William Petty*, Cambridge, 1899.
PIGOU, A.–C., *Employment and Equilibrium*, London, 1941.
PIGOU, A.–C., *Industrial Fluctuations*, London, 1927.
PIGOU, A.–C., *Keynes' General Theory: A Retrospect*, London, 1950.
PLEKHANOV, G., *Selected Philosophical Works*, London, 1961.
PREOBRAZHENSKY, E., *The New Economics*, Oxford, 1965.
PROUDHON, P.J., *Oeuvres complètes*, Paris, 1867–70.
RADCLIFFE Committee, *Report on the Workings of the Monetary System*, CMND 827. London, 1959.
RODBERTUS-JAGETZOW, J.K., *Schriften*, Berlin, 1890.
RODBERTUS-JAGETZOW, J.K., *Zur Beleuchtung der sozialen Frage*, Berlin, 1890.
RUEFF, J., *A l'âge de l'inflation*, Paris, 1963.
SAMUELSON, P., 'Understanding the Marxist Notion of Exploitation', *Journal of Economic Literature*, June 1971.
SARTRE, L., *Esquisse d'une théorie marxiste des crises périodiques*, Paris, 1937.
SAY, J.–B., *Letters to Robert Malthus on Political Economy and Stagnation of Commerce*, London, 1936.
SAY, J.–B., *Traité d'économie politique*, Paris, 1841.
SAY, J.–B., *Treatise on Political Economy*, London, 1821.
SCHMITT, B., *La Formation du pouvoir d'achat*, Paris, 1960.
SCHUMPETER, J.A., *Capitalism, Socialism and Democracy*, London, 1943.
SCHUMPETER, J.A., *Theory of Economic Development*, Cambridge, Mass., 1934.
SCROPE, G. Poulett, *Political Economy for Plain People*, London, 1879.
SISMONDI, J.–C.–L., *De la Richesse Commerciale*, Geneva, 1803.
SISMONDI, J.–C.–L., *Nouveaux principes d'économie politique*, Paris, 1819.
SISMONDI, J.–C.–L., 'Sur la balance des consommations avec les productions', *Revue encyclopédique*, May 1824.
SMITH, A., *An Inquiry into the Nature and Causes of the Wealth of Nations*, Oxford, 1976.
SMITH, A., *The Theory of Moral Sentiments*, Oxford, 1976.
STERNBERG, F., *Capitalism and Socialism on Trial*, London, 1951.

STEUART, J., *An Inquiry into the Principles of Political Economy,* London, 1767.
SWEEZY, P., *The Theory of Capitalist Development,* New York, 1956.
TOOKE, T., *An Inquiry into the Currency Principle,* London, 1844.
TORRENS, R., *An Essay on the Production of Wealth,* London, 1821.
TRIFFIN, R., *Gold and the Dollar Crisis,* New Haven, 1960.
TUGAN-BARANOVSKI, M., *Les Crises industrielles en Angleterre,* Paris, 1913.
TUGAN-BARANOVSKI, M., *Theoretische Grundlagen des Marxismus,* Leipzig, 1905.
VAUBAN, S. Le Prestre de, *A Project for a Royal Tythe,* London, 1708.
VINER, J., *International Trade and Economic Development,* Oxford, 1953.
VINER, J., *Studies in the Theory of International Trade,* New York, 1937.
XENOPHON, *Scripta Minora,* London, 1946.

Index

QUEEN MARY
COLLEGE
LIBRARY

WITHDRAWN
FROM STOCK
QMUL LIBRARY

QMC 703517 6

a30213 007035176b

WITHDRAWN
FROM STOCK
QMUL LIBRARY

DATE DUE FOR RETURN

NEW ACCESSION

08. FEB 85.

21 JUN 1985

24. MAY '88